P9-DNL-979

TANKS & WEAPONS OF WORLD WAR II

BEEKMAN HOUSE, NEW YORK

10

TANKS & WEAPONS OF WORLD WAR II

BEEKMAN HOUSE, NEW YORK

Introduction

By 1939 the Germans, forced to start from scratch after their defeat in 1918, had completely replanned their army. Their strategy was based largely on the work of British military thinkers such as Liddell Hart and General Fuller, who had stressed the importance of the tank, used in massed formations, in giving mobility and concentration of firepower to an attacking force. The French meanwhile had been content to modernize the tactics which had brought them victory in 1918, and still conceived of the tank as basically an infantry support weapon–while the British, slow to adopt new ideas, and hampered by financial stringency in the inter-war years, stood somewhere between the two.

In this context, the success of the German Blitzkrieg had a shattering effect, and the tank soon came to be seen as the dominant weapon in ground warfare. In other fields, too, the war stimulated much research and experimentation, and in spite of the ever present obstacles to scientific progress–political apathy, financial restrictions and bureaucratic interference– development was rapid.

By 1945 the armaments of the major powers were sophisticated indeed, and in this book we present the full story of the weapons of World War Two. The authoritative text deals with the weapons of all classes developed by the powers involved, and their military application, including first hand accounts of the actual fighting in various theatres. It is supported by drawings, diagrams and photographs of the weapons themselves: tanks, artillery and infantry weapons, as well as the more spectacular tools of destruction the war inspired–the guided missiles, rocket bombs, and chemical and atomic weapons that have shaped the arms systems of today.

*Published by Beekman House, New York,
a division of Crown Publishers, Inc.*

First published in Purnell's History of
the Second World War

First published in this form 1973

ISBN: 0-517-130904

Printed in Belgium - H. Proost & Cie p.v.b.a. Turnhout - Belgium

Contents

1939

ARMOURED BALANCE

The tank was to be decisive in the coming campaign. But the Germans did not have more or even markedly better tanks than the Allies. They just used them more imaginatively

Although the end of the First World War in November 1918 seemed outwardly to symbolise an Allied victory and total defeat for the German army, it did not in fact reflect the real balance of fighting power at the front nor illustrate the state which the revolution in warfare had reached. For in the last months of that war the Germans were still retiring in good order towards their homeland. Indeed they were beginning to stabilise the front as the offensive power of the Allied armies declined as a result of their losses and of the difficulties they were experiencing in maintaining men and material at increasing distances from their bases. Indeed, it was becoming progressively harder to drive the war-winning weapons – artillery and tanks – to the front, and there maintain them to fight in mass. And without their presence a relatively thin screen of machine-gunners could delay and hold up infantry and cavalry for sufficiently long to enable successive lines of defence to be prepared in the rear. By the beginning of November 1918, the Allied progress was getting slower and more feeble.

Yet the turning point had come in August and September when the defeats inflicted on the Germans signalised the failure of their own offensive, and underlined the war-weariness of the nation and army. The most decisive of these defeats occurred at Amiens on August 8, 1918, when 430 British tanks – in conjunction with cavalry and infantry – broke through the German lines, and thus convinced General Ludendorff, the controller of the German military machine, that the war had to be ended. The British tanks, fighting in close co-operation with the cavalry and infantry, did not penetrate much deeper than the forward German defences, but their employment in such numbers, carrying them forward 5 miles in one day, administered a shock to the German soldiers and their leader from which they did not fully recover.

The tanks of 1918 were neither fast enough nor sufficiently reliable to break through the enemy lines and then penetrate deep into his rearmost tactical areas. But the tanks under construction for use in 1919 were meant to be capable of doing this very thing, and the Allied plans for that year were based on this kind of strategy. Against these new, faster, and more reliable machines, the Germans would have only been able to deploy conventional artillery, a number of inefficient light anti-tank rifles, and a few clumsy tanks of their own.

For Ludendorff had rejected tanks, thinking it unlikely that the early, slow, clumsy vehicles would ever become viable weapons of war. Anyway, when given new machines, armies take a long time to acquire the techniques necessary to keep them running and to use them to their best effect, so the lead which the Allies had built in two years could not be overtaken in a few months.

Atrophy

Thus the First World War ended at a moment when victory in the field was not clear-cut and its causes not sharply delineated. Many Germans were in no doubt that the surprise use of tanks, in large numbers in the least-expected sectors, had been a paramount factor in their defeat. General von Kuhl, who had been a staff officer in the army group attacked and defeated at Amiens, wrote ten years after the event that, in achieving surprise, the most important and decisive factor had been the tanks.

But the Allies were not similarly convinced and, gripped by inertia linked to their own war-weariness, were content to allow their military thinking to atrophy after 1918. As for the French, for over 20 years they persisted in a policy that compelled tanks to act merely as an adjunct to infantry on the one hand, and as a substitute for cavalry in the scouting role on the other. They envisaged all offensive operations taking place in a manner similar to those of 1918, and so locked themselves behind the fortifications of the Maginot Line, developing a purely defensive mentality. They could not believe that a war of manoeuvre fought by tank armies would take place on their soil. Their tanks were therefore organised into battalions, the bulk of them (33 of between 45 and 60 tanks each) ordained to work in small groups in conjunction with infantry divisions.

The experiments carried out by the French army, starting in 1932, were based on their existing cavalry divisions. There evolved from these experiments three light mechanised divisions – with a fourth being formed in May 1940 – each with 220 tanks, armoured cars, and a brigade of infantry. But this well-balanced force the French threatened to squander because the old cavalry doctrine dictated that it should be employed as a dispersed screen, or advance guard, ahead of the Allied armies when these advanced beyond the frontier to meet the Germans in Belgium.

After the destruction of the Polish army in September 1939, largely as the result of action by German tanks in conjunction with aircraft, the French hastily began to form four new tank divisions in which the machines were heavy ones and the infantry few in proportion to tanks. These were still not proper armoured divisions: their envisaged role was to breach a front through which other conventional formations could pass. They were thus merely an extension of the policy which tied tanks to infantry, and were not conceived as a balanced formation capable of driving deep into the enemy rear to strike at his nerve centres and his supplies – the very heart of his war-making capacity.

The British did not suffer from the same stagnation as the French, but in 1918 the nation that told itself that it had won the war, also persuaded itself that it could rest on its laurels. The heavy losses of tanks in the last few months of the First World War made a case for those who argued that the machine could not replace the horse as the agent of the decisive, mobile arm; the sentiment generated by a lifetime's comradeship with the horse was strong – and so rejected change. Moreover, the formidable bills in-

French

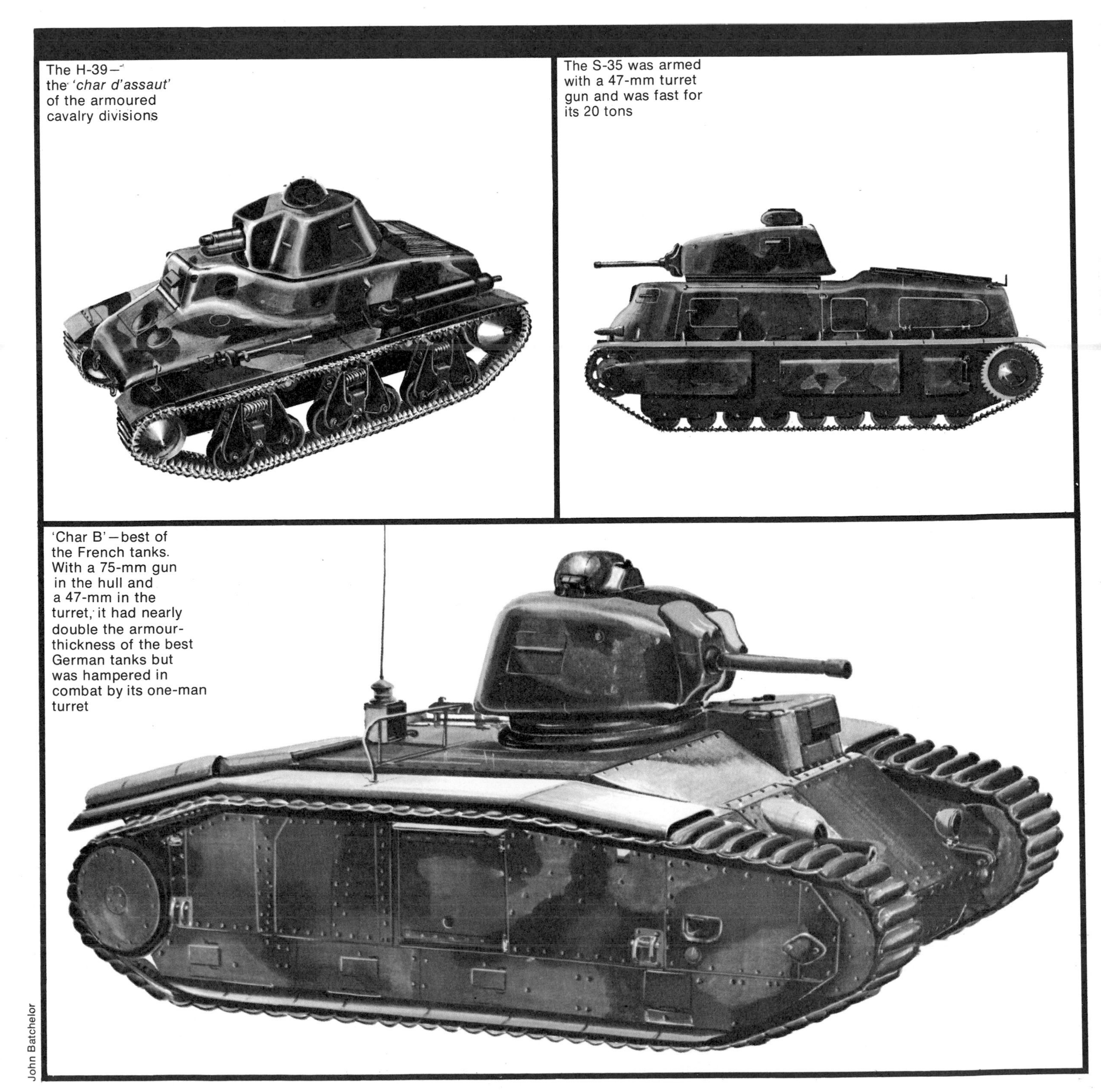

The H-39—the *'char d'assaut'* of the armoured cavalry divisions

The S-35 was armed with a 47-mm turret gun and was fast for its 20 tons

'Char B'—best of the French tanks. With a 75-mm gun in the hull and a 47-mm in the turret, it had nearly double the armour-thickness of the best German tanks but was hampered in combat by its one-man turret

John Batchelor

The 'Tank Idea' versus the horse

curred in the manufacture and running of tanks, when presented to taxpayers who had had enough of war, were striking deterrents to new construction and expansion.

The 'Tank Idea'

Nevertheless, real progress was made in Britain. The discovery that tanks and armoured cars offered a cheaper and better way of policing the more turbulent parts of the Empire encouraged experiment. And the persistence of a few enthusiasts projected the 'Tank Idea' as an element in warfare that intruded beyond the tactical battle into the realms of strategic decision. The names of Captain Liddell Hart, Generals Fuller, Lindsay, Broad, Pile, Hobart, and Martel appear at the head of the short list of pioneers who envisaged armoured forces becoming the decisive element in war, as well as being a straightforward economy of force when compared with the old horse and foot armies.

These men designed and trained tank units and formations that were unique both in their concept and technical proficiency. By the end of 1934, Hobart, as commander of the 1st Tank Brigade, had conclusively underlined what Broad and Pile had demonstrated in earlier years, namely that a mobile tank force could out-manoeuvre conventional forces by advances of prodigious length. And they showed that tanks could dominate the infantry of the day. These men were not dreamers. They were practical soldiers who based their judgements on the bitter experience gained by witnessing four years of slaughter during the First World War. They were often impatient with those who could not or would not understand, and who, by their slowness of mind, could not keep up with the pace demanded by mechanised forces.

Hobart, above all, with a ruthless driving force that he used to push his ideas ahead, would not permit the speed demanded by tank action to be slowed down by artillery, cavalry, and infantry units that were unable to keep up with his machines and their tempo of operation. By his requests for outstanding efficiency and speed, he frightened his more conventionally minded colleagues.

Eventually, there came about a reaction, accusing Hobart of demanding an all-tank army to the exclusion of the traditional arms. This was not entirely justified, since Hobart and his staff are clearly on record as having said they wanted infantry and artillery suitably mounted in armoured vehicles to go with their tanks; but the impression had been given they wanted an army based on armour, and the forces of reaction were quick to seize on this for use as a brake on the progress of the tank enthusiasts.

The traditionalists were also successful in acquiring political support; the Financial Secretary to the War Office, Duff Cooper, stated in Parliament in 1934: 'The more I study them [military affairs] the more I become impressed by the importance of [horsed] cavalry in modern warfare.' In 1935 Duff Cooper became Secretary of State for War.

The traditionalists also insisted that some tanks should be designed and set aside for work in conjunction with the infantry, rather in the manner of the French. Thus Britain began to develop armoured forces of two kinds: the fast moving, all-arms groups, that were the genesis of future armoured divisions; and tank battalions designed for infantry work, equipped with so-called 'I' tanks.

But by investigating the entirely new problems inherent in mechanised forces, the British did train a small cadre of experts whose knowledge and experience were to be invaluable when war, and the need to expand, came. On the other hand, when at last, and too late, it was decided in 1937 to give tanks to a large number of cavalry regiments—instead of expanding the existing Tank Corps—another temporary brake was placed on improvements in quantity and quality at a moment when time was short in the race to catch up with German rearmament. Thus only a small proportion of the British tank units that went to war in May 1940 were experienced and imbued with an insight into mechanised warfare.

Of the British armoured forces ready for action in Europe in May 1940, there was only one armoured division and this was still training in England. In France there was a formation known as the 1st Army Tank Brigade comprising two battalions of the new 'I' tanks designed for close co-operation with the infantry. Of these units—the 4th and 7th Battalions, Royal Tank Regiment—the latter arrived in France on May 1 and was not as well-trained as the 4th. In addition there were with the BEF seven cavalry light armoured regiments mounted in light tanks. Their tasks of reconnaissance and co-operation with the infantry divisions were akin to the traditional cavalry role.

German enthusiasm

The restraints imposed on the French and British after 1918 were totally different from those imposed on the Germans. Because the Treaty of Versailles forbade Germany to have her own tanks, she was reduced to carrying out a few sporadic and subversive experiments, mostly under cover in Russia. But because the Germans had been defeated, as they thought, by the tank as much as any other weapon, they were more anxious than anything else to acquire knowledge of mechanised armoured forces. The same traditional reactions that beset the British innovators held back the progressive German soldiers too, but with the advent of Hitler the political atmosphere became the reverse of Britain's.

As he cast aside the restrictions of Versailles, Hitler gave his enthusiastic backing to the soldiers whose ideas and experience were devoted to tanks. Those generals who had been associated with the early tank investigations—Guderian, Thoma, Lutz, Brauchitsch, Blomberg, and Reichenau—were now brought to the fore.

These men possessed imagination and insight, the appreciation of the strategic and psychological effect of deep thrusts, and the zest for speed and decision demanded by the nature of armoured operations. They were unanimous and generous in their acknowledgement of the profit they gained after studying, and often copying, the British experiments (Guderian is said to have toasted Hobart's name in champagne after a successful German tank exercise before the war). They paid little attention to the French—not even to de Gaulle, who had published a short work on the 'Army of the Future'. As a result, by 1936 the Germans were catching up fast in numbers and quality of machines, and had taken a clear lead in organisation and application over the British and the French, who two years before had been ahead in every department of armoured warfare.

The Germans concentrated their armour from the start in special armoured divisions comprising a balanced force of tanks, artillery, infantry, engineers, and administrative services. No consideration was given to the idea behind the French and British 'infantry' tanks and the doctrines associated with them. The tanks, supported by their own artillery and infantry, were to operate as a concentrated strategic force directed against the enemy's weakest spots and well ahead of the main, slower, infantry army.

This tank army, trained as a team, consisting of ten armoured divisions by May 9, 1940, contained at all levels a wealth of experience. Many of its officers and men were members of tank units which fought on Franco's side in the Spanish Civil War. Here they gained battle practice: they tested new techniques and the mechanical capabilities of their machines; and they saw the fate that befell tank forces that were put into battle dispersed in 'penny packets'. Moreover, intensive peacetime exercises in Germany had been supplemented by the bloodless occupations of Austria in 1938 and Czechoslovakia in 1939. In rapid, long-distance thrusts through these countries, the armoured forces taught themselves essential administrative lessons without having actually to engage in combat.

In September 1939, when the fighting began, the administration worked well and the armoured divisions outfought the old-fashioned Polish army in a matter of days, showing that the quality of the highly specialised, mechanised forces was master of the quantity mustered by the larger, traditional conscript armies. It also confirmed what had been long understood: that the air arm, working in close co-operation with tanks, conferred a powerful element of heavy fire-support on forces operating deep in the enemy rear. The aircraft were in fact a substitute for heavy artillery.

Singers without song

Thus on May 9, 1940, the relative overall condition of the opposing armoured forces can be summarised as follows. The French, saddled with a technique that was 20 years out of date, and with machines operated by men who lacked experience of the pace and scope of modern battle conditions, were partnered by the British, whose techniques were far more up-to-date, but who were attempting to practise them with too few machines, and with a number of officers and men who had not yet had time to grasp the significance of their new role. Indeed, it was this lack of experience that most seriously bedevilled the fighting quality

The Allies, in theory, could oppose the 3,000 German tanks with 3,600 of their own. The British infantry tanks, both the Mark I and the 'Matilda' Mark II, could stand up to the heaviest German tank fire, as could the French 'Char B'. No British tank, however, combined speed with hitting power, as with the more advanced German concept of tank design. The British light and cruiser tanks in particular were vulnerable

British

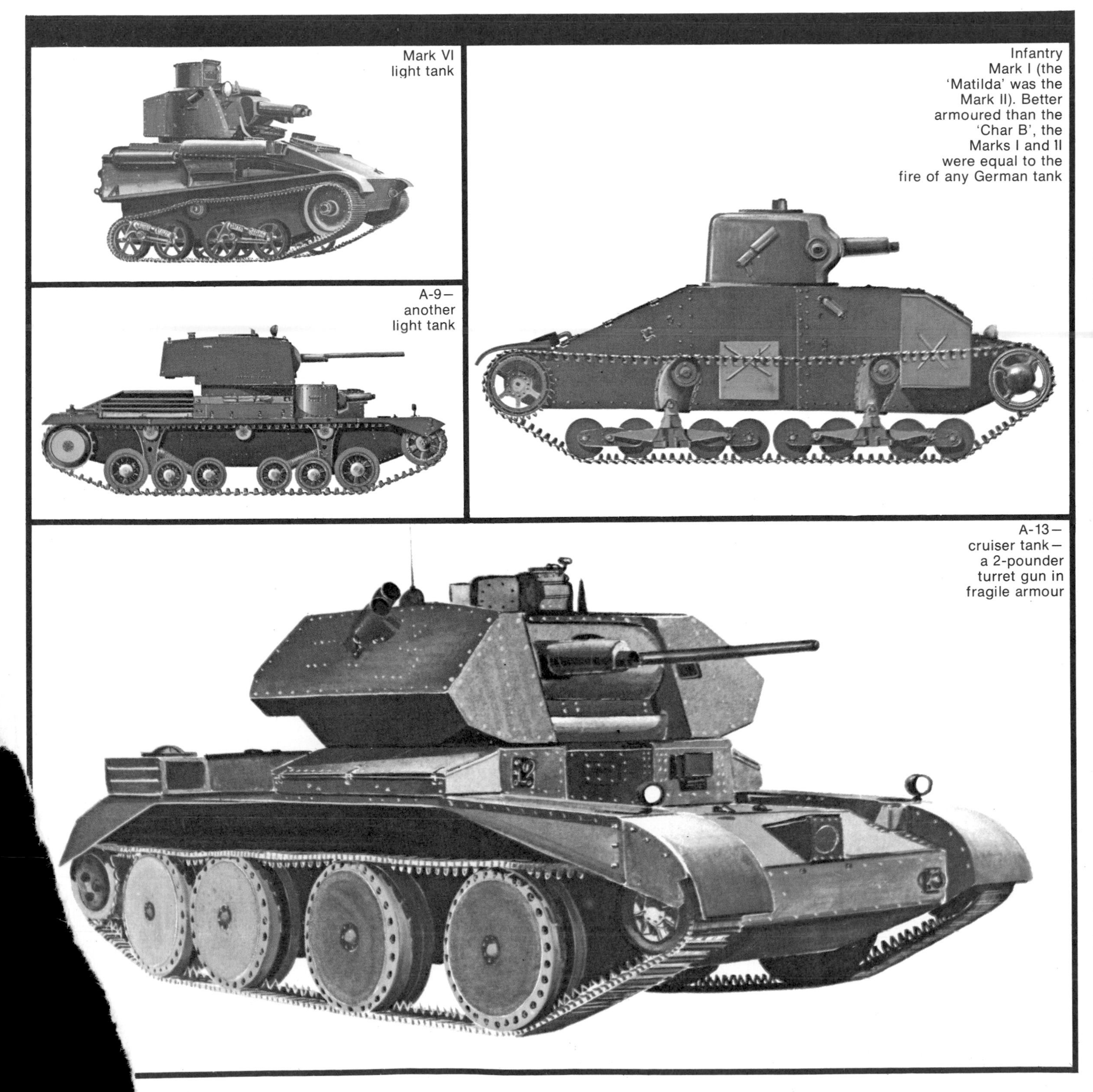

Mark VI light tank

Infantry Mark I (the 'Matilda' was the Mark II). Better armoured than the 'Char B', the Marks I and II were equal to the fire of any German tank

A-9—another light tank

A-13—cruiser tank—a 2-pounder turret gun in fragile armour

of the Allies. Their armoured formations, either through reasons of policy, doctrine, or lack of machines, had not practised together. Nor was there close co-operation with the air arm in the forefront of the land battle. So they were in fact singers without a song.

Fatally linked with their limited use of tanks was the failure of the Allied command to understand and make adequate strategic preparations to defeat the German attacks when they eventually came. There was a belief, sincerely held, despite warnings from men of practical experience, that some terrains were naturally tank-proof and others could be made secure by the erection of concrete and steel fortifications. It was thought that mechanised armies would not be able to pass through the narrow lanes, forests, and valleys of the Ardennes; that the Maginot Line would be impenetrable, and that the extensions of the Maginot Line along the Belgian frontier, certain inundations, and large built-up areas would also be serious obstacles to tank action.

Therefore the Allies made no elaborate plans for tank counterthrusts in the localities they had classified as tank-proof. The best, mobile armoured portions of the French army were not deployed in a manner permitting them to launch an immediate, concentrated counterstroke – even if their doctrine had envisaged such action. As we have seen, no such doctrine existed and as a result it was quite conceivable – even probable – that the light mechanised divisions and the new tank divisions could be flung in piecemeal (and therefore outnumbered) against superior enemy formations.

Their opponents, the Germans, lacked neither doctrine, equipment, training, nor experience. They were masters of a new war-winning technique that brought speed and mobility to the battlefield. By a combination of speed, thrust, and shock action they could bring a completely new momentum to the battle. The impact of the German armoured divisions could not be compared with that of the basically cavalry- and infantry-oriented methods of the Allies: they had in fact – with their range and striking power – introduced a new dimension to warfare.

Types of tank

Yet inevitably the balance of material was in favour of the Allies, who had more tanks than the Germans and many that were technically superior. In their ten armoured divisions the Germans had only 627 of the good Mark III and IV tanks, armed respectively with a 37-mm and a 75-mm gun, and protected by armour not more than 30-mm in thickness. The remaining 2,060 tanks were lightly armoured machines, mostly armed only with a 20-mm gun – although 381 of these were the sound Czech light T-38, equipped with a 37-mm gun. In addition to the 2,690 tanks with the armoured divisions, there were some 800 machines, mostly light ones, in reserve.

Against this array the French fielded about 3,000 machines, of which 500 were in units in the course of formation, plus older reserve machines. Of these 3,000 tanks, 1,292 were with the light mechanised divisions and the new tank divisions; the remainder were split up among the infantry armies. To this total should be added the British. On May 9 they had in France 210 light tanks in the light armoured regiments, and 100 'I' tanks in the 1st Army Tank Brigade. A further 174 light tanks and 156 of the new cruisers, belonging to the Armoured Division, were ready to cross the Channel as the battle started. Thus the Allies could oppose 3,000 German tanks with something like 3,600 of their own – if they chose.

On balance, the quality of the machines possessed by the two sides was about equal. The best French tank, the Char B, mounted the excellent 47-mm gun in a fully rotating turret and had a 75-mm gun mounted in the hull. The 20-ton Somua had a 47-mm gun, too, and was fast. The armour of these tanks was from 40 to 60 mm thick, compared with the best German armour of 30 mm. There were 800 of these new machines and even the older ones compared well with the German lighter vehicles. The 384 light British tanks were certain to be severely outclassed in a stand-up fight, because their guns could not penetrate armour, although their high speed and small size might serve them well when engaged on reconnaissance. But the 100 infantry tanks, of which 23 were the new Matilda, were covered by immensely thick armour (up to 70 mm) and quite safe from the fire of the German tank guns. And the 2-pounder gun, mounted in the thinner cruisers of the Armoured Division and also on the Matilda, was a weapon capable of penetrating any of the German machines at battle ranges.

But while the German and British machines (with one exception) were designed with two- or three-man turrets, the French machines had a single man in the turret confronted with the difficult task of commanding the vehicle, loading and firing the gun, and sometimes controlling the tactics of sub-units. The single British exception was the Mark I infantry tank, and this too presented terrible problems of combat efficiency and command.

This technical factor meant that the German and most of the British crews would be able to fight as teams within the all-embracing organisation of the armoured formations to which they belonged – but would also give the Germans an important advantage when their tank formations clashed with the French. This would make up for the fact that the majority of their tanks were vulnerable to the enemy tank guns, while their own guns would not penetrate the armour of a large proportion of the Allied tanks.

Leadership

The importance of personal command and direction is far more apparent to the fighting man in a climate of military opinion that insists that the generals should remain in the fore-front of the battle, in close touch with the leading tanks both visually and by radio. The Germans practised this method more than the Allies. The French kept their command posts further to the rear in accordance with the practice of 1918, and in any case did not possess a control system suited to high-speed combat. This fact, when combined with the separation of the tank-crew commander from the rest of his crew, would be liable to foster a drop in morale among the French tank units (there is evidence to support this – noted by British tank crews working alongside the French later in the campaign). It was clear, they said, that when faced by German tanks the French crews became cautious and were almost paralysed; and this exaggerated respect for the enemy was a result of the drubbing they had received in their first encounters with the German tanks. Even if the balance of morale between the contestants was equal on May 9, a week later the defects in organisation, leadership, and tactics had swung the scales irrevocably in favour of the Germans.

The overriding superiority of the Germans over the Allies was inherent in their intention to make use of well co-ordinated, massed, all-arms formations, launched into battle at the critical points, commanded by inspired men of vision and determination. Men of the stamp of Guderian and Reinhardt led the armoured corps from the van of the battle (with Rommel leading one of the divisions) – and this wealth of talent could not fail to overwhelm lesser men with old-fashioned ideas. For on the Allied side, none of the generals of 1940 had a deep knowledge of armoured warfare; with a startling lack of foresight, those men who had made a study of the subject had been distributed to positions where their talents lay unused. Martel commanded an infantry division; Broad, Pile, and Lindsay had been sent – some say deliberately – to posts unconnected with armoured warfare; and Hobart had been removed from the Active List, though he was ultimately to be recalled. De Gaulle was only just in the process of assembling a brand new and totally inexperienced tank division.

Let it be admitted that men such as these were not easy to live with. They had learned to be ruthless in the face of long-established tradition, that out-dated rules must be broken whatever the personal and immediate consequences, and that these circumstances applied in all armies. Men insufficiently imbued with spirit failed in the face of military 'vested interests'; those who stood up to them but were unblessed by fortune were removed – as Hobart was; those who fought, and were lucky, followed their stars to success in war in the forefront of the armoured battle.

In 1940, it was the Germans whose spirit and good fortune had combined – and so they dominated. Most of the French armoured commanders were ineffective, and the grossly outnumbered British tank men could not, except on one outstanding occasion, make a decisive contribution.

In numbers the Allies were superior to the Germans; in quality of equipment they were, on balance, about equal; in strategic and tactical application, they were markedly inferior.

The sheer superiority of German armoured technique ensured the certainty of thei[r] victory before the frontiers were crossed.

JOHN H. BATCHELOR is a te[chnical] nical artist with a special inte[rest] in military equipment of all [...] Study of his drawings fro[m the] age of five years shows th[...] clearly. A collector, exp[ert] shooter of antique an[d ...] firearms, he has always been consci[ous of the] expertise and artistic skill required [...] them. After service in the RAF he rea[...] profession in the technical publ[ications de-] partments at Bristol Aero Com[pany, ...] Bakers Ltd., and Saunders Roe Ltd[...]

German tank crews were well matched by the British but the defects of the French designs gave the Germans, relying on a firmer teamwork in battle, a definite advantage over French tank formations. The thinner German armour was the sacrifice made for other advantages which tipped the scale against the superior strength of individual Allied types. Similar use of armour in mass was therefore denied to the Allies

German

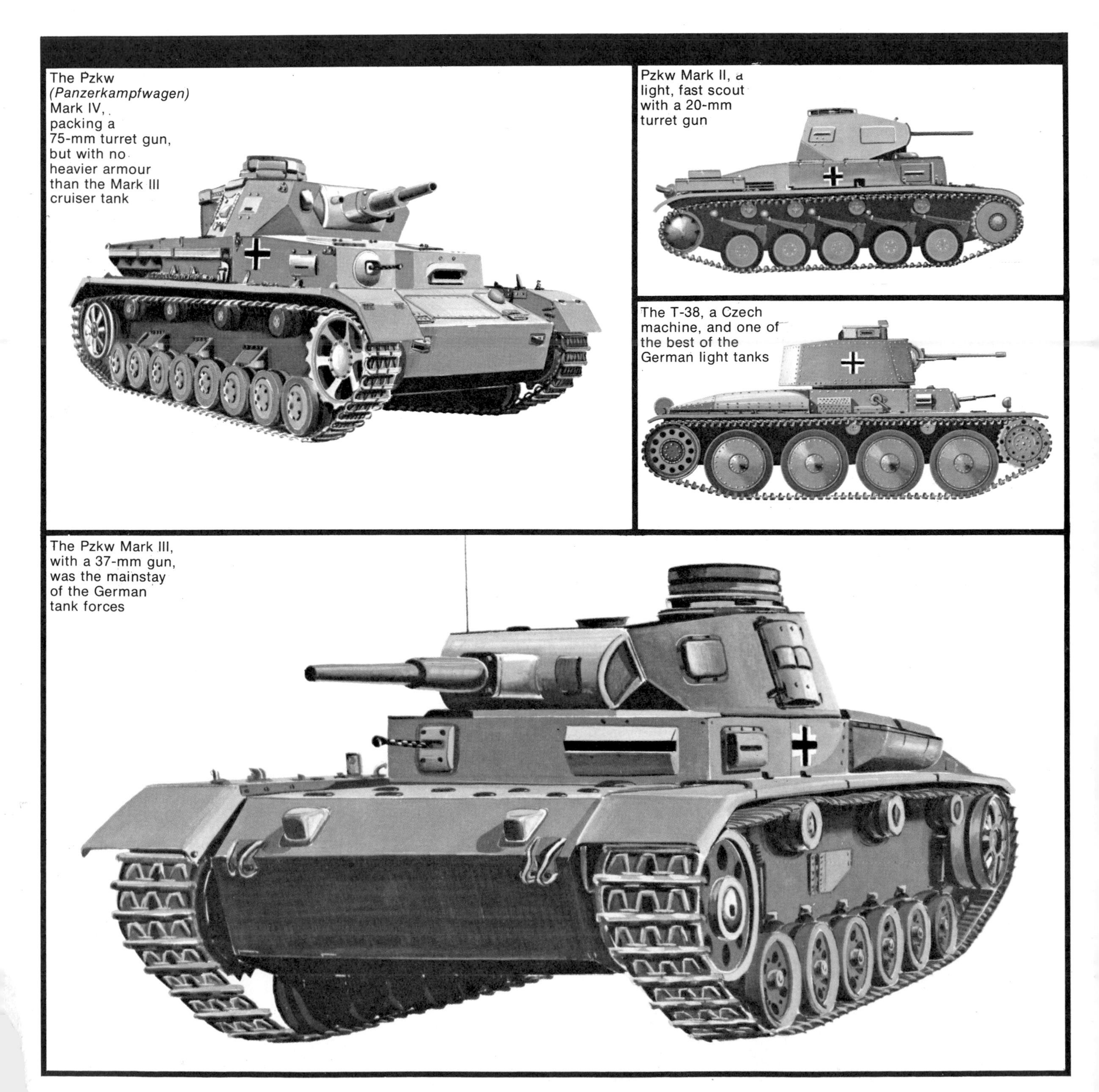

The Pzkw *(Panzerkampfwagen)* Mark IV, packing a 75-mm turret gun, but with no heavier armour than the Mark III cruiser tank

Pzkw Mark II, a light, fast scout with a 20-mm turret gun

The T-38, a Czech machine, and one of the best of the German light tanks

The Pzkw Mark III, with a 37-mm gun, was the mainstay of the German tank forces

the guns

As with the tanks, so with the guns: the artillery designers of the Second World War found themselves caught up in a ceaseless race to outmatch the ever-improving enemy defences. **Ian Hogg** shows how this affected the gunners' war, and how it resulted in the artillery revolution of greater ranges, mobility and fire control.

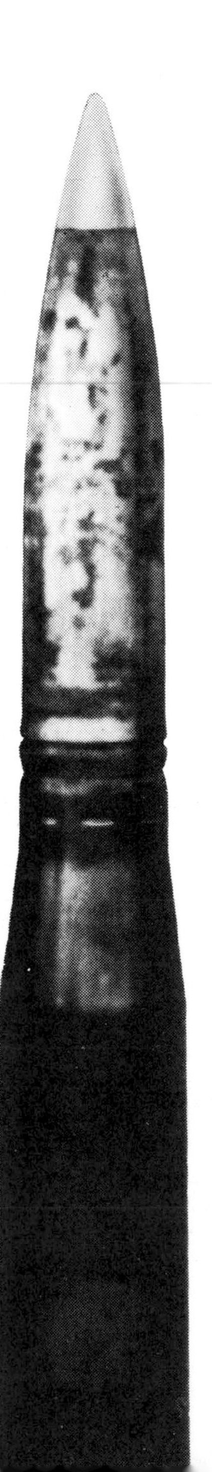

A thorough discussion of the history and development of every artillery weapon used in the Second World War would need several volumes, for the sheer size of the subjects is incredible; the German forces alone disposed over 200 land service weapons in 51 different calibres, without considering experimental models. Britain and America between them fielded about 100 artillery weapons, again not counting experimental models but only those which found their way into the hands of troops. Instead of trying to catalogue every weapon used, therefore, this section merely outlines the principal features of the research which developed during the war, and also brings to light one or two of the more unusual and less well-known weapons which were produced.

There are three main subjects to be explored:

- The routine improvement of weapons, in order to bring them into line with changing tactics and concepts of employment or to counter improvements in enemy defences;
- The improvements in ammunition introduced to step up the performance of existing weapons;
- The application of hitherto untried scientific principles.

In many cases these topics tend to overlap, but rather than try to develop a chronological story with these three aspects jumbled together, it is best to consider them as separate fields.

First, routine improvement. A good example of this in action is the history of the celebrated German 88-mm Flak Gun. This was originally conceived in the late 1920s by Krupp designers attached to the Bofors Company in Sweden. When in 1931 they returned to Essen with the design, the political climate seemed right. A prototype was built in 1932; and due to thorough paperwork it was an immediate success and was issued in 1933 as the 8·8-cm Flak Model 18. It should be stressed, in view of the exaggerated tales which became current in later years, that there was nothing unorthodox about this weapon at all—it was simply a good, sound, conventional anti-aircraft gun. It was taken to Spain by the Kondor Legion during the Civil War and tested in action; its potentialities as an anti-tank gun were also seen, though not advertised. This experience showed that there were a few weak points in the design and as a result, minor modifications were made in the mounting to improve stability and facilitate mass-production. This modified version became known as the Flak 36. In the following year an improved sighting and fire-control system was fitted, and the gun became the Flak Model 37. The 36 and 37 remained in service throughout the Second World War, being used in their primary role as an anti-aircraft gun; as an anti-tank gun, when fitted with shields and direct-fire sights; fitted to coastal craft and U-boats; used as a coast defence gun; and even mounted on a 12½-ton half-track as a self-propelled gun (though this was not one of its most successful applications).

By early 1939 though, in spite of its excellence, it became obvious that bombers were going to fly faster and higher than before, and the gun's performance would have to be improved. And so in 1939 Rheinmettal-Borsig were given a contract for an improved model, to be known as the Flak 41. Prototype trials began in 1941 and it was found that the gun, although a most efficient design, had a lot of teething troubles which were going to take time to eliminate. Since no one else had a contract for the gun, the Luftwaffe (which was responsible for Germany's anti-aircraft defences) was forced to use it or else do without. Consequently the next year saw a great deal of effort thrown in and by March 1943 the first issues were made.

The Flak 41, as finally produced, was a considerable improvement over the 18, 36, and 37. By using a turntable to carry the gun, instead of the more usual pedestal mounting, a much lower silhouette was achieved. The muzzle velocity and ceiling were both improved by adopting a more powerful cartridge, and the stability in action was excellent. The only fly in the ointment was the difficult extraction of the fired cartridge case, which is a flaw of major proportions in a quick-firing anti-aircraft gun. Different designs of barrel were produced in an effort to overcome the trouble, and a special brass cartridge case was developed; but none of these palliatives made much impression and the gun was never the success it might have been.

Some time after Rheinmettal had received their contract, a similar specification had been given to Krupp. Their development, sometimes referred to as the Flak 42, became more and more entangled with their concurrent development of 88-mm tank and anti-tank guns in the hopes of producing a family of weapons which would use interchangeable parts and common ammunition. Before the Krupp version had got off the drawing board, the Luftwaffe was demanding more performance than the design could produce, and in February 1943, not without a certain amount of relief, one feels, Krupp dropped the Flak 42 to concentrate on the tank and anti-tank weapons.

While the 88 shows an example of improvement of a particular calibre, the more common approach was to improve a particular class of weapon by raising the calibre; most anti-tank weapons display this technique. The British army began the war with a 2-pounder; followed it by a 6-pounder and then a 17-pounder; and finally had a 32-pounder in preparation when the war ended, having toyed briefly with a possible 55-pounder. America began with a 37-mm, took over the British 6-pounder and called it the 57-mm; then moved to a 3-inch based on a redundant anti-aircraft gun; then a 90-mm, also based on an AA gun, and was working on a 105-mm when the war ended. Germany also began with a 37-mm and progressed through 28, 42, 50, 75 and 88-mm to arrive at a 128-mm as the war closed.

All these series show steady progression in conventional guns, all intended to beat the forthcoming increases in enemy armour. However, the flaw in this system becomes apparent on looking at the British 32-pounder or the German 12.8-cm Pak 44—bigger calibres may mean a bigger punch, but they invariably mean bigger guns as well, and this means more weight to move about. This is a considerable drawback for an anti-tank gun which usually has to be emplaced by manpower, and certainly the 32-pounder was too big for its task; even had the war continued, it is doubtful whether it would have been accepted into service.

Anti-aircraft guns tend to show a similar pattern among all nations, always striving to extract more ceiling and greater velocity; the increased ceiling meant that higher-flying aircraft could be engaged, while higher velocity meant a shorter time between firing the gun and the shell arriving at the target, and hence less room for error in the prediction of the target's position at the time of the shell's arrival. The two groups of anti-aircraft weapons in common use were the light guns, such as the German 37-mm and the British and US-employed Bofors 40-mm, and the heavy guns, such as the German 88, 105, and 128-mm guns, the British 3.7-inch, 4.5-inch, and 5.25-inch guns, and the American 90-mm, 105-mm, and 120-mm types. The light guns relied on throwing up a heavy volume of fire at a high rate, to counter the low-flying attacker. The heavies fired at slower rates, threw heavier shells, and had higher ceilings to deal with the high-level bomber. But strangely enough, all the combatants had a gap in their defences, which lay between the maximum ceiling of the light guns—about 6,000 feet—and the minimum effective ceiling of the heavies—about 10,000 feet. Below this figure the heavy gun could not swing fast enough to follow a fast low flyer. In an endeavour to fill this gap, development took place in both Britain and Germany to provide a medium AA gun. As far as Britain was concerned, a paramount feature of any weapon proposed in 1940 was to avoid usurping production already hard at work with the more basic weapons needed for simple survival. In view of this, the first question the designers asked themselves was: 'What existing gun can be worked over to fill the bill?' After a few false starts the design coalesced around the existing coast artillery 6-pounder gun, the same calibre as the anti-tank gun but using a heavier cartridge and capable of greater range. This was adapted to a twin-barrel mounting on a three-wheeled trailer, and work then began on designing a suitable automatic feed system to get the rate of fire thought necessary, and a fire-control system to put the shells where they were needed. Since the guns were originally designed for hand loading, the adaptation to autofeed turned out to be more difficult than had at first been imagined; then Allied air superiority gave the project less priority; and, in the event, the twin 6-pounder never entered service and Britain never had a medium AA gun.

The German development was not restricted to an existing weapon, since the 'gap' had been appreciated before the war, and in 1936 Rheinmettal was given a contract to develop a 50-mm gun. This was eventually introduced in 1940 in limited numbers for an extended troop trial to assess whether such a weapon was desirable and whether the Flak 41, as it was known, would fill the requirement. For a variety of reasons the gun was not a success, but the experience showed that the medium AA gun was needed, and a great deal of thought went into the design of a completely integrated weapon system, probably the first such system to be conceived as a complete entity. It was to comprise a 55-mm automatic gun, with matched radar, predictor, displacement corrector, and full electro-hydraulic remote control of a six-gun battery. By the time all these theories and designs had been put together it was mid-1943, and the production of such a far-reaching concept was so difficult that the war ended before the weapon was completed. To act as a stop-gap, the now-obsolescent 50-mm anti-tank gun was fitted with an automatic loading system, but this idea fell by the wayside, and it is doubtful if any were ever made. All in all, the medium AA gun story is remarkable in the similarity of British and German experience.

Imperial War Museum

The much-feared German '88'. Disliked equally by Allied armour and infantry the Pak 43 was both versatile and hard-hitting

Imperial War Museum

US crewmen fire a 120-mm AA gun. The largest American AA gun, it could be fired by remote control as well as manually

Imperial War Museum

The British 4·5-inch static AA gun is seen here being loaded by its crew, its 55-pound shells ready to hand

In the field artillery world practically all development was simply a matter of improvement on existing designs. No nation in its right mind would attempt a major re-equipment of its standard weapons in the middle of a war. The British 25-pounder served valiantly, and modifications to meet special demands included the self-propelled 'Bishop' (on a Valentine chassis) and 'Sexton' (on a Ram chassis); the Australian-developed 'Short' or 'Baby' 25-pounder with a truncated barrel, no shield, short trail and castor wheel for easy manoeuvring in the jungle; it was tried as a self-propelled gun (SP) in many vehicles including the Lloyd carrier, which was asking too much of such a light vehicle; it was strapped to the cargo bed of a DUKW for supporting amphibious landings; and it was even considered for the armament of submarines. Similarly, the American 105-mm howitzer was tried in a variety of SP mountings, starting with a half-track, until the Sherman-based M-7 became standardized as the 'Priest'; it was shortened and placed on a light carriage for use by airborne units; it was mounted in tank turrets as a close support gun; and, like the 25-pounder, mounted on the long-suffering DUKW.

The German 1E FH 18, more or less the equivalent of the 25-pounder and 105 howitzer, suffered similar, though more drastic, changes. First it was given a muzzle brake and a heavier charge with a long-range shell; then in an attempt to reduce the weight, like the 'Baby 25-pounder', the barrel and recoil system were mounted on the carriage of the 75-mm Pak 40 anti-tank gun; the wheels were removed and it was dropped bodily into a tank hull to provide an assault gun; it was grafted on to a variety of tracked mountings. But eventually a complete re-design was called for and Rheinmettal was given a contract. Before their offering was ready, the experiences of the Russian Front had shown that certain features were mandatory in the next generation of field guns. Briefly, these were that the gun must have a good anti-tank performance for self-protection; at the same time it had to be capable of hiding in forests and firing out at high angles; the range had to be at least 8 miles without demanding special ammunition; it had to have all-round traverse, since Soviet partisans could attack from any direction; and it had to weigh less than 2,200 pounds. Now even today a designer would have a hard time meeting that specification, but in 1943 both Krupp and Skoda rose to the challenge.

The Skoda version, the 10.5-cm 1E FH 43, was most ingenious: the carriage had virtually a normal split trail at the rear, plus another split trail at the front, beneath the barrel, and a firing pedestal beneath the axle. In action, the equipment rested on the two rear trails and the pedestal, and the front trails were laid on the ground to form a cruciform stable platform above which the gun could rotate through 360 degrees, the four legs giving stability at any angle of the barrel. The novelty of this carriage lay in the fact that the two front legs were not rigidly attached to the carriage; to compensate for eneven ground they were permitted to lie at any convenient angle. A hydraulic system was arranged so that slow movement of the legs – as during folding and unfolding to and from the travelling position – was freely permitted, but fast movement – as the firing shock – would cause the legs to lock rigidly to the carriage and give the desired stability.

Krupp, under the same nomenclature, produced two models; one was very similar in general design to Skoda's, though without the hydraulic system, while the other was based on a more or less conventional cruciform platform of the type familiar in AA guns. However, none of the designs, Krupp or Skoda, were ready for production before the war's end, and only prototypes existed.

The German super-guns

The heaviest field equipments seen during the war were the German self-propelled howitzers generically known as 'Karl Morsers'. These were of two calibres, 540-mm and 600-mm, mounted on the same type of carriage. Six carriages were made and the exact disposition of barrels between them is in some doubt; the carriages were numbered I to VI; Vehicle V was captured by the US 1st Army and found to have a 540-mm barrel, yet photographs captured later showed this same carriage to have a 600-mm barrel. It is probably safe to assume that three of each calibre were made. The date of introduction is also a little vague, but it seems fairly certain that the 600-mm version was introduced in 1942 and the 540-mm in 1944.

The carriage of 'Karl' was a simple rectangular box, divided into three compartments. The first held the Mercedes-Benz engine and transmission; the second carried the gun; and the third held the carriage raising and lowering gear. After driving into position on its tracks the engine was used to drive the lowering gear, which rotated the anchorages of the suspension torsion bars so as to allow the chassis to be lowered to the ground until the suspension and track were relieved of the weight. For long-distance moves the gun and recoil system were removed from the carriage, dismantled, and loaded on to special trailers; the carriage was then winched on to a special tank-transporter. For very long distances the complete gun and carriage assembly could be slung between two railway flat wagons by means of special trusses.

In the use of railway artillery Germany virtually had the field to herself. This class of weapon is really the prerogative of the Continental nation with a well-developed rail system by which it can readily deploy them to any front. In contrast, Britain and the USA, while possessing railway guns, used them solely as mobile coast defence units, since the problem of transporting two or three hundred tons of railway mounting across the Channel was not a trick to be undertaken lightly. Indeed, the British and American weapons were almost entirely relics of the First World War which had been in mothballs. 1940 saw a few more mountings hastily cobbled together from available spares and hurried to cover the Channel, just as in similar fashion American guns were mobilised and deployed in 1941. In 1944 reports from France indicated that heavy railway artillery might be of use in demolishing strongpoints to be expected in the final assault in Germany, and designs were hastily prepared by the Americans for a number of 16-inch guns, but within a few weeks it was seen that heavy artillery of this class had been rendered superfluous by the quality and quantity of air support available, and the demand was cancelled.

The German army had a vast range of railway guns from 150-mm upwards, but two were really outstanding and deserve closer examination. The first was the 28-cm K5(E) – Kanone, Model 5, *Eisenbahnlafette* – which became their standard super-heavy railway gun and was probably the finest design of its kind in the world. The basic arithmetic and paperwork had been done in the late 1920s and early 1930s, and work began on the gun in 1934. (It is worth noting that every German railway gun was designed and built by Krupp – Rheinmettal did design two, but they were never made.) First, a 150-mm barrel was produced for tests; it had been decided that to obtain the great range demanded, a conventionally rifled barrel was out of the question. A design was prepared with 12 deep grooves and having a shell carrying 12 ribs, or splines, to match. The theory behind this was that the engraving of a conventional copper driving band on the shell gave rise to very high pressure in the gun chamber; by using the spline and groove method to spin the shell, this resistance was removed, and the shell would step off more smartly, allowing a bigger propelling charge to be used without over-straining the gun. The 150-mm test barrel proved that the theory was right, and a full-calibre 280-mm barrel was built.

The mounting was a simple box-girder assembly carried on two six-axle bogies, with the front bogie slung so as to allow the front of the box-girder to be swung across it for aiming the gun. For large angles the whole weapon was mounted on a special portable turntable built at the end of a short spur of track laid at the desired firing point. Each gun was supplied with a special train which included wagons for carrying the turntable, light-anti-aircraft guns for local defence, air-conditioned ammunition wagons, living quarters and kitchen for the gunners, and flat wagons to carry their entitlement of motor transport.

By 1940 eight of these complete equipments were in service, and production continued throughout the war, 25 being built in all. The German gunners called them 'Slim Bertha', but to the Allies in Italy one at least became famous as 'Anzio Annie'.

With the 561-pound pre-rifled shell the gun could reach to 68,000 yards. A rocket-assisted shell was later developed which increased this range, with a certain loss of accuracy, to 94,000 yards. Finally, the Peenemünde Research Establishment designed a 300-pound dart-like projectile which was fired from a special 310-mm smooth-bore barrel and which ranged to 170,000 yards. Although coming too late for general issue, these 'Peenemünde Arrow Shells' were issued for troop trials in the field, and some were fired against the US 3rd Army at ranges of about 70 miles.

The second railway gun, 'Gustav', was the biggest gun the world has ever seen – the Krupp-designed 800-mm Kanone. The idea was conceived in 1937 of a pair of super-guns; they were of quite conventional design, except for their immense size. Too large to be moved in one piece, they were transported piecemeal in special trains and assembled at the selected sites by travelling cranes. When assembled, the mounting straddled two sets of standard-gauge rails, with 80 wheels taking the 1,350-ton weight. An armour or concrete-piercing shell of 7 tons was propelled by a 1¾-ton charge to a range of 23 miles, or a 5-ton high-explosive shell to 29 miles. The first equipment, 'Gustav', was proved at the Rugenwalde range in March 1943, in Hitler's presence. The only record of its use was at the siege of Sebastopol; the gun was sited at Bakhchisary and fired some 30 to 40 rounds. One shot is recorded as having penetrated through 100 feet of earth to destroy a Soviet ammunition dump at Severnaya Bay. The subsquent history of the gun is un-

The short 25-pounder Mark I was developed by the Australians. Its lighter construction allowed its use in jungle terrain

The German 12.8-cm K44 anti-tank gun. Luckily for Allied armour this powerful and sophisticated gun saw no service

Several versions of a self-propelled 25-pounder were produced. This version, mounted on a Lloyd carrier, was not adopted

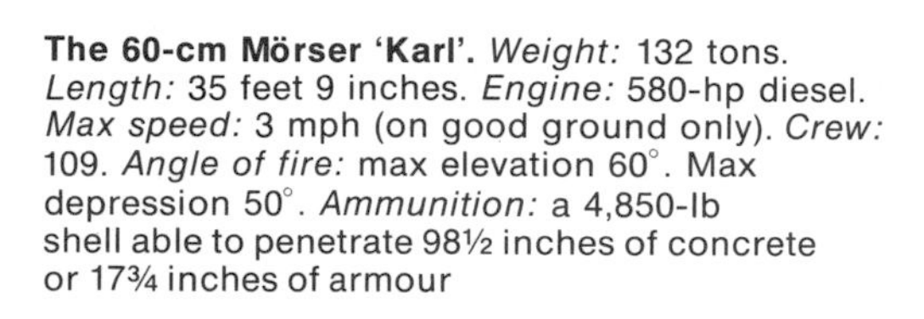

The 60-cm Mörser 'Karl'. *Weight:* 132 tons. *Length:* 35 feet 9 inches. *Engine:* 580-hp diesel. *Max speed:* 3 mph (on good ground only). *Crew:* 109. *Angle of fire:* max elevation 60°. Max depression 50°. *Ammunition:* a 4,850-lb shell able to penetrate 98½ inches of concrete or 17¾ inches of armour

The 80-cm Kanone(E) Dora L40·6. *Range:* 51,040 yards (29 miles). *Crew:* 250 (for assembly and firing), 4,120 in all. *Ammunition:* one 10,500-lb shell, 25 feet long (plus case). *Rate of fire:* 2 rounds-per-hour

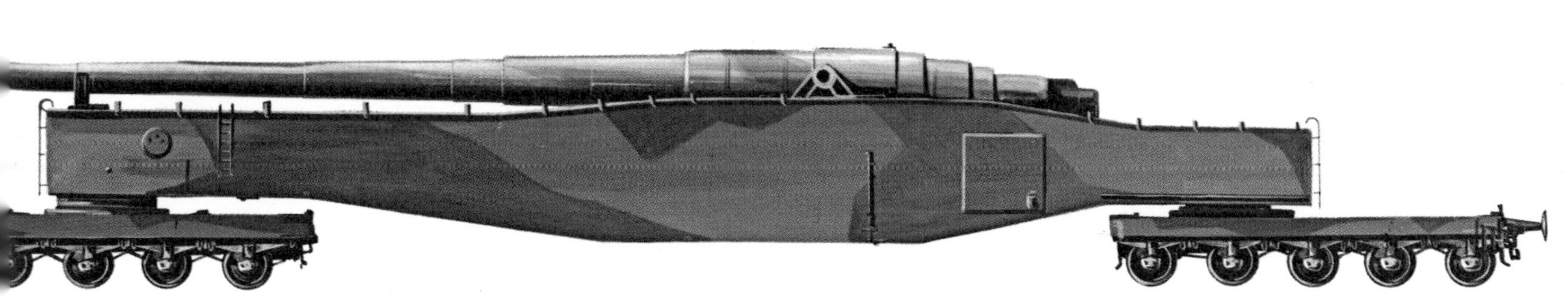

The 28-cm K5(E). *Weight:* 479,600 lb. *Length:* 96 feet. *Range:* 66,880 yards (38 miles). *Crew:* 10 (for firing)

The guns of Germany

The 10·5-cm Leichte Feldhaubitze 18m L/28. *Weight:* 4,488 lb. *Range:* 13,377 yards. *Crew:* 6. *Rate of fire:* 6-8 rounds-per-minute

The 10·5-cm Leichte Feldhaubitze 43 L/28. *Weight:* 5,060 lb. *Crew:* 6. *Range:* 17,875 yards. *Rate of fire:* 6 rounds-per-minute

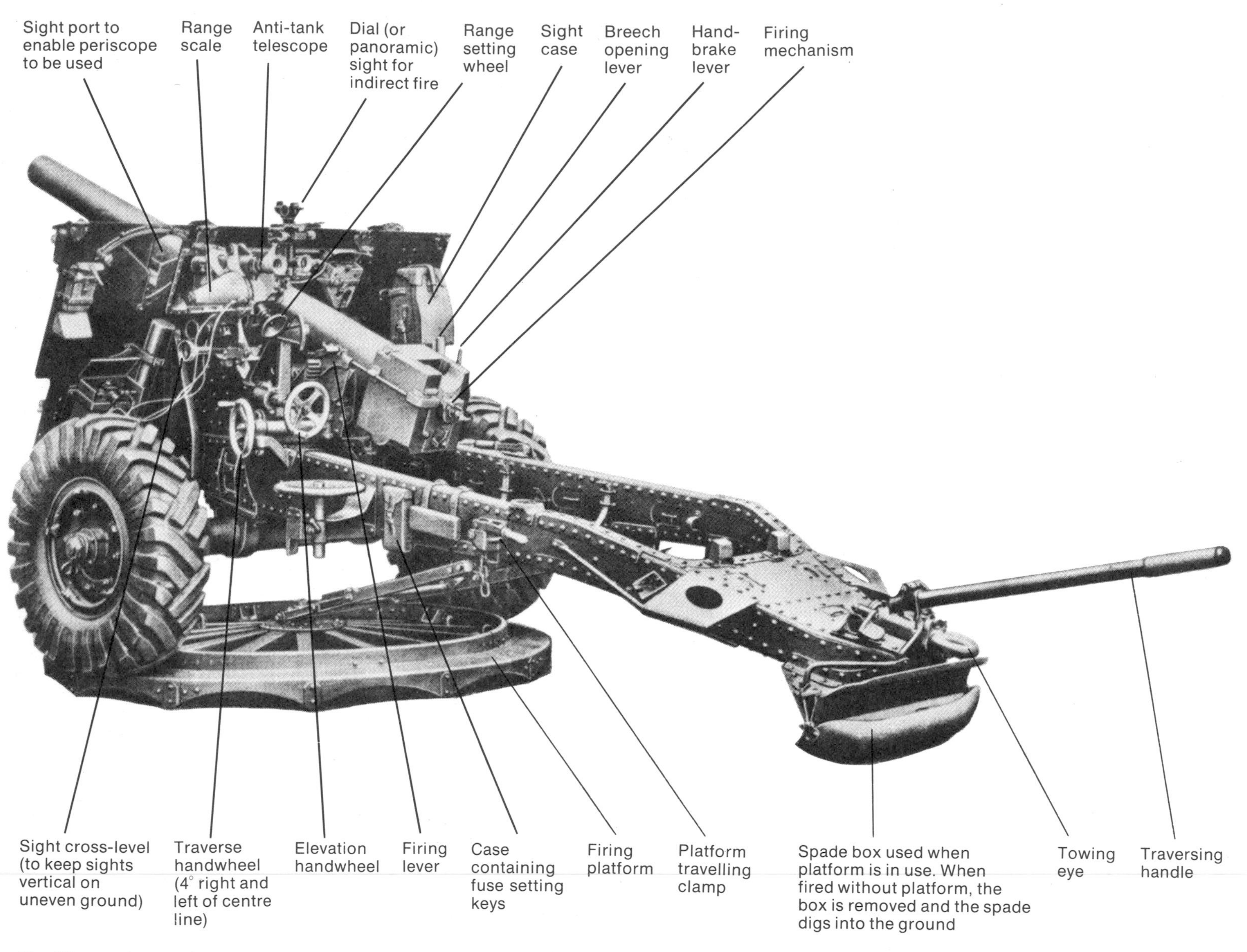

The 25-pounder gun-howitzer. Manoeuvrable, hard-hitting – it was one of the most reliable artillery pieces of the war

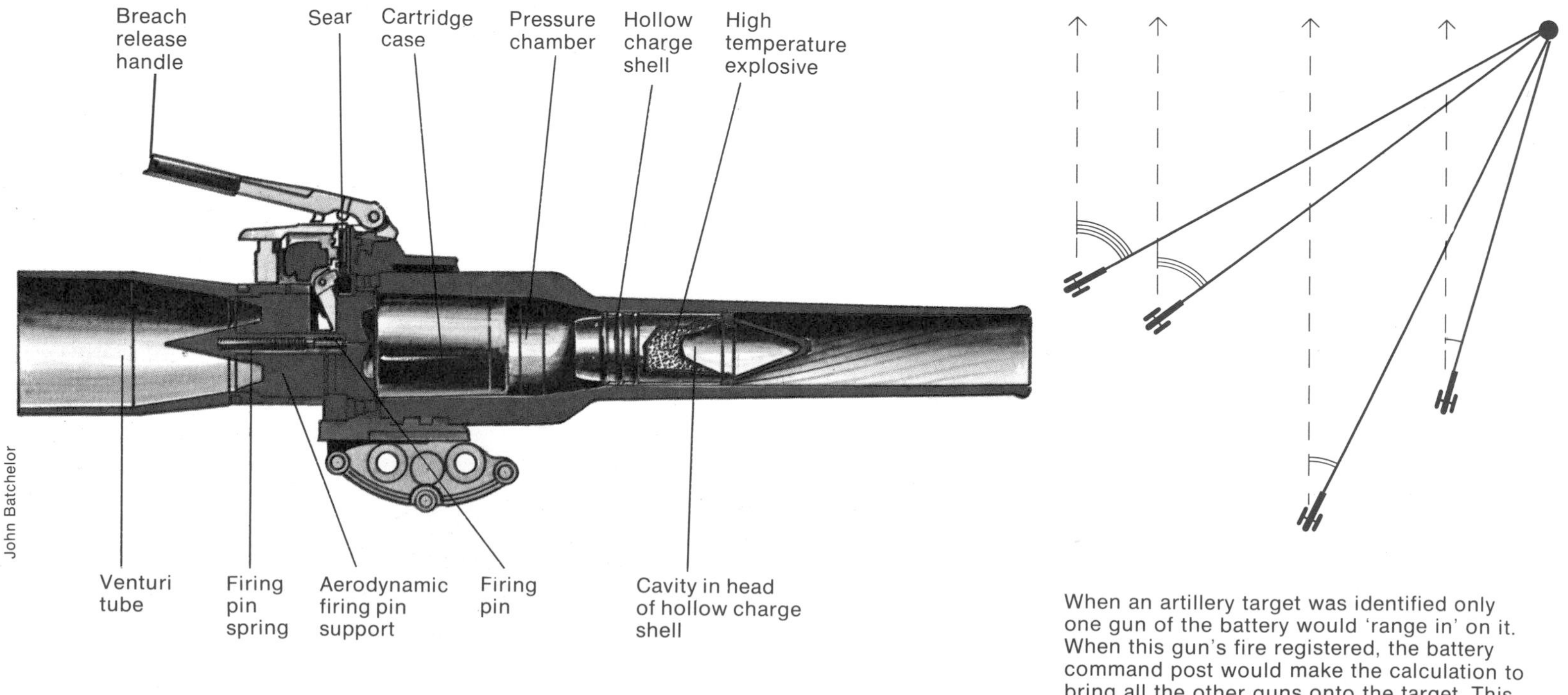

The working parts of a recoilless rifle. Part of the blast travels backwards out of the venturi, thus eliminating recoil. The hollow-charge shell could blast a hole through thick armour

When an artillery target was identified only one gun of the battery would 'range in' on it. When this gun's fire registered, the battery command post would make the calculation to bring all the other guns onto the target. This principle could be extended to include any number of guns, the key to success being good communications

known (it was presumably captured by the Red Army).

The second equipment, 'Dora', so far as is known, never left the proving ground, though what happened to it at the end of the war is a minor mystery (some ammunition and a spare barrel were found at Krupp's proof establishment at Meppen near the Dutch border).

The detachment necessary to man, maintain, and give local protection to Gustav was 4,120 men strong, commanded by a major-general. The actual fire-control and operation of the gun demanded a colonel and 500 men, and the construction or dismantling of the weapon took between four and six weeks. A long-range 'Peenemünde Arrow Shell' was developed for Gustav, but, so far as is known, was never fired. This was to weigh 2,200 pounds and range to 100 miles. There was also a proposition to mount a 520-mm gun on the same carriage to fire rocket-assisted shells and 'Peenemünde Arrow Shells' to a range of 118 miles for cross-channel bombardment, but this never got past the drawing-board.

If it is accepted that it is not a good idea to tamper with a good gun design in the middle of a war, then the only way to render the gun more effective is to improve the ammunition, and this technique was frequently adopted during the war. And in no field is this seen to greater effect than in the battle against the tank. The reason for this is fairly self-evident: personnel targets remain more or less the same—once the anti-personnel projectile is perfected it can stay as it is. On the other hand, once a new anti-tank projectile appears, it is only a matter of time before the enemy put thicker armour on his tanks.

At the outbreak of war there were two types of anti-tank projectile: the armour-piercing (AP) shot, and the AP shell. The difference is basic. Shot are solid, with no explosive filling, and rely purely on their speed to smash through the armour and do damage inside the tank by their impact, the fragments of plate they knock off during penetration, and their own effect when they penetrate the plate and bounce around inside the tank. AP shells, on the other hand, have a small cavity filled with high explosive and are fitted with a fuse in the base. The shell penetrates, similarly to shot, by brute force, but the fuse is activated by the impact and, after a short delay to allow the shell to pass through the plate and enter the tank, the explosive is detonated, shattering the shell into fragments and adding to the shot-like damage already caused. On paper the shell is the better proposition, since there is the bonus of the explosive filling. But paper figures tend to be deceptive, and in fact the shot is probably the more practical projectile, because the high-explosive (HE) cavity weakens the shell, and the fuse is precariously supported against the hammer-blow of impact. Britain held firmly to the shot theory for anti-tank work, though many years of experience in producing AP shells for naval use was available. Several other nations preferred AP shell, bewitched by the HE bonus.

Most of the belligerents entered the war with a plain shot or shell and relied on throwing it hard enough to penetrate the opposing tanks. So long as the target was relatively lightly armoured this was successful; but, naturally, each side began to increase armour thickness on each succeeding generation of tank. The quick answer to this was to increase the gun charge or even the calibre, and thus throw the projectile harder, but there comes a time when the impact is too much for the projectile, and instead of piercing, it merely shatters on the outside of the target without doing any damage.

The answer to this was to protect the tip of the shot or shell with a softer cap, which tended to spread the impact stresses over the shoulders of the projectile, instead of concentrating them into the tip. This preserved the piercing action to higher velocities, and the gun was again winning the battle. The next move belonged to the tank designers who made their armour thicker, and so it went on until the projectile was once more shattering, cap or no cap. At this point the projectile designers were faced with a new problem: if it was futile to throw the projectile harder, might it not be possible to throw a harder projectile? And what was harder than an armour-piercing projectile? Tungsten carbide, a diamond-hard alloy, provided an answer, but it was about one-and-a-half times as heavy as steel, so that it could not easily be made into a projectile. Furthermore, it was expensive and in short supply.

The first application of tungsten to an anti-tank projectile was by the German army in their 28-mm *Schwere Panzerbuchse* 41, a weapon with a unique tapered barrel. The shot consisted of a small core of tungsten carbide held in a light alloy casing of 28-mm calibre. As the shot was fired down the gun barrel, so the calibre diminished and the light alloy casing was ground down, until it emerged as a 21-mm shot. This squeezing enhanced the velocity and changed the ratio of shot diameter to weight. The velocity reached was 4,000 feet per second, and, on impact with the target, the hardness of the core was impervious to impact shock and penetrated successfully.

About the same time—late 1940—a similar idea had been put forward by a Mr Janáček, a Czechoslovakian weapon designer working in England. While his idea was still under consideration, a specimen of the German weapon was captured in North Africa and flown home for trials: the idea was seen to be feasible. The British version was in the form of a taper-bore adapter to be fitted to the existing 2-pounder gun, together with a special tungsten-cored shot, known under the code name of 'Littlejohn', an Anglicised version of Janáček. The advantage here was that the adapter could be removed to permit firing normal explosive shells, but could be refitted quickly for the special shot, whereas the German design required a special pattern of high-explosive shell to be developed, a difficult feat in such a small calibre. The 'Littlejohn' attachment and its shot were not used in towed artillery, since by the time they were ready for service the anti-tank units were armed with 6-pounders, but it was used on 2-pounder and American 37-mm guns mounted in armoured cars.

To use tungsten in a conventional gun, a different approach was needed. The first attempt, for the 6-pounder, was the 'AP Composite Rigid' (APCR) shot, a tungsten core mounted in an alloy sheath of approximately the same dimensions as the conventional steel shot for the gun. By virtue of its light alloy content the APCR shot was somewhat lighter and thus had a higher velocity when fired. Unfortunately the ratio of weight-to-diameter was unfavourable, giving a poor ballistic coefficient or 'carrying power', and while the short-range performance was impressive, the velocity soon dropped, and at ranges over 1,000 yards, steel shot was just as good, sometimes better. Some German weapons were also provided with the same type of projectile, and one was designed for use in the Soviet 76.2-mm field gun which the Germans captured in large numbers and converted into an anti-tank gun. Unfortunately for them, by early 1942 the shortage of tungsten in Germany began to be felt, and in the middle of that year a ban was placed on the use of tungsten in ammunition; what scarce supplies there were had been earmarked for machine tool production, not for throwing about the Russian steppes. After strong remonstrations, the 5-cm Pak 38 anti-tank gun was specifically exempted from this ban, since at that time it was the only weapon capable of stopping a Russian T-34 tank, provided it was supplied with tungsten-cored shot.

Although the 6-pounder APCR shot seemed reasonably successful, it was not the ideal answer. The ideal, in fact, sounded ridiculous: what was wanted was a shot which in the barrel was large-calibre and light, so as to pick up speed quickly and leave the gun at high velocity, but which outside the barrel should be small in diameter and heavy, so as to have good 'carrying power' and keep up its high velocity for a long range. These two conflicting requirements were fused into one projectile by two British designers, Permutter and Coppock, of the Armaments Research Department. Even before the 6-pounder had received its APCR shot they were at work, and in March 1944 their 'AP Discarding Sabot' shot was provided for the 6-pounder. In this design, the tungsten core is contained in a streamlined steel sheath or sub-projectile; this in turn is carried in a light-alloy framework or 'sabot' of the full gun calibre. On firing, this sabot holds the sub-projectile centralised in the bore and gives the whole thing the combination of light weight and large area which is wanted for velocity. But firing actually 'unlocks' the sabot, and as the shot leaves the gun muzzle, so the sabot is thrown clear, allowing the sub-projectile to race to the target at velocities of the order of 3,000 feet per second. Now, since the sub-projectile's sheath is virtually a skin round the tungsten core, it follows that the weight is high in relation to the cross-section—the ideal condition for good carrying power and thus long-range performance. A similar projectile for the 17-pounder followed in September 1944, and one was under development for the 20-pounder tank gun when the war ended.

More punch from the hollow charge

Running parallel with this unfolding story of piercing projectiles was the development of the hollow-charge principle into a viable weapon. This illustrates the adaptation of a well-documented scientific phenomenon to a weapon of war: almost 200 years ago a Norwegian engineer had observed that hollowing out the face of an explosive charge made it cut deeper into rock when blasting. In the 1880s an American experimenter, Monroe, found that when firing guncotton slabs against armour plate, the initials 'USN' engraved in the guncotton reproduced themselves in mirror-like form in the face of the armour plate. From his observations and reports the phenomenon became known as the 'Monroe Effect' and was a scientific curiosity for many years. Just before the First World War one or two inventors toyed with the idea of employing this effect in mines and torpedoes, but since no one really understood why it did what it did, it was difficult to engineer the idea into a

Two sorts of armour-piercing shot. *Left and centre:* the British Armour-Piercing Discarding Sabot which shed its lightweight casing and *(right)* the Armour-Piercing Composite Rigid, which kept it until impact

The German airborne 28-mm PzB-41 gun had a barrel which tapered from 28-mm to 20-mm, giving its tungsten steel shot a muzzle velocity of 4,600 feet per second

Recoilless: the British 3·7-inch RCL saw no service in the war

practical form.

Just before the Second World War broke out, a Swiss consortium approached the British government to offer a 'new and powerful explosive' for anti-tank use—at a high price. The inventors refused to divulge any information until cash was forthcoming, but were prepared to demonstrate their projectile being fired. An astute observer from the Research Department of Woolwich Arsenal went to Switzerland to watch the firing; being a well-read expert on ammunition development and history, he realised that what he was watching was not a new and powerful explosive so much as a practical application of the Monroe Effect. Upon his return to Woolwich he duly reported this, and, since it appeared that the Monroe Effect could be made to work, research immediately began into applying it to a light anti-tank grenade which the infantry soldier could fire from his rifle. Before the outbreak of war, this '68 Grenade' had been perfected and was in production, and carries the distinction of being the first weapon ever to reach the hands of troops which relied on the Monroe Effect, or as it came to be known, the Hollow-Charge Principle.

What is this Hollow-Charge Principle? Put simply, it consists of forming the forward surface of the shell's explosive charge into a cone or hemisphere and then lining this with a thin metal liner. The shell is then fitted with a suitably shaped nose, for ballistic effect and also to give the vital 'stand-off' distance. This is the distance from the target—a matter of a few inches—at which the explosive must be detonated in order for the hollow charge to work effectively. On detonating the explosive at its rear end, the detonation wave exerts an immense pressure on the metal of the liner; the cone shape virtually 'focusses' the explosive energy and causes the metal of the liner to be shaped into a jet of finely-divided metal and explosive gas, shooting toward the target at speeds of up to 20,000 feet per second. The stand-off distance is necessary in order to allow this jet to form and accelerate. When the jet strikes the target plate, the pressure exerted is so great as to blast a hole through the armour, blowing splinters of metal from the inside and permitting the white-hot jet to pass into the tank where it will set fire to fuel or ammunition, and, of course, kill or injure the crew.

The great virtue of the hollow-charge shell is that its performance is always the same, irrespective of the velocity at which it strikes. Even if the shell were standing still when detonated, the penetration would be the same. Because of this, it could be fired from guns too small to fire the large cartridges needed to give the necessary velocity to normal piercing projectiles. As soon as the 68 Grenade was seen to be successful, design began on other hollow-charge projectiles. A great deal of work went into producing one for the 25-pounder, though in the end it was never issued, since the AP shot issued for that gun was quite satisfactory and there was no real need for a hollow-charge shell. Then came a request from India to produce an anti-tank projectile for the 3.7-inch Pack Howitzer, the modern version of Kipling's immortal 'screw-gun'. This gun, a small and portable weapon, could not be made to fire a piercing projectile at anything like the velocity needed to defeat even Japanese tanks, and a hollow-charge shell was designed and placed in production. The same shell was used in the 95-mm howitzer, an abortive infantry support gun which never saw service as a towed weapon, though it was employed as a self-propelled support weapon by the Royal Marines in Normandy and by the Armoured Corps.

By 1944, though, sufficient basic research had been done into this principle for it to be seen that a spinning shell was not the ideal method of employing hollow charges, since the spin tended to spread the jet out and give poor penetration. Finned projectiles were more effective, and consequently no more artillery shells were designed around the hollow charge; it was extensively employed, instead, for infantry weapons such as the PIAT, the Bazooka, and a variety of rifle grenades.

The Germans, and later the Russians, embraced the hollow-charge shell wholeheartedly. The Germans began issuing shell in late 1940 and eventually almost every German field and tank weapon had a hollow-charge shell, thus giving every gun or howitzer an anti-tank capability. Indeed, so short were the Germans of anti-tank guns after the Russian invasion got under way, that they hastily collected up all the French army's 75-mm guns and assembled hundreds of them on to redundant anti-tank gun carriages of German design. A hollow-charge shell was produced and these makeshift weapons were deployed in Russia to stem the advancing Soviet tanks until 75-mm and 88-mm anti-tank guns were in sufficient supply. Judging from appearances, the Soviet hollow-charge shells were developed as virtual copies of German designs which had been captured.

In addition to artillery shell Germany also used the principle for infantry weapons such as the *Panzerfaust*, rifle grenades, and even a small shell which could be fired from a signal pistol. They also employed the principle in an ingenious attempt to prolong the life of the prewar 37-mm anti-tank gun, whose piercing projectile was, by 1942, no longer effective against current tanks. A large hollow-charge bomb was fitted with a hollow tail carrying fins; within this tail was a stick which fitted snugly into the barrel of the 37-mm gun, allowing the tail and fins to slide over the barrel. A blank cartridge completed the outfit, and this was used to fire the stick bomb to ranges of 300 to 400 yards. The bomb's warhead was about 6 inches in diameter and carried about 8 pounds of explosive, giving a devastating effect at the target. In all fairness, it must be pointed out that Lieutenant-Colonel Blacker, inventor of the PIAT and the 'Black Bombard' of Home Guard fame, had proposed a similar 60-pound stick bomb in 1940, to be fired from the 25-pounder, but the idea was turned down on the grounds that it might lead to mis-employment of the gun as a purely anti-tank weapon. (This mis-employment theme was not confined to the British side: many German Flak commanders bewailed the loss of their valuable 88-mm Flak guns as they were whittled away to provide anti-tank defences.)

The third subject is the application of new principles to gun design. The first of these to be unveiled was the taper-bore anti-tank gun, which has already been touched upon. This was the child of a German engineer called Gerlich, who, advocating his principle of attaining high velocity without attracting any buyers, had been stumping the world for several years. He was briefly employed by both the US War Department and the British War Office at various times, but his ideas on improving shoulder arms were felt to be impractical. He eventually settled in Germany and saw his idea accepted as an anti-tank weapon. The 28/21-mm came first, then a 42/30-mm and finally a 75/50-mm. Unfortunately, the lack of tungsten carbide for the special projectiles spelled the demise of these weapons, but experiments continued with coned bores and coned muzzle-adapters for guns of various calibres up to as large as 280-mm, in order to boost velocity and range. These were intended to use high-explosive shells, which were more practical in the larger calibres, though the development of a shell which would stand up to being squeezed down the gun barrel was no easy task.

The second, and more widespread, new line of thought was the recoilless gun. Like most weapon ideas, there was nothing really new about it: Commander Davis of the US Navy had produced a recoilless (RCL for short) gun during the First World War which was adopted by Britain as an anti-Zeppelin aircraft weapon. The virtue of an RCL gun is that by having no recoil one needs no complicated hydraulic buffer system to absorb the firing shock: one need only make the gun-carriage strong enough to take the weight of the gun, instead of being strong enough to withstand being fired from—an ideal state of affairs for an aircraft weapon, particularly in the stick-and-string era. Davis's idea is worth looking at, although outside our time scale, since it is the classic recoilless weapon. He simply provided the gun with two barrels, one pointing forward which fired a normal shell, and one pointing rearward which fired an identical weight of grease and buckshot. When the central cartridge was fired the shell and countershot departed at equal speed in opposite directions and cancelled each other's recoil. From this it can be seen that if you make the countershot (say) one-fifth of the weight of the shell and fire it out at five times the speed, then the gun will still be in balance. Taking this idea to its logical conclusion one finishes up firing out of the back of the gun a fast, light stream of gas, still balancing the recoil since the weight times speed of the gas is the same as the (greater) weight times (slower) speed of the shell.

Cutting down the recoil

This was the principle which the Germans revealed in Crete when their troops appeared armed with a 75-mm RCL gun. The shell was the standard 75-mm shell, but the cartridge case had a frangible plastic base which held for long enough to allow pressure to build up and start the shell moving, then blew out through a hole in the breech-block, releasing the balancing stream of gas. The all-up weight of the gun, on its ex-machine gun tripod, was only 320 pounds, whereas the weight of the standard 75-mm field gun was about 1½ tons—no mean saving for airborne carriage. A 105-mm version soon followed, weighing 855 pounds as opposed to the 105-mm 1E FH18's 4,312 pounds, and many more developments began in this field to provide light weapons for mountain troops and infantry, particularly for anti-tank use. (It ought perhaps to be pointed out that the *Panzerfaust* was in fact a recoilless gun, and not, as generally supposed, a rocket launcher). Eventually RCL guns of up to 380-mm calibre were under development, including many for slinging beneath aircraft to carry artillery aloft for the battle against the Allied bombers, but none of these came to fruition.

US Army

A cheap substitute for the field gun was the mortar, with its high rate of fire. This specimen is the American 155-mm, seen in action in the Pacific theatre. It could throw a 60-lb bomb with great accuracy between 200 and 2,205 yards' range

In Britain, the RCL gun development during the war is a scarcely-known story of one man's persistence. Sir Denis Burney, airship designer and prolific inventor-engineer, began to be interested in the recoilless principle early in the war. In order to prove his theories he converted a four-bore gun into a recoilless weapon and proceeded to fire it from the shoulder with ease; it must have been the world's most comfortable duck gun. Having proved his point he proceeded to design a series of RCL guns ranging from 20-mm to 8-inch calibre. In addition to designing the guns, he expanded his theories and designed special ammunition to take advantage of the ballistic peculiarities of the weapon. He argued that since the rearward blast was taking place, the pressure within the gun would be less than with a conventional type, and the shell would be subjected to a more steady thrust. In which case it would be possible to make shells with thinner walls, which would carry greater charges of explosive than previously possible. He then went further, and reasoned that, since the shell walls were thin, if the shell were to be filled with the then new plastic explosive, it would spread on to the surface of the target like butter; a fuse fitted in the base of the shell would then detonate this plaster and blast in the target. His envisaged target was either the concrete emplacements of the European coast, or the palm-reinforced Japanese bunker, and he called his shell the 'Wallbuster'.

In 1944 his designs were accepted and a 3.45-inch (the same calibre as the 25-pounder) shoulder-fired gun, a 3.7-inch towed gun, a 95-mm towed howitzer, and a 7.2-inch towed howitzer were prepared for production. The 95-mm was also jeep-mounted—the first application of what has since become a standard method of carrying these guns. The 7.2-inch soon fell by the wayside, since it had been intended solely as a means of defeating the Atlantic Wall emplacements, but other weapons were found to do all that was needed. The 3.45-inch was intended as an infantry weapon in the jungle, enabling one man to carry what was virtually a 25-pounder punch on his shoulder. The 3.7-inch was proposed as the future infantry anti-tank weapon, and the 95-mm was contemplated as the airborne field gun to replace the US 75-mm howitzer and the 25-pounder. However, before the guns were produced in sufficient quantity for issue, the war came to an end; some 3.45-inch and 3.7-inch guns were issued to selected infantry units to obtain their reaction to RCL guns as a general thing, and the 95-mm was abandoned altogether.

The principal difference between the Burney guns and the German type was that the Burneys had much longer barrels, and used cartridge cases which, instead of the plastic blow-out base, used many perforations in the sidewall to release the gas into a surrounding chamber, from whence it was passed back to a number of vents around the breech.

Concurrently with Burney's work in Britain, American designers began on similar weapons. A 105-mm howitzer T-9 was developed on similar lines to the German 105-mm, having a blow-out base to the cartridge. Another team developed 57-mm and 75-mm weapons which used perforated cases similar to the Burney pattern but having more and smaller holes, and also had the shell driving band pre-engraved in order to reduce the pressure inside the gun. Both these latter weapons were accepted for service early in 1945, saw service with the US Army in the Pacific theatre, and remained in service for many years. A third team, this time under the auspices of the National Research and Development Council, developed a 4.2-inch RCL mortar, an unlikely-sounding weapon which, so as to be able to fire direct at the target at low angles, carried a small rocket on the nose of the shell to push it down the barrel and fire the propelling cartridge in the usual mortar fashion. Due to the blast of the rearward jet, it could only be fired at low elevations; there was a certain amount of enthusiasm for this weapon but it never entered service.

Perhaps the best summing up of all wartime development on RCL weapons was made in a wartime report: 'Undoubtedly a number of effective recoilless weapons have been developed, but they are being accepted with reserve, and will only be considered as supplementary to older and more orthodox weapons which have proved their accuracy and reliability in service.'

There is, unfortunately, no space here to delve into more recondite stories of research and development: the British 13.5-inch gun linered-down to 8-inch calibre which, fired from Dover, reached a range of over 100,000 yards; the British and American development of flying artillery, which culminated in the mounting of a 32-pounder anti-tank gun in a Mosquito; the German V-3 multiple-chamber gun which was intended to shell London; the American 36-inch mortar 'Little David', designed to batter Japanese strong-points; the German rocket-assisted and ramjet-assisted heavy artillery shells which promised vast increases in range; or the Anglo-American development of the electronic proximity fuse which proved the answer to both 'Doodlebugs' and kamikaze pilots. These and similar stories may only interest the specialist, but they, together with what has been written here, serve to illustrate the incredible range of inventions brought into play in the war waged between the designers and inventors of each side, each endeavouring to get one step ahead of the other, if only temporarily.

IAN HOGG was born in 1926 in Durham City, enlisted in the Regular Army during the war, and became a Master Gunner in the Royal Artillery. After serving in Europe and the Far East, including duty with a Field Regiment during the Korean War, he became a member of the Instructional Staff of the School of Artillery, Larkhill. He later joined the Ammunition Branch of the Royal Military College of Science as an Assistant Instructor, where he stayed until 1972. He has made a study of the history and development of modern artillery equipment for several years, with particular emphasis on ammunition. He is now living and writing in Portugal.

Shot and Shell – Howitzer and Gun

The main difference between guns and howitzers is that guns fire 'directly' at their targets, while howitzers fire 'indirectly' at high angles, dropping their shells on to targets which are hidden by hills or fortifications in the target area. The plunging fire of howitzers is also ideal for cracking open heavy gun emplacements and defences. Howitzers usually fire at shorter ranges than guns, which means that the propellent charges of howitzer shells are comparatively small. And this in turn means that howitzers have shorter barrels than guns, for howitzer charges have a shorter-burning fuse.

This basic distinction was narrowed by 1939 with the appearance of the multi-purpose gun howitzer, of which the classic example is the British 25-pounder: it had exactly the same calibre as the German 88-mm gun, and could serve as an efficient anti-tank gun with a 20-pounder shot. The chart below shows the comparative ranges of guns and howitzers of various calibres; note the longer reach of the gun. At the foot of the page is an array of some of the most used shells of the war – from the armouries of the main combatant powers – compared to a standard rifle round*, to show the scale

M = Mortar
H = Howitzer
G = Gun

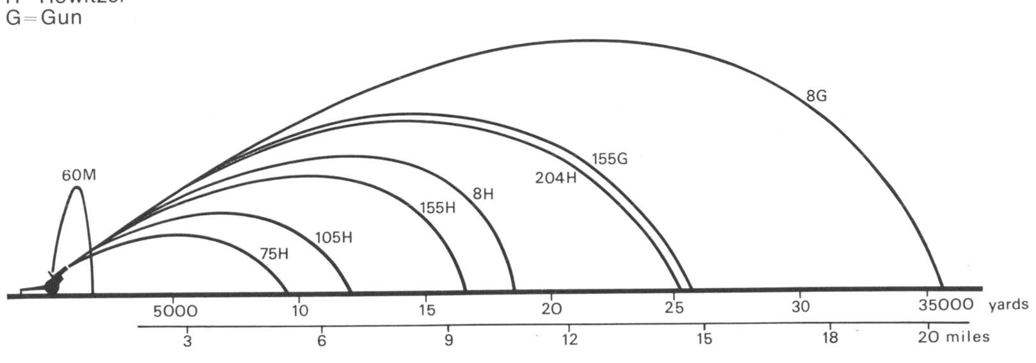

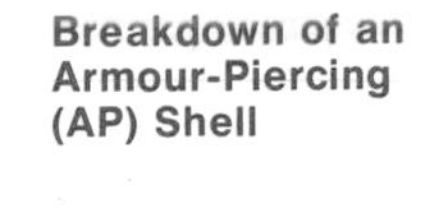

These shells were designed to drill through a tank's armour and shatter after penetration

AA = Anti-aircraft
AP = Armour-piercing
A/TK = Anti-tank
HE = High-explosive
Chem = Chemical

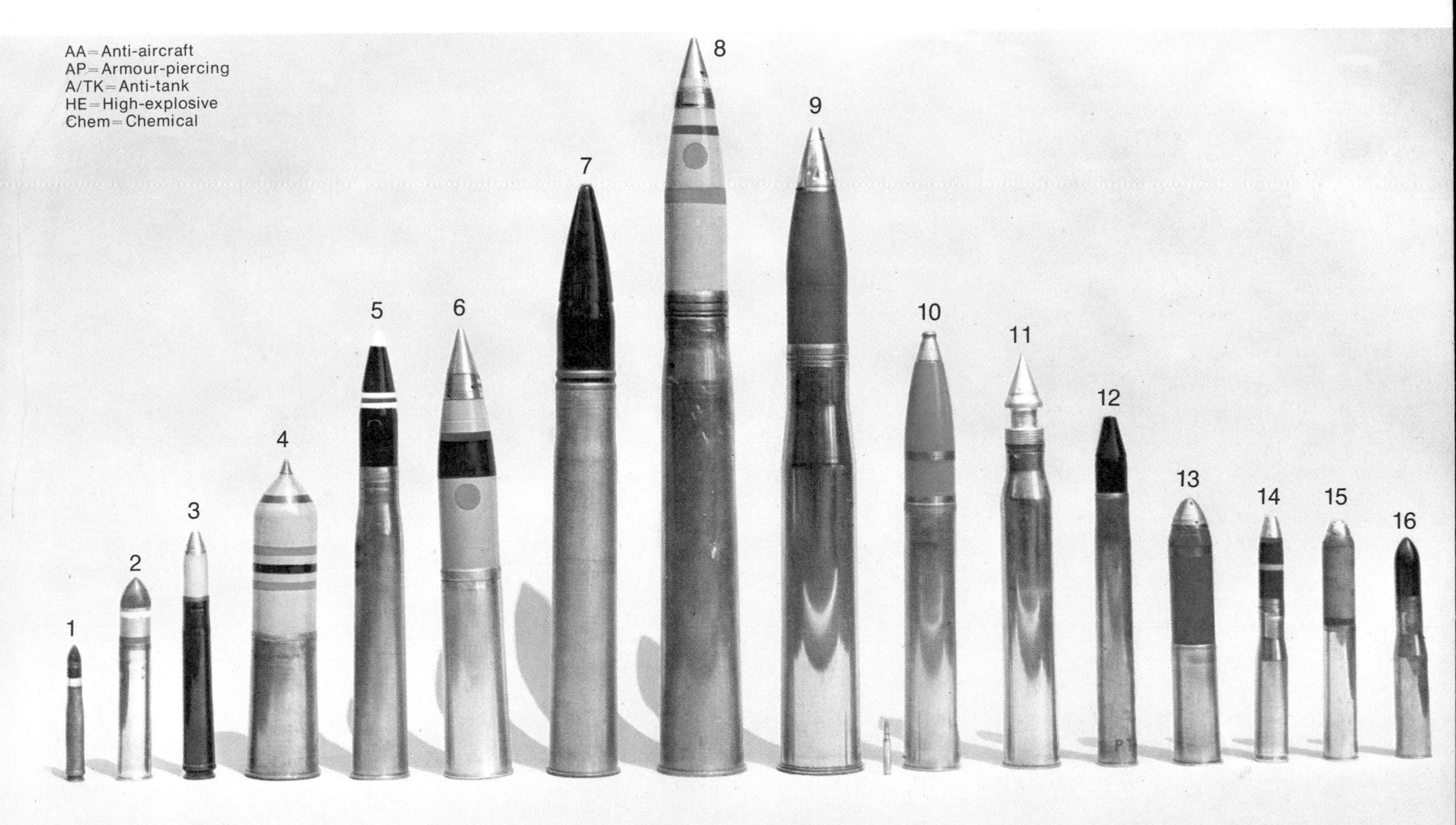

1. Italian 20-mm AA, AP
2. Italian 47-mm AP, HE
3. German 37-mm AA, HE
4. British 95-mm A/TK, HE
5. British 6-pdr AP
6. British 25-pdr (chem)
7. German 88-mm AA, AP
8. British 3·7-inch AA, HE
9. US 90-mm AA, HE
10. Russian 76·2-mm HE
11. Russian 57-mm AP
12. German 47-mm AP, HE
13. Italian 65-mm shrapnel
14. Italian 37-mm AA, HE
15. Italian 47-mm A/TK, HE
16. US 37-mm AP

ARTILLERY—THE RED ARMY'S GOD OF WAR

As Stalin's saying, 'Artillery is the God of War', shows, the artillery has always been the élite arm of the Red Army. But it was not until the beginning of the Second World War that the Russians were forced to incorporate major innovations in their use of artillery. They were the first to develop the concept of the 'artillery division'—a large independent unit with guns of all calibres, which could be used en masse to bring great pressure to bear on a selected part of the front. And the Red Army was the first to use mortars (such as the regimental 120-mm illustrated below) as the standard support weapon for large infantry formations. These developments were precipitated by the enormous losses of the first months of the war: the remaining equipment had to be husbanded and used to the greatest effect; and production had to be concentrated on a few simple designs which would be easy to mass-produce, and which could be operated by the inexperienced and ill-educated conscripts who now formed the mass of the army

122-mm Type 31/37 Howitzer
Range: 22,000 yards
Weight of shot: 55 lb
Firing weight: 15,500 lb

45-mm Type 32 Anti-tank Gun
Range: 9,850 yards with anti-tank shot
5,200 yards with high-explosive
Weight of shot: 3·25 lb (anti-tank)
4·75 lb (high-explosive)
Firing weight: 950 lb

120-mm Type 38 Mortar
Range: 6,600 yards
Weight of shot: 35·5 lb
Firing weight: 445 lb
76·2-mm Type 39 Howitzer
Range: 14,766 yards
Weight of shot: 13·75 lb
Firing weight: 3,500 lb

US artillery: designed for world-wide service

△ **37-mm anti-tank gun**
The US 37-mms were invaluable on all the US fronts; on Guadalcanal, firing anti-personnel canister shot, they had smashed repeated Japanese attacks. **Max range:** 12,850 yards. **Rate of fire:** four rounds per minute

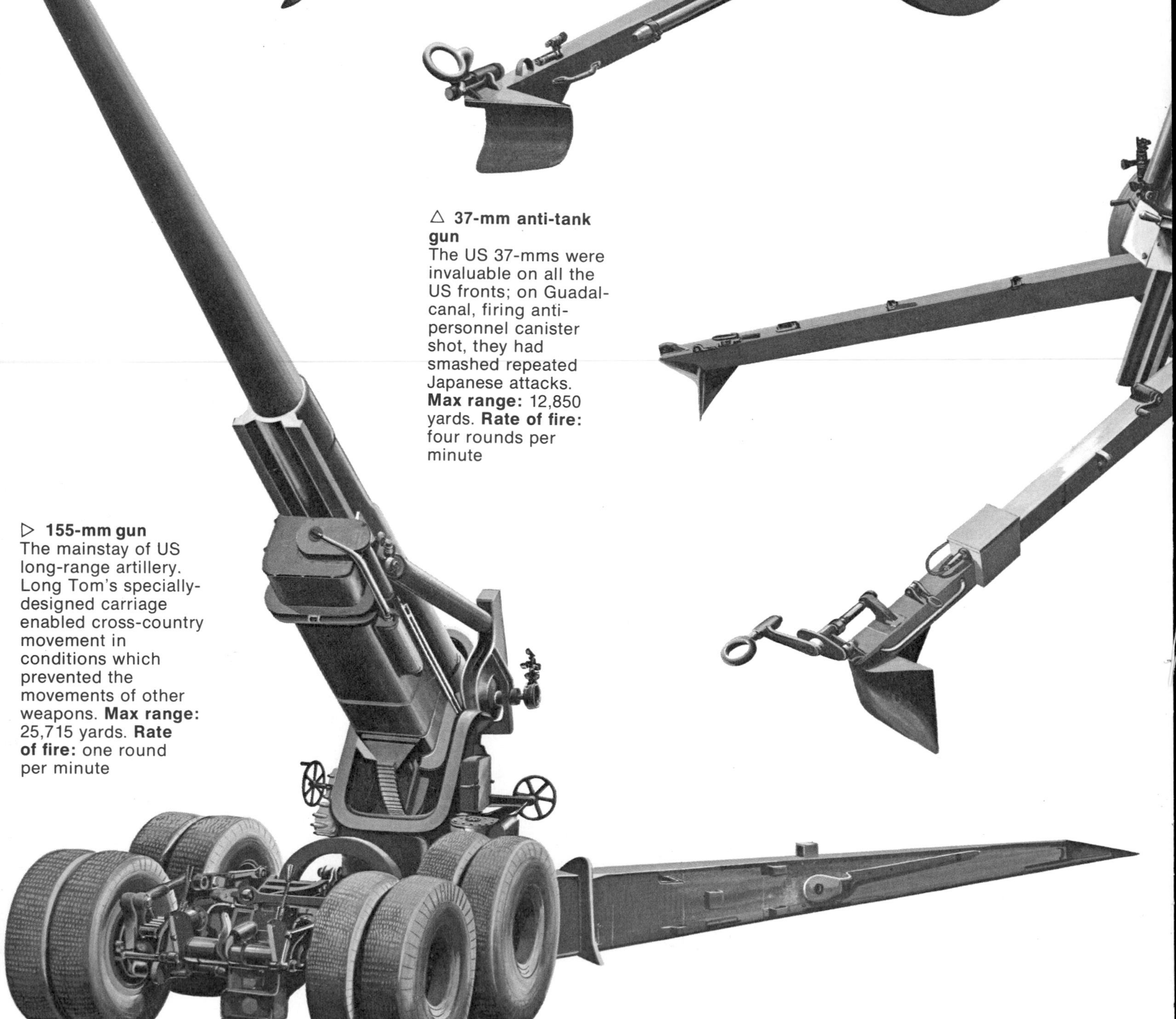

▷ **155-mm gun**
The mainstay of US long-range artillery. Long Tom's specially-designed carriage enabled cross-country movement in conditions which prevented the movements of other weapons. **Max range:** 25,715 yards. **Rate of fire:** one round per minute

△ **M-10 tank-destroyer**
The M-10 was correctly known as a 'gun motor carriage', and consisted of a 3-inch gun in a special turret, mounted on a Sherman hull. A potent tank-destroyer, its AP shells could penetrate 4 inches of the toughest armour at a range of 1,000 yards. **Crew:** five. **Armament:** one 3-inch gun; one ·50-inch machine-gun; five ·30-inch carbines

◁ **105-mm howitzer**
The light weight of the 105's projectile was ideal for a light artillery weapon and was easy to handle; troops reported that the 105 stood up to the toughest conditions on the field. **Max range:** 12,500 yards. **Rate of fire:** four rounds per minute

◁ **155-mm howitzer**
Designed to use the same carriage as the 4·7-inch gun, the 155-mm howitzer was considered by many to be the ideal weapon. It had uncanny accuracy at all ranges and was universally popular with the troops. **Max range:** 16,000 yards. **Rate of fire:** two rounds per minute

John Batchelor

FROM THE JAPANESE ARSENAL

The Japanese army was primarily an infantry force, and consequently its field units were relatively well supplied with artillery. The equipment compared well with that in other armies, being soundly constructed, reliable in action, and with good range and hitting power. All these howitzers had their gun counterparts, but these were less widely used because the terrain made the plunging fire of howitzers and mortars of higher value in the Pacific War

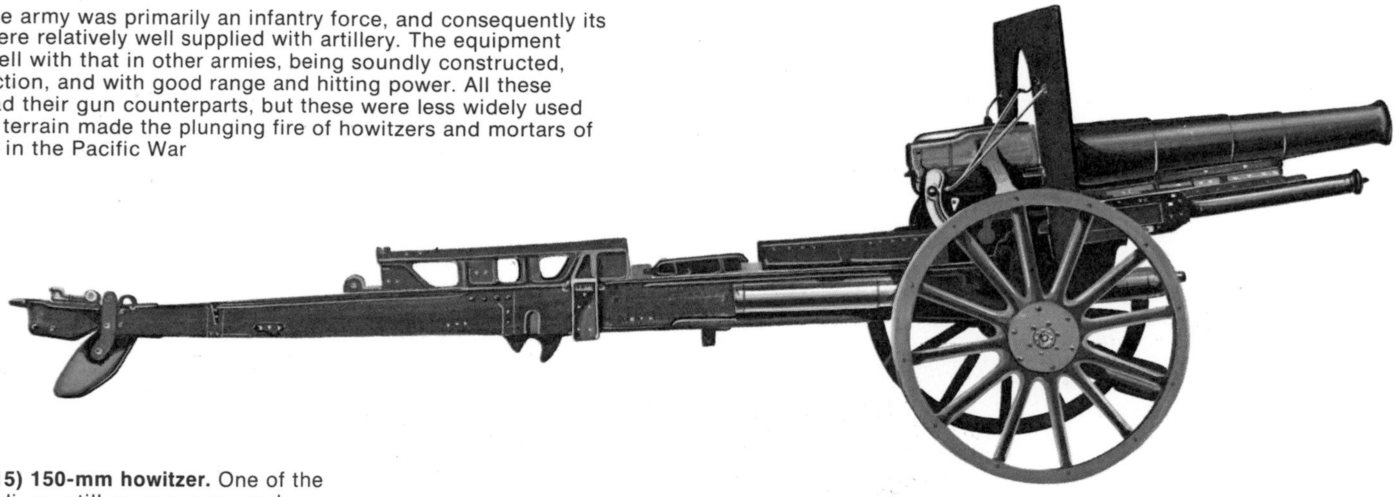

Model 4 (1915) 150-mm howitzer. One of the standard medium artillery weapons; each battalion had three companies with four '150s' apiece. The newer model 96 (1936) could be fired at the unusually high elevation of 75° if a deep loading-pit were dug beneath the breech. **Total weight in action:** 6,100 lb. **Max range:** 10,500 yards

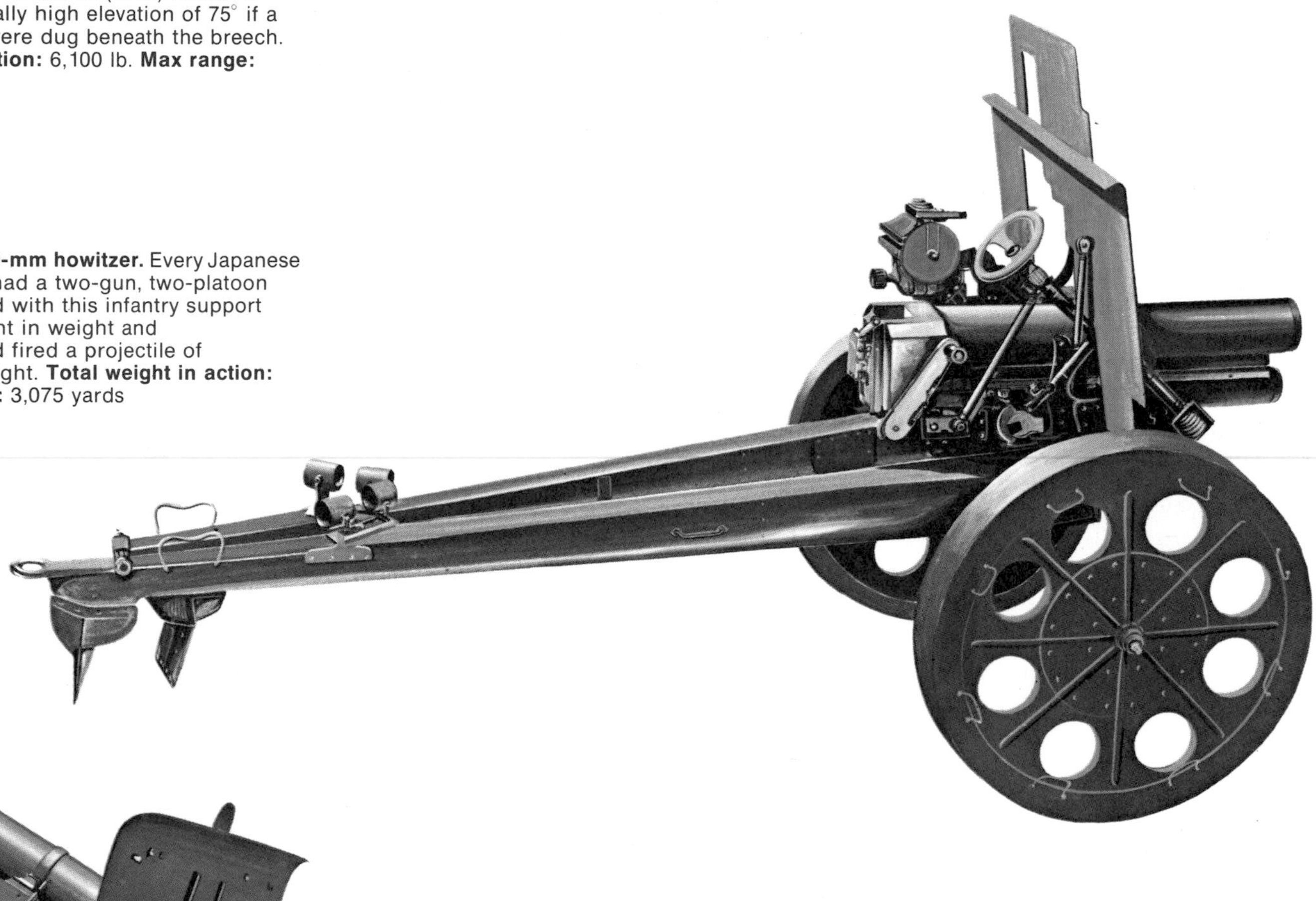

Model 92 (1932) 70-mm howitzer. Every Japanese infantry battalion had a two-gun, two-platoon company equipped with this infantry support weapon. It was light in weight and manoeuvrable, and fired a projectile of relatively large weight. **Total weight in action:** 468 lb. **Max range:** 3,075 yards

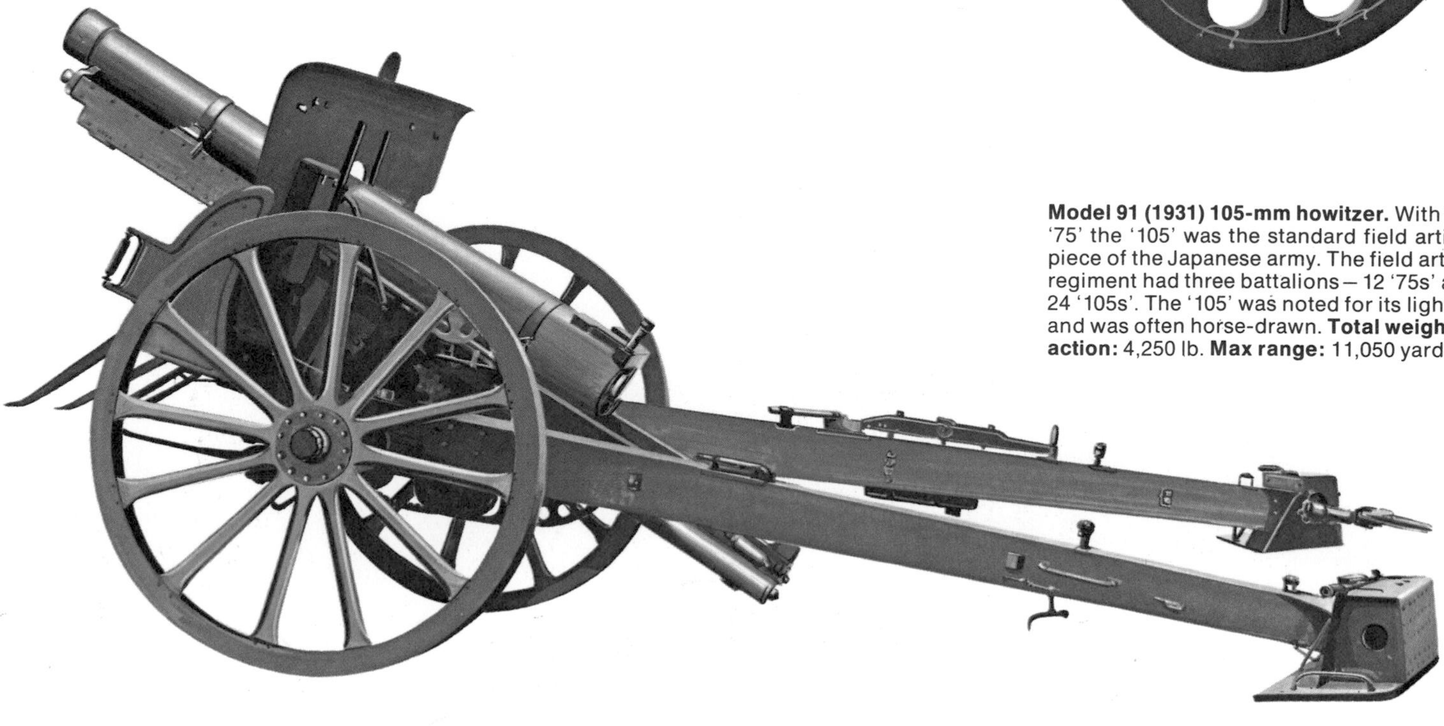

Model 91 (1931) 105-mm howitzer. With the '75' the '105' was the standard field artillery piece of the Japanese army. The field artillery regiment had three battalions – 12 '75s' and 24 '105s'. The '105' was noted for its light weight, and was often horse-drawn. **Total weight in action:** 4,250 lb. **Max range:** 11,050 yards

John Batchelor

The Japanese army which invaded China was well-provided with modern equipment. It compared well with that used by other armies.
(1) Model 11 (1922) 6·5-mm Light Machine-Gun: a modification of the French Hotchkiss. *Weight:* 22½ lb. *Rate of Fire:* 500 rpm. *Ammunition:* hopper holding 30 rounds.
(2) Model 38 (1905) 6·5-mm Rifle: produced in three standard lengths for issue to different types of unit. *Weight:* 9·4 lb. *Magazine:* Five rounds.
(3) Officer's Sword
(4) Model 94 (1934) 8-mm Pistol. *Magazine:* Six rounds.
(5) Model 14 (1925) 8-mm Pistol: ammunition interchangeable with the Type 94. *Magazine:* Eight rounds.
(6) Standard Hand-Grenade

CHI HA Type 97 (1937) Medium Tank. Used in China during the latter part of the war, this tank embodied features learned from tankette and light-tank designs. It was also encountered in Burma and on Guadalcanal. *Weight:* 15 tons. *Length:* 18 feet. *Armour:* 25-mm maximum. *Crew:* Four. *Armament:* One 57-mm gun, two 7·7-mm MG. *Speed:* 25 mph. *Range:* 120 miles.

John Batchelor

The Focus of Infantry Firepower

By the end of the First World War the massive firepower of the new machine-gun had brought a radical change to military thinking by giving defenders a great superiority over attacking forces. With the opening of the Second World War, new weapons restored mobility to the battlefield, but throughout the war the infantry of all the main combatants were supplied with automatic weapons which were now the focus around which they were organised. These weapons fell into two main categories: light machine-guns (such as the British Bren gun, the US Browning Automatic Rifle, and the Russian 'Degtjarev' LMG) which were the main armament of an infantry section (between six and ten men); and heavy machine-guns (some of which are illustrated here) which were issued to battalion support companies. These were used to supply heavier, more sustained, and more accurate fire, and usually had a larger, steadier mounting and a more sophisticated gun-sight

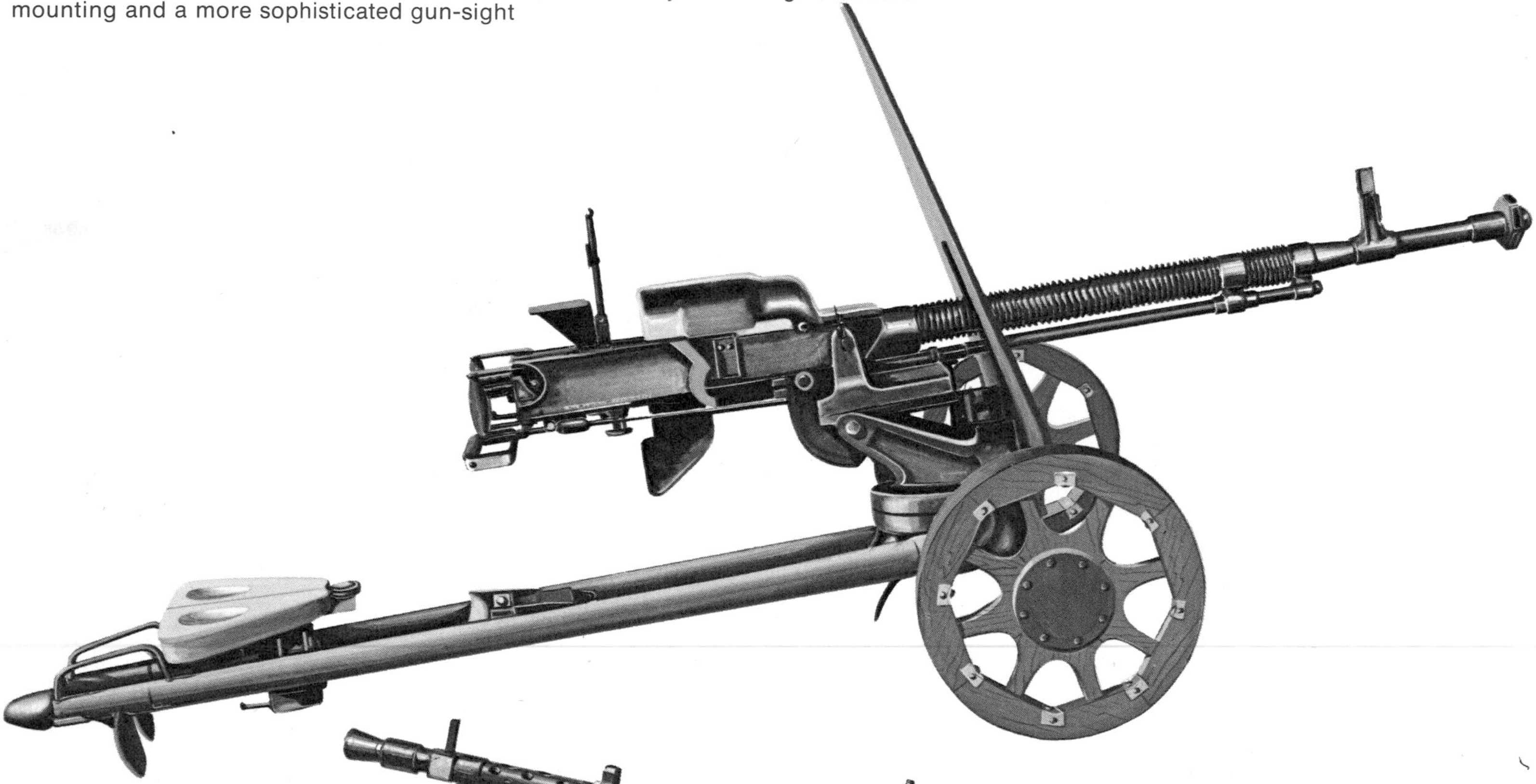

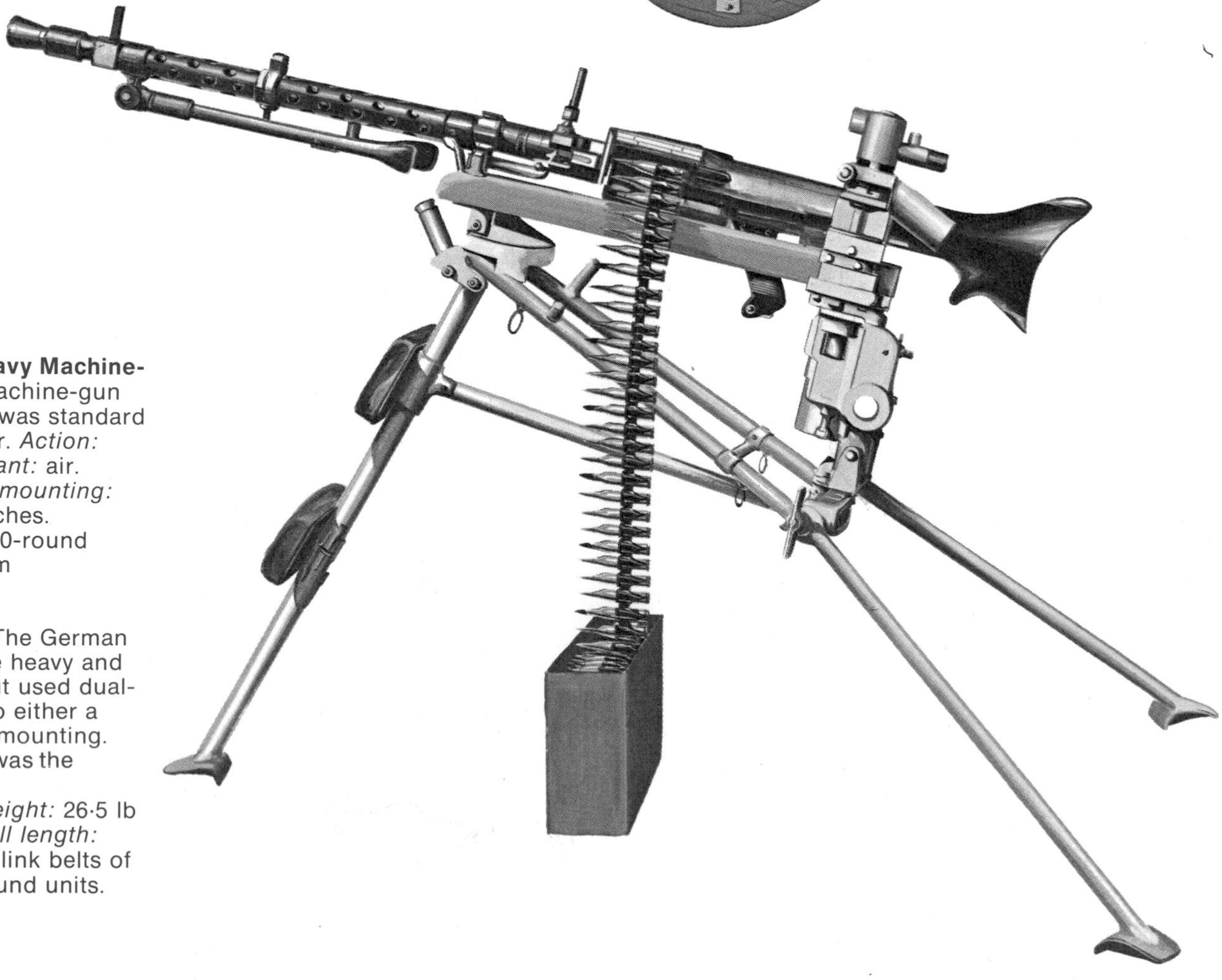

(1) Russian 12·7-mm 1938 Heavy Machine-Gun: The first Soviet heavy machine-gun to be produced in quantity, it was standard equipment throughout the war. *Action:* automatic gas-operated. *Coolant:* air. *Weight:* 78·5 lb. *Two-wheeled mounting:* 259 lb. *Overall length:* 62·5 inches. *Ammunition:* metal link belt, 50-round units. *Rate of fire:* 540-600 rpm

(2) German 7·92-mm MG-34: The German army never produced separate heavy and light machine-gun designs, but used dual-purpose weapons adaptable to either a bipod or an adjustable tripod mounting. (Their other standard weapon was the MG-42, illustrated on page 34.) *Action:* recoil. *Coolant:* air. *Weight:* 26·5 lb (bipod), 42·3 lb (tripod). *Overall length:* 48 inches. *Feed device:* metal link belts of 250 rounds, made up of 50-round units. *Rate of fire:* 800-900 rpm

(3) US Browning ·50-inch M-2 Heavy Machine-Gun: This formidable weapon was not only used as infantry support, but became a standard anti-aircraft gun. It was fitted with a heavy-weight barrel to provide adequate cooling when firing long bursts. *Action:* recoil. *Coolant:* air. *Weight:* 82 lb. *Overall length:* 65 inches. *Ammunition:* metal link belt, 100-round units. *Rate of fire: 450 rpm*

John Batchelor

(4) Japanese 7·7-mm Type 99-1 Heavy Machine-Gun: A standard Japanese weapon which was developed from the French Hotchkiss design. *Action:* gas-operated. *Coolant:* air. *Weight with tripod:* 70 lb. *Overall length:* 42·4 inches. *Ammunition:* 30-round clips. *Rate of fire:* 550 rpm

(5) British ·303-inch Vickers Machine-Gun: The standard British heavy machine-gun during both world wars, the Vickers was renowned for its reliability—in an experiment it once fired non-stop for seven days. It is shown here with ammunition box and steam-condensing radiator assembly. *Action:* recoil, with gas boost from nozzle booster. *Coolant:* water. *Weight:* approx. 40 lb with water. *Tripod:* 50 lb. *Overall length:* 43 inches. *Ammunition:* 250 rounds per box, in canvas belts. *Rate of fire:* 450-550 rpm

THE MORTAR:
VITAL FACTOR IN JUNGLE COMBAT

In the close-quarter fighting in the jungle and hills of northern Burma, the infantry mortar came to be one of the most vital weapons. Light and hard-hitting, it was widely used by the British and Japanese to fire high explosive, smoke, and flare projectiles. △ **British 2-inch Mortar:** one was issued to each platoon. *Weight:* 23·5 lb. *Length:* 25 inches. *Effective range:* 470 yards. *Weight of projectile:* 2 lb. *Rate of fire:* 20/30 rounds per minute

△ **Japanese Model 97 (1937) 81-mm Mortar:** a heavier weapon, its shells could be fired with a delayed-action fuse. *Weight:* 145 lb. *Length:* 49·5 inches. *Effective range:* 3,100 yards. *Weight of projectile:* 6·93 lb

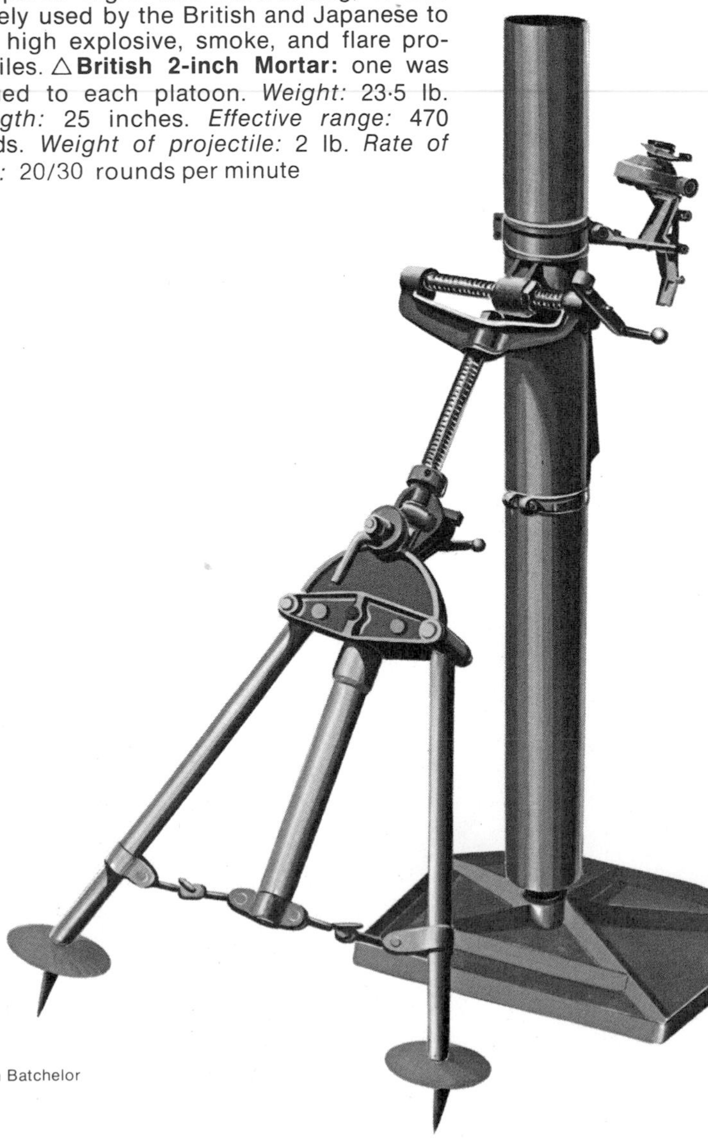

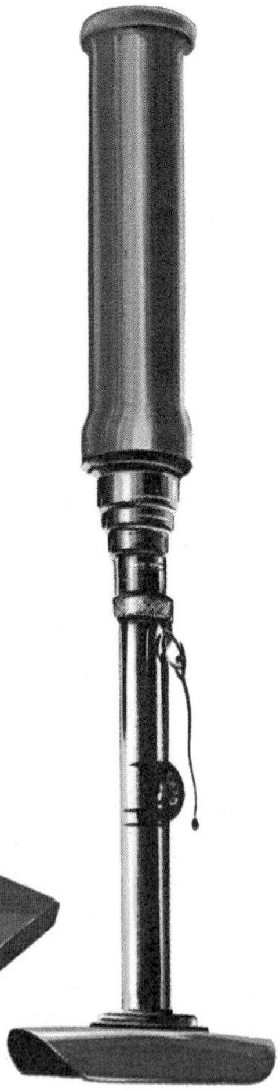

◁◁ **British 3-inch Mortar:** a larger and more accurate weapon used by battalion heavy weapon companies. *Weight:* 124 lb (Mortar: 42 lb, Mounting: 45 lb, Base plate: 37 lb). *Length:* 51 inches. *Effective range:* 1,600 yards. *Weight of projectile:* 10 lb. *Rate of fire:* 20/30 rounds per minute

◁ **Japanese Model 10 (1921) 50-mm Grenade Discharger:** a light platoon weapon mainly used for firing flares. Sometimes known by the Allies as the 'knee mortar', due to the belief that the base plate was rested on the knee. If tried, this resulted in a broken leg. *Weight:* 5·5 lb. *Length:* 20 inches. *Range:* 65-175 yards

John Batchelor

British infantrymen firing a 3-inch mortar

Imperial War Museum

A Japanese 81-mm mortar crew in action

Associated Press

Weapons of the British Infantry

British infantry weapons were noted for their toughness and reliability: **(1) Bren ·303 light machine-gun.** *Weight:* 22 lb. *Effective range:* 800 yards. *Magazine:* 30 rounds. *Rate of fire:* 500 rpm. **(2) Sten 9-mm submachine-gun.** *Weight:* 7·8 lb. *Effective range:* 200 yds. *Magazine:* 32 rounds. *Rate of fire:* 500-550 rpm. **(3) Lee Enfield ·303 rifle No. 4 Mk 1/2.** *Weight:* 8·8 lb. *Maximum range:* 2,000 yds. *Magazine:* 10 rounds. **(4) Lee Enfield ·303 rifle No. 5 Mk 1** (a jungle-warfare version of the standard rifle). *Weight:* 7·15 lb. **(5) Webley ·380 revolver.** *Weight:* 2 lb 6 oz. *Effective range:* 50 yds. *Magazine:* six rounds. **(6) Enfield ·380 No. 2 Mk 1* revolver.** *Weight:* 1·7 lb. *Effective range:* 50 yds. *Magazine:* six rounds. **(7) Browning FN 9-mm automatic pistol No. 2 Mk 1.** *Weight:* 2·06 lb. *Range:* 50 yds. *Magazine:* 13 rounds

The Light Machine-Gun

'Intense Machine-gun Fire'
Light machine-guns played a vital and devastating role in the battle for Dieppe. **Below:** The German MG-42; one of the most remarkable general-purpose machine-guns ever designed, the MG-42 was introduced in 1942 to replace the MG-34. It was cheap and simple to operate, and could be used as a section LMG, a sustained support weapon, or a light AA gun. It had one major drawback when used as a section weapon—its rate of fire was so high that many rounds were wasted and it was difficult to carry adequate ammunition. *Calibre:* 7·92 mm. *Weight:* 25 lb. *Ammunition:* 50-round belts which could be clipped together. *Maximum rate of fire:* 1,100-1,200 rpm. **Bottom:** The British Bren Mk III; standard section LMG throughout the war, the Bren was noted for its ruggedness and reliability. It originated from the Czech ZB-26 which was designed at BRno and developed at ENfield. The Bren was usually used to fire single shots or bursts of four or five rounds and was thus very economical. *Calibre:* ·303-inch. *Weight:* 19·3 lb. *Ammunition:* 30-round boxes. *Maximum rate of fire:* 480 rpm.

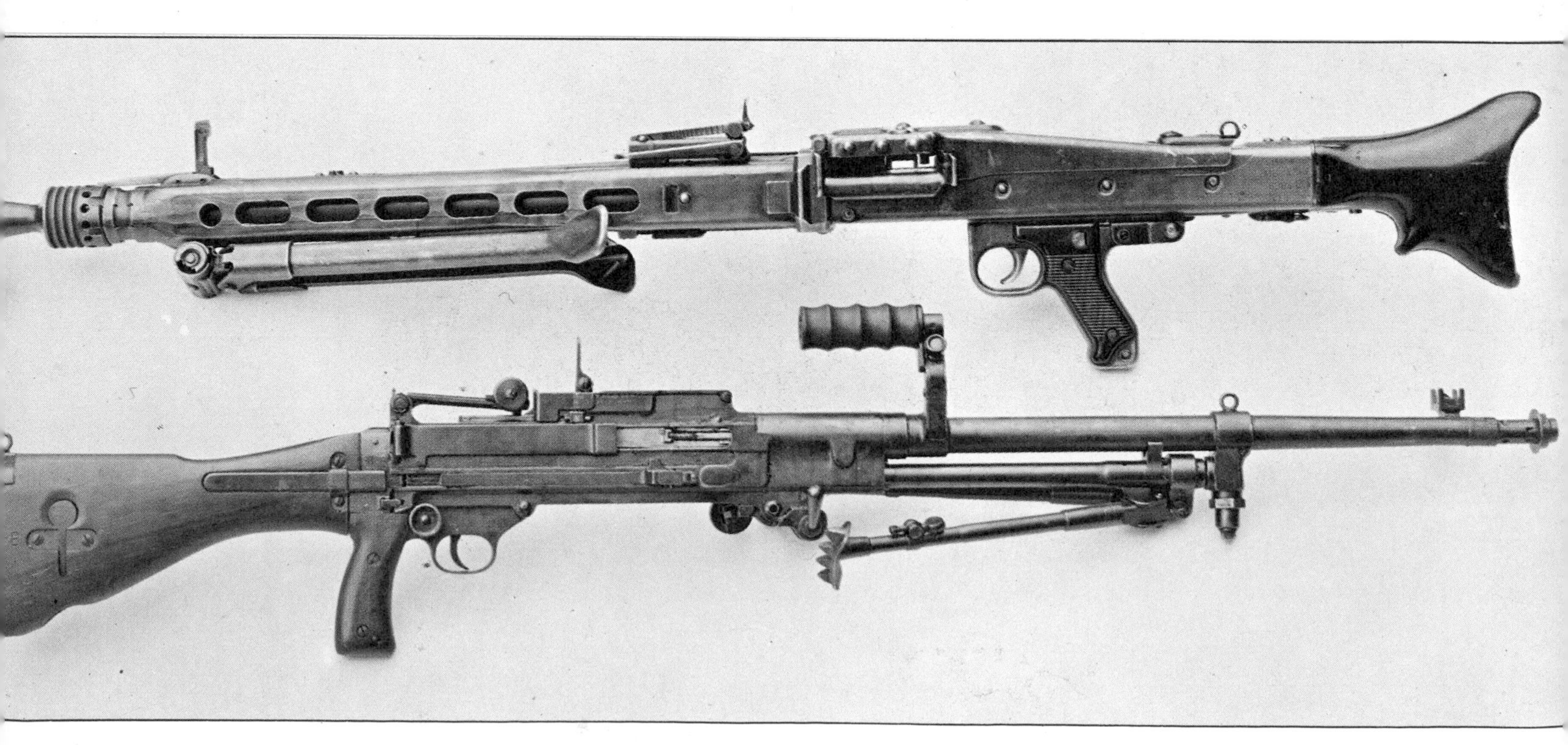

Arms from America

1. A P-14 ·300-calibre rifle (P-17 in USA)
2. A ·45-calibre Thompson sub-machine-gun (M-1)
3. A Colt ·45 automatic pistol (1911 model)
4. A Colt ·45 revolver (1917 model)

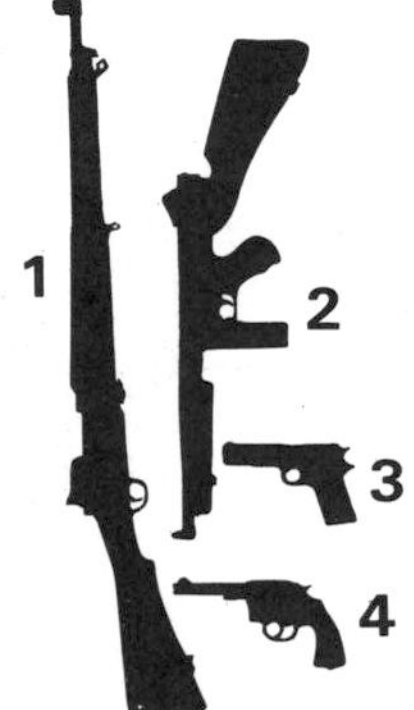

Stalemate at Stalingrad: The Hand-to-Hand Battle

At Stalingrad each separate battle resolved itself into a combat between individuals. In the jumble of ruins—which the fighting widened daily—the tommy-gun and hand-grenade ruled supreme. Below are illustrated typical fighting men of both sides with their key weapons

1. KAR-98K 7·9-mm rifle (5 rounds in magazine)
2. MP-40 machine-pistol (32 rounds in magazine)
3. Walther P-38 9-mm automatic (8 rounds in magazine)
4. Standard hand-grenade

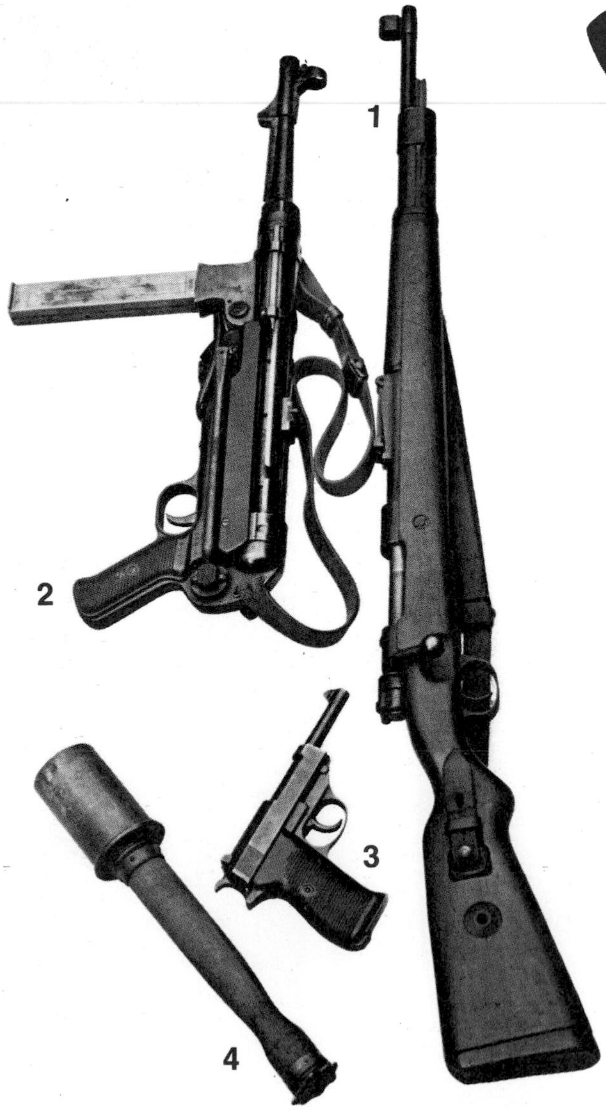

1

2

3

4

At Stalingrad the Germans were baffled by a situation hitherto outside their military experience, and they reacted to it characteristically—by the application of brute force in heavier and heavier doses. Paulus was reinforced by a variety of specialist troops, including police battalions and engineers skilled in street fighting and demolition work. But the Russians, although heavily outnumbered, remained their masters in the street-to-street, house-to-house, room-to-room, fighting

The Russians in Stalingrad had perfected the use of 'Storm Groups', small bodies of mixed arms—light and heavy machine-guns, tommy-gunners, and grenadiers usually with anti-tank guns—who gave one another support in lightning counter-attacks; and they had developed the creation of 'killing zones', houses and squares heavily mined and to which the defenders knew all the approach routes, where the German advance could be canalised, met with savage fire, and blunted

Even with the three firearms shown here, the impressive standardisation of the Red Army's equipment is strikingly obvious in their use of 7·62-mm calibre weapons

1. M-1930 7·62-mm rifle (5 rounds in magazine)
2. PPSH 7·62-mm submachine-gun (71 rounds in magazine)
3. Tokarev TT 7·62-mm automatic (8 rounds in magazine)
4. Standard hand-grenade

Deirdre Amsden

The 'Leatherneck' and his weapons

'Don't worry about food, Japs eat it too . . . all you have to do is get it' had been a Marine watchword since Guadalcanal. And as the US Pacific offensives developed, the few Marine divisions which carried the weight of every major Pacific attack added more and more glory to the US Marine Corps, now aided by newer and more hard-hitting firearms

Deirdre Amsden

1. *M-1941 Johnson Rifle:* a semi-automatic infantry rifle like the Garand, but with a novel magazine design. This was of rotary action and had two more rounds than the Garand, but was only used for a limited period. *Calibre:* ·30-inch. *Magazine capacity:* ten rounds

2. *M-1 Carbine:* introduced as a semi-automatic weapon to weigh little and hit hard. Assessment reports said that troops were 'very enthusiastic . . . impressed by its high rate of automatic fire'. *Calibre:* ·30-inch. *Magazine capacity:* 15 rounds. *Effective range:* 300 yards

3. *M-1 Garand Rifle:* Patton called it 'the greatest battle implement ever devised'. Its high rate of fire earned it the same reputation as the British Lee-Enfield. *Calibre:* ·30-inch. *Magazine capacity:* eight rounds

4. *M-3 Submachine-gun:* replaced the famous Thompson submachine-gun in Marine and army service. It was produced in great quantities—with an extra barrel for captured German ammunition. *Calibre:* ·45-inch. *Magazine capacity:* 30 rounds. *Rate of fire:* 400 rounds per minute

5. *·45-inch Automatic:* this veteran of the First World War was eclipsed as an important infantry weapon by the carbine. But it retained its role as a personal defence weapon. *Magazine capacity:* seven rounds

6. *Smith and Wesson ·38-inch Revolver:* another well-trusted 'hand gun' used as a side-arm by officers, but whose importance ended with the general introduction of the machine-pistol

Marine firepower

In the amphibious landings the worst moment of all was at the moment of contact with the shore, when the first wave of the landing force came under the fire of enemy beach defences with no heavy firepower of their own in support. The British met this problem with the DD swimming tank—but in the Pacific war the Americans preferred to improve on the well-tried 'Landing Vehicle, Tracked'—the Buffalo. Two armed versions helped the Iwo Jima landings, one armed with twin cannons for light support and one with a 75-mm howitzer for heavy support. The former was able to fire at ground targets while acting as a troop transport, while the howitzer version played the same role as the DD tank

LVT(A) (Howitzer)
Weight: 13·7 tons. *Crew:* four. *Speed:* 20 mph on land, 7½ mph afloat. *Armament:* one 75-mm M-3 howitzer, two ·50-inch Browning machine-guns

LVT(A) (Twin Cannons)
Weight: 12·5 tons. *Crew:* six. *Troop capacity:* six. *Speed:* 20 mph on land, 7½ mph afloat. *Armament:* two 20-mm cannon, two ·50-inch Browning machine-guns

BLOODED AT DIEPPE

CHURCHILL MK 1: Fourth in the British series of infantry support tanks, it was first used in action at Dieppe, and later proved a successful and reliable design. It had the heaviest armour of any British tank in service in 1942, and an adequate cross-country speed with excellent cross-country ability. But, like its predecessors Infantry Mark I, Matilda, and Valentine, the Churchill suffered from inadequate armament. Its inability to fire high explosive, except from the close support howitzer in the hull, was a serious weakness and only a few were actually equipped with the howitzer, the majority mounting a 7·92-mm machine-gun in the hull instead. **Weight:** 38·5 tons. **Armour:** 102-mm maximum. **Crew:** Five. **Speed:** 17 mph. **Range:** About 100 miles. **Armament:** One 2-pounder in the turret with a co-axial machine-gun, and a 3-inch howitzer or a 7·92-mm machine-gun in the hull.
Below: For the landing, the tanks were water-proofed and fitted with special attachments to allow them to wade ashore from a depth of about 7 feet.

Baby & Co Ltd

the tanks

Speed, hitting-power, and mobility were the immutable factors that the pre-war tank designers had to reconcile. Those, like the Russians, who put considerable time and thought into their pre-war tank research and development, found that their efforts paid dividends when war overtook them—although not necessarily at first. **Kenneth Macksey** shows how the race between armament and protection shaped the development of wartime tank design

Shortly after the fall of France a picture showing men of the Waffen-SS *Totenkopf* Division examining a captured British Matilda tank appeared in a German journal called *Damals*. Beneath ran the caption *'Immer Wieder Lernen'* which, loosely translated, meant 'There is always something to learn'. The picture had more than symbolic importance, for it brought the Germans face to face with a new dimension in armoured warfare—one of which they were always aware but which they had hoped would be slower to appear: the advent of a sharp intensification of the race between hitting power and protection, between gun and armour.

Matilda carried a 2-pounder gun with a muzzle velocity of 2,650 feet per second, a little more than that of the 37-mm gun mounted in the German Pz Kw III and 38t tanks, and twice that of the short 75-mm in their Pz Kw IV. But whereas the heaviest German armour plate was only 30 mm thick and easily penetrated by the 40 mm's solid armour-piercing (AP) shot, the Matilda's 80-mm armour (much of it cast) was quite impervious to the shot from German tank guns. Of course there were too few Matildas in 1940 to affect the issue, and the victory by the German Panzer divisions had been won by tactical *technique* rather than technology—speed, mobility, the use of men, better control, and superior employment of mounted and dismounted men working in close co-operation with the fire support given by aircraft and artillery—overcoming less well co-ordinated French and British opponents. The campaigns in Poland in 1939 and in Western Europe in 1940 established the armoured division as a fundamental weapon of decision, yet the German victories came largely from exploiting deficiencies in the enemy's armour, for within the Panzer divisions themselves there were many defects yet unrevealed.

Russia takes the lead

Building an armoured vehicle is a prolonged and specialised business. At the end of the First World War the British and French knew most about the art, the United States was learning at its customary competitive speed, Germany knew next to nothing, and other nations depended upon what they could glean from Britain and France. Until 1933 the overall level of each nation's knowledge stayed in that order, for while the Versailles Treaty forbade Germany to own tanks, the other nations hung on to old war stocks and spent trivial sums on research into new machines. In Britain, under the auspices of the Vickers firm, radical advances were made in the design of tanks and infantry and artillery carriers, extending the British lead over France, who merely stretched and 'beefed up' existing designs. In America, however, the dynamic J. Walter Christie invented his own version of a fast, lightly armed and armoured cruiser that was one day to dominate world-wide tank developments—except those of his own country.

In Russia the Red Army's strong belief in the future of armour led to large-scale experiments and the production of versions of Vickers and Christie designs in the early 1930s, while in Germany, with the rise of Hitler, an entirely new tank-building industry came to life. Largely because the Russians were the first to start wholesale tank development and production, followed by Germany, Britain, and America, the national index of quality linked to quantity in 1940 stood in that order of merit. In the late 1930s the Germans had to catch up an enormous amount of technical and manufacturing leeway, which is why their first tanks were relatively crude and unreliable; the British, slow to start rearmament, had then to rush into production using well-tried but outdated design techniques; and the Americans, who had been starved of research funds even more severely than their competitors, found themselves in appalling straits.

Yet, as it happened, nearly every improvement in design that took place during the Second World War had been foreseen and provided for in the preceding years of peace. Every major nation had envisaged the coming demand for heavier guns capable of firing high-explosive shells as well as solid, armour-piercing shot, and the main reasons why the production of these larger guns was delayed were economic and the priorities of industrial procurement. When the facilities for tank manufacturing were in their infancy, and the need for quantity overrode the need for quality, and when a tank construction programme competed, for instance, with naval construction in its calls on materials, labour, and finance (as it did with all the warring powers except Russia), less sophisticated weapons had to be accepted. For example, the priority given to the German Panzer divisions had to be concentrated on the production of its primary weapon—the tank. The need for armoured, cross-country infantry and artillery carriers was clear but sufficient production facilities were just not available in Germany. So in the Panzer (or 'armoured') division, only tanks, plus a few multi-wheeled armoured cars for reconnaissance, were wholly 'Panzer': the rest of the division, less some half-tracked armoured personnel carriers and artillery tractors, was unarmoured, wheeled, and therefore road-bound whenever the ground became softened by the rain. In consequence the tanks tended to draw away from their supporting arms in mobile operations since the latter could neither keep up in bad going nor survive in the open when brought under direct fire.

Compromises of this sort were commonplace in every army and never completely eradicated; what most countries wished to avoid was falling too far behind their opponents in technical fighting power. It was the task of technical intelligence, when it briefed general staffs and industry, to forecast the latest possible moment at which each new up-gunning or up-armouring had to take place, always trying to give at least 18 months' warning, since, in those days, it took approximately that length of time to bring a new gun or vehicle into service. Of course, a competent, foresighted design team also had a duty to project fighting vehicles that could later accept bigger guns and heavier armour with the least possible redesign, since taking one type of tank right out of production and starting another in its place was costly in every way—and, on occasion, unacceptable due to other demands.

Before the war the Germans made full allowance for up-gunning: both Pz Kw III and IV in their final form carried 75-mm guns of about three times the power of the original weapons, absorbing increases of weight (including that of thicker armour) from, respectively, 15 to 23 tons and 17 to 25 tons and accepting engines that, in the case of IV, were raised from 250 to 300 hp.

The British found themselves to have been less well served when it was discovered that their prewar tanks were hard pressed to accept heavier guns or armour. The Matilda was quite incapable of being up-gunned and had to go out of production when the gun/armour race got too hot: the Valentine needed a completely redesigned turret, as did the Centaur/Cromwell series later in the war. The French, of course, fell out of the race in 1940 though all their front-line tanks had by then reached the ultimate point of development. The Italians, using their M-13s (an improved Vickers design), never approached comparison with friend or foe, and the Japanese (who were also developing basic Vickers designs) had only a secondary need for armoured vehicles because of the terrain over which they fought.

Thus the Matilda gave the Germans a surprise in 1940 and the impulse to press urgently ahead with a more powerful 50-mm gun in Pz Kw III (a long established intention), as well as speeding up work on bigger versions of the 50-mm and 75-mm guns on field mountings. Nevertheless, the rate of the gun/armour race only marginally quickened. For although the 37-mm anti-tank guns had frequently failed against Anglo/French armour, field artillery had then filled the tank-killing gap while the 88-mm anti-aircraft gun had emerged as a most potent anti-tank weapon capable of settling with even the Matilda at ranges beyond 1,000 yards.

The Tiger II, or 'King Tiger'. Its 88-mm gun had great range and accuracy. Its turret armour was 7 inches thick

US Army

The gun/armour race did not really get into top gear until the Germans met the Russian T-34/76 and KV-1 tanks in July 1941. These were tanks whose 76-mm gun outmatched every German tank gun, and whose frontal armour generally resisted every field-mounted anti-tank gun except the new long 50-mm and the 88-mm anti-aircraft gun. It was combined action of the German battle-groups—when they skilfully outfought the poorly co-ordinated Russian forces—that led to the striking initial German victory, but the very magnitude of that victory then exposed the vulnerabilities of armoured forces in yet another way.

Something like a 25% unreliability rate in tanks had always been allowed for by the Germans, but this rose sharply—and dangerously—during protracted operations because the vehicles depended upon centralised maintenance and servicing based in Germany to put machines right, after a campaign, rather than at the time at the front. The short campaigns before 1941 had not fully tested this system, but Afrika Korps in the desert, and then the rest of the Panzer divisions in Russia, found their strengths severely reduced once the campaign had gone on longer than Hitler's prescribed six weeks' maximum. Breakdowns and heavy losses that could only slowly be replaced slashed tank strengths below the level of safety.

Then there were the inescapable restrictions imposed by logistics. Each campaign and each major advance started close to well-stocked depots that could usually maintain the invaders up to a distance of about 400 miles, so long as a reasonable road network, one that could carry the wheeled supply vehicles, existed. Despite the hideous state of Russian roads which collapsed whenever it rained, the Germans rode forward over 400 miles in four weeks—but then stopped dead, their axes of advance littered with broken-down vehicles, the Panzer spearheads grounded from shortage of fuel and ammunition.

As the war progressed every other mechanised army was to meet, and be defeated by, this same problem to some extent. Even though the supreme aim of all mechanised operations was perpetual motion, logistics, in the end, inevitably imposed a halt in order to give the supply services time to stock new, advanced bases ready to support the next main leap forward. And this usually gave the enemy time to recover his strength and composure.

In 1941 the Germans had to rethink their armoured technology while the Russians reconsidered their tactical methods and tried to improve the training of commanders and crews whose abilities had been found sadly deficient. Busy on the periphery of the major conflict, the British, aided by the Americans, sought to build more and better vehicles and reach the standard of professional perfection displayed by the well-trained German formations before engaging them in Europe.

Now the time and money spent on prewar study and research paid off—those with a real lead usually retained it. Indeed, the Russian lead in production facilities was never overtaken: in the quickest time imaginable they could reassemble masses of vehicles to outnumber the Germans on every front. The Germans, however, were the equal of the Russians in technological quality and were able, with the knowledge at their disposal, to up-gun the Pz Kw IV to match the T-34/76 and, by producing even bigger guns and fitting them to their second generation of heavier tanks (Panther and Tiger), to defeat the T-34/85 and the KV's successors, the heavy JS (Josef Stalin) tanks. But the creation of these two new German machines named Panther and Tiger (both of which had been first thought of before the war) demanded a vast increase in industrial outlay, linked with the introduction of new manufacturing techniques that were close to the frontiers of knowledge when the German economy was coming under extreme pressure.

On the battlefield tactical methods were constantly under review. The German concept of all-arms battlegroups originated in the First World War when infantry groups acquired increasingly close support from organic artillery and machine-gun elements and withstood the tests of combat. In the Panzer divisions, which were fundamentally offensive in employment, even when engaged in strategically defensive operations, tanks predominated, and the Panzer divisions themselves acted independently, though in conjunction with infantry divisions. This did not leave the infantry divisions devoid of armour, however, for besides the indirect support given by Panzer divisions when they wove mobile patterns around infantry positions, the infantry divisions possessed their own direct armoured support from the self-propelled assault gun known as the *Sturmpanzer*.

The *Sturmpanzer* first came into being in 1940. The earliest production model was a 47-mm gun mounted high on a Pz Kw I chassis, followed by versions with bigger guns built mostly on obsolete German, French, and Czech chassis that came into use by stages throughout the war. At the same time the need to give the infantry formations a more mobile anti-tank defence than that provided by towed guns (the gigantic field-mounted 88-mm Pak 43 guns were far too large and clumsy) led to the introduction of SP (self-propelled) anti-tank guns—*Jagdpanzers*—which, though organised as army or corps troops, could readily be allocated to close support of both Panzer and infantry formations.

But the dividing line between *'Sturm'* and *'Jagd'* vehicles was thoroughly blurred when it came to battle. Both could, and did, carry out the function of the other, just as did similar variants in other armies—the Semovente in the Italian army, the M-3 in the American, the Archer in the British, and the SUs of the Russians. However, the Americans and British were most strict in defining the role of tanks when in support of infantry: both earmarked particular armoured formations to act primarily in this role (at one time the British actually substituted a tank brigade for an infantry brigade within the infantry division but gave up the experiment in 1943 after it failed in Tunisia). Critics of the British infantry tank system say it was wasteful, forgetting that the German use of SP guns was even more wasteful, since SPs were only defensive in concept whereas tanks could be used for offensive as well as defensive operations.

In any case, the underlying reason for the Russians and Germans operating SP guns was one of quantity linked with quality. It was quicker and cheaper to produce a new, more powerful gun on an existing chassis, giving it only a limited traverse, than to produce a chassis to carry a fully rotating turret.

By 1943 the evolving trends of manufacturing techniques were plain for all to see. Where nations with vast industrial resources could lay down new plant at speed, major armoured components, such as turrets and parts of the hull, were made of cast steel—a technique used in the T-34, with its three-man, 85-mm-gunned turret, and in the three-man turret of the American Sherman with its 75-mm gun. In Germany and Britain, where industrial capacity had less means with which to expand, the technique of welding armour plate (which had been developed for AFVs only shortly before the war) gradually took over from bolting or rivetting.

Protection was further increased by sloping armour: in 1939 most German, British, and American tanks carried vertical plates, but the example set by the Russian T-34 persuaded the Germans to adopt sloping plate, and they were closely followed by the Americans and, last of all, by the British who endured with the theory that, since no shot ever arrived at 90 degrees to the vertical plate, that sort of plate gave the better protection. At the same time few tanks anywhere entered service with frontal armour of less than 80 mm—and some carried more than twice that thickness.

Automotive powerplants increased their output in proportion to the increasing size and weight of vehicles and the kind of

Imperial War Museum

The British Comet retained the lay-out and engine of the Cromwell, but had better armour and a 77-mm gun

Christie's system: independent suspension, enhancing speed and allowing a tracked vehicle to run exclusively on its road wheels

Imperial War Museum

The Russian BT medium tank series incorporated Christie's system, but it was somewhat under-armoured and under-gunned

Imperial War Museum

A later development, the T-34 featured a Christie-style suspension, a powerful 76.2-mm overhanging gun, and well-sloped armour

Imperial War Museum

Germany's Pzkw-V Panther was designed to outclass the T-34, and indeed it proved itself to be one of the war's best tanks

engines that happened to be available. Most tank powerplants derived from aircraft engines. The light Russian diesels, the British Liberty engines, and the American Wright radial engines—all came from this source, though there were some, like the 12-cylinder Bedford engine in the British Churchill, and the 30-cylinder Chrysler engine in some makes of Sherman, that grew with the needs of the occasion from improvised commercial vehicle engines.

Few engines were specifically designed for tank use. Range and performance were then conditioned by national fuel policies: the Americans, British, and Germans mostly insisted on their tanks being fuelled by petrol (though many US and British diesel-engined tanks were built), while the Russians settled for diesel, characterised by greater range, reliability, safety—and by the plumes of white smoke that betrayed vehicles when engines were started or put under high power. It is to be noted, however, that national policy was decided by the availability of fuel—not operational desirability.

Each increase in vehicle weight was accompanied by a corresponding increase in the size and weight of suspension. The cross-country mobility of a tracked vehicle is mostly dependent upon its power/weight ratio, and the track-to-ground pressure. Wider tracks give a lower ground pressure and a lower rate of sink—a tactical advantage over soft ground that was to be decisive in Russia, at one time, when Soviet tanks with a lower ground pressure were able to manoeuvre while their German opponents were bogged down.

Tracks also were fundamentally important, for not only did they give grip (the American rubber tracks were actually of low gripping efficiency on wet ground), but they also wore out very easily. At one time low track life was the bane of British cruiser tanks, but the introduction of manganese steel tracks, or, in other nations, rubber-bushed pins, did much to improve track life. Changing a track may be laborious, but to demand excessive life in one component of a fighting vehicle whose life is almost bound to be of short battlefield duration is often economically wrong—a fact that was well recognised in tank design circles. Finally, let it be noted that wheeled vehicles continued to be made—mostly for reconnaissance purposes—but it was generally felt that their simplicity, silence, and speed did not compensate for shortcomings in cross-country ability.

No other aspect of armoured development was more important than that of hitting power, although protection ran it a close second, and the needs of quality control to achieve improved reliability nagged every phase of design. It could be argued that armour was bound to be penetrated eventually at some range or another, and this was acceptable providing it was always possible to penetrate the enemy at an equivalent range. The idea of what distance actually constituted the 'normal battle range' at which penetration would occur was fundamental to decisions about the ratio of gun size to armour strength. In the early stages of the war few effective engagements against armour took place much beyond 500 yards, but in the desert and on the steppes this range increased to nearly 2,000 yards. However, poor visibility and the problems of identifying friend from foe brought the *average* range of engagements, even in the latter stages of the war when a Russian JS III could kill a Tiger I at 2,000 yards, down to as little as 1,000 yards.

Increases in the size and effectiveness of guns represented the most striking advances in fighting vehicle technology during the Second World War, and affected most profoundly tactics and crew training. Longer barrels and the greatly increased pressures exerted by the firing of much more powerful ammunition imposed immense strains on turret mountings, leading to increases in their size, diameter and, consequently, in overall vehicle weight. Bigger ammunition demanded more room for stowage and inevitably resulted in fewer rounds being carried, with a corresponding rise in demands upon supply echelons stretching back to the sources of production and supply. Bigger ammunition also multiplied the physical problems of a tank gunloader working in a cramped space, causing lower rates of fire that got still lower when the sheer weight of an individual round had to be divided by separating projectile from charge. The 88-mm gun carried by the Tiger II had fixed ammunition: the 128-mm gun in the Jagdtiger was separated.

As more hard armoured targets began to appear on the battlefield, related to a sharp increase in the number of tank-versus-tank actions, it became essential to hit and penetrate the enemy at as long a range as possible. Guns became far more accurate because design and manufacture grew more precise and gave rise to higher muzzle velocities; the velocity of 1,265 feet per second given by the short L/24 75-mm German gun in 1940 is to be compared with 3,950 feet per second reached by the armour-piercing (with discarding sabot) round fired from the British 17-pounder in 1944. The need to judge distance was simplified at the shorter ranges because the shot's trajectory was so flat that an accurate lay by the tank gunner might ensure a first round hit. But observation of the fall of shot at longer ranges (with higher trajectories), to enable corrections to be made to the lay, was still mandatory—and the flash and dust thrown up by the discharge of bigger guns could easily obscure the fall of shot, as it arrived at its target before the flash and dust subsided. Yet even at the short ranges a miss was possible, either because sights were not fully integrated with guns, the gunner had made a poor lay, or because the gun itself lost accuracy from excessive wear. Improved optical devices could and did help reduce inaccuracies but in the final analysis straight shooting was the result of true weapons and well-trained crews.

Into the design of shot and shell went enormous research. Simple armour-piercing shot (and even larger calibre high-explosive shells) was able to penetrate or disrupt light armour, but thicker armour with specially hardened faces could only be defeated by sophisticated shot moving at very high velocities. For instance, early British shot was found to break up against German face-hardened armour, a process that could be prevented if the shot were made stronger, fitted with a protective cap, or given a higher velocity—usually a combination of all three. Rises in velocity were the most common solution as we have seen, brought about either by increasing the size of charge relative to projectile (costly in space) or squeezing the round. One type of squeeze could be applied by firing a tungsten round through a tapered barrel, but German experiments in this field were curtailed by shortage of tungsten: another, British, method involved adding an attachment to the end of a 40-mm 2-pounder—but this 'Littlejohn' device imposed almost unacceptable restrictions on firing anything other than armour-piercing shot—high explosive and smoke were excluded.

Usually the gun designers chose to squeeze the shot 'within itself', either (as with the Germans and Russians) by using composite rigid (APCR) shot that placed a hard core within a soft outer sheaf that caused the core to accelerate on striking the target, or (as with the British and Americans) by casing the round with a 'sabot' wrapped round the hard core, acceleration being imparted to the core as it was squeezed by the sabot during their passage down the gun barrel. This round was called an armour-piercing discarding sabot (APDS).

But a quite different approach to armour penetration from that practised by the brute force of high-velocity, kinetic-energy rounds came with chemical-energy ammunitions—the hollow charge or high-explosive anti-tank (HEAT) round. These low-velocity projectiles (which inevitably imposed a range assessment problem on the crews) exploded on the hostile armour and then directed a jet of molten debris to cut a thin hole at something like 27,000 feet per second. Not only could they be fired from ordinary guns, but also from the hand-held infantry weapons such as Bazooka, Piat, and Panzerfaust; and though they had a somewhat lower chance of killing a tank than shot, they could cut through the thickest armour, and, being cheap and easy to make, proliferated the number of anti-tank weapons infesting the battlefield. They would also have been the warhead fitted to the first anti-tank guided missile ever produced—the experimental German X-7.

It can be seen that most innovations brought added complexities in their train—throwing an additional load on manufacturing capacity when increased numbers of tanks were being demanded at the front. Every nation wanted more tanks, but each had to overcome different problems, besides those of research and development, to get them. America, blessed with limitless labour and materials, and quite undisturbed by enemy action, produced the most tanks once her industry got into gear—as it did by 1942. Russia made vast strides in production despite losses and the interruptions caused by removing factories beyond the reach of the German advances. Britain made great numbers of tanks despite hostile activities and labour shortage. But Germany's case was easily the most interesting, for she redoubled and almost completely reshaped her tank factories during the war, although hampered by material shortages, destruction by air raids, disruption of transport, and the vagaries of foreign labour.

Quality and reliability varied between and within each nation's products. None, except the Russians, achieved a very high level at the outset and the Russians shunned sophistication in their search for basic simplicity. Some German designs started unreliably and were improved, and the same could be said of the British, while the Americans started well and kept it that way, in no small part because they stuck to thoroughly proven components.

In the last years of the war armoured vehicles were still predominant on the battlefield, but could no longer operate with impunity. The increased power and number of anti-tank weapons deterred tanks from charging defended localities in mass, forbade ▷

Imperial War Museum

British Cruiser Mk I (A-9) was designed as a fast tank for armoured divisions; its suspension was inferior to the Christie

Imperial War Museum

The Mk III (A-13), developed by Nuffield, used Christie's suspension and had a 2-pounder gun as main armament

Imperial War Museum

Cruiser Mk V, the 'Covenanter', dogged by mechanical faults, was never used in action but was useful as a training vehicle

Imperial War Museum

The Cromwell type entered service in 1944, two years late—to find itself outclassed by the Panther

Kenneth Macksey

In the Battle of France on May 21, 1940 Matilda tanks struck the flank of Rommel's motorised infantry regiments, where they created havoc. In Rommel's own words: 'The anti-tank guns which we quickly deployed showed themselves far too light to be effective against the heavily armoured British tanks.' The strength of the 'Matilda's' armour was a revelation to the Germans and opened their eyes to serious deficiencies in their own armour strength that had not been rectified when Afrika Korps met them again in the desert

Pzkw-IVs pass a captured British Bren-gun carrier in the Western Desert. The *Panzerkampfwagen* IV was the only German tank that remained in both production and service throughout the war, forming the backbone of the German armoured corps until replaced by the Pzkw-V Panther

T33417

Kenneth Macksey

The British Crusader tank (the Cruiser Mk VI) first saw action in the Western Desert in June 1941. Its performance was marred by mechanical unreliability and the low power of its 2-pounder gun. This picture shows the Mark III version firing the bigger 6-pounder which came into service in 1942

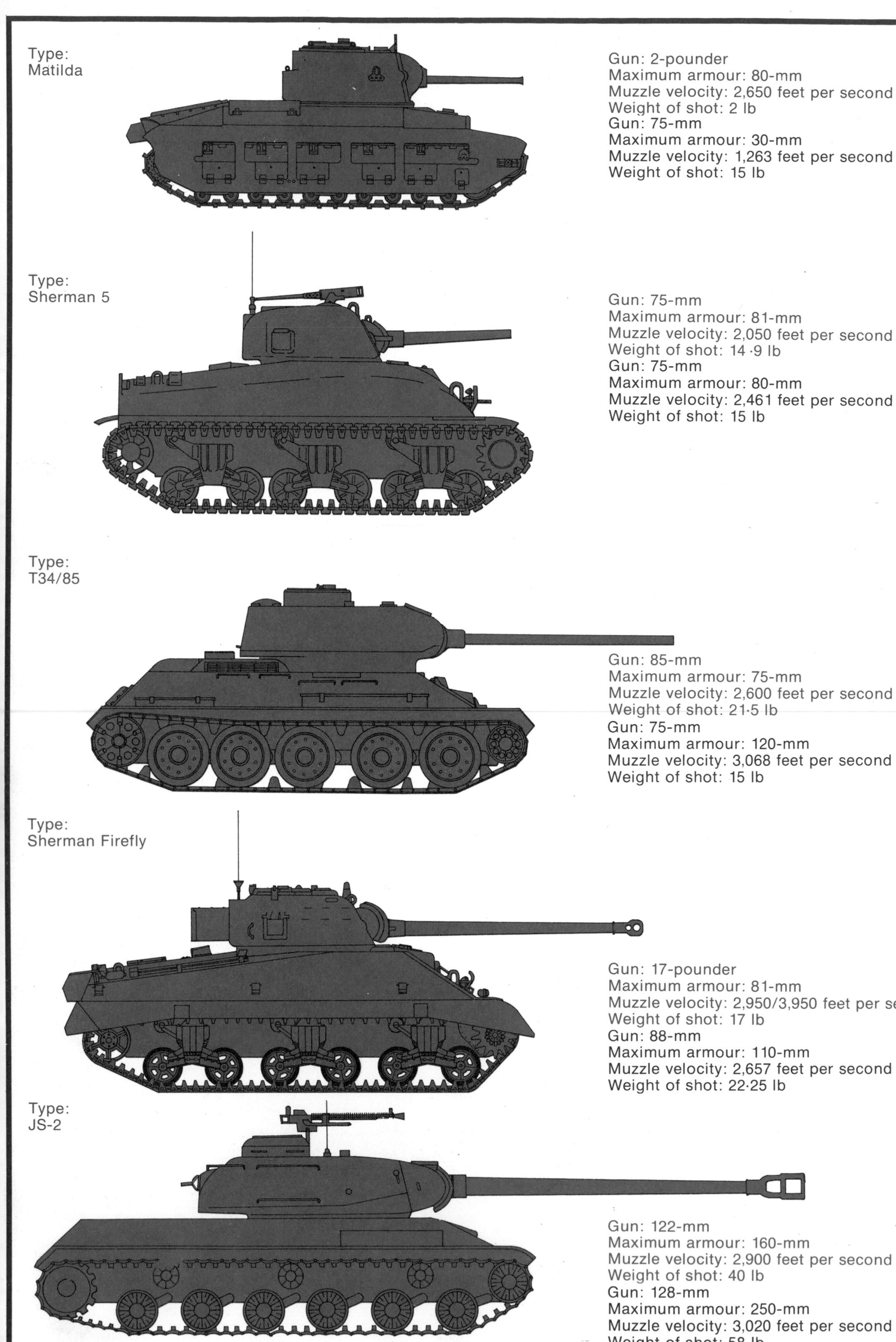

Type:
Matilda

Gun: 2-pounder
Maximum armour: 80-mm
Muzzle velocity: 2,650 feet per second
Weight of shot: 2 lb
Gun: 75-mm
Maximum armour: 30-mm
Muzzle velocity: 1,263 feet per second
Weight of shot: 15 lb

Type:
Sherman 5

Gun: 75-mm
Maximum armour: 81-mm
Muzzle velocity: 2,050 feet per second
Weight of shot: 14·9 lb
Gun: 75-mm
Maximum armour: 80-mm
Muzzle velocity: 2,461 feet per second
Weight of shot: 15 lb

Type:
T34/85

Gun: 85-mm
Maximum armour: 75-mm
Muzzle velocity: 2,600 feet per second
Weight of shot: 21·5 lb
Gun: 75-mm
Maximum armour: 120-mm
Muzzle velocity: 3,068 feet per second
Weight of shot: 15 lb

Type:
Sherman Firefly

Gun: 17-pounder
Maximum armour: 81-mm
Muzzle velocity: 2,950/3,950 feet per second
Weight of shot: 17 lb
Gun: 88-mm
Maximum armour: 110-mm
Muzzle velocity: 2,657 feet per second
Weight of shot: 22·25 lb

Type:
JS-2

Gun: 122-mm
Maximum armour: 160-mm
Muzzle velocity: 2,900 feet per second
Weight of shot: 40 lb
Gun: 128-mm
Maximum armour: 250-mm
Muzzle velocity: 3,020 feet per second
Weight of shot: 58 lb

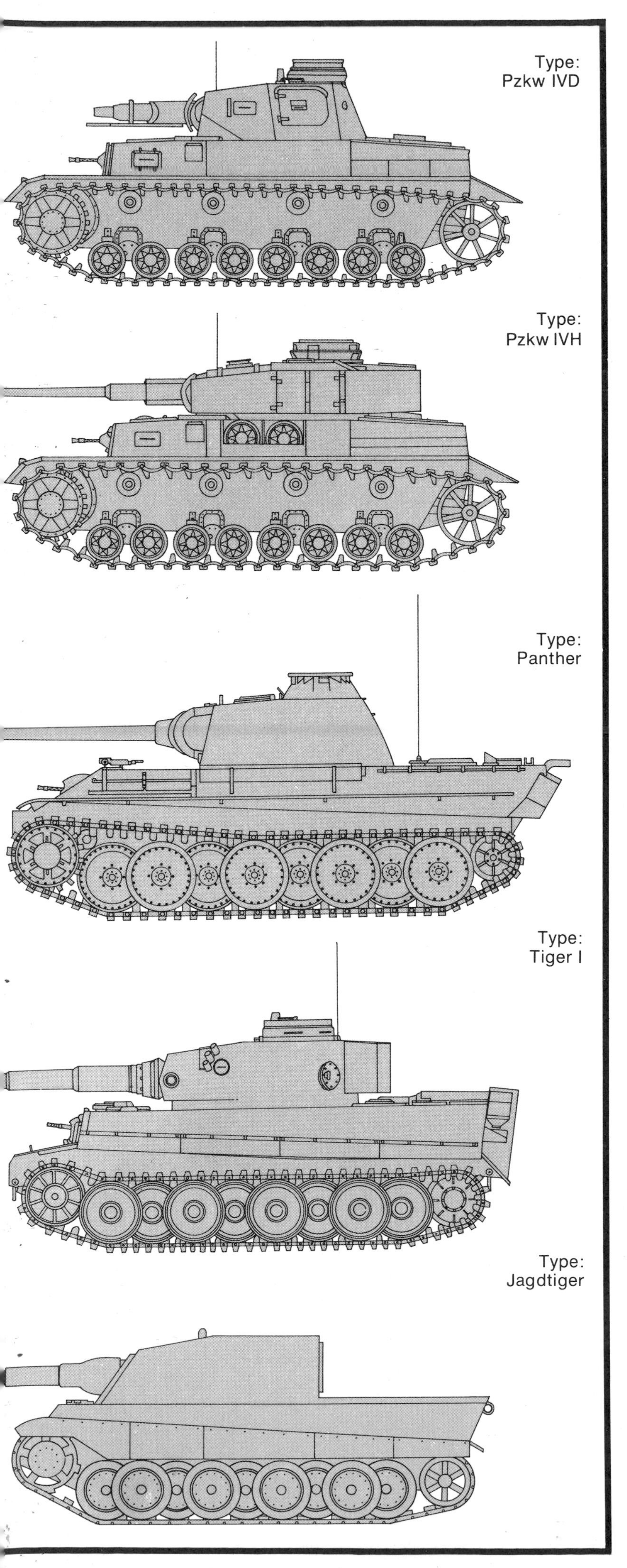

them entering close country or towns, and demanded that they should be still more closely supported by infantry and artillery and, if possible, directed away from heavily entrenched positions—in fact, striking with even more care than the tank practitioners of 1940 had demanded.

Armoured operations were hampered still further by air attacks and mines. The former, as they multiplied in number and improved in technique, were less successful as tank killers (it was imperative to hit a tank to kill it and most difficult to achieve by rocket or bomb) than as disrupters of vital supplies. Mines were laid in belts and in countless numbers as the Germans reverted ever more to the defensive. Linked with natural obstacles such as rivers, they could account for up to 20 or 30% of all tank casualties; they could impose critical delays; and they channelled tanks into killing zones of interlocking anti-tank fire.

Tank tactics had to be modified with each new technical innovation. By 1943 armour could no longer race ahead unsupported by other arms. It had to move with care, searching hard to avoid opposition, using high-explosive shells and machine-guns to neutralise and destroy anti-tank weapons, supporting each shift of position by fire and hiding in well-concealed ambushes in order to surprise careless enemy moves. Infantry on foot or in armoured carriers had to give close support to tanks to knock out opposing infantry anti-tank weapons, which by the end of the war were accounting for increasing numbers of tanks. Tanks, in their turn, had to support the infantry's every step, shooting up machine-gun positions that might wipe out unarmoured men in a trice. Massed artillery fired immense volumes of ammunition in support of every operation, while air power took part with sufficient success to compel armoured forces to introduce special anti-aircraft tanks

Though armoured forces could and did take part in every engagement where they could be thrust into the front line (even in the mountains and valleys of Italy and, as the result of immense feats of engineering, through the jungles of Burma or across the beaches of Pacific islands) their principal purpose remained the quest for a strategic stroke to the enemy brain. No better example of this came during the invasion of France in 1940; thereafter the great armoured drives into the Balkans, through the desert, deep into Russia and, reciprocally, back into Germany from east and west, lost their outright stunning nature because the novelty had worn off and armies and nations had learned how to weather these storms. Armour's battle-winning capability, however, was in no way reduced.

Each operation of war had need of men surrounded by armour for the same reasons as it had always been required to give protection against the effects of an omnipotent firepower that could not itself be entirely destroyed by counter-firepower. So in the attack, following reconnaissance by armour, infantry (many in armoured carriers) and tanks led the assault, each picking the routes and tasks best suited to their characteristics, fully supported by artillery drawn by wheeled or tracked vehicles, some of them armoured and many in the assault gun class and moving in the second wave of attack. In defence or withdrawal, however, it was the assault guns that found their place in the front rank along with infantry, backing away out of trouble, their battleworthiness no longer seriously circumscribed by lack of all-round traverse, while, in this phase, the tanks were to be found as part of a counterblow force, held in depth ready to pounce on the enemy's flank or rear when he had become entwined with and over-extended by the main infantry defensive positions.

Finally, there appeared an increasing proportion of specialised armour, developed to overcome the obstacles imposed by nature or raised by man. Bridge-laying tanks to cross streams and obstacles; flail, roller, or plough tanks to destroy mines; flame-throwing and bomb-throwing tanks to smash fortifications; and swimming tanks to land on an enemy shore or cross wide rivers—each a relatively costly device since its application was specialised and not universal, but each one tactically essential since, like armour itself, nothing else could ensure man's continued survival on a battlefield smothered by weapons of widespread effect.

By the last months of the war there was evidence to suggest that the future of the tank might be limited by the dominance of anti-tank weapons. At the same time every nation was making plans to invent tanks that would exploit the lessons of six years of armoured warfare—a demand for relatively cheap, universal machines competing with the beliefs of those who considered a degree of specialisation unavoidable for both tactical and technological reasons. Compromise being the essence of armoured vehicle design, it has shaped the plans for the future as it did in the war. Only the pace has been reduced, to match the needs of a peacetime economy, when a fighting vehicle can be expected to last 20 years instead of 20 weeks.

Tank Firepower

Much has been written about the increase in tank firepower during the war years, but to the layman calibre sizes usually have little meaning. Some idea of the rapid growth in actual striking potential can be gathered from the two groups of ammunition below. These represent the full range of British and German tank guns that saw service. Generally, size for size, German weapons were ahead of those fitted to the various Allied tanks; it was not until the appearance of the 17-pounder that we had something to fight back with on equal terms with the Panther and Tiger I. But even the 17-pounder was not in the same league as the powerful long-barrelled 88-mm KwK 43 of the Tiger II and the enormous 128-mm gun of the Jagdtiger. Although the latter was a self-propelled tank destroyer and not a true turreted tank, at least two super-heavy German tanks were under development at the end of the war using the same weapon. The complete round for this gun was too heavy to manhandle as a single fixed item, and so the shells and cartridges were loaded as separate units. The armour-piercing projectile weighed 62½ pounds, which was 42 times the weight of the 37-mm projectiles fired from the early Mk III guns. For close support work, some British tanks were armed with the 3-inch howitzer at first and later a larger 95-mm howitzer. The 77-mm was basically a shortened version of the 17-pounder designed to fit into tanks that could not accommodate the longer breech mechanism. In actual size the British 17-pounder case (23 inches long) is about 2 inches shorter than the 75-mm KwK 42 case of the Panther tank. (This information was provided by Mr L. F. Thurston.)

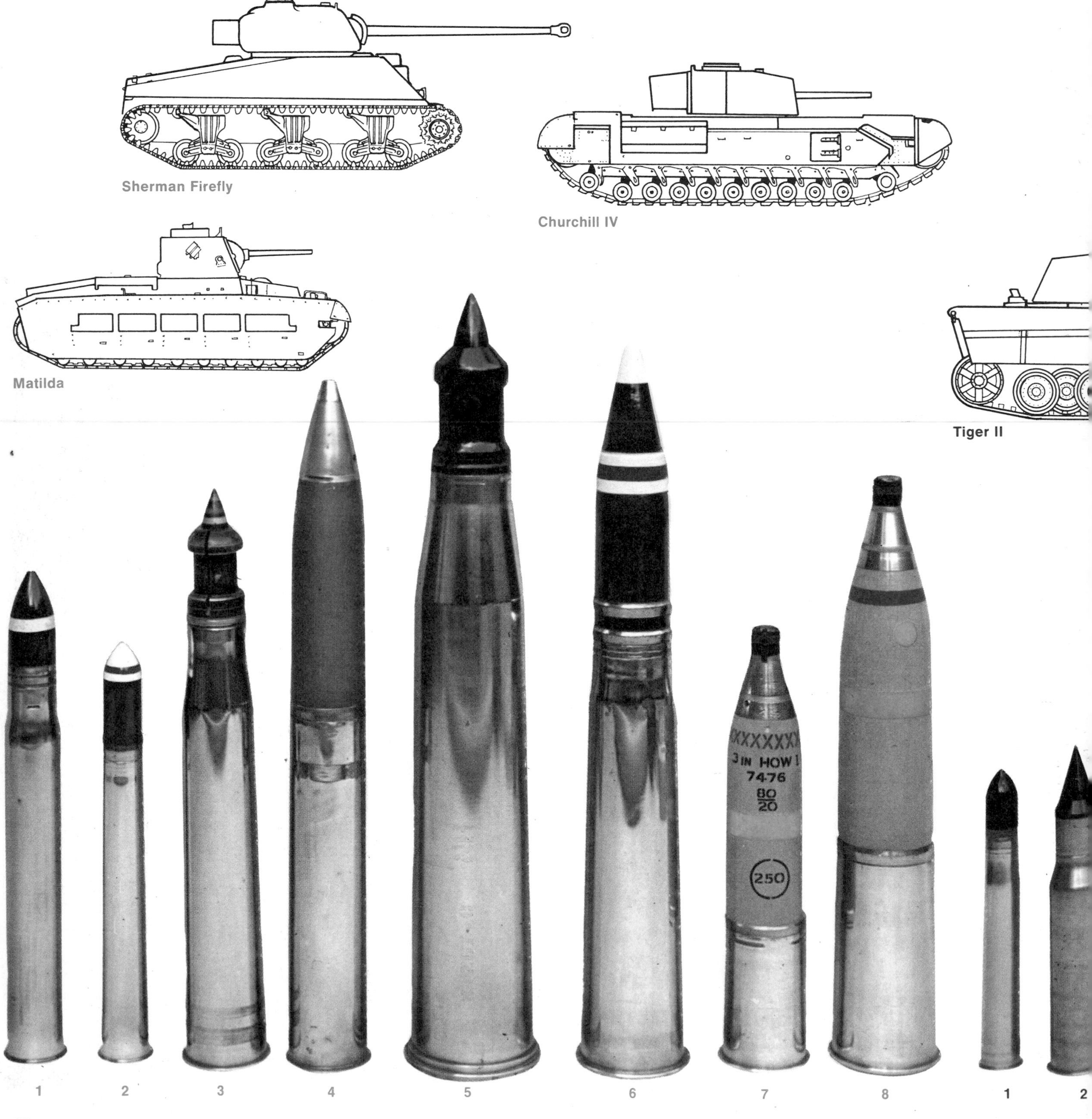

British Tank Ammunition
1 3-pounder Practice. (Cruiser A-9)
2 2-pounder Armour-Piercing. (Tetrarch, Crusader I and II, Matilda)
3 6-pounder Armour-Piercing Discarding Sabot—a light-weight high-velocity projectile with a very hard tungsten carbide core. The outer sabot construction breaks up in the bore, but is held together until clear of the muzzle, when the pieces are spun free of the smaller centre projectile. This then travels to the target at higher than normal velocity. (Cromwell I and III, Centaur I, Valentine VIII and IX)
4 75-mm High-Explosive (Cromwell IV, V, and VII, Centaur III, Churchill IV)
5 17-pounder Armour-Piercing Discarding Sabot. (Challenger, Firefly, 17-pdr Archer)
6 77-mm Armour-Piercing. (Comet)
7 3-inch Howitzer High-Explosive. (Churchill I, III, and IV Close-Support, Crusader CS)
8 95-mm Howitzer High-Explosive. (Cromwell VI and VIII, Centaur IV, Churchill V and VIII)

German Tank Ammunition
1 3·7-cm KwK* Armour-Piercing. (Mk III)
2 5-cm KwK (Short) Armour-Piercing. (Mk III)
3 5-cm KwK 39 (Long) High-Explosive. (Mk III)
4 7·5-cm KwK (Short) High-Explosive. (Mk III and IV)
5 7·5-cm KwK 40 High-Explosive. (Mk IV)
6 7·5-cm KwK 42 Armour-Piercing. (Panther)
7 8·8-cm KwK 36 High-Explosive. (Tiger I)
8 8·8-cm KwK 43 High-Explosive. (Tiger II)
9 12·8-cm PAK 44 Armour-Piercing Projectile and Cartridge. (Jagdtiger)

KwK* = Kampfwagenkanone (Tank Cannon)

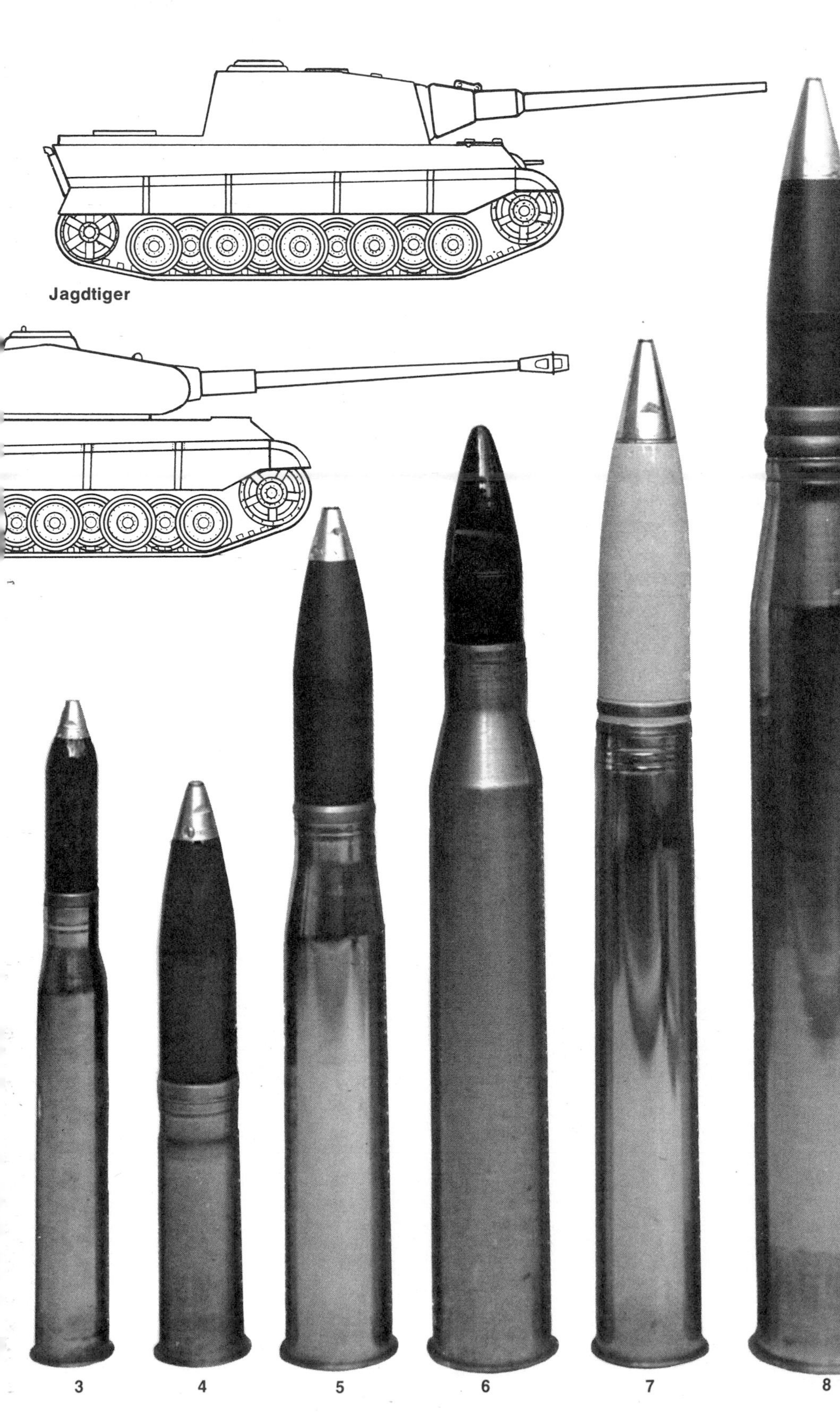

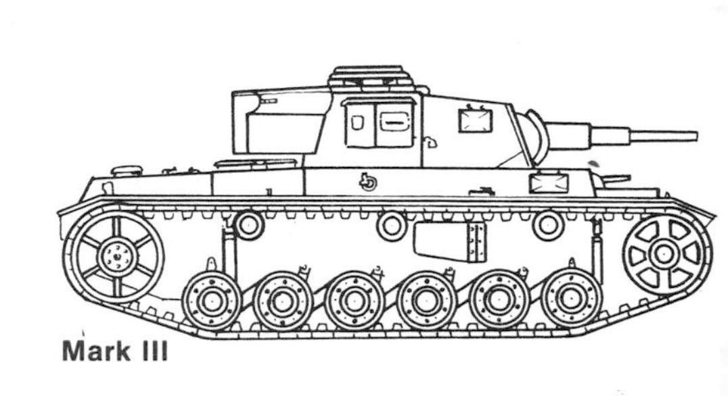

Japan's obsolescent armour

Japanese tanks in 1941 were light – none of their designs for models over 22 tons were developed – thinly armoured, cramped, uncomfortable, and out-dated. But in the Pacific war, the scope and role of armoured units were very different to those in Russia and the Western Desert – a fact which favoured Japan in 1941/42. The light Japanese tanks were easily transportable for the initial attacks on the 'Southern Area', and for the later amphibious warfare in the Pacific islands. And because the British forces in the Far East found themselves at the bottom of the list for replacement with the newer tanks and anti-tank weapons, the Japanese armoured attacks faced little positive opposition. Here was yet another contribution to Japan's runaway victory.

Light Type 95 (1935). With the Type 94, the '95' saw action both in Malaya and in later Pacific campaigns, remaining operational until 1943. Typical of the Japanese light tank designs, it was cramped and very lightly armoured. **Weight:** 10 tons. **Crew:** three. **Armour:** 14-mm (max). **Armament:** one 37-mm; one 7·7-mm machine-gun on rear of turret, one 7·7-mm machine-gun in hull. **Speed:** 28 mph. **Ammunition:** 130 rounds 37-mm, 2,970 rounds secondary armament. **Engine:** 110 hp Mitsubishi diesel. **Range of action:** 100 miles.

Medium Type 94 (1934). This model was extensively used in China after the unsatisfactory performance of its predecessor – the Type 89B. The '94' was also used in Malaya and Burma, as late as 1942. **Weight:** 15 tons. **Crew:** five. **Armour:** 17-mm (max). **Armament:** one 57-mm; one 7·7-mm machine-gun on rear of turret, one 7·7-mm machine-gun in hull. **Speed:** 28 mph. **Ammunition:** 100 rounds 57-mm, 2,750-mm rounds secondary armament. **Engine:** 160 hp Mitsubishi air-cooled diesel. **Range of action:** 100 miles.

ITALIAN
M13/40 (above): standard Italian medium tank during and after the 'Wavell campaign'. Armour: 40-mm. Turret gun: 47-mm. **Autoblinda 40** (right): medium armoured car of the Italian desert army. Turret gun: 20-mm. Machine-gun: 8-mm. **CV3/35** (below): equivalent of the British machine-gun carrier, from which it was developed. Armour: 14-mm. Armament: two 8-mm machine-guns

Desert Armour

BRITISH
Infantry Mk II (left): the 'Matilda'. Infantry tanks decided the battle for the Italian bases. Armour: 78-mm. Turret gun: 2-pounder. **Rolls-Royce Armoured Car** (below, right): as worthy a First World War veteran as the battleships of the Mediterranean Fleet. Armour: 7-mm. Machine-gun: ·303-in. **Bren-gun Carrier** (right): maid-of-all-work of the infantry. Armour: 11-mm

John Batchelor

Newcomers to the Desert War

By November 1941, the 'second generation' of British infantry and cruiser tanks, together with the American light Stuart tanks, had reached the desert theatre—but they met with mixed success in 'Crusader'. The Allies were painfully learning the tactics of the German Panzer divisions, but the reliability of the older German designs was still superior

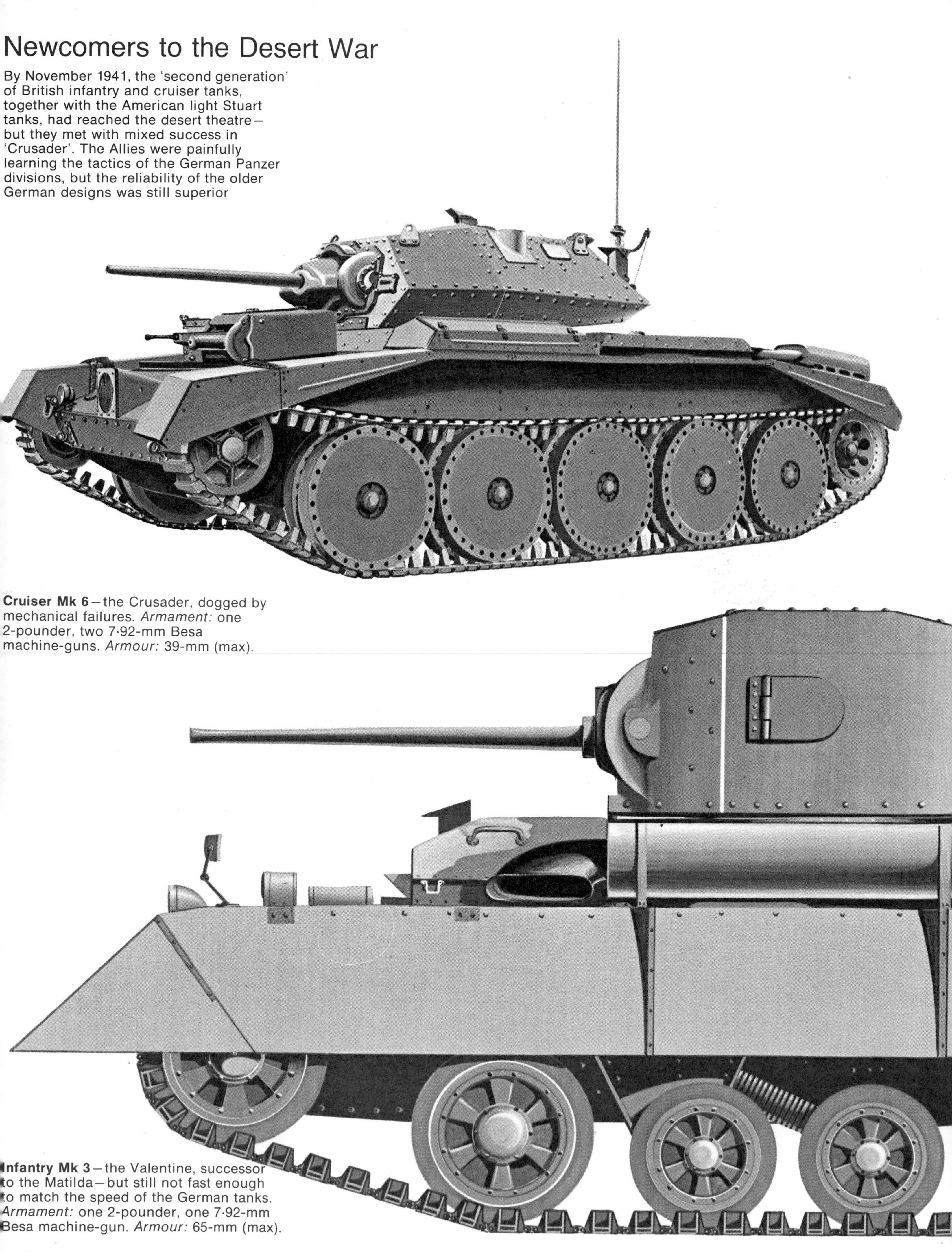

Cruiser Mk 6—the Crusader, dogged by mechanical failures. *Armament:* one 2-pounder, two 7·92-mm Besa machine-guns. *Armour:* 39-mm (max).

Infantry Mk 3—the Valentine, successor to the Matilda—but still not fast enough to match the speed of the German tanks. *Armament:* one 2-pounder, one 7·92-mm Besa machine-gun. *Armour:* 65-mm (max).

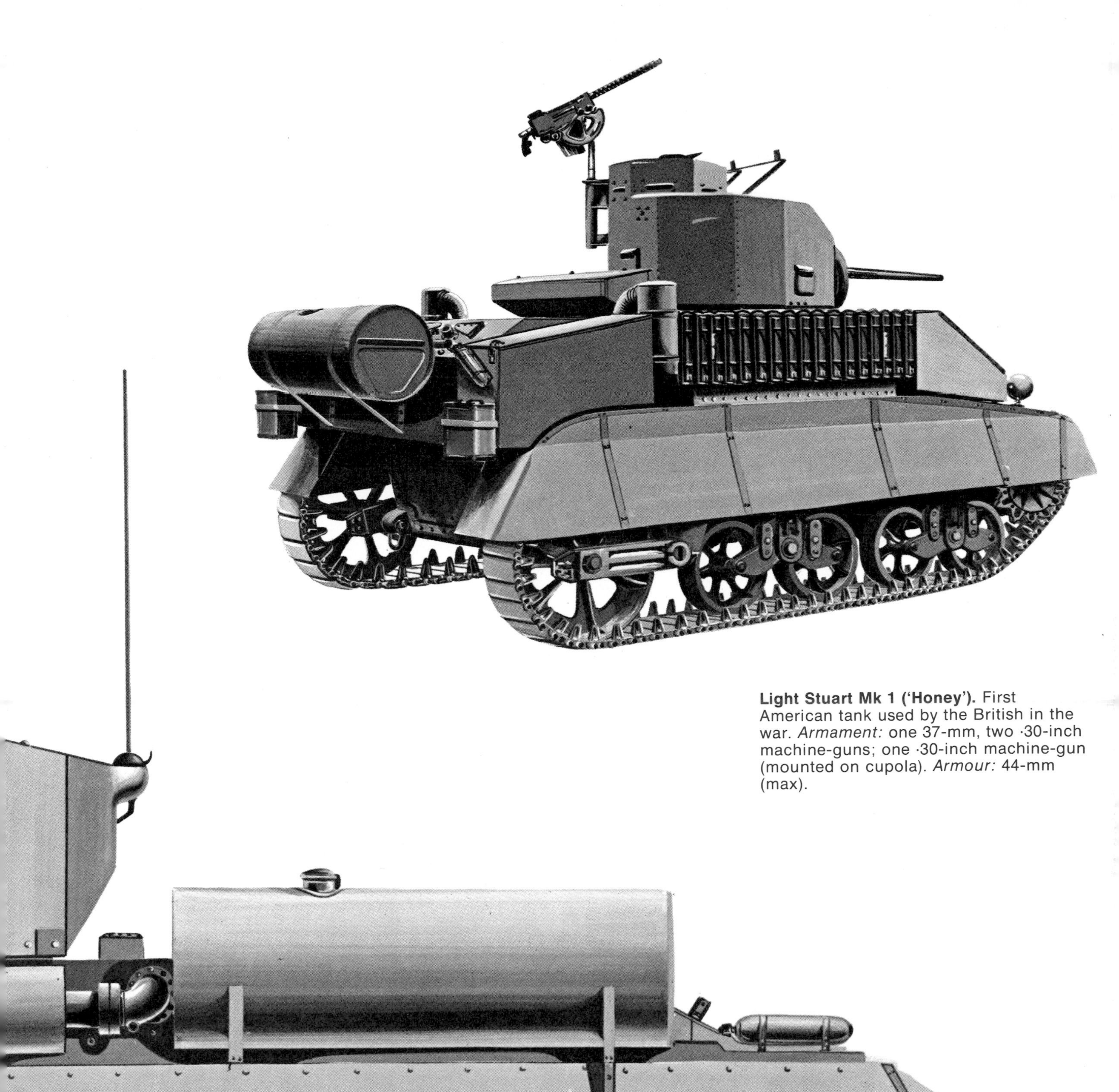

Light Stuart Mk 1 ('Honey'). First American tank used by the British in the war. *Armament:* one 37-mm, two ·30-inch machine-guns; one ·30-inch machine-gun (mounted on cupola). *Armour:* 44-mm (max).

John Batchelor

AXIS

Apart from receiving some Mark III Specials (see below) the Germans concentrated mainly upon improving equipment which had already proved reliable and battle-worthy. The Panzer Mark III, with its short-barrelled 5-cm gun, was the most numerous German tank, and its armour was strengthened by bolting plates of face-hardened steel on to various parts of its anatomy. Although the majority of the Italian armoured formations were still equipped with their 'mobile coffins', as Axis soldiers called the M13/40, they had begun to receive some new equipment like the self-propelled gun below

Italian 75/18 Semovente (self-propelled gun): although much Italian equipment during the early years of the war was obsolete and ill-suited to desert warfare, by 1942 they had begun to produce somewhat improved weapons. The 75/18 Semovente first saw action with the Ariete Division early in 1942. **Weight:** 12 tons. **Speed:** 20·5 mph maximum. **Crew:** Four. **Armament:** One 75-mm gun, and one 6·5-mm machine-gun. The main armament had a maximum range of 10,280 yards, and a maximum rate of fire of four rounds a minute. It had an elevation of 22½ degrees and depression of 11 degrees, with a traverse of 17 degrees left, and 20 degrees right

Panzer Mark III Special: by mid-1942 the Afrika Korps had begun to receive a new version of the Mark III. It was equipped with the long-barrelled 5-cm gun, similar to the formidable Pak 38, and was also designed with 'spaced armour'—an extra frontal plate separated from the basic armour by an air space of 4 inches, and intended to break up the armour-piercing cap of an anti-tank shell and thus reduce its power to penetrate the plate behind. **Weight:** 22 tons. **Armour:** 57-mm maximum, with a 20-mm spaced plate. **Speed:** 25 mph road speed. **Radius:** 100 miles maximum. **Crew:** Five. **Armament:** One 5-cm long-barrelled gun, and two 7·9-mm machine-guns

ALLIED

For the Allies the lull before the Battle of Gazala saw the introduction of equipment which went some way toward counteracting the grave deficiencies which had become apparent in the earlier battles. But these new weapons were still in very short supply, and although individual pieces compared well with their enemy counterparts, their performance was jeopardised by serious deficiencies in other equipment—particularly the failure to develop an armour-piercing warhead which could penetrate the new thicker German armour at extreme ranges

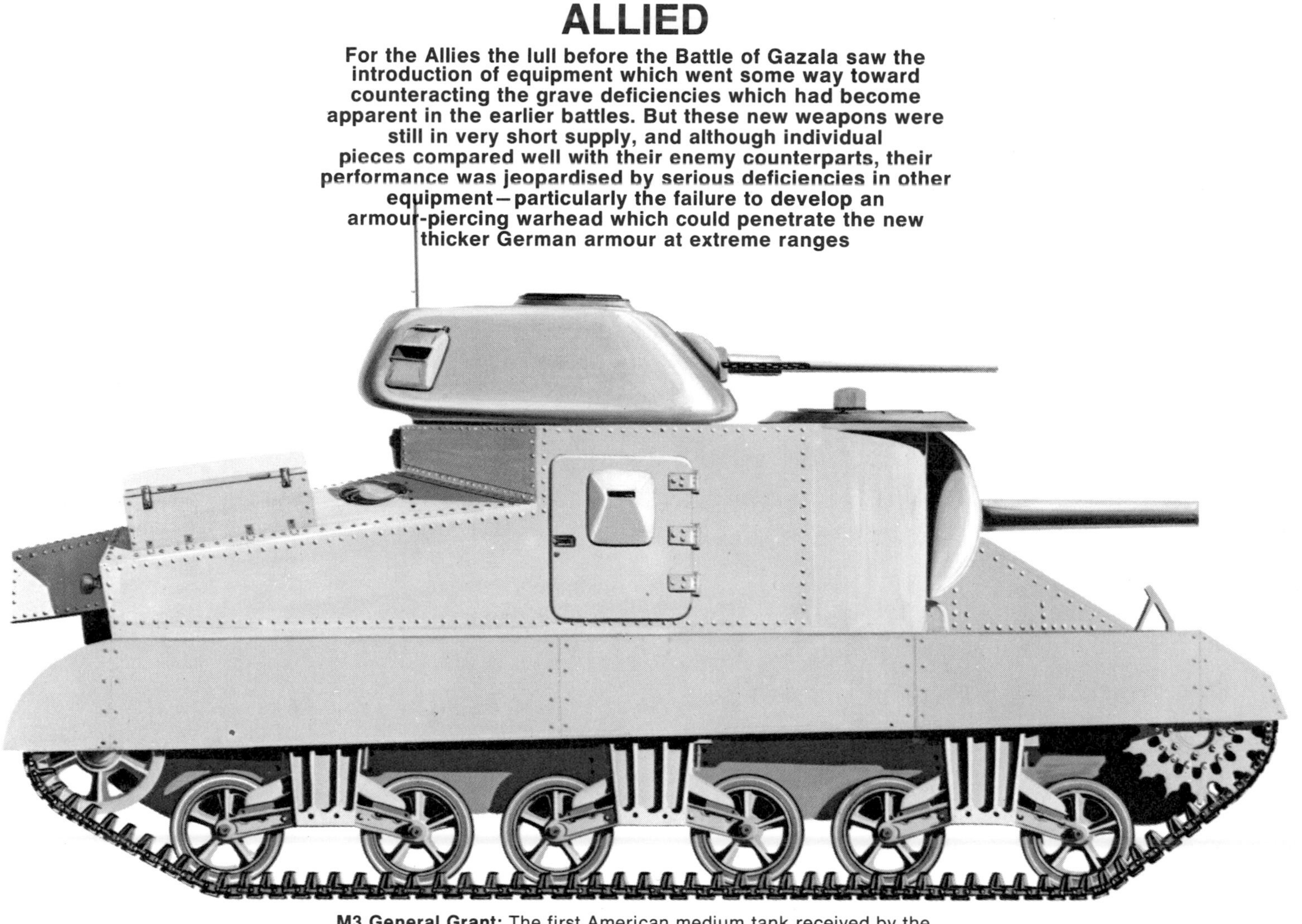

M3 General Grant: The first American medium tank received by the British forces. Its arrival was greeted with enthusiasm, for the 8th Army now had a tank with a gun capable of engaging German tanks and anti-tank crews on equal terms—and this could be done from behind the heavier armour of a reasonably fast and very reliable tank. Its major weakness was that the vital 75-mm gun was mounted in one side of the hull and thus had a very restricted arc of fire. **Weight:** 28·5 tons. **Armour:** 57-mm max. **Speed:** 28 mph maximum on roads. **Radius:** 108 miles maximum. **Crew:** Six. **Armament:** One 75-mm (hull) and one 37-mm (turret) gun, and four ·30-inch machine-guns

Six-pounder Anti-Tank Gun. The development of a larger gun to replace the 2-pounder had begun in 1938, but the stress of general rearmament had meant that the gun was not ready for trials for two years. Its delivery was further delayed by the fact that it was decided to use the tried 2-pounder to re-equip the army after Dunkirk. As a result the 8th Army had only 112 of the new guns by mid-1942. **Crew:** Five. **Weight in action:** 2,560 lb. **Range:** Up to 5,000 yards. Could fire either armour-piercing shot or high-explosive shell—but the latter was in limited supply

John Batchelor

Allied armoured units during their long wait for the infantry to clear the corridors

Camera Press

Western Desert, October/November 1942

George Greenfield

But what was it like to be fighting at the Battle of El Alamein? The author served with The Buffs in 13th Corps, whose task was to distract German attention, and to tie down forces vitally needed elsewhere. Here is his version of this important but often overlooked phase of the battle

The full moon was very bright on October 23, 1942. Moving up to our start-line, I picked up a piece of paper that had blown against the camouflage scrim of a 25-pounder. It was one of the printed broadsheets that the Army Commander had had distributed to (it seemed) every man in the 8th Army. I read the schoolboy prose once again by the light of the moon and then handed it to the Battalion Intelligence Sergeant. He tossed it away with one short, sharp comment.

General Montgomery was no stranger to 2nd Battalion, The Buffs, for they had served under him in Britain for a year when he had been South-East Army Commander. We had not loved him then and on this particular night our affection had, if anything, diminished. Marching up to a start-line for a battle under the radiant moon that threw strange black shadows across the humps and hollows of the desert did not strike us as an occasion for cricketing slogans like 'hit the enemy for six out of Africa'. It was not too hard, we thought, to sit in the pavilion of Army Headquarters and urge the others out to face the fast bowling.

Our sector was the extreme south of the Alamein Line, with the impassable Qattara Depression on our left. At H-Hour, 131st (The Queens) Brigade would advance through our protective minefields along lanes that had been previously prepared and then camouflaged, cross the few hundred yards of No-Man's-Land, and attack through the enemy minefields to carve a gap in his defensive position. Behind their forward screen, teams of sappers were to open up lanes in both minefields for 7th Armoured ▷

THE FIGHTING AT ALAMEIN

During the savage fighting in the 30th Corps sector: the crew of one of Rommel's precious Panzers surrenders to a British infantryman

Imperial War Museum

 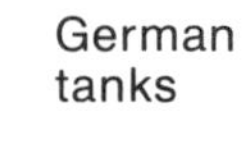
German tanks

British tanks attacking

British tanks

German 50-mm gun

Burned-out British tanks

German 88-mm gun

British mine-clearers

Minefield

 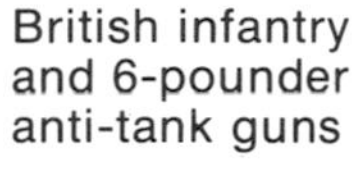 
British infantry and 6-pounder anti-tank guns

British 25-pounder shell-bursts on German positions

A Set-Piece Desert Battle

Alamein was the first set-piece battle the 8th Army had to fight against an enemy firmly entrenched behind minefields which could not easily be turned. Although on a far larger scale than most subsequent engagements, it set a pattern for a series of later actions in which the 8th Army had to breach the defence lines set up by the retreating Panzerarmee. This diagram shows a typical desert engagement. In the foreground a corridor has been cleared through the Axis minefield, the armour (Crusaders, Grants, and Sherman tanks) has passed through; and one formation is waiting to go in on the near side of a ridge. Meanwhile, infantry are coming up in trucks with their 6-pounder anti-tank guns and the engineers are clearing a second lane. In the centre another tank unit is launching an attack; well spaced out—at least 100 yards between vehicles—they move against the Axis troops who have their 50-mm PAK anti-tank guns in front, and their 88-mm guns lying back. Axis armour waits on the flanks of the position which is being shelled by British 25-pounders

Diagrammatic representation

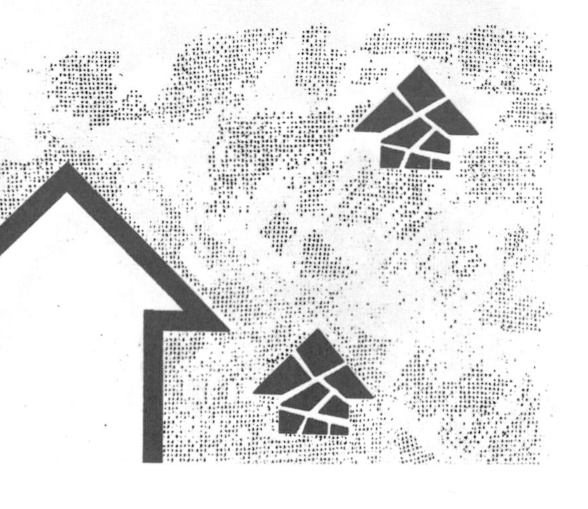

Peter Sarson

Two Rulers of the Desert Battlefield

To achieve a decisive breakthrough, 8th Army had to breach and clear strong Axis defence lines and minefields. Thus in the early stages new mineclearing vehicles – like the Scorpion – played an important part, although clearing by hand was still the most reliable and common method. But when the tank-to-tank battles began, in spite of Allied re equipment and material strength, the Germans still had the outstanding mobile weapon – their Mk IV tank with the devastating long-barrelled 75-mm gun

SCORPION. A mine-sweeping tank built on the hull of a Matilda, with two additional engines to drive the revolving drum which carried the chains. The tank would be driven at 2 mph with the drum revolving at 72/80 revolutions per minute
PZKW Mk IVG: *Weight:* 24 tons. *Crew:* Five. *Speed:* 25 mph. *Range:* 130 miles. *Armament:* One long-barrelled 75-mm KWK 40 (L-43) gun, and two 7·92-mm Type 34 machine-guns

John Batchelor

Division—the original 'Desert Rats'. If the Queens Brigade gained enough space for them, the tanks would rampage behind the enemy lines. But we all knew that it was a limited attack, a feint to keep the German Panzer divisions alert in the south, which would take some of the pressure off the 8th Army's main thrust in the north.

The 132nd Brigade, which consisted of two battalions of Royal West Kents as well as The Buffs, had the follow-up role to the 131st: either to leapfrog through them, if their attack went well, and open the salient wider, or to consolidate whatever ground they had gained if their attack lost momentum. As Battalion Intelligence Officer, I knew that our own minefields stretched up to quarter of a mile in depth and that the enemy's were reckoned to be half a mile deep in places. The enemy forces in front of us were reported to be mainly Italian, which would normally have been a comforting thought. But these Italians were the Folgore division, a grounded paratroop force who had fought ferociously against us in one of those 'straightening the line' engagements a few weeks earlier. We did not assume that they would just run away on this occasion.

Hitler's order to Rommel: 'In the situation in which you find yourself there can be no other thought but to stand fast'

Imperial War Museum

The barrage began. It was a shattering fantastic sound, drowning the subdued whispering of boots in the sand and the occasional clink of a rifle or bayonet as the infantry moved up. The din of over 1,000 field guns firing along the front was like gigantic drumbeats merging into one great blast of noise. As we went forward, we could hear the sighing whistle of the shells overhead and the flicker of their bursts on the dark horizon and beyond, as they sought out the enemy gun positions to nullify their return fire. Part of the fire plan was also to keep the enemy infantry crouching in their slit-trenches and sangars while our own forward troops probed the minefields. Bofors guns on fixed lines were lobbing tracer shells in a lazy curve towards the enemy lines ahead of us, to help the Queens Brigade maintain the correct axis of advance.

A chaotic curtain-raiser

We reached the start-line, which was marked with long strips of white tape laid out across the desert, and began to deploy in battle order as we had rehearsed in the last day or two. Up till then, all had been quiet, purposeful, following smoothly a practised drill. But now there was a shambles. Troops of the Queens Brigade were milling around in the dark looking for their officers, stretcher-bearers were scurrying to and fro, there were walking wounded adding to the confusion, and, here and there on the moonlit sand, the ominous dark patch of a dead body. A wounded Queens sergeant told me that the opening barrage from the guns had landed smack on the start-line. Whether this was so or whether the infantry had pushed ahead too far and been caught by the barrage that was meant to shield them, I never learned. But it was not a happy curtain-raiser to the Battle of Alamein to realise that the first casualties had been caused by our own guns.

The Second Buffs moved delicately through our own quarter-mile-deep minefield along the lanes where the mines had already been lifted—or so we hoped. The barrage had long since stopped except for spasmodic firing from individual batteries, but ahead of us in the night we could hear the hammering of Bren guns and the higher-pitched rattle of German Spandaus. The noise they made was like that of a child running a stick along the railings. We could also hear the thudding of mortar bombs ahead. The enemy had got over the initial shock of the barrage and was hitting back. We fanned out into No-Man's-Land, scraped out slit trenches, and settled down for what remained of the night. But there were few that slept soundly.

At first light, the battalion commander, Lieutenant-Colonel Williams, and I went forward for a reconnaissance. No-Man's-Land was about half a mile wide at that point. It sloped gently down to a hollow about mid-way and then rose equally gently towards the enemy minefield and forward defensive positions. In the grey dawn it was bleak and strangely lifeless. But as we neared the gap that had been cut through the minefield, marked with white tape strung between lines of angle irons, there were more signs of life—or mainly death. Askew inside the minefield, where it had strayed off the path, lay a blackened Sherman tank, smoke still drifting away lazily in the still morning air. In a wadi, just short of the track, were a group of wounded men from The Queens, waiting patiently to be evacuated. One bareheaded youngster, who appeared unwounded, was wandering about, muttering to himself. There were ten or twenty bodies, lying where they had fallen, near or in the minefield. At the far end of the gap, sitting on the ground with his back propped against the very last angle iron, was a young Queens officer, staring straight ahead. I was about to say to my CO that it seemed odd to be sitting around in the middle of a battle when I looked again. The young officer was dead.

The commander of 132nd Brigade, Brigadier Whistler, always known as 'Bolo', who two months before had been a major, second-in-command of a Royal Sussex battalion, and who, a few months later, was to be a Major-General commanding the famous Desert Rats, summoned his O Group. 'Bolo' Whistler was a tall, quiet man with a humorous glint never far from his eyes; however chaotic the situation, he always seemed relaxed and confident. He told us that the Queens Brigade had taken a hammering in its night attack. They had managed to cut through the minefield and had captured the first line of enemy defences but had received heavy casualties and were only just hanging on. When darkness fell, we would move in and relieve them and at the same time open up the bridgehead. We would get supporting fire from our own divisional artillery and from those tanks of 7th Armoured Division still hull down inside the bridgehead.

After the O Group ended, I asked the Brigade Intelligence Officer what had happened to Buffalo Force. Someone at Corps Headquarters, reputedly the Commander himself, General Horrocks, who later found a second and more celebrated metier as a television performer, had had the brilliant idea of brigading the Bren-gun carriers from the division and using them as light tanks accompanying the first assault. A Bren-gun carrier is noisy, cumbersome, and, to anything heavier than a rifle bullet, about as much protection as a paper bag. Each battalion commander had had to nominate a few of his best officers to help man the carriers and two of my friends had been selected. Buffalo Force, I was told, had taken a real beating.

That night the Queens Brigade—or what was left of it—came out and we went in. The moon still shone serenely but the scenes it illuminated have a dark, nightmarish quality in the mind's eye. I remember the sour, animal smell of the sangars: Italians were believed to be too lazy to dig trenches, so they rummaged around for loose boulders and built them into low walls, known as sangars, behind which they crouched. I remember seeing one of our men in a kind of blood-frenzy jabbing his bayonet time and again into an enemy corpse that was already stiff and cold. I remember my sergeant being seriously wounded in the legs when he was helping to move a dead Italian paratrooper. One of the enemy had booby-trapped the body by placing a live grenade beneath it. When the weight of the body was shifted, the grenade went off. The Intelligence section was so enraged at the thought that a good friend should be wounded through an act of decency that they would cheerfully have killed the booby-trapper on the spot if they had ever found him.

As the retreat began, all those Axis infantry who had no transport were quickly overrun by the 8th Army

I remember the Battalion Medical Officer, a chunky, amusing Canadian of Russian origin named Shragovitch, shouting to me to give him a hand. A splinter from a mortar bomb had hit one of our men in the thigh, almost slicing his leg off. It was only attached by a few shreds of flesh. The doctor told me to hold the leg steady while he snipped it clear before applying a tourniquet to the stump. When this rough-and-ready operation was complete, the doctor's quick action saving the man's life, I was left squatting on the sand, stupidly holding the unattached leg, still in its stocking, webbing gaiter, and boot, across my knees. I had never realised before the utter dead weight of a solitary leg.

And the last thing I remember about that strange night was snatching a few hours' sleep after the moon had set. Having been on my feet for close on two days, I just wrapped a blanket round myself and sank down on the hard desert. My head nestled against something lumpy but it might have been the best down pillow. I awoke at first light to find that I had been reclining on the chest of a dead Italian.

I was just in time to see the last squadron of Sherman tanks belonging to 7th Armoured Division rumbling away down the minefield gap, their wireless aerials whipping in a thin arc against the grey dawn sky as they bucked and lurched down the uneven track. There was not enough room inside the bridgehead which, as I learned later that day, was only about 500 yards deep at its furthest point, for the tanks to deploy. Besides, they were needed to regroup and stand by to reinforce the main attack in the north.

But it was a cheerless moment to face the dawn on an empty stomach and know that the total defence in the extreme south of the sector was two infantry brigades, strung out along some 2,000 yards of front, with a badly knocked about remnant of the Free French Brigade in reserve somewhere to our left rear. The Free French had mounted a brave attack against the bare sandy hill of Himeimat and had actually got a few of their troops on to the summit, only to be driven off by a swift enemy counterattack. So the Germans still had their observation post on top of Himeimat, which looked down into our positions. We were slap in the path that the German Panzer divisions had taken six weeks before when Rommel attacked in the south and had been flung back at Alam Halfa. As the last of our own tanks disappeared into reserve, I had the fervent hope that history would not repeat itself.

The waiting begins

For a couple of days we dug in deeper and waited. Battalion headquarters was occupying a steep-sided wadi that ran diagonally across the front for about 40 yards and which had been used by the Italians before us. Although we kept our heads down as much as possible in daylight, it would have taken no keen military brain on the other side to realise that such a useful natural feature would be put to use. So on the first day of our occupation and every subsequent day at irregular intervals, we were greeted by mortar-bomb attacks. Casualties were few as long as one happened to be lying at the bottom of a deep slit-trench but the scream and thud of each bomb, which if it happened to land close enough might cause a small avalanche of sand down the side of one's slit trench, tended to fray the nerves after a while. Once, a runner at Battalion HQ nearly suffocated to death when a mortar bomb landed almost on the lip of his trench and the whole side caved in on him. He was only just dug out in time.

The ground rose for a few yards behind the wadi and then dropped away sharply. The HQ latrines were sited on the reverse slope. They were under cover from the enemy but the visitor had to appear in full sight for a second or two on his way there and back. The Italian commander opposite must have deduced what was happening and, with a sense of humour we failed to appreciate, had a rifle on a fixed sight aimed at the path to the latrines, loosing off at intervals. No one was ever hit but the ever-present possibility was a great cure for constipation.

So we fell into the routine of stalemate. By day movement was kept to a minimum and the troops sat tight in their trenches. At night rations came up from B Echelon behind the minefield, men stretched their legs and both fighting and reconnaissance patrols probed the enemy defences. Fortunately, the Italians were never very keen on carrying out night patrols themselves but we kept sentries on the alert just in case. Part of my duties was to visit the forward companies every night; it was important to have a bump of direction and not go wandering past our own positions into the enemy lines. I used to hear from the company commanders what had happened in their immediate locality that day and in return pass on the news of the battle in other sectors to our north. As far as we could piece together the facts, things were not going too well. Some ground had been gained in the north but at heavy cost and there were still over 1,000 yards of dense minefields and a resolute defence to be overcome. Up to that time General Montgomery had

ALLIED

Throughout the war the Allies made great use of armoured cars for reconnaissance, and at no time were they more useful than during the long pursuit of the Afrika Korps. The Humber illustrated right was widely used throughout the desert war. These cars were adapted on the spot to carry a wide variety of weapons. The Daimler was used in almost every theatre in which British troops were engaged.

DAIMLER Mk II: Speed: 50 mph. **Range:** 150/250 miles. **Crew:** Three. **Armament:** One 2-pounder gun, one 7·92-mm machine-gun.

Sd.Kfz-251: Half-track reconnaissance vehicle. **Speed:** 31 mph. **Range:** 185 miles. **Crew:** Two. **Armament:** Two 7·92-mm machine-guns.

AXIS

At the outbreak of the war, German forces had been well supplied with armoured cars and half-track reconnaissance vehicles and personnel carriers. The vehicles illustrated below were used throughout the war, and formed the mainstay of the Afrika Korps' light-armoured forces during the fighting in the desert. Their speed also made them particularly useful during the initial moves into Tunisia.

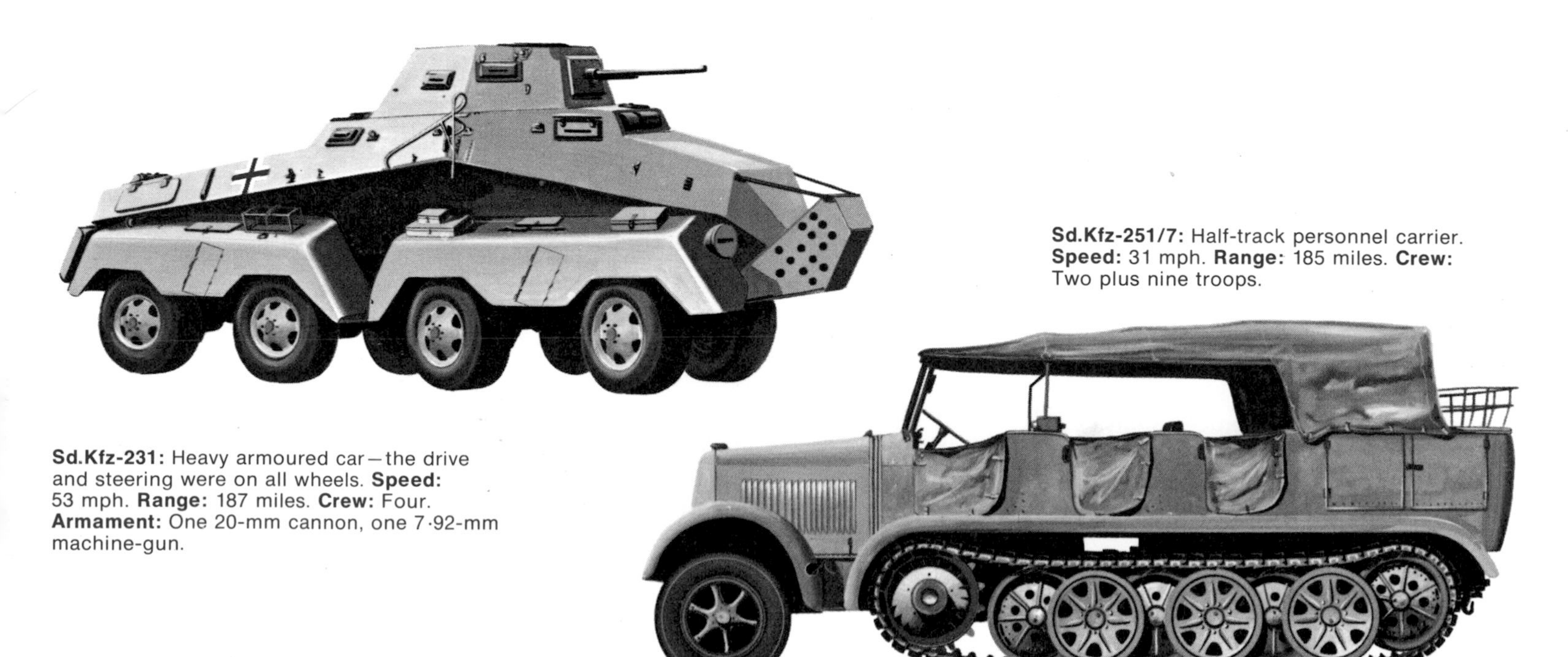

Sd.Kfz-251/7: Half-track personnel carrier. **Speed:** 31 mph. **Range:** 185 miles. **Crew:** Two plus nine troops.

Sd.Kfz-231: Heavy armoured car—the drive and steering were on all wheels. **Speed:** 53 mph. **Range:** 187 miles. **Crew:** Four. **Armament:** One 20-mm cannon, one 7·92-mm machine-gun.

HUMBER MK1: Speed: 55 mph. **Range:** 360 miles. **Crew:** Three. **Armament:** One 2-pounder gun, one ·303-inch Vickers machine-gun.

Sd.Kfz-222: Light armoured car. **Speed:** 50 mph. **Range:** 180 miles. **Crew:** Three. **Armament:** One 20-mm cannon, one 7·92-mm machine-gun.

not really justified himself, except as a fire-eating commander back in Britain with a strange passion for self-denial and physical fitness. Many of us wondered—and were to go on wondering for another week—whether he had the capacity to command troops in a successful action.

Our battalion commander, Lieutenant-Colonel Williams, was one of those very brave men who utterly fail to understand how anyone else could be other than brave. He had been in the desert with the 1st Battalion The Buffs ever since the outbreak of war and had joined us a few weeks before Alamein when our previous CO had been wounded in the Alam Halfa action. We soon had a taste of his mettle. On the first afternoon that we took over from The Queens, he summoned his company commanders and myself for a forward reconnaissance. This consisted of walking—almost marching—straight towards the enemy lines. I was tagging along discreetly in the rear, lugging a large map board covered in talc, which glittered far too brightly in the sunshine for my taste. The CO kept yelling to me not to lag behind, as he strode on, all six feet of him, with shoulders squared and head held high. The inevitable happened. An Italian machine-gun opened up and, before the first burst had sped past our ears with that sharp, whipcracking sound made by a near-miss, I had hit the protecting sand. The various company commanders were not much slower to take cover. Only the Colonel stood his ground and looked down on us with a cool surprise.

Two days later, this indomitable man ordered me to reconnoitre the area on our northern flank with him in a Bren-gun carrier. A map trace supplied by brigade showed an 88-mm anti-tank gun dug in on that flank and I was not wildly anxious to be wandering about in daylight in a thin-skinned Bren-gun carrier when a lethal, armour-piercing weapon like an 88 was reputed in the neighbourhood. I stood in the front compartment, alongside the driver, and, whenever he changed gear, took advantage of the noise by muttering to him to go slower. Colonel Williams, who was in the rear compartment, soon grew impatient with our tardy progress. He told the driver to halt and ordered me to take his place at the rear while he stood in front to give the driver directions. We moved around and the carrier started off again, with the CO urging us on at an unseemly pace towards the enemy.

We had not gone 50 yards when there came a bang like a thunderclap. The carrier lurched to its left and the day went black with a cloud of smoke and dust. I baled out and lay flat on the ground behind the carrier, shoulders hunched, awaiting the next shell from what must be the suspected 88 mm. But nothing happened and I cautiously climbed to my feet, peering round the side of the vehicle.

There was a trough into which the left-hand side of the carrier had dipped. Over 10 yards away, a chunk of track, as long and several times as heavy as a man, had been hurled by the force of the explosion. We had gone over a Teller mine. The whole blast had been taken by the flat steel floor of the left-hand front compartment. Both the CO's legs had been smashed—the left one, I heard later, broken eleven times between knee and ankle.

Captain Shragovitch, our MO, arrived with stretcher bearers to evacuate the Colonel and the driver, whose left shin was broken by the gear lever when the blast wrapped the solid metal bar around his leg. When the casualties had been taken away, 'Shrag' stood near the smashed carrier, wiping his brow for the sun was fierce. I happened to notice a taut wire almost brushing the backs of his sturdy calves and said in as casual a tone as I could muster: 'Don't step back—you're almost leaning on a booby trap!' The Germans had an unpleasant habit of planting anti-personnel mines among their anti-tank varieties and these could be set off if anyone stumbled into the wire 'triggers' that were stretched a few inches above the ground.

Then we all had a large gulp of brandy.

So the battle in the south went on, compounded of dozens of small incidents, a 'phony' war except for the mounting list of killed and wounded. On one occasion, in the middle of the day, after they had first broken in on our wireless wavelengths with an appeal, the Italians sent a small delegation across No-Man's-Land, carrying a large white flag. They were seeking a short truce, so that they could send out burial parties to collect and bury their dead. We had long since collected our own dead by night and those of the enemy who had fallen near our trenches. (My worst memory was coming across a smashed Bren-gun carrier that had belonged to the ill-fated Buffalo Force and finding the body of one of my friends in it. An 88-mm shell had blasted through the front bulkhead, through the driver, through the officer behind him and out through the steel plate at the back. In the clear light of the moon, you could look right along the neat series of holes, like looking through a rifle barrel.)

The truce was refused and the Italians told that it was up to them to collect their dead by night, as we had done. By the end of the second day's occupation of our present lines, the unburied dead had already gone black and bloated under the high, bright sun.

Another week went by. Then we heard that 10th Corps had broken through in the north, rolling up Rommel's left flank. The mortars and machine-guns in front of us fell silent: there were fires and explosions by daylight in the Italian lines as they tried to destroy equipment they could not carry off in retreat. Under infantry escort our sappers cut lanes through the last of the minefields ahead but they met with no resistance. The enemy had run. We were ordered to pursue and the battalion transport, which had been hidden away in the rear throughout the battle, came lumbering up.

There were only two narrow gaps through the minefields in front of us allotted to The Buffs, and vehicles were ordered to go through one at a time with longish intervals between, just in case the Luftwaffe managed to raise a Stuka or two for a sneak raid. So it was a long and tedious business getting the hundred or so vehicles through the minefields.

Too long and tedious for the Free French, who were to follow us through. A squadron of them in Bren-gun carriers formed up in line abreast at about 10-yard intervals along the edge of the minefield. There was no question of bothering about gaps where the mines had been lifted. Their leader blew a blast on his whistle and the column charged into the minefield. There were thunderclaps of bangs and crashes as one Bren-gun carrier after another blew up. Some went up within the first few yards; a few dodged their way ahead for 50 yards or more. But one after the other, with the inevitability of doom, the carriers smashed themselves to grounded hulks on the mines. It was magnificent and it was futile, a fitting epitaph to a famous victory.

GEORGE GREENFIELD was educated at King's School, Rochester, and Downing College, Cambridge. When the war broke out, he joined the Lincolnshire Regiment as a private and was later commissioned into The Buffs, with whom he served in the Western Desert and elsewhere in the Middle East. Towards the end of the war he went on to the General Staff, and ended up as GSO II, Cyprus. After the war he spent seven years in book publishing and then became a partner in a leading literary agency. He has virtually given up writing, but his published novels include *Desert Episode* (which won the Macmillan Centenary Award), *This World is Wide Enough,* and *At Bay.*

Graves: El Alamein

Live and let live.
No matter how it ended,
These lose and, under the sky,
Lie befriended.

For foes forgive,
No matter how they hated,
By life so sold and by
Death mated.

John Pudney

(From *Collected Poems* of John Pudney (Putnam)) Central Press

MINES: A DEADLY FACTOR IN DEFENSIVE WARFARE

It was during the pursuit of the Panzerarmee that the 8th Army encountered the widespread use of anti-personnel mines—a facet of warfare which the Germans developed to a fine art. Elaborate mining was the quickest way of setting up a defensive position and making up for lack of personnel: mines could be used as standing patrols to guard an area, to channel attacks into special zones, to prevent the enemy using observation posts, and to make all enemy movement difficult and costly. The most pestilential of the German types was the 'S' mine (in action below), which would be sown thickly over an area with only the detonation trips showing above the ground. When activated, there was a short delay before the ejector-charge hurled the mine about seven feet into the air where the main charge exploded, scattering pieces of mine and ball-bearing over an area of about 150 feet. A soldier of the 8th Army describes some typical German methods: *They were laid with cunning and imagination. One night a truck-load of Middlesex hit an anti-tank mine; the survivors, jumping clear, found themselves in an 'S' minefield and were killed. During the night some Camerons sent out a patrol to bring in the bodies; they were fired on, took cover in a crater, and found it full of mines—six of them were killed. Once more the Camerons tried, but this time the Germans had attached 'S' mines to the bodies, and three more lives were lost. That particular spot is said to have cost 36 lives before it was cleared*

Chris Harrison

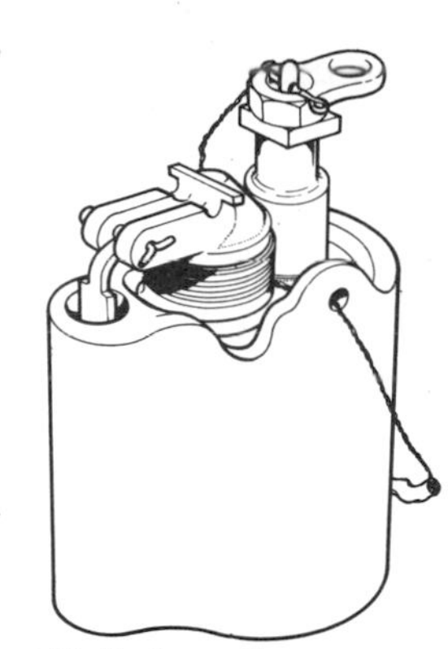

British Shrapnel Mine Mk II: An anti-personnel mine weighing 10 lb and containing 1 lb of Amatol. A pull of 4 lb on the trip-wire set off a charge which caused casualties up to 30 yards

British No. 75 Hawkins Grenade Mine, Mk I: This small anti-tank mine weighed 3 lb and contained $1\frac{1}{2}$ lb of Nobel's Ammonal 704 explosive. Capable of destroying light tanks and vehicles

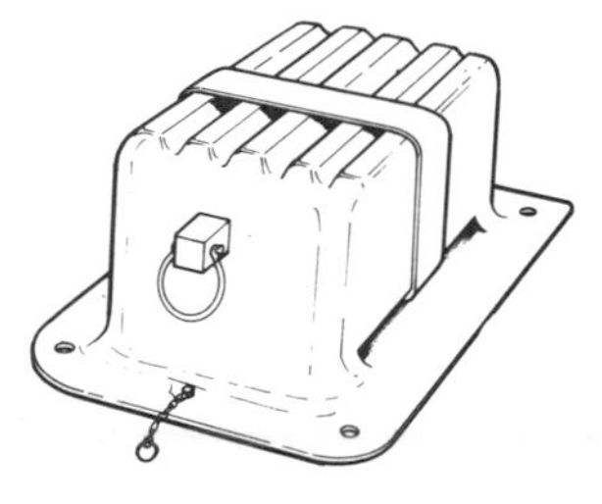

French Light Anti-Tank Mine: This mine weighed $14\frac{1}{2}$ lb and contained $5\frac{3}{4}$ lb of explosive. It needed pressure of 300-500 lb to set it off

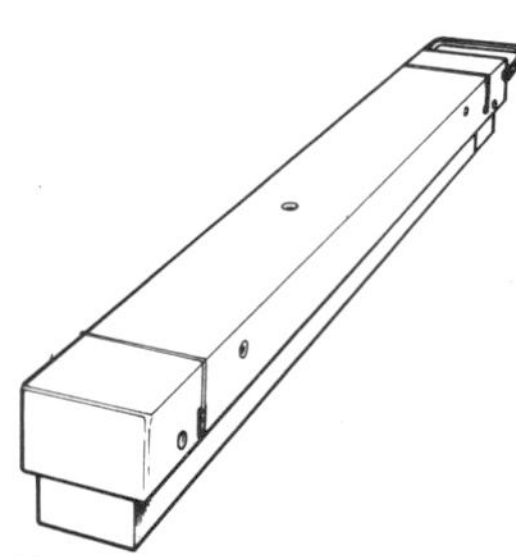

German Riegel Mine 43: An anti-tank mine which weighed 20·5 lb and contained 8·8 lb of explosive

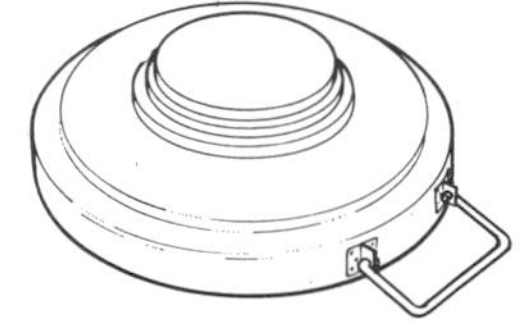

German Tellermine 42: This anti-tank mine weighed 20 lb and contained 12 lb of TNT. It needed pressure of 240-400 lb on the top plate to set off the charge

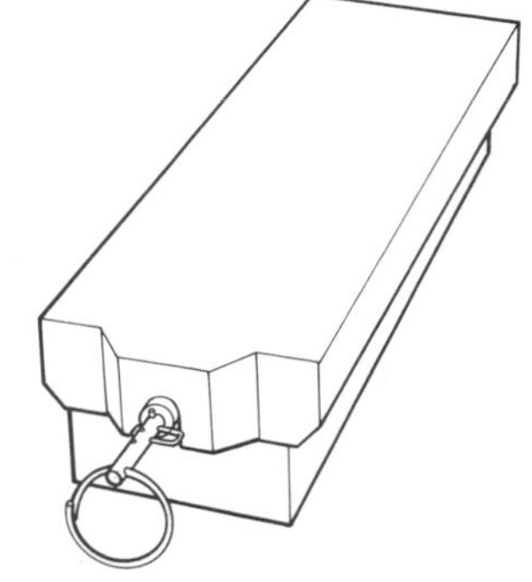

Italian Anti-Personnel Mine: This mine weighed 1 lb and had a case made of Bakelite containing $\frac{1}{3}$ lb of explosive

John Batchelor

LATECOMER TO THE DESERT WAR

'NEBELWERFER' 150-MM ROCKET-LAUNCHER: The most widely used of the family of launchers developed by the Germans, the six-barrelled Nebelwerfer ('fog-thrower') was used to lay down extremely heavy short-range bombardments or smoke screens. As compared with conventional artillery, the Nebelwerfer fired a heavy projectile (below) from a light carriage, and was thus very manoeuvrable, but it was far less accurate. The six barrels had to be fired separately (this took 10 seconds) to prevent the carriage overturning; the tubes could be reloaded in 90 seconds. *Weight of launcher:* 1,195 lb. *Range:* 7,330 yards with high explosive, 7,750 yards with smoke shells. *Weight of rocket:* 75·3 lb (high explosive), 78 lb (smoke)

▷ One of the deadly '88s' of the Halfaya garrison. Before its transfer to Rommel's desert army, this particular gun (as indicated by the rings on the barrel) had fought in the Polish, Belgian, and French campaigns, with an impressive total of kills to its credit

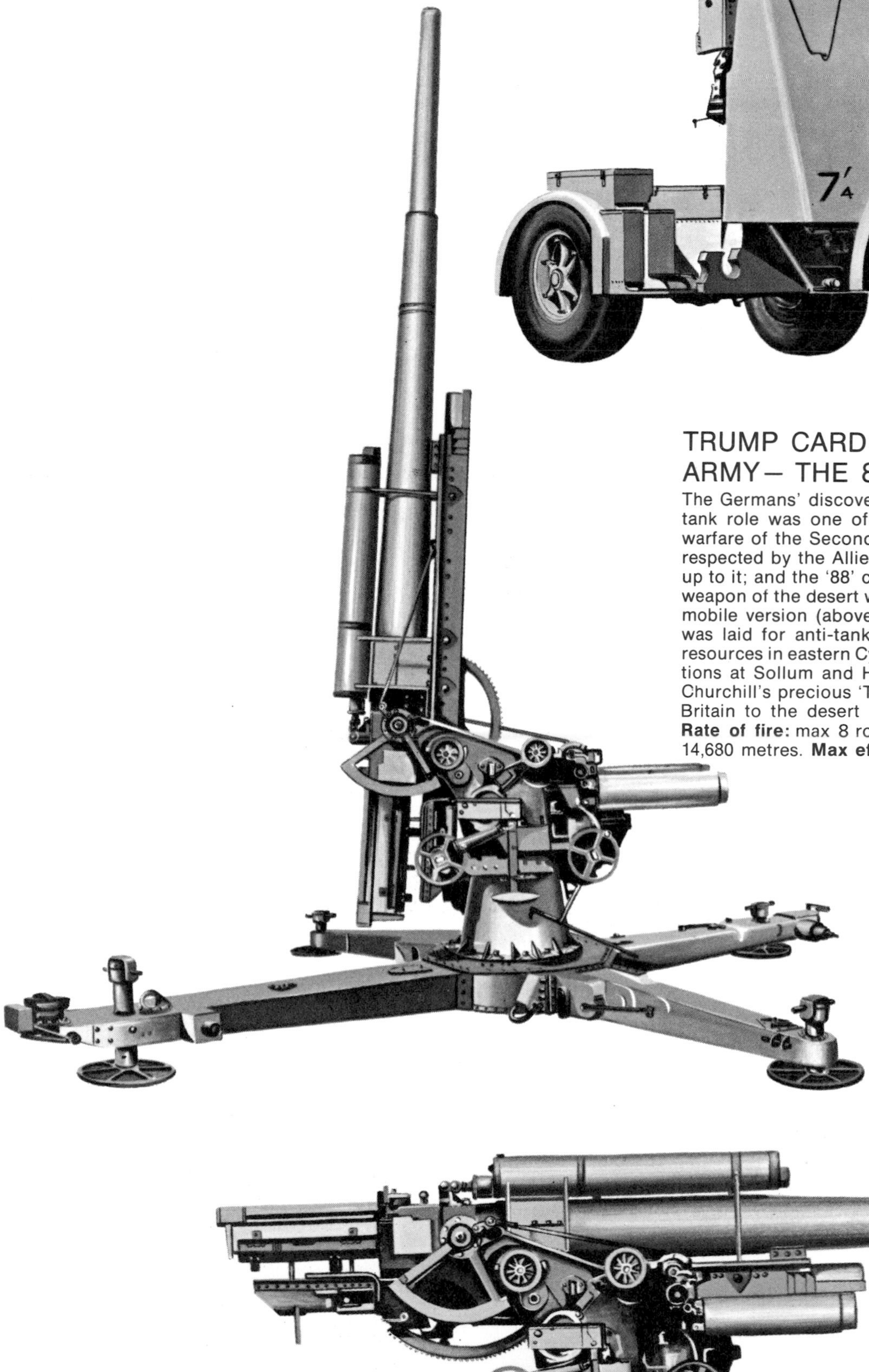

TRUMP CARD OF THE GERMAN DESERT ARMY– THE 8·8-CM FLAK GUN 18

The Germans' discovery of the potency of their heavy flak guns in an anti-tank role was one of their most startling contributions to the armoured warfare of the Second World War. The '88' was a weapon both feared and respected by the Allied forces in the Western Desert; no tank could stand up to it; and the '88' came to be regarded as the ultimate German wonder-weapon of the desert war, with almost mythical powers. It is here seen in its mobile version (above), in its normal anti-aircraft position (left), and as it was laid for anti-tank use (below). Rommel eked out his over-stretched resources in eastern Cyrenaica by digging-in '88s' to hold his front-line positions at Sollum and Halfaya; and these guns reaped a rich harvest when Churchill's precious 'Tiger Cubs' were rushed from the training-grounds of Britain to the desert battlefield. **Calibre:** 8·8-cm. **Overall length:** 25 feet. **Rate of fire:** max 8 rounds per min. **Crew no:** 6. **Max effective altitude:** 14,680 metres. **Max effective horizontal range:** 10,600 metres

John Batchelor

Weapons for the Final Desert Drive

The first British attempts to produce efficient self-propelled guns were not encouraging. The Bishop *(below)* was weak in design and construction, slow, uncomfortable, and usually more trouble than it was worth; the Sexton *(right)* was better, being constructed from more reliable components. But in the 5·5-inch and 3·7-inch guns the British artillery had two splendid weapons, which were equal to any of their Axis counterparts; and although the 3·7 was never allowed to give of its best in the anti-tank role, the 5·5 served with distinction, proving invaluable in the interminable bombardments among the Tunisian hills

Bishop Self-Propelled Gun
No two variants were ever exactly alike, but the type basically consisted of a 25-pounder mounted in a Valentine hull. It was not a happy combination, as the two components were usually battle-weary from past campaigns. *Weight:* 18 tons. *Crew:* four. *Max armour thickness:* 51-mm

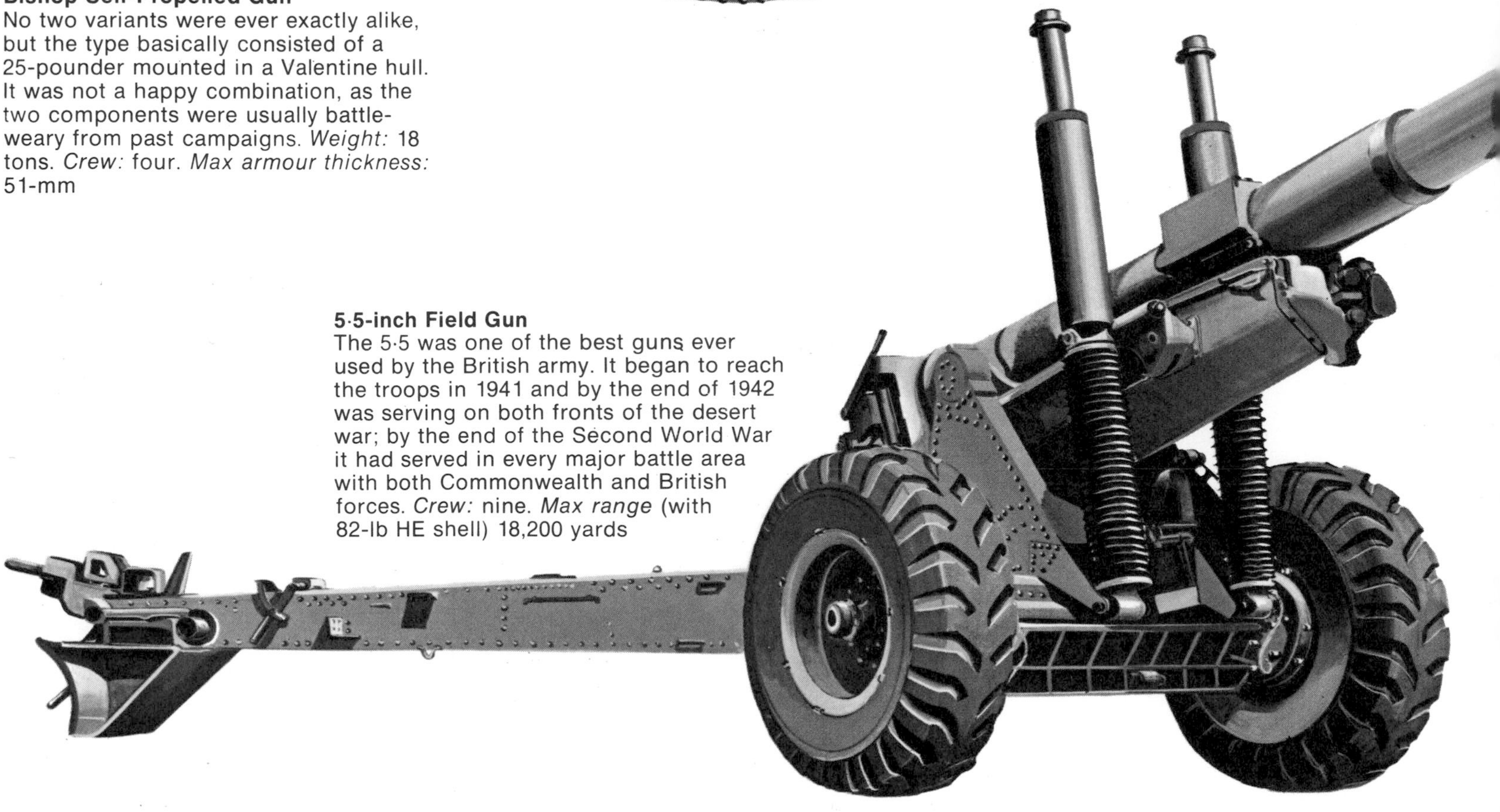

5·5-inch Field Gun
The 5·5 was one of the best guns ever used by the British army. It began to reach the troops in 1941 and by the end of 1942 was serving on both fronts of the desert war; by the end of the Second World War it had served in every major battle area with both Commonwealth and British forces. *Crew:* nine. *Max range* (with 82-lb HE shell) 18,200 yards

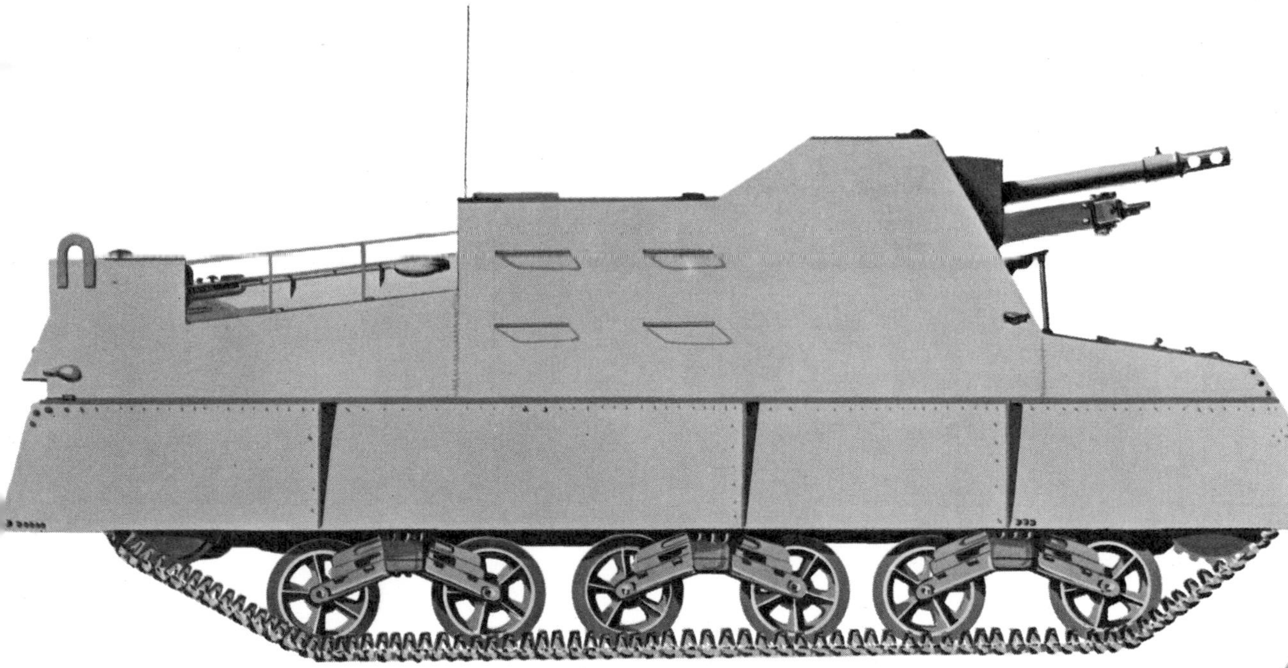

Sexton Self-Propelled Gun
The Sexton began to appear when the flood of American equipment had reached the desert theatre; it was constructed along the same lines as the Bishop, with a 25-pounder or 75-mm gun mounted in a Grant or Sherman hull. *Weight:* 25 tons. *Crew:* four. *Max armour thickness:* 65-mm

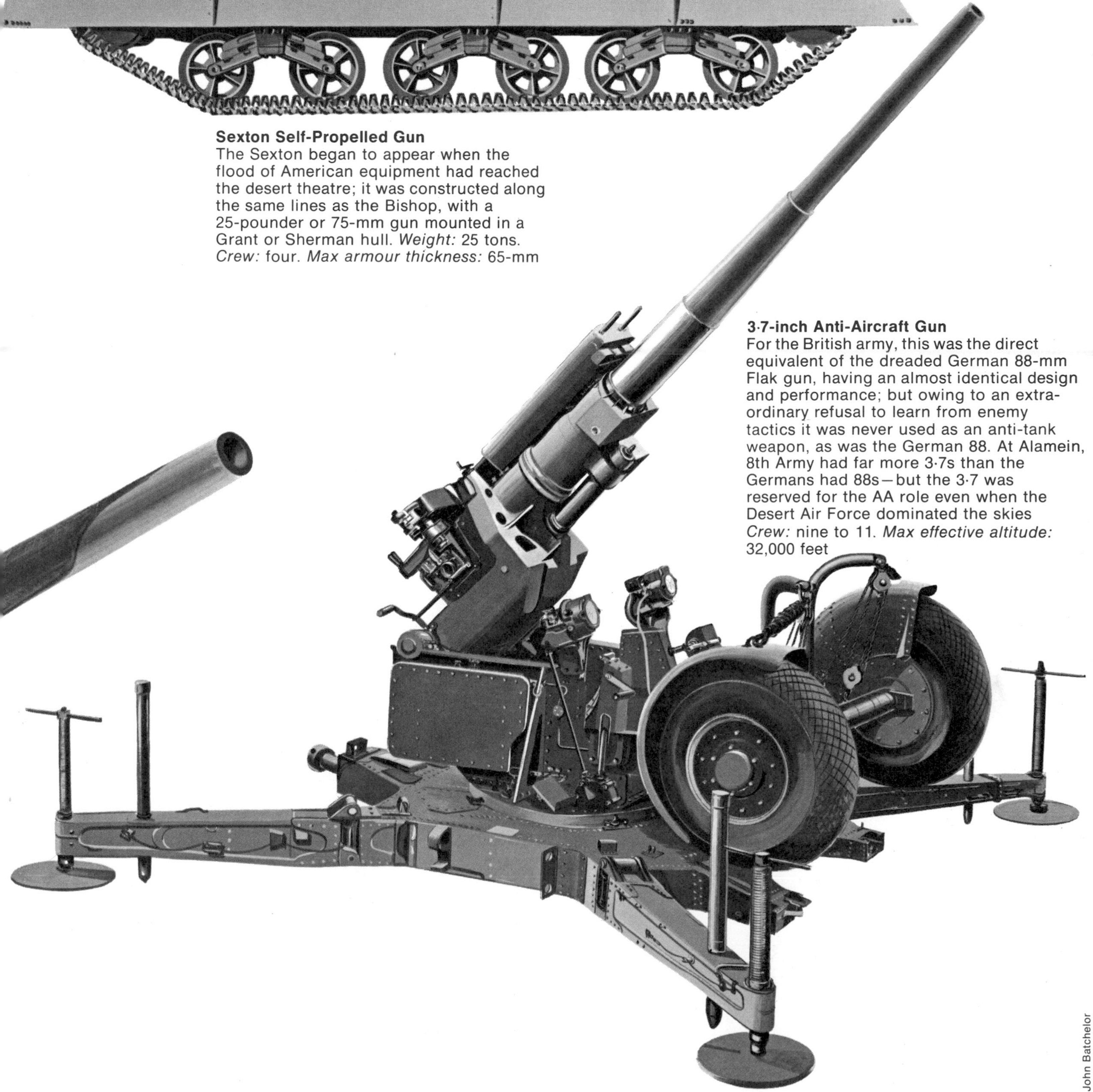

3·7-inch Anti-Aircraft Gun
For the British army, this was the direct equivalent of the dreaded German 88-mm Flak gun, having an almost identical design and performance; but owing to an extraordinary refusal to learn from enemy tactics it was never used as an anti-tank weapon, as was the German 88. At Alamein, 8th Army had far more 3·7s than the Germans had 88s—but the 3·7 was reserved for the AA role even when the Desert Air Force dominated the skies *Crew:* nine to 11. *Max effective altitude:* 32,000 feet

John Batchelor

THE PANZER

Germany, February 1943

Geoffrey Jukes

While the Russians were ruthlessly streamlining their armament industry and concentrating their production on a few battle-proven designs, the Germans continued to act as if the war was nearly over and wallowed in the luxury of research and experimentation. They thus wasted vital industrial capacity on a multitude of rival designs and failed to concentrate on any one type, even though most of their armour had been rendered virtually obsolete by the Soviet T-34. At last Hitler was forced to recall Colonel-General Guderian (below) to restore some sanity to the Panzer army — but his work was still hamstrung by professional jealousy and inter-departmental rivalry. Article begins overleaf

Ullstein

One of many obsolete designs

PANZER SPÄHWAGEN II 'LYNX': A light reconnaissance version of the Pzkw-II. Although the Pzkw-II was obsolete by the beginning of the war, this version remained in production until the early part of 1943, and was widely used on the Russian front. **Weight:** 11·8 tons. **Armour:** 30-mm maximum. **Speed:** 40 mph. **Range:** 150 miles. **Crew:** Four. **Armament:** One 20-mm gun, one 7·92-mm machine-gun

John Batchelor

PROBLEM

Germany's newest heavy tank
PZKW-VI 'TIGER I': The heavy tank design of the programme. As compared with other tanks in service during the war the Tiger was outstandingly well armed and protected. It was well designed internally, but suffered from its great width when being transported to the front by rail or road. **Weight:** 55 tons. **Armour:** 110-mm maximum. **Speed:** 25 mph. **Range:** 60 miles. **Crew:** Five. **Armament:** One 88-mm gun, two 7·92-mm machine-guns

Untried in battle, but promising
PZKW-V 'PANTHER D': The medium tank design of the new German programme. The design of the Panther D was greatly influenced by the T-34 and was partly based upon a study of the Russian tank. The Panther D suffered from considerable teething trouble, but later models proved to be more than a match for any Allied tank, including the T-34. **Weight:** 43 tons. **Armour:** 120-mm maximum. **Speed:** 30 mph. **Range:** 100 miles. **Crew:** Five. **Armament:** One 75-mm gun, two 7·92-mm machine-guns

Despite the urgent need to find a rival to the Russian designs *(right)*, production of the German Pzkw-IV, their most useful tank, was bedevilled by wasteful experimentation. As a result, in October 1942, only 100 Mark IVs were produced, against about 900 T-34s

Evolution of the Self-Propelled Gun. SPGs had first been designed to form a balanced part of an armoured division, providing anti-tank and close-support for the forward elements. But with the desperate need for large numbers of vehicles with heavier guns to combat Russian tank superiority, Hitler insisted that their production should take precedence over tanks themselves. SPGs were certainly less complicated than tanks and thus absorbed less production facilities, but they were also basically inferior weapons. Their gun traverse was limited, and each succeeding model was more cumbersome, and thus less manoeuvrable, than the last

(Below left) Panzer Jäger 1: Germany's first SPG, introduced in 1940. Built on a Pzkw-1 chassis. *Weight:* 6·4 tons. *Crew:* Three. *Speed:* 25 mph. *Range:* 90 miles. *Armament:* One 47-mm gun. **(Below) StuG-III:** A low, compact assault gun, introduced in 1940. *Weight:* 24 tons. *Crew:* Four. *Speed:* 25 mph. *Range:* 65 miles. *Armament:* One 75-mm gun, one 7·92-mm MG

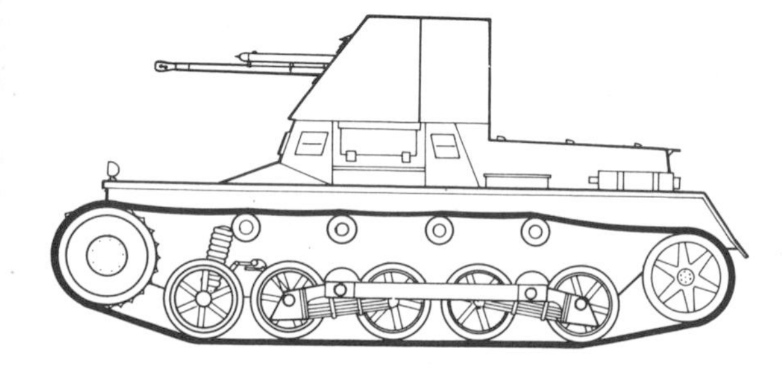

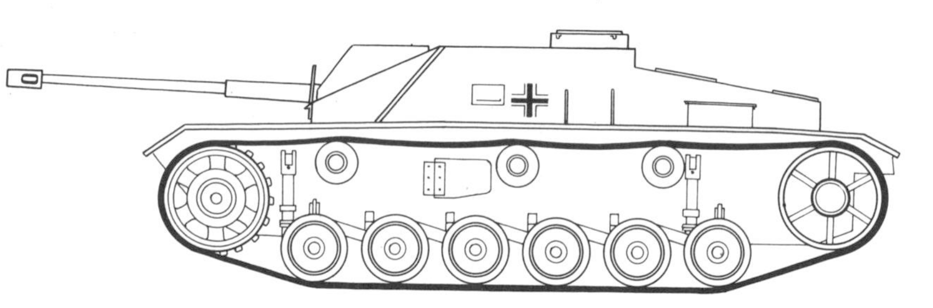

John Batchelor

Imperial War Museum

Russian T-34

Russian KV-1

Imperial War Museum

By the time of Stalingrad, the once-unquestioned superiority of the German Panzer arm had almost disappeared. The main reason for this was the Soviet T-34 medium tank. This tank, though not revolutionary in its details, except perhaps for its diesel engine, represented by far the best solution yet devised to the problem of combining mobility and fire-power with ease of maintenance in the field.

The T-34 was nearly impervious to the standard German 37- and 50-mm anti-tank guns, and of the two main German tanks (Mark III and IV), it outclassed the Mark III in all respects and the Mark IV in all except gun power, where the newer Mark IVs equalled it. It mounted a 3-inch gun with a high muzzle velocity, and was a serious headache to the Panzer commanders—as early as the autumn of 1941 the most outstanding Panzer leader, Colonel-General Guderian and many of his officers, had suggested that the best solution to Germany's problem would be to copy it with the minimum of modification. For a number of reasons, this was not done. Various alloy steels used in the T-34 were in short supply in Germany; its powerful and compact aluminium diesel engine was a novelty—and so, in those days, was the extensive use in T-34 assembly of electric welding. No doubt, racial pride also played its part: even leaving normal vanity aside, to copy the products of the 'sub-human' Slav designers of the T-34, Koshkin and Morozov, accorded ill with the doctrine of the 'Master Race' which lay at the foundations of Nazi philosophy.

Throughout 1942, the design and limited production of new types of tank had gone fitfully ahead. Hitler took such close personal interest in tank matters that he constantly interfered in matters of detail, and from time to time insisted on diversion of effort into super-heavy tanks of 100 tons and more (even authorising design of a 1,000-ton 'land-monitor'). In January 1942, under the influence of his artillery officers, he ordered the diversion of much tank-chassis production into self-propelled guns, while at the same time increasing tank production to 600 a month.

The self-propelled guns had no complicated turret mechanism, and no secondary armament, and though lack of these features put them at considerable disadvantage when fighting tanks, it was easier to produce them in quantity. Furthermore, the gunners succeeded in persuading Hitler that the hollow-charge shell, recently developed, would reduce the tank's advantage over the artillery, and this lent additional impetus to the self-propelled gun programme, to the detriment of tank production.

By mid-1942, the situation was one of baffling complexity. In the design and development field, there were three main designs—a heavy tank (Tiger), a medium (Panther), and a light reconnaissance tank (Leopard). Both Tiger and Panther existed in two competitive versions, and it had not yet been decided which versions should go into quantity production. The eccentric genius from Krupps, Dr Porsche (the man who conceived the Volkswagen) was working, at Hitler's invitation, on a design for a 100-ton tank. The Krupp version of the Tiger was about to spawn a variant —the Ferdinand—with a 100-mm fixed gun. Numbers of Czech tank chassis were being fitted as self-propelled guns with a 75-mm gun, and the standard Mark III was about to be up-gunned to the same calibre. Modifications to improve the armour of the Tiger and Panther tanks had just been issued, though the tanks were not yet in quantity production. Meanwhile, on the Soviet side, almost all tank production consisted of two types only—the T-34 medium and the KV heavy—and was running at over twice the German rate.

It could not be said that the situation in Germany improved during the rest of 1942. In August, it was decided to look into the possibility of putting into the Tiger the German gun which had proved most successful in coping with T-34's—the 88-mm, originally designed as an anti-aircraft gun but found to be remarkably versatile. In September it was decided to modify the self-propelled guns by thickening their frontal armour to 100 mm (nearly 4 inches) and putting in a long-barrelled 75-mm gun. A battalion of the Henschel version of the Tiger was tried out on the Leningrad Front, but unsuccessfully, because of unsuitable terrain. The design, however, was adjudged promising, though in need of further modification.

All this frenzied experimentation was bound to affect production unfavourably. In October, production of Germany's most useful tank, the Mark IV, reached the hundred mark for the first time; in the same month, close on nine times as many T-34s came off the assembly lines. In November, Tiger production was doubled from 13 to 25 a month, and at the beginning of December a decision was taken to stop production of the Mark III. But this did not mean an increase in the production of the more modern tank types, as Hitler ordered that all the production facilities released were to be devoted to turning out chassis for self-propelled guns.

The Army General Staff was being deluged with complaints over the spare parts problem, created by the multiplicity of types and modifications. Field commanders found it impossible to get new tanks (since these, inadequate in numbers as they were, went primarily to new formations in Germany) and were unwilling to send their damaged vehicles back to Germany for heavy repairs. They preferred to patch them up locally, on the grounds that a patched tank in hand was worth two properly repaired ones in the German bush from which they might not be returned. Inevitably this policy meant that they would have a high proportion of non-runners at any given time.

On top of the deterioration in quality of the hardware, compared with that of the Red Army, there had been a dilution of numbers. In 1940 the standard strength of a Panzer division had been 400 tanks in four battalions; by 1941 the fourth battalion had disappeared; and by the end of 1942 the third had been replaced by self-propelled guns, which were not only inferior weapons from the Panzer commander's point of view but also remained in the artillery chain of command, thus complicating problems of control.

As Soviet production mounted, as the Red

(Below) Jagdpanzer 38(t) 'Hetzer': A light tank-destroyer designed at Guderian's request. It was one of few SPG designs which relied on manoeuvrability rather than massive armour for its protection. *Weight:* 16 tons. *Speed:* 26 mph. *Range:* 135 miles. *Crew:* Four. *Armament:* One 75-mm gun, one 7·92-mm MG

(Right) Jagdpanzer Tiger (P) 'Elephant': A heavy, powerful tank-hunter which represented the other extreme of German SPG design. Built in 1943 on the chassis of the Porsche Tiger design. *Weight:* 68 tons. *Speed:* 24 mph. *Range:* 50 miles. *Crew:* Five. *Armament:* One 88-mm gun, one 7·92-mm MG

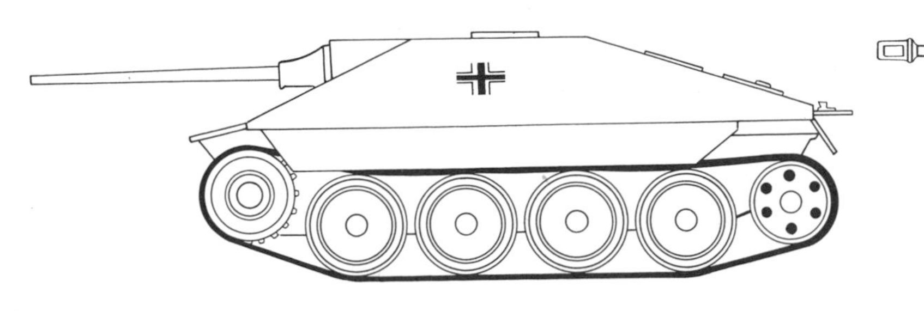

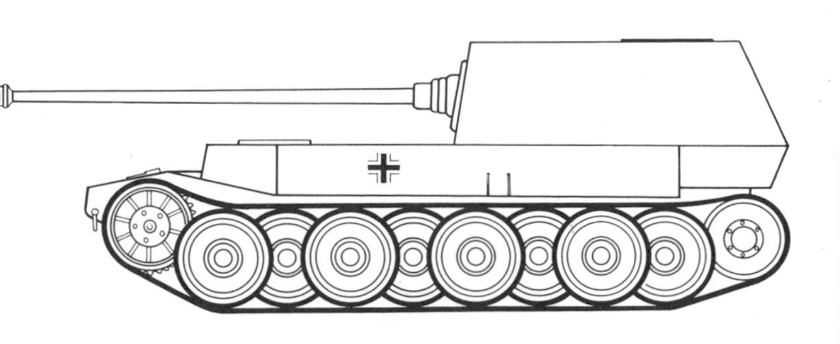

As a stop-gap, self-propelled guns were produced by mounting captured Russian 76·2-mm guns on the Czech 38(t) chassis

Army gained experience in the kind of swift-moving warfare hitherto monopolised by the Germans, and as the second-generation Panzers designed to cope with the T-34 and KV failed to materialise, discontent spread throughout the Panzer armies, and it became clear to the General Staff at OKH that something drastic had to be done. In an attempt to break the log-jam in new tank production, OKH in early February 1943 requested the abandonment of all tank production except that of Tigers and Panthers.

Coming from soldiers as professional as those at OKH, such a request could only be read as a gesture of despair, for the Panther was not yet in quantity production, and until it was, fulfilment of their demand would have temporarily reduced Germany's monthly production of tanks to the 25 Tigers authorised the previous November—at a time when T-34 production was moving steadily towards *1,000 a month*. The remedy would have been worse than the disease, as the Mark IV, at any rate, could still do useful work in skilled hands.

Guderian returns

While the state of Germany's armoured forces was going from bad to worse, their progenitor, Colonel-General Heinz Guderian, was sitting in enforced idleness in Germany—an idleness to which he had been condemned by Hitler, along with most of his colleagues of Army Group Centre, after the failure before Moscow in December 1941. With the growing discontent in the Panzer forces only to be assuaged by someone cast from the same mould, since their confidence in the High Command had reached a very low point, it was arranged that Hitler should be induced to read some of Guderian's pre-war writings, in the hope that he would draw the appropriate conclusions and put Guderian back in harness. And so it turned out.

On February 17, 1943, Guderian was summoned to meet Hitler at Supreme Headquarters Vinnitsa in the Ukraine. He made his way to Rastenburg by train, and there was met by Hitler's adjutant, Colonel Schmundt, who explained the situation to him. Guderian agreed to take on the assignment provided that he was subordinate direct to Hitler, not to OKH or the commander of the training army; that he was able to influence the development of equipment both with the Army Equipment Office and the Armaments Ministry; and that his control extended to the armoured units of the Luftwaffe and the Waffen-SS, the tank schools, and the tank units of the training army. That same afternoon (February 20, 1943), he was summoned to Hitler and offered the post of Inspector-General of Armoured Forces on the terms he had outlined to Schmundt.

A directive setting out his terms of reference was signed by the Führer on February 28, and it showed that the new Inspector-General would not lack for opponents. The armoured forces over which he was to have jurisdiction had been defined originally as including 'assault gun units'—the self-propelled gun formations within the Panzer, infantry, and Waffen-SS divisions.

This was a point of great importance, for it was relevant to questions of self-propelled gun versus tank production, to the number and role of self-propelled gun formations, and to questions of control of self-propelled gun units. Because of the fact that they remained in the artillery chain of command, there had been a tendency to send self-propelled gun units to the infantry and Waffen-SS divisions, where they retained greater freedom of action than was the case in the tightly integrated Panzer divisions. As a result the self-propelled gun elements of Panzer divisions were often seriously under strength, a factor which had contributed to the decline of confidence within the Panzer arm.

In the course of drafting the directive, some unknown hand inserted the word 'heavy' before 'assault guns', thus excluding about 90% of the self-propelled guns from Guderian's control. All his efforts to restore the situation failed, and the self-propelled guns remained a part of the artillery. Nevertheless, a great step forward had been taken in restoring the confidence of the Panzertruppen. They would henceforth have a spokesman at Supreme Headquarters who thoroughly understood their difficulties. Unity of direction would replace the chaos which had existed up to now in the tank programme. 'Mad scientists' like Dr Porsche would find it less easy to sell wild ideas for super-heavy tanks. There would be some limit put to the amount of tinkering with designs that should be frozen for mass-production. Coupled with the replacement of the incompetent Armaments Minister, Dr Todt, by the very able Albert Speer at the end of 1942, Guderian's new appointment would mark a new epoch in providing Germany's most important arm with the tools it needed.

The Kursk offensive, now being planned, would be the greatest tank battle of all time, and would make demands on the Panzers which they had not yet had to face, even in their toughest campaigns. It was high time their problems were taken in hand, because their greatest trial would soon be upon them. The assault on the Kursk salient was to open at the beginning of June if enough Panthers and Tigers could be produced in time. The Tiger had already proved itself in the recent Donets counteroffensive; the Panther was completely untried but promised well.

Guderian was opposed to *any* large offensive in 1943: his objective was to restore the Panzer divisions to their original strength of 400 tanks each, so as to be able to launch large-scale attacks with good prospects of success in 1944. But he was overruled, and that being so would do his utmost to ensure the success of the operation.

A race was now on between the planners of the German offensive and of the Soviet defence of the Kursk salient. If Guderian could not win the race for the Panzers, nobody could.

A new Panther D leaves a factory followed by a Tiger I. The development of these tanks, which were the only ones which could hold their own with the T-34, was undertaken in an extremely leisurely and haphazard manner. And due to the obsession with self-propelled guns, their production was on a very limited scale

Camouflaged German Pzkw Mk 111 tanks on the move during the second phase of Hitler's assault on Moscow. Early frosts had improved the going, but the tremendous drop in temperature which accompanied the approach to Moscow crippled all movement. Machine-guns and motor engines froze up in the paralysing cold

SP Guns of the Eastern Front: Hybrids versus Heavyweights

In their efforts to enable supporting artillery to follow their tracked, armoured vehicles across the muddy Russian steppes, both Germans and Russians turned out a wide range of self-propelled artillery pieces carried on the hulls and chassis of obsolescent or captured tanks. The two German 'hybrids' illustrated below were in fact based on the hulls of the French army light and heavy tanks (shown on page 7), using field-calibre guns as artillery pieces. The Russian 'heavyweight' SP guns *(right)* were different. They were designed primarily for the direct support of tanks, and were closer to the category of tank destroyers—such as the German Jagdpanther and Jagdtiger—although they carried high-explosive shell as well as armour-piercing shell

German *Panzerfeldhaubitze* 105 (ex-Char B)
Another former mainstay of the French tank forces, the Char B had earned respect from Panzer crewmen in the 1940 campaign, because of its good armour. Specimens of the Char B, like the Hotchkiss, were pressed into service with the Wehrmacht as SP guns. *Crew:* four. *Weight:* 31 tons. *Armour:* 60-mm (max). *Armament:* one 105-mm gun, one 7·02-mm machine-gun. *Speed:* 16 mph. *Range:* 112 miles

German *Panzerfeldhaubitze* 105 (ex-Hotchkiss)
This machine—an 'armoured field-howitzer'—was tailored to the hull of the French Hotchkiss H-35 tank, large numbers of which were captured in the French defeat of 1940. *Crew:* four. *Weight:* 12·2 tons. *Armour:* 34-mm (max). *Armament:* one 105-mm gun. *Speed:* 15·6 mph. *Range:* 75 miles

Soviet JSU-152
The Russians were among the first to evolve a medium SP gun—the JSU-152, based on the JS-1 tank, then being superseded by later marks. Produced in relatively large numbers, it gave added weight to the fire support for the Red Army's armoured spear-heads. *Crew:* five. *Weight:* 46 tons. *Armour:* 90-mm (max). *Armament:* one 152-mm gun, one 12·7-mm machine-gun. *Speed:* 23 mph. *Range:* 137 miles

Soviet SU-122
The Russians followed the practice of other armies in using the hulls of successful tank designs as carriages for SP guns. But in general the Red Army was able to use larger and heavier guns on more sophisticated hulls. The SU-122 used the T-34 tank hull. *Crew:* five. *Weight:* 30·9 tons. *Armour:* 45-mm (max). *Armament:* one 122-mm gun. *Speed:* 34·5 mph. *Range:* 375 miles

John Batchelor

Pzkw-IV: heavyweight of the German forces

KURSK: THE CLASH OF ARMOUR

In the summer of 1943, one of the greatest clashes of the war took place on the Eastern Front: the Battle of Kursk. Like the Moscow and Stalingrad battles, it was vast in scale and terrible in intensity. Armies millions strong on each side were locked in a fierce and stubborn struggle which went on for 15 days—and the tank battles which took place were the largest in the war. The German attacks, aimed at regaining the strategic initiative in Russia and turning the course of the war, were utterly shattered

Novosti Press Agency

Kursk Salient, Russia, July/August 1943

Colonel G. A. Koltunov

By the summer of 1943 there had been a radical strategic change on the Eastern Front—the decisive front of the war. After the offensive which followed the battle of Stalingrad, the Red Army had snatched the initiative from German hands, and had held it. The Soviet attacks had not only expelled the German invaders from the territory gained by them in 1942, but had liberated many of the towns and districts captured in 1941. Millions of Soviet citizens had been liberated from Nazi oppression, and the Red Army had begun the massive expulsion of the invaders from Soviet territory.

The defeats at Stalingrad and in the Soviet winter offensive at once raised for the German High Command the problem of how the war in the East was to be carried on. Germany could forego an offensive and remain on the defensive. But what would the effect of this be on Germany and her allies? To forego an offensive would finally disclose to the whole world—and above all to the people of Germany herself—the dark prospect of losing the war. Only by an offensive could the Axis coalition be preserved from disintegration, faith in victory be maintained among the German people, the enslaved peoples of Europe be kept in fear, and the illusion of the might and invincibility of the German army be kept alive before the world.

That is why the German leaders decided to carry out a large summer offensive on the Eastern Front, aimed at recapturing the strategic initiative and changing the course of the war in Germany's favour. They hoped thus to cement their bloc and revive Germany's fallen prestige. The Chief-of-Staff of OKW, Field-Marshal Keitel, expressed this view openly, when he said, at one of the conferences in the Reichschancellery: 'We must attack, on political grounds.'

Germany's military and political leaders also assumed that successes in the East would shake the foundations of the Allied coalition and cause it to disintegrate by increasing the dissatisfaction of the Soviet government and the whole of Soviet society at American and British delays in opening a second front in Europe. As the West

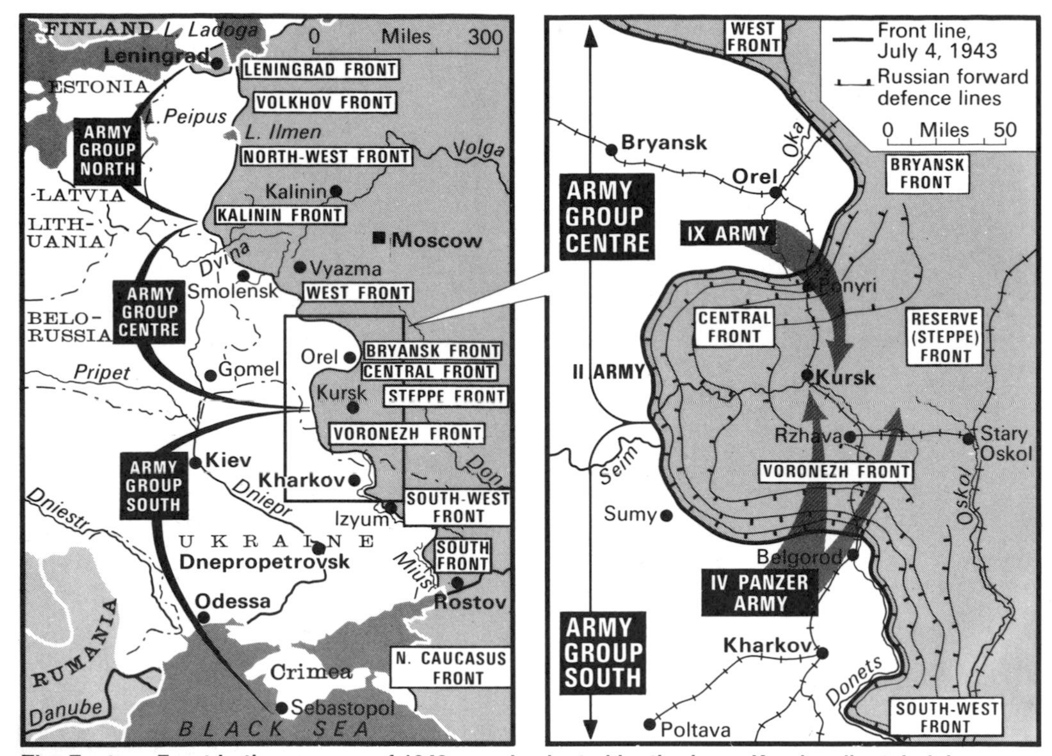

The Eastern Front in the summer of 1943 was dominated by the huge Kursk salient, bulging westwards between Orel and Kharkov. This the Germans were determined to eliminate in their third Russian offensive: huge Panzer concentrations under Model and Manstein were to pinch it out and exploit the breakthrough as far eastwards as possible. But the defences in the salient – in eight concentric belts – were the strongest yet tackled by the Wehrmacht in Russia

German historian Walter Görlitz writes, Hitler believed that 'the sooner a heavy new blow is struck at the Russians, the sooner the coalition between East and West will fall apart'.

In planning the summer offensive, the German leaders could not ignore their economic capabilities. Germany's economy, and above all its war industry, was growing unceasingly. Production of medium and heavy tanks, 5,700 in 1942, was 11,900 in 1943, and that of aircraft went up from 14,700 to 25,200. Twice as many guns and mortars were produced in 1943 as in 1942, and most of them were of new types. Ammunition production was almost three times as much in 1943 as it had been in 1940. And so the German High Command could not only replace its losses in arms and equipment, but also equip the new formations which were being established.

Great hopes were placed in the new equipment, particularly in the new tanks and assault guns whose production had greatly increased by summer 1943. The Pzkw-VI Tiger was a powerful machine, weighing 57 tons and carrying an 88-mm gun and two machine-guns. Its frontal armour was 4 inches thick, and that of the King Tiger was 6 inches. The new Pzkw-V Panther medium tank had also gone into mass production, and the new Ferdinand self-propelled gun, with frontal armour 8 inches thick, a quick-firing 88-mm gun, and one machine-gun, was also being produced.

The Germans had also paid much attention to re-equipping the Luftwaffe, which had already begun to receive new aircraft – the Focke-Wulf 190A fighter, with a maximum speed of over 375 mph, and the Henschel 129 for direct support of infantry on the battlefield. Both these aircraft were powerfully armed.

While they supplied their armed forces with new equipment, the German High Command was hastily replenishing its divisions which had been seriously thinned out in their battles with the Red Army. By July 1943 the total manpower of the German armed forces was 10,300,000, almost exactly the same as in 1942. And so though the quality of the Wehrmacht had deteriorated considerably, it remained a powerful force with first-class equipment and capable of hard fighting.

Germany's situation was eased by the fact that no second front had yet been opened in Europe, and the High Command took advantage of this to transfer more and more formations and units to the Eastern Front. About 196 of the best German divisions (two-thirds of the German army) were fighting here, together with 32 divisions and eight brigades from Germany's allies, around 56,200 guns and mortars, 5,800 tanks and assault guns, and 3,000 aircraft.

The Soviet-German front remained as it had been, the chief and decisive front of the war, as at the time only seven German divisions and two brigades – 2·7% of the German army – were in action against Anglo-American forces. The rest of that army – 91 divisions and three brigades – was on duty in occupied territory.

The Germans decided to strike on a narrow sector in the area of the Kursk arc, to cut off the so-called 'Kursk salient' which had formed during the Soviet offensive in spring 1943. This idea was favoured by the shape of the front in that area. The German forces concentrated in the Orel and Belgorod regions hung over the flanks and rear of the Soviet troops in the salient. At the same time, this salient, which jutted deep into the German defences, was important for the Soviet forces as from it they too could strike, at the flank and rear of the German forces at Orel and Belgorod (see map).

The Germans began their preparations at the end of the winter. After the plan had been considered from all angles at the highest level Hitler issued an order on April 15, 1943, for an offensive operation, code-named 'Citadel', in the area of the Kursk salient. The order stated:

This offensive is of decisive importance. It must end in swift and decisive success . . . On the axis of the main blow the better formations, the best weapons, the better commanders, and a large amount of ammunition must be used. Every commander, every private soldier, must be indoctrinated with awareness of the decisive importance of this offensive. Victory at Kursk will be a beacon for the whole world.

According to the plan of Operation 'Citadel' the main blows at the Soviet forces were to be struck from south of Orel by IX Army of Army Group Centre, and from north of Kharkov by IV Panzer Army and Operational Group 'Kempff' from Army Group South. By striking in the general direction of Kursk, the German High Command reckoned to surround and destroy the forces of Central and Voronezh Fronts, defending the salient, to straighten the front line and, in the event of success, to develop their offensive into the rear of South-West Front (Plan 'Panther'). Nor did they exclude the possibility of a subsequent strike to the north-east, to outflank Moscow and come out behind the whole of the Soviet forces in the centre of the front.

In the zone facing Voronezh and Central Fronts the Germans concentrated a large force amounting to 50 divisions, 16 of which were Panzer or motorised, and totalling about 900,000 men, with around 10,000 guns and mortars, and 2,700 tanks. An additional 20 divisions on the flank of the strike force could be redeployed to support the assault troops. Therefore the Germans could use for the assigned mission about 70 divisions, more than one-third of all the German strength on the Eastern Front, and about a quarter of these were Panzer or motorised divisions. Air support was to be provided by a force of over 2,000 aircraft. Elite Luftwaffe units were transferred to the area – JG-51, the 'Mölders' fighter wing; the 'Condor Legion'; and others.

Since such special importance was attached to the forthcoming battle, OKH reviewed and revised the Citadel plan several times, and Hitler stated more than once 'there must be no failure'. Divisions which were to take part in the offensive were rested and made up to full strength in men and material. Particular attention was given to the terrain and the Soviet defensive system in the salient, and according to the German General Mellenthin, every square yard of it was photographed from the air. As he wrote in his book *Panzer Battles, 1939-45*: 'No offensive was ever prepared as carefully as this one.'

Training was made as realistic as possible, and practice firings and tactical exercises carried out regularly. In April General Guderian, at that time Inspector-General of the Armoured Forces, inspected the Panzer troops. As General Erfurth, a former member of the staff of OKW, later wrote: 'All the offensive power which Germany could assemble was thrown into Operation Citadel.' So everything possible was done to win the Kursk battle and turn the course of the war to the advantage of the Axis coalition.

After the winter battles of 1942-43, the Red Army had also begun to prepare a great summer offensive. But it soon became known that the German High Command was also preparing for a decisive offensive on the Soviet-German front. Thanks to good Intelligence, Russia's Supreme Command was ▷

The deployment of German armour from the air. By July 5, nearly 2,700 tanks and assault-guns, spearheaded by the new Tigers and Ferdinands and stiffened by the medium Panthers, were moving up for the attack on the salient

ARBITERS OF THE ARMOURED BATTLE

The gun-crew of a German *Panzerjäger* unit, in action against Soviet armour

Jagdpanzer Tiger (P) 'Elephant'
Originally named 'Ferdinand' after its designer, Professor Porsche, this assault-gun version of the Tiger tank was a solidly armoured, hard-hitting, but sluggish beast. It was easily out-manoeuvred, and could be attacked from the flank where its armour was thinner. **Crew:** six. **Armour:** front 200-mm, sides 90-mm, rear 80-mm. **Armament:** one 88-mm Pak gun, one 7·9-mm machine-gun. **Weight:** 68 tons

SU-76 Self-Propelled Gun
Far more thinly armoured than the 'Elephant', the SU-76 (which fielded the standard 76-mm and 7·6-mm calibres of the Red Army) was therefore obliged to 'lie back' instead of taking part in the forefront of the battle. Thus its role, unlike the 'Elephant's', was one of support rather than of direct assault. **Crew:** four. **Armour:** 26/35-mm. **Armament:** one 76·2-mm gun, one 7·62-mm machine-gun. **Weight:** 11 tons.

△ A German *Panzerkeil* (tank wedge) sweeps across open country towards the Russian lines

△ A German Pzkw-III Special advances through steppe grass set on fire by Russian shells. **Right:** The attack moves on

able to find out not only the general concept and direction of the main strikes to be made by the German forces, but also how many of them there were, what resources they had, what possible reserves there were, when they were to arrive and, subsequently, when the offensive was to begin.

When they had analysed the German plans, the Soviets decided to go purposely on to the defensive in the Kursk salient, to wear out the enemy forces in defensive battles on previously prepared lines, and then to complete the destruction of the Axis shock groups by a counteroffensive in the Orel and Belgorod areas. If the counteroffensive developed successfully, it was to grow into a general Soviet offensive on a vast front, to crush the so-called 'Eastern rampart' of the Axis, and also to liquidate their Kuban bridgehead.

The actual defence of the Kursk salient was entrusted to Central Front (General K. K. Rokossovsky) and Voronezh Front (General N. F. Vatutin). Bearing in mind that the offensive which the enemy was preparing was large and had far-reaching aims, STAVKA concentrated large reserves in the area of the salient, and joined them into a Reserve Front (later renamed Steppe Front), under the command of Army General I. S. Koniev. The forces of this Front, which constituted a major STAVKA Reserve, were destined to reinforce Central and Voronezh Fronts on the sectors where a threat to them was being built up, to establish a solid defensive front east of Kursk, and later to take part in the counteroffensive, once the enemy had been exhausted and bled white. On-the-spot co-ordination of the fronts was conducted by the Deputy Supreme Commander, Marshal G. K. Zhukov, and the Chief of the General Staff, Marshal A. M. Vasilevsky.

Elaborate steps were taken to prevent an enemy breakthrough. The fronts were reinforced with large numbers of guns, tanks, and aircraft, the greatest concentration being made on the most likely axes of attack. For example, on the sector held by 13th Army, which was covering the most vulnerable axis, along the Orel-Kursk railway, almost half the artillery regiments of Supreme Command Reserve allotted to the Front were placed. The army was also given the 4th Breakthrough Artillery Corps, which had 484 guns, 216 mortars, and 432 field rocket-launchers. This made possible a hitherto unprecedented concentration of artillery in defence of about 155 guns and mortars of calibre exceeding 76 mm per mile of front—one and a half times the density established by the Germans for the coming offensive.

In the sectors held by 6th and 7th Guards Armies of Voronezh Front were 67% of the guns and mortars of the front, and about 70% of the artillery allocated from Supreme Command Reserve. The defensive system of the Soviet forces in the salient was deeply echelonned, saturated to the maximum with weapons, provided with a good system of trenches, and with many other engineer installations and obstacles.

Soviet 'hedgehog' defences

As the Germans hoped to attain their objectives by the massed use of tanks, the front commanders took special care over anti-tank defences, based on anti-tank strongpoints and areas and a system of minefields. Artillery reserves were allocated and trained in good time, as were mobile obstacle detachments. As a rule the strongpoints were allocated three to five guns each, up to five anti-tank rifles, two to five mortars, between a section and a platoon of sappers, and a section of submachine-gunners. On the most important axes, the anti-tank strongpoints had up to 12 guns each. Anti-tank and anti-personnel obstacles were widely used.

The depth of defence of Central and Voronezh Fronts on the axes of probable attack reached 95-110 miles. Adding the defence line of Steppe Front and the defence line along the Don river, it came to 160-180 miles, and comprised eight defence belts and lines. To picture the scale of the work done in the preparatory period, it is enough to mention that on Central Front's sector more than 3,100 miles of trenches and communication trenches were dug, approximately enough to reach from Moscow to Irkutsk. On the same front, the engineers laid about 400,000 mines and ground bombs, and the average density of minefields on Central and Voronezh Fronts reached 2,400 anti-tank and 2,700 anti-personnel mines per mile of front—six times that of the defence of Moscow, and four times that of Stalingrad.

Anti-aircraft defence of the forces was given great attention. Nine anti-aircraft artillery divisions, 40 regiments, 17 batteries, five troops, ten anti-aircraft armoured trains, two fighter aircraft divisions of the 'Air Defence of the Homeland' were concentrated in the salient. In addition more than a quarter of all heavy and light machine-guns and anti-tank rifles in the main defence belt, and up to half of them in the other belts, were allotted to air defence.

Responsible tasks were laid on the tactical air forces, which were to co-operate with the ground forces to repel the German attack and to seize air superiority. Even while the operation was being prepared the air armies made a series of attacks on Axis airfields, rail junctions, and concentration areas.

All personnel were trained for the forthcoming battles under an intensive programme in which priority was given to countering enemy tanks and aircraft and to skill in counterattacking enemy forces which had penetrated the defences. The Military Councils of the Fronts and Armies, commanders, political organs, party and Communist Youth organisations undertook an intensive effort to raise the political standard and morale of the troops. They organised discussions for them on various themes, including ways of countering the new German tanks.

The civilian population of those parts of the Kursk, Orel, Voronezh, and Kharkov regions adjacent to the front line gave active assistance to the Soviet forces in preparing for the coming battle. By April 1943 some 105,000 people from the Kursk area—collective farm workers, white-collar workers, housewives—were already building defence works, and by June there were 300,000 of them. Workers from the liberated areas gave invaluable aid in building a railway from Stary Oskol to Rzhava, which was most necessary for the supply of Voronezh Front's forces. In the three months of preparation the workers of the frontal areas dug thousands of miles of trenches throughout the salient, and with their help about 250 bridges and more than 1,800 miles of roads and tracks were repaired.

By the start of the defensive battle a large Soviet force was present in the salient. On a sector 345 miles long (13% of the Soviet-German Front), the Red Army had concentrated more than 20% of its manpower, nearly 20% of its artillery, about 36% of its tanks and self-propelled guns, and over 27% of its aircraft.

Unlike the Stalingrad and Moscow battles, the Soviet forces in the Kursk salient had a general superiority of 1·4 to 1 in men, almost 2 to 1 in guns and mortars, 1·3 to 1 in tanks and self-propelled guns, and almost 1·2 to 1 in aircraft. However, as the Germans were counting on a swift breakthrough, they had grouped most of their Panzer and motorised divisions in the first line, so that on the narrow breakthrough sectors in Central Front's zone they outnumbered the Soviets by more than 2 to 1 in tanks and almost 2 to 1 in men, and on that of 6th Guards Army (Voronezh Front) the German superiority was almost 2 to 1 in men and 6 to 1 in tanks. Consequently the German High Command expected to break the defences by a strong initial Panzer blow with strong air support.

The night before the offensive opened, an address by Hitler was read out to the troops. 'From tomorrow,' it said, 'you will be taking part in great offensive battles, whose outcome may decide the war. Your victory will convince the whole world more than ever that all resistance to the German army is, in the end, futile.'

But the offensive did not turn out as the Nazi war leaders would have liked. They had miscalculated, and failed to take the Soviet forces by surprise. As early as July 2, 1943, STAVKA, acting on Soviet Intelligence information, had warned the commanders of Voronezh and Central Fronts that the enemy offensive was likely to begin in the period July 3/6, and demanded increased vigilance and readiness to ward off the enemy strikes. And indeed, prisoners captured on July 4 stated that the offensive by the shock groups had been set for dawn on the 5th and that the units had already taken up their starting positions.

The Soviet command decided to undertake a powerful artillery and air counterpreparation against the Germans who were preparing to attack. Central Front's main artillery target was the enemy batteries. Voronezh Front also bombarded German batteries which were active, but in addition it directed its artillery counterpreparation against the Germans tanks and infantry.

At 0220 hours on July 5 hundreds of Soviet guns brought down a hurricane of fire upon the positions of the Germans as they prepared to attack. The calm before the July storm was ended.

The counterbombardment caused losses in men and equipment, and adversely affected German morale. It became clear to them that their plan had been uncovered, surprise had been lost, and the Russians were ready to meet them. The offensive had to be put off 1½ to 2 hours, to put the units in order. But the counterbombardment could not disrupt the offensive completely on either the north or the south face of the salient, and this is how events developed:

On the Orel-Kursk axis, the German IX Army (Colonel-General Model) began its artillery bombardment at 0430 hours—90 minutes behind schedule, and large bomber forces took off at 0510 hours. Under this artillery and air cover the tanks and infantry went into the attack on a 25-mile front at 0530 hours. The main blow was directed at the Soviet 13th Army (Lieutenant-General N. P. Pukhov) and the 48th and 70th Armies on either side of it. Three Panzer and five infantry divisions were thrown into the battle, and the main effort was concentrated

Novosti Press Agency

Soviet Pakfronts smashed the Panzer attacks on Kursk
The basis of the Soviet anti-tank defence system lay in the artillery and tank concentrations which barred the way to Kursk. All other Soviet arms were secondary, merely supplementing their fire. As a rule, the anti-tank strongpoints contained 45-mm (above) and 57-mm anti-tank guns, seconded by 76·2-mm field-guns firing armour-piercing shot

against the left flank of 13th Army, on the Olkhovatka axis, where the defence was in the hands of 15th (Colonel V. N. Dzhangava) and 81st (Major-General A. B. Barinov) Rifle Divisions.

About 500 German tanks attacked on the main axis, Tigers and Ferdinands in groups of ten to 15 in the first echelon, medium tanks in groups of 50 to 100 in the second echelon, and the infantry following behind. About 300 bombers, operating in groups of 50 to 100, were thrown against 13th Army at the same time.

The Soviet Front Command directed the bulk of 16th Air Army (Lieutenant-General S. I. Rudenko) to the support of 13th Army, and fierce battle was joined on the ground and in the air. Four times the Germans tried and failed to break through in the course of the day. The Soviet troops beat them off stubbornly, holding on as long as possible to every piece of ground and putting in counter-attacks. The Germans were able to penetrate 13th Army's main defence belt only at the price of colossal efforts and casualties. During the battles of July 5/6, they moved forward up to 6 miles, losing in the process over 25,000 killed and wounded, about 200 tanks and self-propelled guns, more than 200 aircraft, and much of their artillery and other equipment. Furthermore, many of the German regiments lost a considerable part of their officers, the 195th Regiment of 78th Infantry Division (XXIII Army Corps) losing all its company commanders in two days of fighting.

Five Germans attacks were repulsed
Since they had failed on the Olkhovatka axis, the Germans decided on July 7 to make Ponyri, a junction on the Orel-Kursk railway, their main objective, and fierce fighting broke out around it. The Soviet forces based there were able to strike at the enemy troops as they advanced, and a German infantry officer was later to describe the fighting here as one of the fiercest battles in the whole Eastern campaign. Five times during the day the Germans launched furious attacks, and five times they were hurled back by Major-General M. A. Yenshin's 307th Rifle Division, which defended Ponyri with a heroism matched by that of the tankmen, gunners, and sappers, who mined the routes along which the German tanks moved. On the morning of July 8, about 300 German tanks supported by sub-machine-gunners attacked positions held by Colonel V. N. Rukosuyev's 3rd Anti-Tank Brigade, the main weight of the onslaught falling on Captain G. I. Igishev's battery.

The Soviet gunners held their fire until the tanks were within 750-650 yards, and then destroyed 17 of them. But only one gun and three gunners were left, and the Germans pressed on again. Soon they lost two more tanks and were forced to withdraw. But the Soviet battery had been completely wiped out, the last survivors having been killed by a direct hit from a bomb. Three hours later, the Germans attacked again, and this time Senior Lieutenant V. P. Gerasimov's battery had to face the main assault.

The situation became so critical that the brigade commander radioed to the army commander: '1st and 7th Batteries have been wiped out, and I am committing my last reserve – 2nd Battery – to action. Please assist with ammunition. We shall hold out or die here.' In this action against odds almost a whole regiment of the brigade was wiped out. But the German tanks did not get through.

By July 10, the Germans had committed almost the whole of their strike force, but had failed in their mission of rupturing the Soviet front and annihilating Red Army forces north of Kursk. The German tank and infantry formations were marking time, and suffering immense casualties while they did so. On their main strike sector they had penetrated no more than 6 miles, and IX Army, having already lost about two-thirds of its tanks, was forced to take up the defensive. Meanwhile the Soviet Central Front, now that it had disrupted the German plan to break through to Kursk

Novosti Press Agency

Even the mighty Tigers could not survive the Russian Pak guns
Hundreds of Tigers met the fate so emphatically described by the picture above. The Russian tanks fielded the 76·2-mm gun which was also serving very efficiently with the Pakfront artillery forces; and the T-34s and KVs eliminated hundreds of Tigers by getting close in and attacking from the sides, where the Tigers' armour was thinner

from the north began to prepare for the counterblow.

The Germans met with no more success on the south face of the salient. Here too they launched forces into the offensive on the first day – five infantry, eight Panzer, and one motorised divisions from Field-Marshal von Manstein's Army Group South. The main assault, against the sector held by the Soviet 6th Guards Army (Lieutenant-General I. M. Chistyakov), was carried out by strike forces of IV Panzer Army, under the command of Colonel-General Hoth, and was directed towards Oboyan, while III Panzer Corps of Operational Group 'Kempff' conducted a secondary attack in the general direction of Korocha, against the 7th Guards Army of Lieutenant-General M. S. Shumilov. About 700 tanks took part in the main assault on the first day of the offensive, and the divisions on the ground were heavily supported from the air, about 2,000 sorties being observed in Voronezh Front's sector on the first day.

The 52nd and 67th Guards Rifle Divisions of 6th Guards Army had to withstand a blow of particularly great force, and their resistance, as well as that of 7th Guards Army, was so stubborn that the Germans found it necessary to commit all the reserves of IV Panzer Army and Operational Group 'Kempff' in the course of the first day.

Voronezh Front Command decided that the Oboyan axis must be securely covered, so on the night of July 5/6 formations of 1st Tank Army (Lieutenant-General M. E. Katukov) and the 2nd and 5th Guards Tank Corps (from Front Reserve) moved into the second defensive belt, and 6th Guards Army was reinforced with anti-tank artillery.

A new German attack began on the morning of July 6, and fighting became especially fierce. Lieutenant-General Popel, the 'Member of Military Council' of 1st Guards Army wrote later in his memoirs: 'I suppose that neither I nor any of our other officers had ever seen so many enemy tanks at once. Colonel-General Hoth had staked everything on a knight's move. Against every one of our companies of ten tanks were 30 or 40 German tanks. Hoth well knew that if he could break through to Kursk, no losses would be too great and no sacrifices in vain.'

By the end of the second day the enemy attack towards Oboyan had penetrated the main defensive belt in the centre of 6th Guards Army and approached the second belt, to which the Soviet divisions withdrew. Here the Germans were halted by the tank corps. Most of the tanks had been dug in, and had become hundreds of armoured pillboxes, which the infantry and artillery used as the foundation of a strong barrier of fire. The German attack towards Korocha fared no better.

The Soviet air forces gave great assistance to the defenders, striking at the German tanks and infantry, and contesting the air fiercely with the Luftwaffe. Lieutenant A. K. Gorovets set up a world record by shooting down nine German aircraft in one dog-fight, but was himself killed. It was in these battles that the Soviet fighter pilot, I. N. Kozhedub, who was to win the award of 'Hero of the Soviet Union' three times by the end of the war, opened his score.

After the failure to achieve success on the Oboyan sector, the German command decided to transfer its main efforts to Prokhorovka, so as to outflank Kursk from the south-east. Here were thrown in the best of the Waffen-SS Panzer forces, headed by the most experienced generals. The German view was that the attack on Prokhorovka should decide the battle in their favour. Altogether the Germans threw into the Prokhorovka area about 700 tanks and assault guns, about 100 of which were Tigers, and Operational Group 'Kempff' with about 300 tanks mounted a secondary attack on Prokhorovka from the south.

Voronezh Front command, in agreement with STAVKA, decided to mount a major counteroffensive against the wedged-in German force. The main role in this was entrusted to two armies which had arrived from STAVKA Reserve – 5th Guards (Lieutenant-General A. S. Zhadov) and 5th Guards Tank (Lieutenant-General P. A. Rotmistrov), supported by 2nd Air Army (Lieutenant-General S. A. Krasovsky), part of 17th Air Army (Lieutenant-General V. A. Sudets), and units of the Long Range Air Force.

The greatest tank battle in history

On July 12 the greatest tank battle in history took place in the Prokhorovka area. Here in the early July morning, on a relatively small area, in black clouds of dust and smoke, two mighty avalanches of tanks totalling some 1,500 machines moved to meet each other. General Rotmistrov, now Chief Marshal of Armoured Forces, in recalling this unprecedented battle, remarks that the first echelon of his 5th Guards Tank Army cut into the German line at full speed, and the diagonal attack was conducted so fast that the leading lines of tanks went through the entire German formation.

The lines became mixed up, with the Soviet tank gunners firing at the Tigers at point blank range, and an immense knotted mass of tanks formed. Over the battlefield swept the roar of motors, the clang of metal, and the flames from hundreds of burning tanks and self-propelled guns. The fierce fighting went on until late in the evening, and the Soviet tank men displayed great courage and skill. Here, too, the Germans failed to break through to Kursk.

In this one day the Germans lost here more than 350 tanks and over 10,000 officers and men, in making an advance of 20-25 miles. This day, July 12, was a turning point in the battle, for Bryansk and West Fronts now opened their offensive against the German forces in the Orel area. It was a day of crisis for the German offensive, for on it they were compelled to go on to the defensive on the southern face of the Kursk salient, and then to begin withdrawing to their start lines. On the 16th, the main German forces began retreating behind strong rearguards, and Voronezh Front launched its pursuit, followed on July 19 by Steppe Front; and by the 23rd the Germans had to all intents and purposes regained the lines which they had held on July 4. The third great German offensive in Russia had failed.

In sum, the offensive battle had resulted in brilliant fulfilment of the tasks set them by the Soviet troops. The Germans had been exhausted and bled white, and the strategic balance had changed even further in favour of the Red Army. The long and carefully prepared Citadel operation, by which the Germans had hoped to get back the strategic initiative, had suffered a total failure.

The question of timing the Soviet counter-offensive had already arisen during the defensive battle. The basis of the Soviet plan for the Orel operation was the idea of dissecting the enemy defence by a number of converging blows, and then destroying the isolated enemy forces unit by unit. Four strong blows were envisaged:

- by West Front (Colonel-General V. D. Sokolovsky) southwards to Bolkhov and Khotinets, so as to cut off the enemy in the Orel salient;
- by Central Front, in the direction of Kromy to meet Western Front;
- by Bryansk Front (Colonel-General M. M. Popov), two deep dissecting blows from the Novosil area, to outflank Orel from north and south.

German forces in the Orel bridgehead comprised 27 infantry, eight Panzer, and two motorised divisions of II and IX Armies of Army Group Centre, totalling some 600,000 officers and men, 6,000 guns and mortars, and about 1,000 tanks and self-propelled guns. Over 1,000 German combat aircraft were available for their support. The area was well fortified, and only on the narrow sector where they had penetrated into the Soviet defences did the first-line forces lack positions prepared in advance. On the sector facing the left wing of West Front and the right and centre of Bryansk Front, as far as the Novosil area, construction of defence lines had begun over a year before in March 1942, and further south, in front of the left wing of Bryansk Front and facing Central Front, construction had begun at the end of March 1943.

Russian guns: 420 to the mile

In view of the importance which they attached to Orel, the Germans had set up a firm defence with a well-developed system of field fortifications protected by obstacles. In the depth of the defence were intermediate and rear belts, and cut-off positions, mostly along the rivers. Most of the villages had been prepared for an all-round defence. The defence lines, prepared in advance, and the large number of rivers in the depth of the defence, were a serious obstacle to the Soviet offensive, and it was the first time that Soviet troops had met with such a powerful defensive system. To break it required great skill, high morale, and offensive élan. The Soviet Command therefore decided to attack in depth, and provided its strike forces with large amounts of artillery. It is worth mentioning here that for the first time in the war a density of artillery of 420 guns and mortars to the mile was achieved, on the sector of West Front's 11th Guards Army (Lieutenant-General I. Kh. Bagramyan).

Preparation for the counterblow required special attention to be given to ammunition and fuel supply, and to training the troops in breaking through permanent defences. Commanders and political workers took care that every soldier knew his sub-unit's mission. Brief meetings and Party and Youth League assemblies took place in the companies and batteries in the front line. Many soldiers wished to go into battle as Communist Party members. Hundreds and thousands of them wrote in the hours before battle: 'I shall justify the party's trust in battle', or 'If I die, count me a Communist.'

By the beginning of the Orel operation, the Soviet superiority over the Germans was 2 to 1 in men, 3 to 1 in guns, 2·3 to 1 in tanks, and 2·7 to 1 in aircraft. By means of bold manoeuvre the superiority was even greater on the breakthrough sectors.

On July 12, after an intensive artillery and air bombardment, the left wing of West and the whole of Bryansk Fronts moved forward, while the German forces in the Belgorod-Kharkov area were still trying to break through the southern face of the salient, and IX Army was preparing to renew the offensive against Kursk from the north.

By the evening of the 13th, 11th Guards Army had broken through after intense fighting, on a front of 15 miles, and the assault force of Bryansk Front's 61st Army (Lieutenant-General P. A. Belov) on a front of 5 miles. The 3rd Army (Lieutenant-General A. V. Gorbatov) and 63rd Army (Lieutenant-General V. Y. Kolpakchi) had penetrated 9-10 miles. But the Soviet forces still faced an organised defence, and had to fight hard to destroy the large numbers of strongpoints in the depth of the defensive system.

The offensive mounted by 2nd Tank Army

Südd Verlag

During the dying offensive of IV Panzer Army: flame-throwers advance, backed by a camouflaged assault-gun and riflemen

was already on the first day causing hasty German redeployment of reserves to threatened sectors, and it was decided to unify the commands of II Panzer and IX Armies in the Orel salient under Colonel-General Model, who enjoyed the Führer's special confidence, and was known in the German army as 'The Lion of Defence'. On taking over command, he issued an order to II Panzer Army on July 14, in which he wrote: 'The Red Army has begun an offensive along the entire Orel salient. We face battles which could decide everything. In this hour, which demands great effort by all forces, I have taken under command your army, experienced in battle.' He issued a number of threatening orders, demanding that his troops stop the Soviet formations and stand to the last man, whatever happened.

But the Red Army's victorious offensive was no longer to be stopped by German orders, nor could the Third Reich any longer preserve its soldiers' faith in victory by the mere issuing of orders. They were haunted by the ghosts of their compatriots who had fallen at Moscow, Stalingrad, Ponyri, and Prokhorovka, and despite considerable reinforcement of the Orel salient at the expense of other sectors of the front, the Soviet counterblow continued to develop successfully.

By July 19, 11th Guards Army, which completely held the initiative, had broken through on its whole front to a depth of 45 miles, and its main forces were driving south towards Khotinets, while Bryansk Front had overcome the German resistance, broken through several intermediate defence lines, and by July 17 made a gap 22 miles wide and 15 miles deep. The Luftwaffe intensified its efforts to stop the Red Army, but the Soviet pilots replied in kind.

The French 'Normandie Niemen' squadron fought side by side with the Soviet airmen, and its volunteer pilots displayed courage, great skill, and determination in the struggle with the Luftwaffe.

By drawing much of the German Orel

With Citadel bogged down north and south of Kursk, Manstein is faced with an immediate Russian counteroffensive

force away from the Kursk direction, the offensive by West and Bryansk Fronts created favourable conditions for Central Front. It finished regrouping late on July 14, attacked on the 15th, and by the 18th its right wing had completely liquidated the German wedge into the Soviet defences on the Kursk axis, regained its former line, and begun to develop its attack towards Kromy.

The fighting grew fiercer and fiercer, and STAVKA decided to attain a further superiority of force over the Germans, so West Front was ordered to commit the 4th Tank Army (Lieutenant-General V. M. Badanov), the 11th Army (Lieutenant-General I. I. Fedyuninsky), and the 2nd Guards Cavalry Corps from reserve to the battle, while Bryansk Front was to commit the 3rd Guards Tank Army (Lieutenant-General P. S. Rybalko).

These reserves were deep in the rear, and to get them into battle proved very difficult, as torrential rains had begun and washed out the roads. The 61st Army of Bryansk Front, in co-operation with 11th Guards and 4th Tank Armies of West Front, liberated Bolkhov on July 29 and developed its advance towards Orel from the north, threatening the enemy's communications from Orel to Bryansk. At the same time Bryansk Front forces deeply outflanked the enemy force in the Mtsensk area and forced it to withdraw. Bryansk Front was simultaneously continuing to advance on Orel from the east. The German position was deteriorating further and further, and Colonel-General Model asked Hitler for permission to withdraw from the Orel bridgehead, warning the Führer uneasily of the danger of 'another Stalingrad'.

Because the general situation on the Eastern Front was serious, and that of the Orel force critical, the German High Command had already on July 26 resigned itself to abandoning the entire Orel area and withdrawing to the 'Hagen Line' (a defence line running east of Bryansk) by a planned retreat through several intermediate ▷

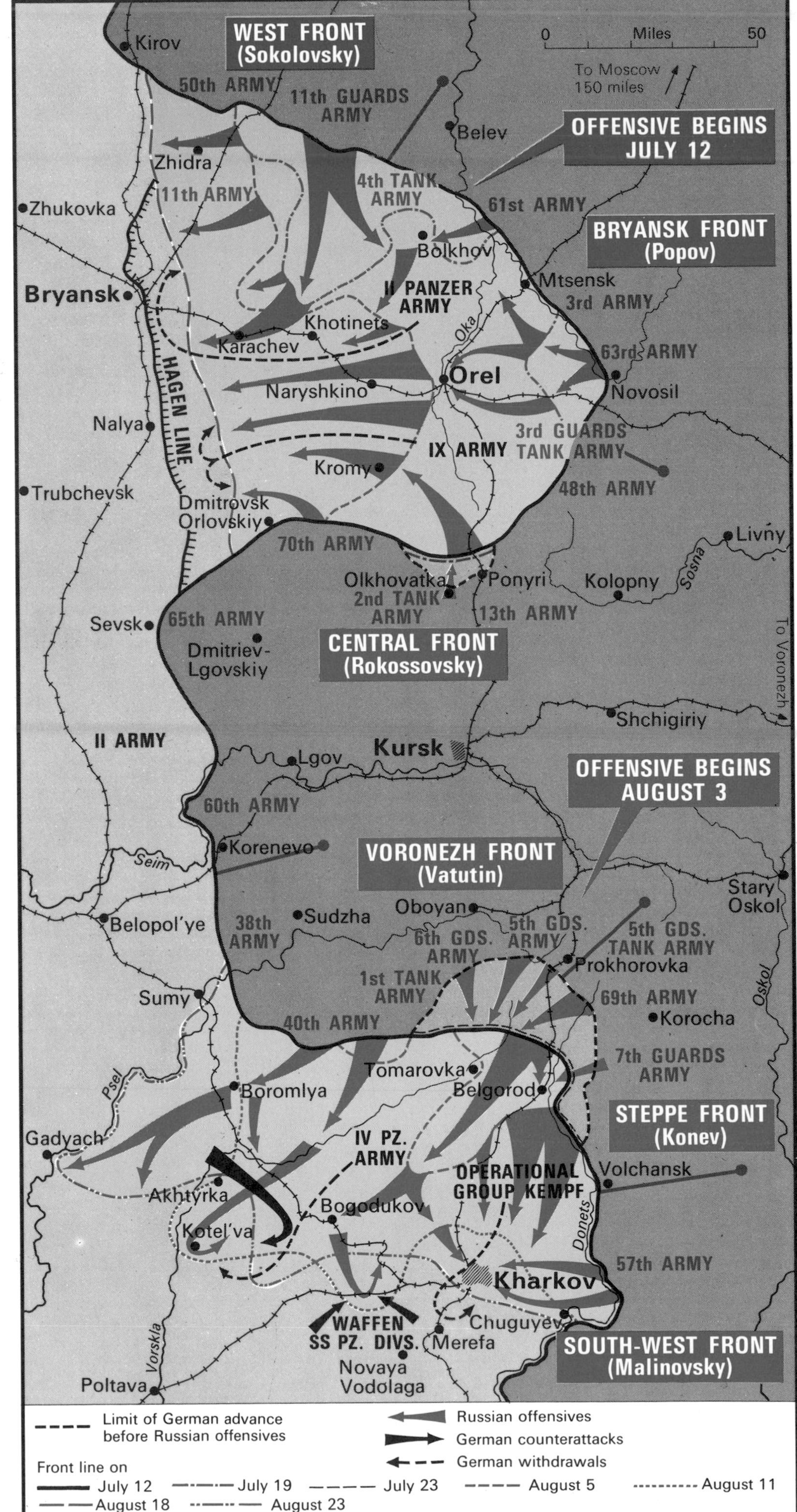

'Citadel' collapses – and the Russians recover Kharkov

SOVIET ARMOUR: MORE THAN A MATCH FOR THE PANZERS

The Germans had tended to underestimate Soviet tank design and production, and they received a rude awakening when the Wehrmacht encountered the new T-34s and KVs, whose existence had not even been suspected. Overnight, the German armour designs were rendered obsolete; not only were the new Soviet tanks formidable fighting vehicles, but the simplicity of their design meant that they could be turned out in large numbers, and operated by relatively inexperienced crews. So long as they were few in number, and used in small formations to support the infantry, the superior German tactics enabled the Wehrmacht to hold its own—but the Russians were rapidly adding to their tank strength—and to their experience

T-34
Probably the outstanding tank of the war, its combination of well-sloped armour, a heavy armament, high speed, and a superb cross-country performance (due to its wide tracks and high power-to-weight ratio) meant that the German Pzkw Mks III and IV found themselves completely outclassed. **Weight:** 26·3 tons. **Range on roads:** 250 miles. **Armour:** 45-mm front, sides, and rear; 75-mm turret front and rear. **Crew:** four. **Armament:** one 76·2-mm; two 7·62 machine-guns

KV-2
An assault-gun version of the KV-1, it proved to be unsuccessful because of the excessive overall height and the general clumsiness of the arrangement. **Weight:** 52 tons. **Range on roads:** 150 miles. **Armour:** 110-mm (max). **Crew:** six. **Armament:** one 152-mm; three 7·62-mm machine-guns

John Batchelor

KV-1
First of the Red Army's new heavy tanks, it was an extremely well-armoured vehicle. A peculiar feature was the rear-firing machine-gun mounted in the turret. **Weight:** 43·5 tons. **Range on roads:** 210 miles. **Armour:** 75-mm front, sides, and rear; 90-mm turret front and rear. **Crew:** five. **Armament:** one 76·2-mm; three 7·62-mm machine-guns

Sado-Opera Mundi

▷ North-east of Belgorod, Panzer Mk IVs advance to the attack through standing grain. The outer sheets of armour were intended to explode anti-tank shells before they could penetrate the tank's vitals

A German 105-mm howitzer hammers back at the Soviet forces during the battle for the Orel salient

Ullstein

The Russians, too, had heavy tank losses: here a T-34 blazes

Sado-Opera Mundi

SS Grenadiers take shelter from a Russian bombardment

lines between July 31 and August 17. An area about 60 miles deep was to be cleared, to release more than 20 divisions by straightening the line, and to decimate the attacking Soviet forces by defensive battles on the new line.

'A question of getting out fast'

In an effort to secure an orderly withdrawal from the tip of the Orel salient, every effort was made to hold its flanks, but the plans were frustrated by Soviet ground and air attacks. Field-Marshal von Kluge, commanding Army Group Centre, wrote in his estimate of the state of his forces in the area: 'The staff of the army group is fully aware that its previous intention to strike the enemy as much as possible during the withdrawal is now impossible to fulfil, because of the over-exhaustion and reduced fighting capacity of the troops. It is now a question of getting out of the Orel salient as fast as possible.' On the night of August 3/4, advance units of the Soviet 3rd and 63rd Armies burst through to Orel, and by dawn on the 5th the town had been completely cleared of Germans.

The 5th, 129th, and 380th Rifle Divisions, the 17th Guards Tank Brigade, and a number of air force units especially distinguished themselves in the fighting for Orel, and were given the town's name as a battle honour. In Moscow on the evening of August 5, an artillery salute boomed out for the first time in honour of the forces which had liberated Orel and Belgorod, and it became customary from that date to mark Red Army victories by salutes in Moscow.

By August 5, Central Front's forces had reached the approaches to the important road junction and German supply base of Kromy, and by the 18th Bryansk Front and the right wing of Central Front had come up to the previously prepared defence line on which the Germans had dug themselves in. The Orel salient had been liquidated, and the German force there, which had been oriented to an offensive against Kursk, had received a shattering defeat.

Soviet partisan activity contributed to the success of the Orel operation. Between June 21 and August 3 alone, the partisans of Orel region blew up more than 10,000 rails, and as a result the rail junctions and stations filled up with German trains, which were then systematically bombed by the Soviet air force.

The Soviet counterblow lasted 37 days, during which time the Red Army advanced westwards about 95 miles, disrupting the German plan to attack Kursk from the north, throwing a strong German force back to Bryansk, destroying about 15 German divisions, and creating good conditions for further westward development of the offensive.

The forces of Voronezh and Steppe Fronts had had to begin the counterblow in difficult conditions. During the defensive battles and then in pursuit of the enemy they had lost heavily in men and equipment. And now they had to face a fight against an enemy in prepared defensive positions in the Belgorod and Kharkov areas.

The Germans were misled by the relative quiet which prevailed on the south face of the Kursk salient from July 24 to August 2. Since they remained in ignorance of the Soviet plans, and since their estimates of Soviet strength and deployment on the south face of the salient were wrong, they were not expecting a large Red Army offensive on that sector so soon. In addition they were short of forces in the Orel salient. Furthermore, South-West Front had begun an offensive out of the Izyum area on July 17 towards Barvenkovo, and South Front had launched one on the Mius river.

In the course of these operations South-West Front had crossed the northern Donets on several sectors, and was threatening to strike down behind all the German forces in the Donbass, while South Front had broken the strongly defended Mius river line and seized a bridgehead on its western bank. The German High Command therefore began transferring forces from the relatively quiet Belgorod-Kharkov area to improve its position in the Orel and Donbass regions, and thus the Soviet High Command's work in organising precise strategic co-operation on the whole front made the conditions favourable for a counterblow by Voronezh and Steppe Fronts aimed at Belgorod and Kharkov.

By now the main forces of the two fronts were concentrated north of Belgorod, well placed for a frontal assault at the junction between IV Panzer Army and Operational Group 'Kempff', against the enemy formations which had been most worn down and demoralised in the unsuccessful offensive against Kursk. Bearing all this in mind, and aiming to reduce the preparation time for the operation as much as possible, it was decided not to attempt any complicated regrouping but to strike hard with forces of both fronts in a south-westerly direction towards Bogodukhov, Balka, and Novaya Vodolaga, so as to cut off IV Panzer Army from Operational Group 'Kempff' and then destroy them.

In this phase Voronezh Front would operate against IV Panzer Army, attacking westwards towards Akhtyrka, while Steppe Front would turn south to Kharkov, simultaneously rolling up the German defence on the right bank of the northern Donets. While Steppe Front was approaching Kharkov the 57th Army of Army General Malinovsky's South-West Front was to strike westwards, so as to outflank Kharkov from the south. The operation was prepared extremely quickly, by great efforts on the part of the command, staffs, and political organs.

German forces in the area under attack comprised 18 divisions, four of them Panzers, totalling about 300,000 men, with over 3,500 guns and mortars and about 600 tanks, supported from the air by the 900 aircraft of Luftflotte IV. They were based on prepared positions with well-developed artificial defences. The tactical defence zone consisted of two belts totalling some 10-13 miles in depth. The main belt included two positions, each provided with strongpoints and focal points of resistance, joined by deep trenches, themselves linked by communication trenches. All villages had been made ready for a prolonged all-round defence, and the cities of Kharkov and Belgorod had been ringed with large numbers of weapons, well protected in wood and concrete emplacements.

By the start of the operation, the Soviet forces had a superiority of more than 3 to 1 in manpower, 4 to 1 in tanks and artillery, and 1·5 to 1 in aircraft. By skilful massing of men and weapons this superiority was even higher on the breakthrough sectors.

Voronezh Front's main striking force was to be made up of formations from 5th and 6th, 1st Tank, and 5th Guards Tank Armies. A high-density deployment of artillery and tanks was arranged, so that the breakthrough of the deeply-echelonned German defence would be rapid, and on the sector of 5th Guards Army, for example, there were about 370 guns and mortars, and up to 112 tanks, per mile of front. A special feature of the operation was Voronezh Front's plan to introduce the two tank armies into the gap made by the two infantry armies, to ensure a rapid and deep penetration.

The counterblow began on the morning of August 3, after a three-hour air and artillery bombardment. At 1300 hours, as soon as the infantry of 5th Guards Army had penetrated the enemy's main defence belt, the tank armies were sent into action. Their leading brigades completed the breaching of the German tactical defence zone and began to develop their success in the operational depth. Hard fighting went on in the whole breakthrough area throughout August 4, with the Soviet shock groups continuing to advance southwards, by-passing centres of resistance. They advanced up to 12 miles, and on August 5, Colonel M. P. Seryugin's 270th Regiment of the 89th Guards Rifle Division led them into Belgorod.

This powerful and unexpected Soviet blow worsened the situation of the Germans in the south. The Panzer divisions so recently moved away to Izyum, Barvenkovo, and the Mius river came hastily back, taking heavy punishment as they came from a series of Soviet air attacks.

The activities of Ukrainian partisans against railways behind the German lines were of great assistance to the Soviet forces, derailing more than 1,000 trainloads of German troops and equipment during the months of July and August.

A letter from the front

The breach made in their defences, and their losses during the first days of battle had a disintegrative effect on the German troops. In a letter to his brother a German NCO, Otto Richter, wrote:

Dear Kürtchen: You know me, I have never been one for losing my head or panicking. I have always believed firmly in our aims and in victory. But now I want to say goodbye to you. Don't be surprised, I really mean goodbye, and for ever. We attacked not long ago. If you only knew how disgusting and horrible it was. Our soldiers went forward bravely, but the Russian devils wouldn't go back for anything, and every metre cost us the lives of our comrades . . . And then those Russian devils came rushing down on us, we started to back off, a real ding-dong began. We abandoned Belgorod yesterday. There aren't many of us left . . . only 18 in our company. But that's not so bad, there are only nine in the 2nd . . . God, how will it all end . . . I know they'll kill me, goodbye, but I don't care, what's the point of living if the war's lost and the future black?

Richter was killed before he could post the letter.

Meanwhile the troops of Voronezh and Steppe Fronts were still pursuing the enemy. Elements of 1st Tank and 6th Guards Armies, after advancing over 60 miles in five days of continuous battle, seized one of the most important centres of enemy resistance, the town of Bogodukhov, on August 8, thus cutting the German Belgorod-Kharkov forces in two.

By the evening of August 11 Voronezh Front's troops had broadened their breakthrough considerably towards the west and south-west, and their right-wing forces had reached the enemy strongpoints of Boromlya, Akhtyrka, and Kotelva, while the left wing had cut the Kharkov-Poltava railway south of Bogodukhov and by-passed Kharkov from the west, thus creating a serious threat to the German forces still stubbornly defending the Kharkov area. Steppe Front's offensive also prospered between August 8/11, and they reached the outer defence perimeter of Kharkov.

The Soviet 57th Army (Lieutenant-General N. A. Gagen), which had crossed the northern Donets and taken the important enemy centre of Chuguyev, approached Kharkov from the east and south-east.

The Germans were now making desperate efforts to stop further Soviet progress and retain Kharkov, whose loss would open the door to a Red Army offensive into the Ukraine. The Soviet forces advancing south of Bogodukhov were especially dangerous, as they threatened to encircle the Germans at Kharkov from west and south. The German High Command therefore decided to use the main forces transferred from the Donbass against them, and on August 11 they assembled in the area three Panzer divisions of the Waffen-SS which had been made up to strength after heavy fighting – 'Das Reich', 'Totenkopf', and 'Viking', and hurled them against 1st Tank Army and part of the left flank of 6th Guards Army.

Fierce fighting went on south of Bogodukhov from August 11/17. The Germans had managed to achieve superiority in tanks by introducing the Waffen-SS divisions, and were able to squeeze the Soviet forces away 12 miles to the north. However, the Soviet Command moved formations of 5th Guards Tank Army in to assist, so the Germans failed in their plan to break through to the rear of Voronezh Front's strike force. By August 17, their losses forced them on to the defensive.

Following this failure, the German High Command began in mid-August to plan an offensive against Bogodukhov from the western (Akhtyrka) side. Their plan was to cut off the salient in the front south of Akhtryka, break through to Bogodukhov, and destroy the bulk of Voronezh Front's strike force. But the Soviet High Command foresaw this counterstrike and moved fresh forces into the Akhtyrka area to repel it. In three days of intense fighting, August 18/20, Voronezh Front shattered this enemy attempt too, first stopping the Germans and then throwing them back to their start line.

Steppe Front broke through the outer defensive perimeter of Kharkov on August 13, but the Germans continued to fight back doggedly from a broad system of defensive positions. They knew that if Kharkov fell, all their forces in the Donbass would be in danger, and had decided to stabilise the front and hang on to the Kharkov industrial region at whatever the cost. Manstein had received orders to this effect.

Between August 18/22 fighting was especially fierce on the flanks of Steppe Front, and the outcome was that by the evening of the 22nd the 5th Guards and 53rd Armies had by-passed Kharkov from west and south-west, while 7th Guards and 57th Armies had done so from east and south-east, thus threatening all the German forces there with complete encirclement. Only the road and railway from Kharkov to Merefa and Krasnograd remained open to them, and this narrow corridor was under constant air attack. The commander of Steppe Front, Marshal Koniev, wrote: 'The question was which solution to adopt. We could, of course, throw in all the forces needed to cut the corridor, surround the enemy in the city, and finish him off there . . . But destroying such a large force in a fortified town would take much time and mean many casualties. There could be another solution – to storm the city, drive the enemy out of it, and polish off what was left of him outside.'

On the afternoon of August 22, the Germans began to pull out. To prevent an orderly withdrawal, save looted property, and avert the destruction of the city, the commander of Steppe Front on the evening of the 22nd ordered a night assault. The task of capturing the city itself was entrusted to 69th Army (General V. D. Kryuchenkin) and 7th Guards Army. Fierce street fighting went on throughout the night of August 22/23. The Germans had turned stone buildings into blockhouses, with medium artillery in the lower storeys and sub-machine-gunners and machine-gunners in the upper ones. All approaches to the city, roads entering it, and streets on its outskirts were thickly mined and barricaded.

But the Soviet troops by-passed the enemy fortified positions skilfully, filtered through his defences, and attacked his garrisons boldly from behind. By midday on the 23rd, after stubborn fighting, the city which the Germans had tormented was completely free of them. Most of the German forces were destroyed in the fighting and the remnants of them fled behind the Merefa and Mzha rivers, with the Red Army in hot pursuit, and leaving behind masses of abandoned equipment. The Soviet forces had destroyed

The generals who fought at Kursk

Rokossovsky

Vatutin

Koniev

Model

Manstein

Weichs

about 15 enemy divisions, and now they hung over the whole south wing of the German front, in an excellent position for a general offensive to liberate 'west bank' Ukraine and reach the Dniepr.

'Germany's last battle for victory'

The Battle of Kursk ended in a brilliant victory for the Red Army over a still strong and cunning enemy. It was one of the most important and decisive events of the whole war. It began during a changing balance of forces, when the Red Army was getting stronger and its command cadres growing in skill as organisers, and in the course of it the Red Army repulsed the last German attempt at a large summer offensive aimed at changing the course of the war in Germany's favour, preserving the Axis bloc from disintegration, and thus reducing the political consequences of its defeat at Stalingrad.

'Germany's last battle for victory', as the Germans themselves called it, was lost by them, and the dread spectre of catastrophe rose in its full height before the Nazi Reich and its Wehrmacht. The Chief-of-Staff of OKW, Keitel, later testified that after the defeat of the German forces in the summer of 1943 it became clear to the German High Command that the war could not be won by military means.

The prestige of German arms was irreparably damaged. Of the 70 German divisions operating in the area of the Kursk salient, 30 were destroyed, seven of them Panzer divisions. In 50 days' fighting the Germans, on their own figures, lost over 500,000 men killed, seriously wounded, or missing. The Red Army grasped the strategic initiative firmly, and retained it for the rest of the war. In essence, Kursk completed the radical turn-about in the war which had begun at Stalingrad.

The failure of the German offensive at Kursk buried once and for all the Nazi propaganda myth about the 'seasonal' nature of Soviet strategy, which alleged that the Red Army could attack only in winter. Reality showed that it could beat the Germans winter and summer. The German High Command had once again underestimated Red Army strength and overestimated its own strength and capabilities. Churchill wrote of the summer battles: 'The three immense battles of Kursk, Orel, and Kharkov, all in the space of two months, heralded the downfall of the German army on the Eastern Front.'

The failure of their offensive strategy in the East caused the Nazi ruling clique to look around for new ways of waging the war. They decided to assume the defensive on the whole Soviet-German front, to impose static warfare on the Red Army, and hence to gain time for an attempt at persuading the USA and Britain to settle for a 'draw', keeping Nazi Germany as a barrier against the 'Red Peril' in Europe. However, the incessant and constantly increasing hammer-blows of the Red Army put an end to this gamble. The Soviet government fought persistently to put into effect the decisions agreed by all the countries of the Allied coalition.

The brilliantly conducted third Soviet counterblow (after Moscow and Stalingrad) forced the Germans to throw all their main forces into the Soviet-German Front. Large fighter and bomber formations, and a number of units and groups from the other services, had to be transferred from the Mediterranean theatre. This made it considerably less difficult for the Allies to land in Italy, and made that country's defeat inevitable.

Germany's relations with the other countries of the Axis became considerably more difficult. When they saw the defeat at Kursk, the rulers of Finland, Hungary, and Rumania intensified the efforts which they had been making since Stalingrad to find a way out of their unpromising situation. The Red Army's victory gave increased impetus also to the struggle of the peoples suffering under the yoke of the Nazi 'New Order' in Europe.

In the countries of the anti-Axis coalition, the Kursk victory had a great influence on the people, enhancing their feelings of solidarity with the Soviet Union. After Orel's liberation, a friendly correspondence grew up between its citizens and those of the English borough of Hampstead, and a message of greeting sent by the 'Aid to Russia Committee' of a block of flats there said:

Citizens of Orel, we greet you. In the grim war both our great peoples are fighting, our friendship is cemented for ever by the blood of our sons, who are bringing death to Nazism. At last we see hopes of victory before us. We have shared the burdens of war—we shall share, too, the beautiful gifts of peace, proud of the fact that we both belong to the Invincible Army of Freedom.

And President Roosevelt, in a speech to the American people on July 28, said: 'The short-lived German offensive, which began in the first days of this month, was a desperate attempt to raise the morale of the German people. But the Russians did not allow themselves to be taken by surprise . . . The world has never yet seen greater devotion, determination or self-sacrifice than that shown by the Russian people and the Russian armies. . . .'

In Western historical writing, particularly in books by former Wehrmacht generals, the events at Kursk are wrongly described in many respects. Some of these authors deliberately keep quiet about the downfall of Citadel. Others write about it, but ascribe the defeat to mistakes by Hitler. By ignoring historical facts, they distort them. *The main point is not that Hitler made mistaken decisions which ruined the Wehrmacht's Russian campaigns. The mistake was in the idea of making war on the Soviet Union in the first place.*

The main cause of the failure of the Wehrmacht's offensive strategy was the steady rise during the war of the power of the Soviet state and its armed forces, and the Kursk battle was a new triumph for Soviet military skill. When they had uncovered the enemy's intentions the Soviet command decided to wear out the enemy strike forces by means of a carefully prepared defence, and only then to begin a counterblow. In the course of the battle it was shown that the Red Army had been more powerfully equipped, and that its officers had become more skilful in making use of all services and arms of service both in defence and in attack. In the air battles which took place here the Soviet air forces won superiority once and for all. The defeat of the Germans at Kursk began a great summer-autumn offensive by the Red Army over a front of 1,250 miles, from Velikiye Luki to the Taman peninsula.

COLONEL G. A. KOLTUNOV, a prominent Soviet military historian, holds the degree of Candidate of Historical Sciences. He was one of the authors of Volume III of the six-volume *History of the Great Patriotic War of the Soviet Union, 1941/45*, of *The Second World War* (Moscow, 1958), and *The Liberation of the Crimea* (Moscow, 1958). He has also published several newspaper and magazine articles.

Operation Citadel

1943 July 5: Operation Citadel, the Wehrmacht's attempt to cut off the Orel/Kursk salient, begins.
July 5/6: Germans push south 6 miles, losing over 25,000 killed and wounded, 200 tanks, 200 aircraft. The southern attack penetrates the first belt of the Soviet defence, then bogs down.
July 6/9: Determined Soviet resistance forces Model to commit the whole of his strike force, but the front holds. Central Front prepares a counteroffensive.
July 12: 'The greatest tank battle in history': the southern German attack struggles forward 20/25 miles for the loss of 10,000 men and 350 tanks. Bryansk and West Fronts take the offensive.
July 15: Central Front takes the offensive.
July 16: German withdrawal begins. Voronezh Front takes the offensive.
July 17: South-West Front takes the offensive.
July 19: Steppe Front takes the offensive.
July 23: German forces have withdrawn beyond their start-lines; Citadel has failed disastrously.
July 26: German High Command orders a planned withdrawal from Orel.
August 4/5: Soviet forces recover Orel and Belgorod.
August 6/11: Voronezh and Steppe Fronts close in on Kharkov.
August 22: Threatened with encirclement, German forces begin to withdraw from Kharkov.
August 23: Soviet forces recover Kharkov, threatening the whole south wing of the German front.

The German answer to the bombers – flak

Just as the Germans had been the first to realise and exploit the offensive power of aircraft, so they were among the first to provide their forces with a wide range of anti-aircraft equipment, ranging from the multiple 20-mm cannon to the legendary 88 and even larger weapons. All the guns illustrated below in their mobile versions could also be used to provide static defence for strategic targets, and combined with radar and searchlights to form a series of defensive belts

105-mm AA Gun: A development of the 88, the 105 was widely used in a fixed defensive rôle. *Ceiling:* 12,800 metres. *Crew:* five. *Rate of fire:* 3 rpm

128-mm AA Gun: When used in a static rôle this heavy AA gun looked very similar to the 105. It is shown here mounted on a railway car. *Crew:* six. *Ceiling:* 14,800 metres. *Rate of fire:* 2 rpm

37-mm Flak 43: The German equivalent of the Allied Bofors 40-mm light AA gun, mounted on a Sdkfz-251 chassis. *Crew:* four. *Rate of fire:* 150 rpm

20-mm Flakvierling 38: This version of the quadruple 20-mm was mounted on a small trailer and could be towed behind a light vehicle

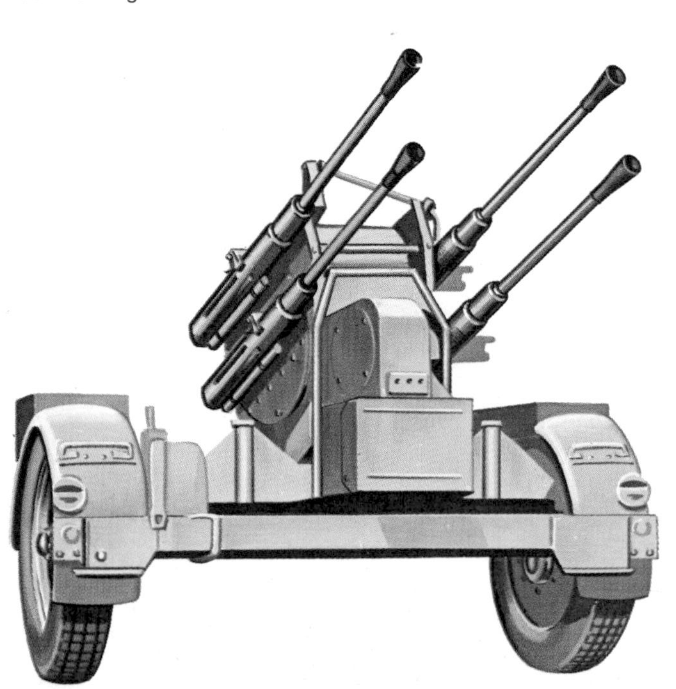

▽There could be no relaxation for the flak crews on the Channel coast, many of whom had scores dating back for over two years

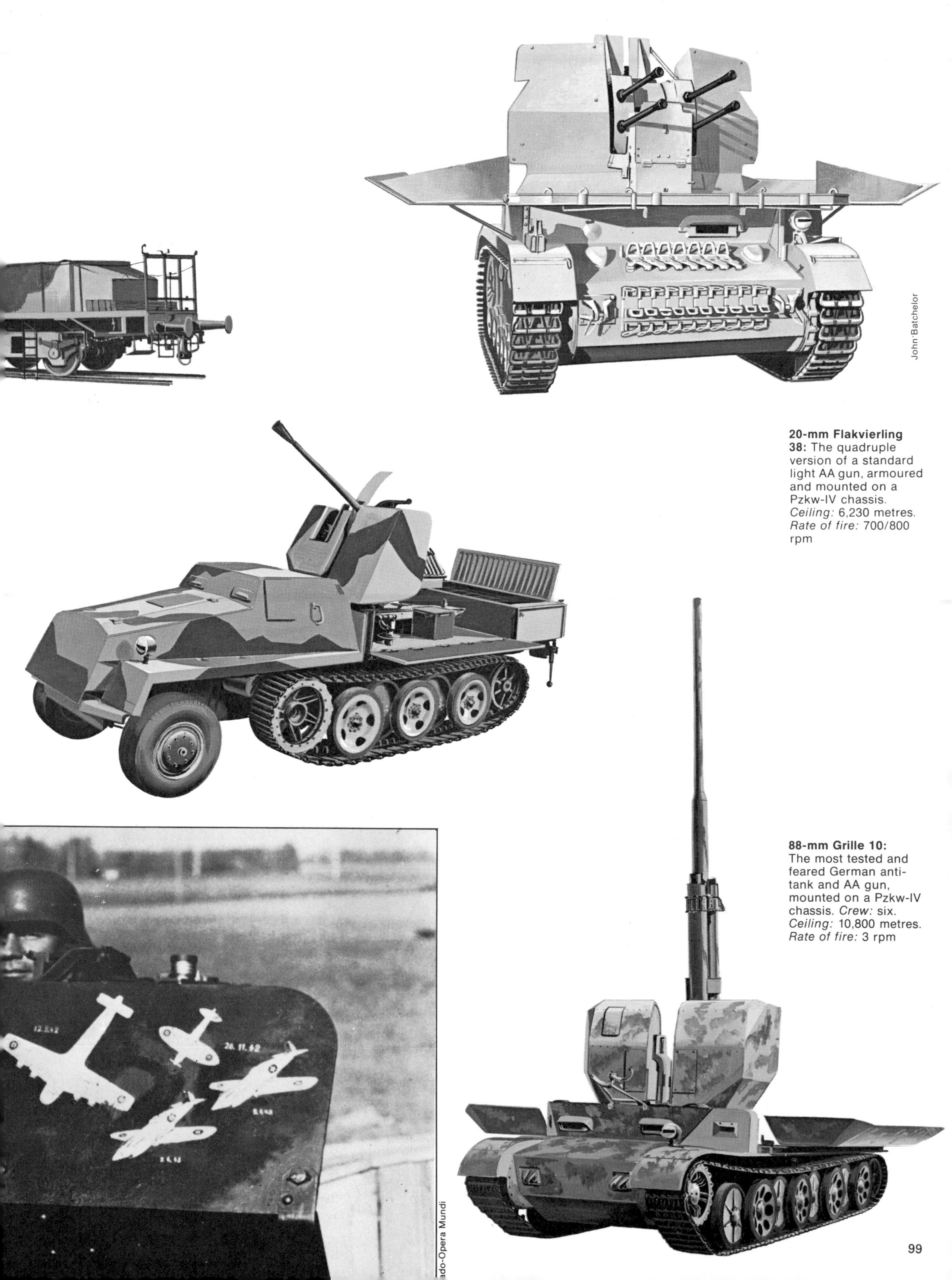

John·Batchelor

20-mm Flakvierling 38: The quadruple version of a standard light AA gun, armoured and mounted on a Pzkw-IV chassis. *Ceiling:* 6,230 metres. *Rate of fire:* 700/800 rpm

88-mm Grille 10: The most tested and feared German anti-tank and AA gun, mounted on a Pzkw-IV chassis. *Crew:* six. *Ceiling:* 10,800 metres. *Rate of fire:* 3 rpm

ado-Opera Mundi

40-mm BOFORS ANTI-AIRCRAFT GUN. The Bofors, designed in Sweden, was one of the most widely used weapons of the war. It was not only an extremely effective anti-aircraft gun, but was also used during night attacks—such as Alamein—to fire tracer as a guide-line for advancing infantry. **Weight in action:** 2·4 tons. **Weight of shell:** 2 lb. **Rate of fire:** 120 rounds per minute. **Effective altitude:** 12,000 feet. **Crew:** Average of six.

From the Allied AA Armoury

Light Flak for the Allies
The 20-mm Oerlikon cannon, here shown on its naval mounting, was one of the most valued guns in Allied use. It served on land and sea, in all theatres, defending the ships on the 'Black-Out Route' to Russia and the Malta convoys, in the Atlantic and the Pacific. It was used to give teeth to amphibious landing-craft. It was mounted in anti-aircraft tanks such as the Skink and the AA Crusader—and it was one of the weapons 'blooded' in the European theatre that was most willingly adopted by the US armed forces. *Crew:* three. *Rate of fire:* 650 rounds per minute. *Magazine capacity:* 60-round drums

John Batchelor

ARMOUR IN ITALY

Lieutenant-Colonel R. L. V. ffrench-Blake

Once the Allies were poised on the edge of Italy's plains, it seemed at last possible that they would be able to use their massive superiority to sweep aside the German defences and crush Kesselring's forces once and for all. But, as the author points out, no theatre of war is more deceptive to the armchair tactician than Italy . . .

In his memoirs Kesselring attributes his successful retreat to three factors: to the failure of the Allied air forces to smash the targets presented to them; to the caution of the ground forces and their distribution over the whole front; and to the failure to attempt a tactical landing in his rear areas by airborne or seaborne troops. Alexander, for his part, first makes it very clear in both his memoirs and his dispatches that General Mark Clark wrongly veered off to Rome after the Anzio 'break-out', instead of seizing Valmontone as agreed—thus failing to close the door of the trap. Secondly, the forces under Alexander's command were hamstrung by the removal, during the pursuit, of four American and three French divisions for Operation Anvil—the invasion of southern France. Thirdly, neither aircraft nor landing craft were available for tactical operations. And yet, with four armoured divisions in hand—US 1st, Canadian 5th, British 6th, and South African 6th—and with complete command of the air, it seems puzzling to the armchair student that the Allied armies were unable to stop Kesselring from passing the remnants of his forces through the

Top: A Sherman burns; the Allies sought an armoured break-through, but the German hill defences dominated the valleys

Middle: Victims of an ambush; the graves of another Sherman crew lie beside the battered hull of their tank

Bottom: Frequent road-blocks and other hold-ups meant that much support work had to be undertaken while under fire

Sado-Opera Mundi

Imperial War Museum

Imperial War Museum

Top: A tank of the South African 6th Armoured Division passes a wrecked German half-track during the race to Florence

Middle: British troops examine one of the mobile steel pillboxes which the Germans used as the focus of their defences

Bottom: Some of the Germans of X Army who did not get away; men of a French armoured division guard a group of prisoners

Paul Popper

Imperial War Museum

Alfredo Zennaro

Tiber bottleneck, and redeploying them in Umbria and Tuscany.

No theatre of war however is more deceptive to the armchair tactician than Italy. Examination of the 'plains' of Tuscany and Umbria proves them to be far from ideal for armoured operations – in 120 miles of coast road between Rome and Livorno there are 60 main river bridges marked on a large-scale map. The whole of Tuscany and Umbria is a maze of rivers and hills, and the 'grain' of the country runs at right angles to the path of the attacker. In addition, a wealth of terracing and cultivation makes cross-country movement extremely difficult.

Beside these natural difficulties, one must set the fact that the day of the tank as king of the battlefield was now passing. First, the power of conventional anti-tank weapons had continued to increase. The towed anti-tank gun was becoming obsolete, since the limited protection which it gave to its crew made it too vulnerable to the high-explosive tank shell – now, at last, standard equipment in all tanks. The place of the towed gun was being taken by special self-propelled anti-tank guns, of low silhouette, without turret, and with a huge gun mounted behind a sloping front plate of immense thickness. Moreover, in fixed defences the Germans had installed a number of Tiger turrets set in concrete. These were extremely hard to knock out, since they were proof against everything but a direct hit from the largest British anti-tank weapon – the 17-pounder.

The introduction of these two types of weapon had forced the Allies back into the policy of using a proportion of tanks with specialised guns, and it was becoming necessary to improvise by putting 17-pounders into Shermans. The Americans were re-equipping with a longer version of the 75-mm, known as the 76-mm. But the higher velocity of this weapon made it far less effective as an artillery weapon, since its flat trajectory raised problems of crest clearance, and it was therefore far more difficult to use from a 'turret-down' position against anti-tank guns. (In firing 'turret-down', the tank is kept completely below the crest of a hill, and the gunner cannot see the target. The tank commander controls the fire from his elevated position on top of the turret, or even by going forward on foot to the crest with a telephone cable.)

New weapons: light, cheap, deadly

To this classic struggle between missile and armour plate was added another element, devastatingly simple and effective. It had been discovered that a charge of explosive moulded into a parabolic shape like a cup, if detonated against armour plate, would blow a hole in it. These 'hollow charges' had first been conveyed to the tank by hand; but as time went on more sophisticated methods were evolved, mostly based on simple rockets. There was now a multitude of these 'personal' anti-tank weapons, either discharged from simple launchers, such as the US Bazooka, or from tubes held in the hand (the German Panzerfaust), or even from Very-light pistols. Every infantryman could carry one. They were light, cheap, and expendable. In open country they were of little use, except at night, but in the tangled vines and orchards of Italy they were deadly.

The mine and the booby-trap, which had already appeared in great numbers in North Africa, were now even more widespread. Above all, in Italy, the chief weapon in defence was the demolition charge. The scale of destruction which the Germans achieved beggars description. It was an administrative miracle how, with their limited transport – much of which was still horse-drawn – they managed to convey such an enormous tonnage of explosives to the right place at the right time. Every variety of demolition known to the engineer was practised: bridges, culverts, and houses were demolished; and extensive 'side-cuts' (the demolition of a road where it passes under a cliff) were found in every mile of road. All these demolitions were mined and booby-trapped.

On the railways a special hooked device, towed behind two engines, tore up the sleepers and distorted the rails irreparably. To advance, *even without opposition,* became a major engineering problem. For example, in 107 days of pursuit after Cassino, the engineers of 6th Armoured Division built 50 bridges totalling 2,500 feet, in addition to filling innumerable craters, clearing thousands of mines, removing booby traps, and improving tracks. As the leading troops approached a demolition, they would be engaged by artillery fire, directed by observers in the hills above, by anti-tank fire from self-propelled guns and from tanks concealed anywhere up to 2 miles from the obstacle, and finally by small-arms fire from infantry dug in near the obstacle.

Before the engineers could reconnoitre the demolition, infantry would have to be deployed to secure a bridgehead round it. The reconnaissance would next have to be made under heavy shell fire; then no work could be started until after dark, when the debris would first have to be cleared of mines and booby-traps before the bulldozers could move in to level and prepare the site. The bridge would have to be brought up and built before daylight, otherwise the enemy would destroy it again next day. The bulldozers – at that period unarmoured – were so precious that they could not be exposed to shell-fire, since if they were knocked out, the advance could be ended.

'Fox and Geese'

The battlefield was like a gigantic version of the old draught-board game 'Fox and Geese', in which the defender tries to withdraw without leaving any gap. The difference in war is that the attacker has the power to destroy a defending piece – *if* he can surround it and prevent its withdrawal. The difficulty in doing this is to generate sufficient speed, power, and above all surprise, to prevent the withdrawing force from slipping away. The trouble is that if the pursuer is steadily gaining ground, without losing many casualties, he may well feel that he is doing well enough.

The Allied divisions in the pursuit were not launched into it fresh from reserve; they had taken part in the 'break-in' battle in support of the infantry, and had already had a week of some of the hardest fighting of the whole war before starting the 'break-out', which took yet another week. They then had three months of continuous fighting advance, 'in the line', without rest, before reaching the outskirts of the Gothic Line. As fatigue and exhaustion set in, it became less and less possible to generate the extra momentum to cut out and destroy any part of the withdrawing forces.

The Germans in the Second World War often criticised the British for their inability to sustain a battle after the first encounter. In fact the history of the war is full of examples of failure by both sides to exploit with sufficient vigour at the moment of success. Part of the reason as far as British troops were concerned lay in the organisation of the armoured division, which was incompletely equipped to enable it to carry out the task for which it was originally intended – to win campaigns by thrusting deep into enemy territory.

In 1939 the standard armoured division had contained two armoured brigades, and a support group consisting of one field artillery regiment and two motor battalions – six tank regiments to two infantry battalions. In 1940 each tank brigade was given its own motor battalion, making three infantry battalions in all. An armoured car regiment was also added. At the King's review of 6th Armoured Division on Lakenheath in 1941 the members of the Army Council were so appalled at the unwieldiness of the mass of 400 tanks that they decided to halve the armoured content to one tank brigade, including its own motor battalion. The division thus contained one tank and one infantry brigade. The artillery was increased to two field regiments, one anti-tank regiment, and one AA regiment.

This remained the basic organisation until the end of the war, but in Italy the use of tanks was so inhibited by the ground, that it was decided to add a second infantry brigade. The 6th Armoured Division therefore consisted of a tank brigade, a motor brigade (Greenjackets), and an infantry brigade (Guards). In theory each armoured regiment could therefore expect the support of a whole motor battalion.

The deficiency of equipment mentioned above lay in the transport for these motor battalions, and for the administrative echelons accompanying the tanks. It is absolutely necessary for tanks to be accompanied by a supply of ammunition, fuel, and a medical unit. This first-line administrative reserve (or 'AI echelon', as it was then called) must be able to follow the tanks wherever they go. In other words, *vehicles accompanying tanks must be both tracked and armoured.* At that date, they were neither. The AI echelon consisted of ordinary 3-ton lorries. The motor battalions at that time were equipped with Bren-gun carriers, a few half-tracked vehicles, and four-wheeled, lightly armoured scout-cars. Even these vehicles had the greatest difficulty in following the tanks through the difficult going caused by enemy demolitions, and by the devastation left by friendly artillery and bombing. Later, a certain amount of improvisation with turretless light tanks, from the reconnaissance troop of the armoured regiment, enabled a small emergency AI echelon to be formed, but this was not capable of supplying a whole tank regiment with both fuel and ammunition. Tanks, incidentally, are self-supporting with food and water, carrying supplies of both for at least a week. Later, whole armoured regiments were equipped with tanks modified as infantry carriers, but these were used as corps troops, and were never an integral part of the armoured division.

The failure to provide armoured and tracked transport vehicles to accompany the tanks cannot be laid at the door of the early pioneers of armoured tactics, who had always advocated such a policy. It can certainly be blamed partly on the inhibiting effect of financial control; and partly on the fact that in the early part of the war all British armoured policy was based on experience of the Western Desert where, on the whole, wheels could move as freely as tracks. Formations training in Great Britain were very restricted in cross-country movement, and never experienced the effect of roads blocked by demolitions. In any case, tank production was so far in arrears that it would have been many years before Great Britain could have afforded the capacity to produce a tracked infantry carrier and supply vehicle.

Obsolete tactics?

Was there also some fundamental deficiency in British staff and command training in the art of exploitation and the pursuit? Were the enormously complicated problems of passing the pursuit force through the gap created by the 'break-in' battle fully understood, and fully practised in training? Was there sufficient planning and study of the Italian theatre, after the end of the North African campaign? Although 6th Armoured Division did not reach Italy until early March, and although the Italian campaign had been opened six months earlier, yet no regimental officers had been sent over to study the new conditions; and training in North Africa continued to be based on experience of battles fought in the immediate past.

The warfare of Italy turned out to be mostly mountain warfare, the rules of which are strict, and inescapable – troops advance in the valleys only at the speed at which the high ground on either side can be secured. The heights must be taken, and held, by resolute infantry action, backed by an efficient supply system to maintain the troops against enemy action and against the effects of the weather. In the valleys, the engineer problems will be paramount. These rules applied from Calabria to the borders of the Po plain, where other problems were to arise.

The Germans, always skilful in defence, made masterly use of the ground in their long withdrawal up the length of the peninsula. More than once their army was on the very edge of disaster, and one must admire the way in which they continued to fight till the very end of the campaign. For the moment, we leave them in the fastnesses of the Gothic Line, in early September, while the Allied armoured divisions rest in the Arno valley, after the long pursuit.

Backing up the Allied advance

In war, mobility is vital: both at the front, and behind it for redeployment and to ensure that supplies and reinforcements keep coming forward. In the Italian campaign – where the terrain with its many steep hills, rivers, gullies, and other obstacles gave the defence a very great advantage – the problems of movement were multiplied. For the Allies, every obstacle had to be cleared under fire and so special vehicles were developed which could withstand considerable punishment while blazing a trail for the troops

▽ **Churchill Ark:** A turretless Churchill Mk III chassis fitted with a ramp over the tracks with extensions 11 feet 9 inches long at front and rear. An Ark could scale a 12-foot wall and span a 30-foot ditch. For vertical obstacles the Ark dropped its ramps on the obstacle and on the ground. Other vehicles drove over it and used fascines if necessary to reduce the drop on the other side. *Weight:* 38·1 tons. *Speed:* 16·4 mph. *Range:* 123 miles. *Crew:* 2. *Armament:* One 7·92-mm MG

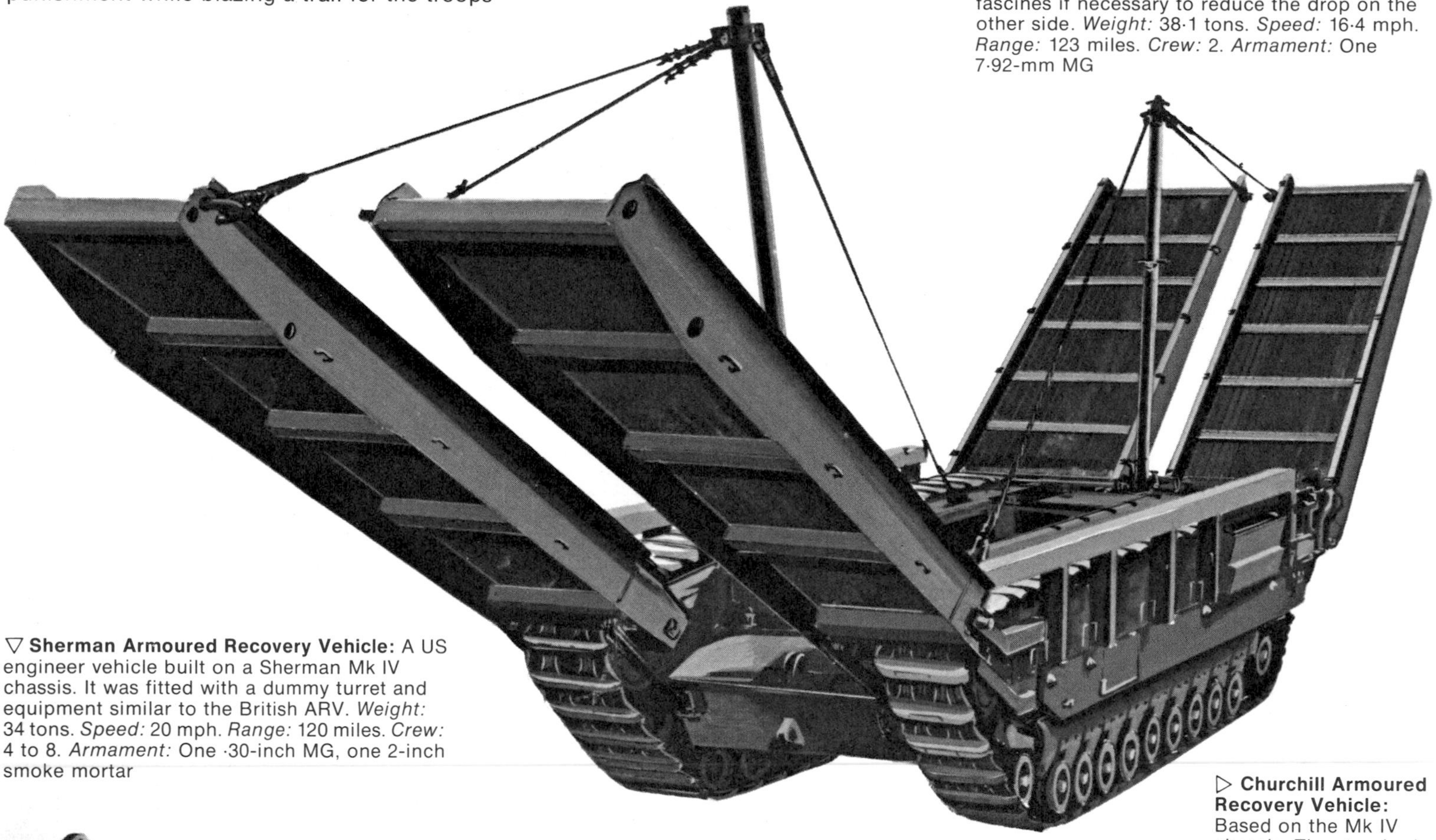

▽ **Sherman Armoured Recovery Vehicle:** A US engineer vehicle built on a Sherman Mk IV chassis. It was fitted with a dummy turret and equipment similar to the British ARV. *Weight:* 34 tons. *Speed:* 20 mph. *Range:* 120 miles. *Crew:* 4 to 8. *Armament:* One ·30-inch MG, one 2-inch smoke mortar

▷ **Churchill Armoured Recovery Vehicle:** Based on the Mk IV chassis. The standard turret was replaced by a fixed turret with a dummy gun and two cupolas. Special equipment included a forward jib with a 7½-ton lift, a rear jib with a 15-ton lift, and a two-speed winch with a 25-ton pull. *Weight:* 33 tons. *Speed:* 16·4 mph. *Range:* 123 miles. *Crew:* 3 to 8. *Armament:* One 7·92-mm MG

Bippa

△ A common sight behind the lines in Italy *(top left)*, the British Bailey Bridge was the most versatile military bridge of the Second World War. It was a heavy fixed bridge in which the decking was laid on two main trusses built of 10-foot panels pinned together with horizontal cross members *(see model top right)*. These basic elements—placed in position by hand and machinery often under fire *(above)*—could be reinforced to carry loads up to 100 tons over spans up to 220 feet wide. The Bailey could also be used as a pontoon bridge laid on 60-foot pontoons. It was also employed by the US Army engineers

John Batchelor

Build-Up for D-Day

BALANCE OF ARMOUR

Major K. J. Macksey

Imperial War Museum

Much had happened in armoured warfare since May 1940, when Germany's Panzer forces humiliated their Allied counterparts. New concepts, new weapons, new leaders had appeared on both sides—and only the showdown at Normandy would prove which were superior. Major Macksey inspects the armoured forces on both sides and explains how 'The Funnies' could tip the balance in the Allies' favour

Upon the day that the German army marched into the Low Countries in May 1940, the balance of armour—that common factor in a war that was to be dominated by armoured fighting vehicles and aircraft—had been struck in favour of the Germans, only because their combat techniques were superior to those of the Allies. It will be recalled that the French and British, between them, possessed more and, in some respects, better tanks than the Germans, but that only the Germans had recent practical battlefield experience in Spain and Poland with armoured vehicles, and had a greater insight into their potentialities.

After that torrid summer, the heat of battle came to play ever more intensely upon the art of making war, fashioning and tempering techniques in the forge of experience and ingenuity; but readers will have seen that battlefield pace still moved no faster than the speed of tracked vehicles and that combat was decided by armoured protection in relation to fire power, salted by the skill and bravery of the fighting men. However, when the whole of the French tank fleet, plus the entire French industrial output, fell into German hands, numerical superiority went the way of the victors. Thereafter the Allies—even when joined by the might of Russia and the USA—had to cut many corners in order to catch up both qualitatively and quantitively.

Combat experience conditioned every armoured technological response after 1939, the British learning by practice in the desert and southern Europe, the Americans studying both sides when forming their embryo armoured forces, the Germans striving to retain their early lead. But the vital incentive to armoured development, despite the wholesale losses in the summer of 1941, turned out to be the quality of the resurgent Russian armoured force: the Russians had constructed an enormous tank army in the 1930s, equipping it with simple, rugged machines ideally suited to crews of peasant origin and the wildly exacting terrain and climate of the steppe. It was the quality of this armoured force (though not the manner of its employment) which drove the Germans to the verge of design and industrial panic measures, as it dawned upon them that the Red Army enjoyed an unexpected technical potential.

In 1931, by purchasing the brain child of a brilliant, but temperamentally awkward, American inventor, J. Walter Christie, the Russians sired the strain of *Bystrokhodye* (fast) or 'BT' tanks which found most potent expression in their T-34. This tank, whether armed as in 1941 with the 76-mm or, after 1943, with the 85-mm gun, was probably one of the finest fighting vehicles ever built, its sloped armour, simple armament, and reliable automotive parts hardly degraded at all by primitive and stark construction. Complementary with the KV series of heavier tanks, the T-34, once it started coming forth in large numbers after 1941, gave the Russians technical equality with their invaders.

Moreover, from the beginning, the Russians exhibited every intention of achieving a technical lead, engaging wholeheartedly in a race by pressing ahead with up-gunning and up-armouring programmes of their heavier, proven vehicles, discarding lighter ones and introducing an increasing number of self-propelled assault guns armed with newer, more powerful weapons than those already in service on the turreted tanks. In short, the Russians accorded the highest priority on the need to 'out-gun' the Wehrmacht, never losing sight of the essential need to outnumber. They claim to have built 30,000 tanks, assault guns, and armoured cars in each of the last three years of the war. When the 11,000 tanks sent to Russia by her allies are added to this figure, the highest-ever German output—19,000 machines in 1944—looks somewhat sick.

Inevitably, the Germans had to retain the bulk of their armoured force in the east to keep the Russians in check, for the Russians threw their tanks into the attack in the same way as they employed massed infantry supported by massed artillery. Perforce, the German armour in the West, notably in France and Belgium (the best tank country) had to be pared to the bone: consequently the quality of machines and crews had to achieve new peaks of performance, to compensate for shortage in numbers, if they were to retain the slightest hope of survival. But the end of the Stalingrad campaign found the size of the Panzer force at its lowest, and with much of the old quality dissipated as well.

So the Germans brought back the old rebel, Heinz Guderian—Hitler appointing him Inspector-General of Armoured Troops, charged with a charter of Guderian's own drafting that gave him power throughout the entire field of armoured organisation and training, with responsibility for fixing the requirements for technical development and production in conjunction with the new Minister of Armaments and Munitions—Albert Speer. Guderian's target lay not one bit short of re-creating the armoured troops into a decisive weapon designed to win the war: how ironic that this should have had to be stated by the Germans in 1943. His powers were immense, for 'Armoured Troops' encompassed each component of the Panzer divisions, including their infantry and anti-tank units—but excluded the assault-gun units, after the artillery arm had fought a successful rearguard action in retaining this element to themselves.

Apart from an intense drive to raise the standard of training, Guderian, with Speer's brilliant and wholehearted support, set about rationalising fighting vehicle production, playing down projects aimed at producing monster tanks (one suggested a 1,500-ton machine). He demanded an instant short-term increase in the production of existing machines, incorporating thicker armour and better guns, concentrating on improving the new, infinitely more powerful models just coming in to service, while Speer speeded up production by a wholesale centralisation of control to focus production on essential items, dismantling the wasteful practice of individual arms of the services being allowed to deal unilaterally with their own 'private' manufacturers. Only the SS escaped Speer's net to any significant extent—but then they, and their Panzer divisions, ran on special, inflated establishments and were almost a law—Hitler's law—unto themselves.

Germany: a new breed of Panzers

Both the original Pzkw-IIIs and IVs had been in course of re-equipment with progressively more powerful guns since 1941, a measure of the foresightedness of their original design that they could afford the extra space and absorb the increased recoil exerted by these bigger weapons. Even larger guns went into assault gun (*Sturmgeschütz*) versions of both Mk III and Mk IV chassis—so there evolved a valuable armoured anti-tank force to act as a defensive pivot, around which the more ubiquitous tanks could manoeuvre.

Highest priority went to rushing the new Tiger and Panther tanks to the front, for even the most lavishly modified Pzkw-IV was hard pressed to match the latest Russian tanks—let alone whatever the British and Americans might unveil. Ironically, that same German High Command which had won its greatest triumphs on the backs of the armoured force, had neglected to press hard enough for new generations of fighting vehicles while those triumphs were in train. Both Tiger and Panther had been projected before 1940, but such was the lack of urgency behind their progress that the heavy Tiger I only began trials in 1941 and the medium Panther did not reach prototype stage until March 1942. Thereafter, under the threat of the T-34, matters quickened and Tiger I-E with its 88-mm gun reached the troops at the front in September 1942, while Panther with its 'long' 75-mm gun came into service early in 1943. But although both enjoyed material superiority over any armoured vehicle then at war, the violent haste of development and production gave vent to a nagging unreliability which, all too often, left undamaged machines in Allied hands during the recurring withdrawals as Germany's frontiers contracted.

By June 1944, however, the German armoured force in the West had largely recovered its strength and composure and could muster ten Panzer divisions (of varying complements and organisation) within reach of the invasion coast, equipped with a mixed collection of Pzkw-IVs and Panthers. In addition, there existed a Panzer Grenadier division, whose armoured strength rested upon 45 assault-guns, and several heavy battalions consisting either of Tigers or Panther assault-guns (Jagdpanther), supplemented by further assault guns of multifarious armament mounted on old Czech and French tank chassis. And just beginning to appear were a few of the formidable Tiger IIs (King Tigers), armed with the 'long' 88-mm gun. Further reinforcements of these units thereafter depended upon the extent to which resources could be spared from other theatres; the immediate presence of reserves at the front to be decided partly upon the workings of Rundstedt or Rommel and partly upon the moody direction of Hitler from afar, though frequently delays imposed by the damage caused by Allied bombing or the Resistance threatened to produce more profound effects than any command decision. Nevertheless, Guderian's restoration had worked miracles on crew training and morale – it remained to be seen if quality could constantly outstrip quantity.

Britain: desperate after Dunkirk

If in no other respect, the British and Americans possessed quantitive superiority in armour, and that, in itself, was no mean industrial achievement when it is recalled that, after Dunkirk, Britain had only 200 tanks fit for battle, while the Americans owned hardly a single operational tank worthy of the name.

Whatever British industry could make in 1940 had to be churned out at once, regardless of quality, to rearm the rescued BEF: indeed, Churchill insisted that, for the time being, all research and development should stop in order to concentrate every ounce of energy on production. So, those tanks already in, or about to enter, production – Matilda, Valentine, Cruisers IV, V, VI, and the new heavy Churchill, all armed with the obsolescent 2-pounder gun – rolled forth in growing numbers while the next generation of vehicles waited in abeyance.

To add further to confusion, the British tank supply organisation tottered on rotten foundations. A month before the outbreak of war, what few tank technologists the War Office boasted had been grabbed by the new Ministry of Supply, isolating the War Office from informed tank advice. A purely politically inspired Tank Board had been set up, to head tank affairs in the right direction, but suffered from a surfeit of responsibility, a lack of power – and a flood of resignations and reappointments. It failed in its task. The last in the line of Britain's great tank enthusiasts, Major-General Hobart, had been dismissed from command of 7th Armoured Division in the desert by Generals Wilson and Wavell, because the former had 'no confidence' in Hobart's way of command. When Guderian proved Hobart right in May 1940, the latter was being promoted to Lance-Corporal in the Home Guard; but by autumn of that year he was on his way back to power, having devised a plan in conjunction with General Pile (another tank expert then in command of the anti-aircraft command) for a new armoured army, governed by a charter strikingly similar to that to be written by Guderian over two years later.

On the insistence of Churchill, Hobart was recalled, ostensibly to raise a new armoured division, but primarily to train all the tank forces. Neither the CIGS, General Dill, nor Commander Home Forces, General Brooke, felt able to accept Hobart's complete plan, so Hobart got his armoured division and General Martel, another of the early tank pioneers, took the watered-down training job, without a charter. For the next two years the tale of British defeat could be linked with mediocre handling of inferior vehicles by officers and men whose courage alone made up for the other deficiences.

Tank production mounted apace with the aim of filling the establishments of ten armoured divisions each of about 400 tanks. However, the insistence of the pre-war General Staff that a large number of slow, heavily armoured infantry support vehicles would be needed to lead a basically infantry army now led to a short-fall in the number of fast cruisers being built for the armoured divisions: not until later, when US production was tapped, could this deficiency be rectified, so, in the meantime, infantry tanks had to fill spaces in the armoured divisions. In any case, the next generation of cruiser – Mark VII called 'Centaur' – ran into technical troubles, never met its specification or delivery date, and was superseded by a revised Mark VIII 'Cromwell', before the former could be brought into action. And Cromwell, when at last it appeared in 1944, went to battle outgunned and incapable of accepting a larger weapon than the comparatively low-powered 57-mm (6-pounder) or 75-mm gun with which it was provided.

Guns versus speed

This semi-permanent state of under-gunning stemmed from the earlier, but untested, belief that tank armament could take lower priority after speed and armour, on the assumption that field artillery would supplement the high-explosive dispensing capability the tanks did not possess – a theory which died an instant death in the first major armoured battles when it was discovered that, in a fast-moving encounter, tanks had to be able to provide all sorts of self-support at short notice and that the slower artillery methods often could not compete. Thereafter the delay in making and mounting 57-mm and 75-mm (and later the 17-pounder) guns occurred mainly because of weakness in communication between the War Office and Ministry of Supply – the former not stating their requirements with sufficient clarity, leading to the army being given whatever the latter thought good for the soldiers. Acrimony ran rife, for instance, when the Ministry of Supply said, in 1942, that it would be impossible to mount the 17-pounder in the Sherman, leaving the War Office to prove it feasible in 1943 and thrust the modification through against protocol barely in time for June 6.

Reorganisation of British armoured forces took place about once a year under the impetus of fresh thought and the demands of front-line soldiers. In 1941 a cry for more armoured divisions to replace infantry ones led to several infantry (including Guards) battalions being converted to armour – an admission that pre-war policy had been wrong, tied to a staunch attempt at retaining old regimental traditions in a changing world. But the disruption in the minds of infantrymen transposed to an entirely new way of thinking and fighting could take at least a year to appease. So when, at last in 1942, the transposition was beginning to make headway, a fresh decision was taken to cut the armoured content of the armoured division by half (and to substitute more lorry-borne infantry) while transferring the redundant armour to independent brigades charged with the task of supporting infantry formations – and this made confusion doubly compounded. Thus British armour multiplied in a state of annual transplantation, the victim of vacillation at the whim of a hierarchy which had never consolidated its concept of future operational procedures.

For the invasion, therefore, the British army, with its large Canadian contingent and the 1st Polish Armoured Division, came to consist of five armoured divisions and eight independent armoured brigades, plus certain specialised armoured formations – of which more later – in all some 3,300 Shermans (barely 1 in 20 with 17-pounders), Churchills (including 100 of the new more heavily armoured Mark VII), and Cromwells – the whole backed by sumptuous material reserves.

America: a New World impulse

The American armour force had not endured the same vicissitudes as the other nations after 1940 because then it hardly existed at all and owned but a few hundred obsolete models, and a small cadre of crews trained in cavalry methods. Its modern battle organisation was of its own devising, but based on a close study of the ideas of the warring nations since, until 1940, American armour had been smothered first by its subservience to the infantry and then the cavalry. The main American battle tank came to be the Sherman armed with either the 75-mm or the slightly superior 76-mm gun. In early 1941 American tank production turned in gestation: in 1942 it gave birth to 14,000 Shermans, followed in 1943 by another 21,000 – the rate still rising at the demand of the sort of mass-production urge so characteristic of New World impulse. Numbers alone, matched by the virtue of mechanical reliability, gave the Sherman (and thereby the Allies) their one significant counter to the German gun and armour superiority; while the seething American training organisation churned out a concourse of mass-trained crewmen, full of confidence but still with much to learn, inspired by the drive of that most colourful of armoured generals – the American counterpart of Guderian and Hobart – George S. Patton.

In 1943, however, the USA could have had – and should have had – a powerful successor to Sherman: the T-20, mounting a 76-mm gun, which could have seen action in 1944. But a belief that Shermans in large numbers would be good enough to saturate the German defences as well as act with reliability and speed in pursuit, prompted a decision to stop production of the T-20 in order not to disrupt the flood of Shermans coming from the factories. It is the privilege of vast nations to employ big battalions regardless of finesse, and to a considerable extent this was American policy in 1944.

Updating the tank tactics

Every combat army had learned the need to combine infantry and artillery with tank action, although the levels at which co-operation took root differed as did the detailed methods of command. The Germans plumped for mixed battle groups of flexible composition within the division; the British tended to draw a line between armoured and infantry formations, regrouping no lower than brigade level if they could help it; while the Americans followed the German example in the main, but enhanced flexibility by refining control through special Combat Commands (two per armoured division) upon mixed battle groups drawn from a divisional tank strength of 270 (including 83 light Stuarts). This was the latest of several variations on the American theme and was in use by the six US and the French 2nd Armoured Division in mid-1944.

However, unlike the Germans who employed their assault gun units purely in the infantry support role, the American philosophy reached towards the British by setting aside specific GHQ tank battalions to work closely with infantry divisions. This reflected the fundamental difference between Allied and German doc- ▷

Imperial War Museum

By 1944 the Western Allies, particularly Britain, had moved away from the idea that the tank was primarily an infantry support weapon – although the Churchill (seen above undergoing waterproofing tests) was to do sterling work in this role – and their main tank, the fast, manoeuvrable Sherman, was well-suited to offensive armoured warfare. But compared with the most modern German designs it was undergunned, and often needed superior numbers to outmatch the opposition. Several attempts were made to mount a heavier gun, the most successful being the *SHERMAN FIREFLY (top)* which carried the British 17-pounder. *Weight:* 32.9 tons. *Speed:* 24 mph. *Range:* 120 miles. *Crew:* Four. *Armour:* 81-mm maximum. *Armament:* One 17-pdr, one .30-inch MG. Meanwhile the Germans, faced with a growing need for powerful defensive equipment which could counteract Allied numerical superiority, had developed larger, less manoeuvrable, but heavily gunned tanks and self-propelled guns – weapons which could be built into a tightly-knit defensive screen. The *STURMPANZER IV (bottom)* had developed out of a requirement for a mobile infantry-support gun, and was to prove its worth in Normandy where the terrain prevented the Allies from exploiting their mobility. *Weight:* 25 tons. *Speed:* 23 mph. *Range:* 60 miles. *Crew:* Five. *Armour:* 80-mm. *Armament:* One 75-mm gun, two 7.92-mm MG. The *JAGDPANTHER (middle),* one of the most potent armoured fighting vehicles produced during the war, was the result of a marriage between the excellent 88-mm gun and the chassis of the Panther tank. *Weight:* 46 tons. *Speed:* 35 mph. *Range:* 125 miles. *Crew:* Five. *Armour:* 80-mm. *Armament:* 88-mm gun, two 7.92-mm MG

John Batchelor

The 'Funnies': a strange menagerie of armoured monsters

Both Allied and German planners had realised that the success of D-Day hinged on the speed with which the invaders could overcome the 'hard crust' of beach defences and move inland. After the disaster at Dieppe, the British had realised that infantry assault troops must be preceded and supported by armour specially adapted to deal with the various types of ob-

1

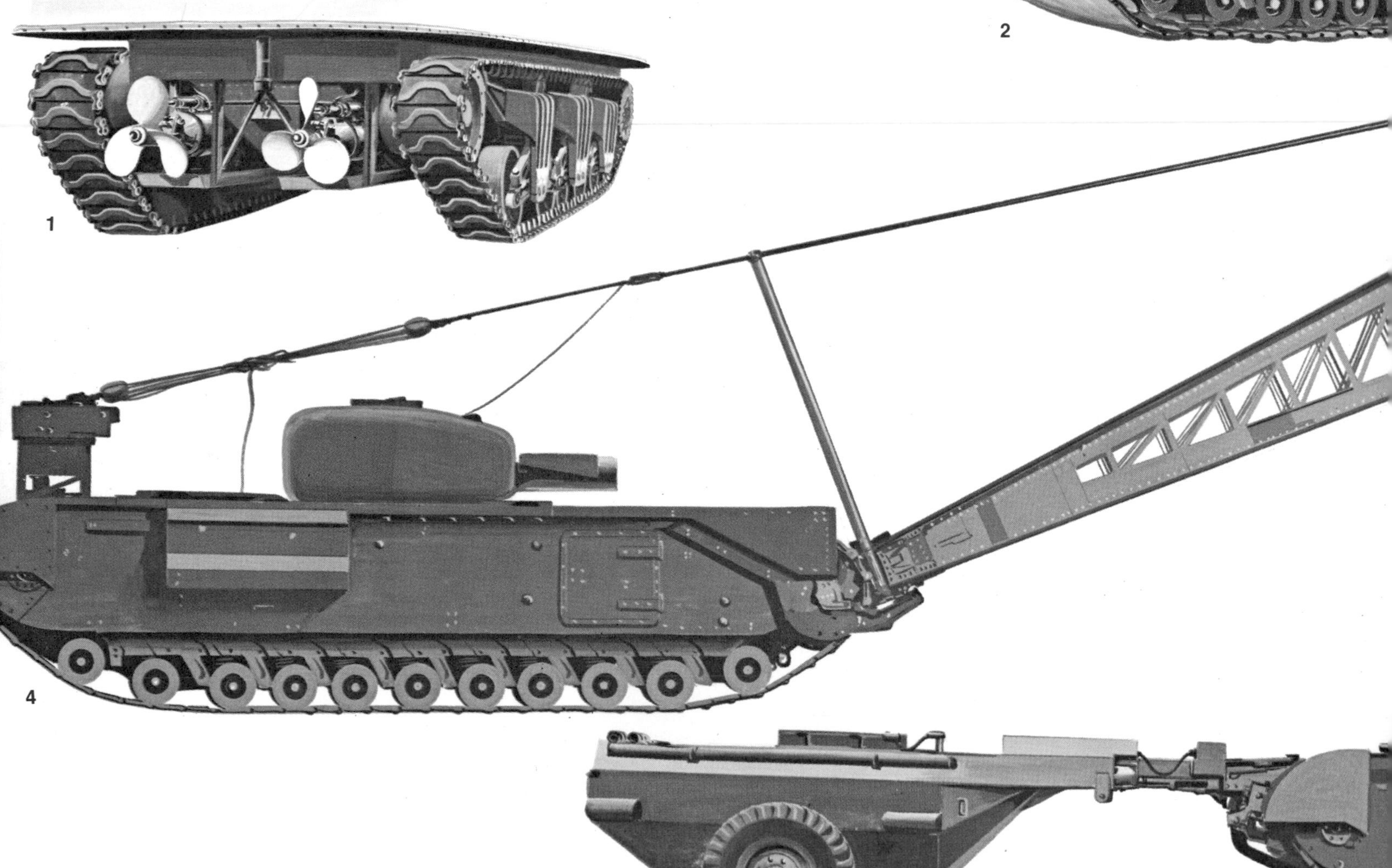

stacles. Thus the 'Funnies', brainchildren of Maj-Gen Hobart, were born: (1) *Duplex Drive* (DD): an amphibious conversion which could be fitted to the normal Sherman. A collapsible canvas screen gave the tank buoyancy and it was driven at up to 4.3 knots by two propellers and its tracks. (2) *Bobbin* on a Churchill chassis; designed to lay a 9 foot 11 inch-wide canvas carpet over soft sand. (3) *Crab:* a mine-sweeping adaptation of the Sherman which could clear a lane 10 feet wide working at 1½mph. (4) *Churchill AVRE* with SBG Bridge: a Churchill chassis adapted to carry a bridge which could be dropped in 30 seconds over a 30-foot gap, or surmount a 15-foot wall while supporting 40 tons. (5) *Armoured Bulldozer:* a specially equipped version of the heavy-duty bulldozer produced by the Caterpillar Company. (6) *Churchill Crocodile:* a flame-thrower conversion of the Mark VII. The flame gun, with a range of about 120 yards, was mounted in place of the hull machine-gun, and 400 gallons of fuel were carried in the trailer. Pressure from compressed nitrogen was used to force the fuel from trailer to gun

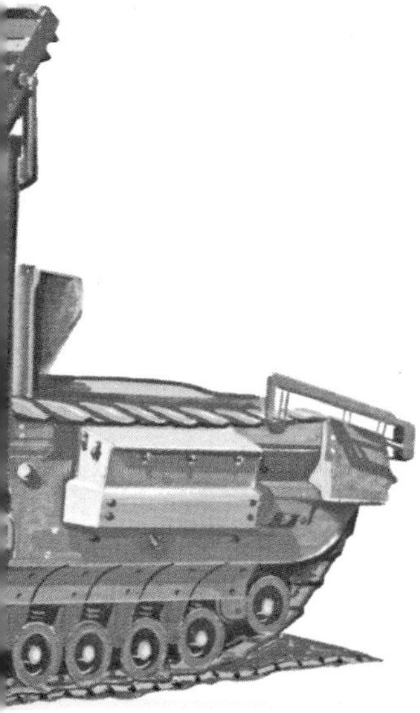

3

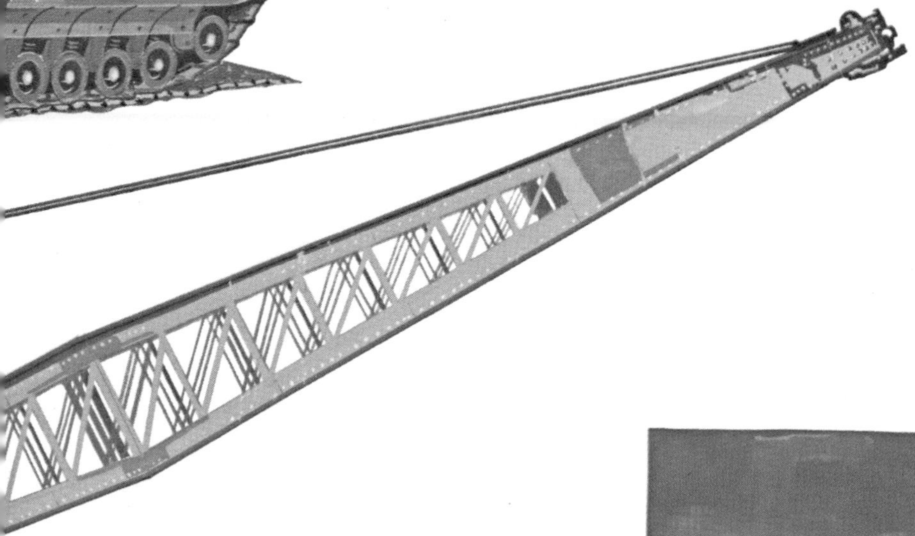

5

6

John Batchelor

New punch for the infantry

One of the most significant developments in weaponry during the latter part of the war was the usage of effective anti-tank weapons by the ordinary infantryman. The Americans were the first to produce a light, portable rocket-launcher, the Bazooka (seen in use during a training exercise in the photograph below), which enabled the infantryman to destroy heavy tanks without having to rely on vulnerable anti-tank guns or artillery. The power of the new weapon was so obvious that soon all the major combatants had introduced similar equipment—such as the British PIAT and German Panzerfaust and Panzerschreck—which could be operated by one or two men and used a hollow-charge high-explosive projectile, effective against fortifications as well as armour

△ *Panzerschreck:* **German 88-mm recoilless rocket-launcher. It fired a 7-lb projectile which was capable of penetrating 4½ inches of armour at 165 yards**

◁ *PIAT:* **British Projector Infantry Anti-Tank. A shoulder-fired weapon which used a 3-lb projectile capable of penetrating 4 inches of armour at a range of 50 yards**

▽ *Bazooka:* **US 2.36-inch recoilless rocket-launcher. It fired a hollow-charge 3½-lb projectile up to 400 yards**

John Batchelor

Imperial War Museum

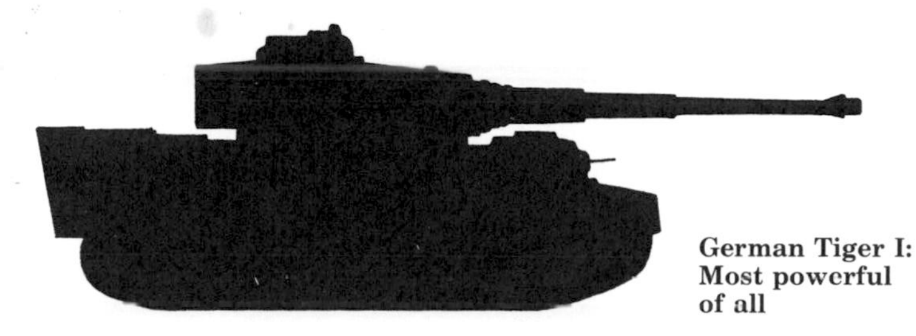
German Tiger I: Most powerful of all

German Panther: Fast and hard-hitting

trine, for the latter insisted on the merits of armoured divisions being grouped exclusively in armoured corps. Each system had its advantages, depending not a little upon the insight of commanders into the potentialities of armour, but not least upon the restrictive nature of ground and room available for manoeuvre. In Russia the rolling steppes favoured the German armoured corps: in Normandy the intensely close bocage threatened to impose an anti-tank barrier infested by well-supported infantry—a situation which favoured the British system.

The greatest changes in the armoured balance since 1940 had been wrought by advances in the nature of field defences, by improvements in the power of anti-tank weapons, and by the proliferation of mines. Whereas the standard towed German anti-tank gun of 1940 had been the 37-mm, by 1944 it was the long 75-mm Pak 40, supplemented by the big, clumsy 88-mm Kwk 43—the latter capable of penetrating 168-mm of sloped armour at 1,000 yards. A German infantry division deployed 31 anti-tank guns augmented by towed 88-mm guns from army resources, this formidable array knitting together the main fabric of an anti-tank curtain behind which hid the mobile reserves of armour. And from the close range of 100 yards, an infantryman had the new-found ability to penetrate the thickest armour using a recoilless *Panzerfaust* or *Panzerschreck* hollow-charge missile—equivalent of the British PIAT and the US Bazooka.

Almost everything favoured the German defence

Of course, the Allies assembled almost as tough a collection of anti-armour weapons in addition to their own assault guns—a US infantry division having both 37-mm and 57-mm anti-tank guns as well as 558 Bazookas; and a British division was no less well equipped and had the well-tried 17-pounder gun. Towed anti-tank guns are strictly a defensive weapon and require time to arrange mutually supporting arcs of fire, to settle in their positions and conceal such protective digging as may be necessary. Hence, anti-tank guns were of more use to the Germans, since they nearly always fought on the defensive from previously established positions. For the same reason, the Germans could make extensive use of minefields to shield their positions and to delay penetrations by Allied armour: thereby they gave their mobile reserves more time to shape counteraction at the critical points of rupture. And on the beaches, the mines lay thickest among a cunning arrangement of artificial obstacles linked with the natural sea defences and inundations.

Every defensive feature favoured the Germans and pulled the balance of armour towards their side of the scales. However, the more powerful weapons are almost inevitably bigger, clumsier, and demanding of increased man- and machine-power resources to move them about the battlefield, culminating in a multiplication of difficulties when seeking satisfactory emplacements. Moreover, the faster a high-velocity shot flies, the greater the difficulty of seeing by what distance it has missed its target (since it gets there before the smoke and dust of discharge have subsided), and so correction of fire is repeatedly made haphazard by this sort of obscuration with a consequent degradation in hit probability. These difficulties all tell against big fieldpieces, the positions of which are compromised once the flash and smoke of discharge appear: ironically they helped restore some of the advantage in favour of armour in 1944.

The German static defences erected along the coastline, set in belts inland and drawn close around vital points—such as the radar station at Douvres in Normandy—raised far more serious hazards to the assault than anything of the sort met so far in the Second World War: they were the products of four years' thought and labour, galvanised by a few months of Rommel's dynamic enthusiasm and his belief in the importance of holding the beaches as a hard crust. Indeed, the Americans seem to have come apathetically to accept these obstacles as a deterrent to the use of massed armour in the lead of the assault: but to the British, recalling their bitter experience at Dieppe, the obstacles acted as a spur to finding ways of destroying them by unconventional methods.

Wholesale slaughter at the water's edge was unthinkable to the British—and the emotions of Churchill ran riot at the nightmare that, once again as at Gallipoli, British infantry might be mown down in heaps at his behest. At Dieppe the Canadians had already suffered something like this fate as, when the tanks came ashore, they were prevented from breaking through the shore obstacles and left the infantry unsupported beyond: while, as the engineers tried to clear pathways for the tanks, the vicious circle drew tight and they were shot down because the unsupported infantry could not subdue the German machine-gun nests.

In March 1943 the CIGS, General Brooke, decided to create special armoured units whose purpose would be to land in the van of the assault, open gaps on their own even before the first waves of infantry got ashore, and then dominate the defences without exposing more than a few unarmoured men to direct fire. Teams of specialised armour were visualised as progressively smothering the German defences with aimed fire, detonating the beach minefields, breaking down the artificial barriers, demolishing or bridging the next row of sea walls, concrete blocks, or deep ditches, then disposing of more minefields, while subjugating the remaining pill-boxes, before accompanying the next wave of assault infantry and armour deep inland. Speed came first in these complex operations, particularly in the British sectors, where the nature of the ground aided German armoured counterattack, since the need quickly to gain depth and space inland, to fight a mobile battle, took precedence over almost every other requirement once a lodgement had been made.

Before 1943, most of the essential kinds of special device needed had reached some form or another of experiment or development—indeed, the ideas for most of them originated from the First World War. Primitive flails had been employed in Africa to detonate mines; an Armoured Vehicle Royal Engineer (AVRE), carrying demolition teams and a variegated selection of bridges or fascines for crossing walls and ditches, had been invented (appropriately by a Canadian, named Donovan) after Dieppe and mounted on the Churchill tank; early efforts to help tanks swim had hardened into a simple arrangement whereby a canvas screen, temporarily erected round the vehicles, displaced the tank's weight while its engine drove two propellers—this was Nicholas Strausler's invention, the Duplex Drive tank (DD); another type of Churchill tank had been fitted with flame-throwing equipment, with pressurised fuel carried in an armoured trailer, the whole device called Crocodile; there were also tanks mounting a powerful searchlight called a Canal Defence Light (CDL). Later a host of other inventions came up for trial, to be rejected or accepted, improved, put into production in quantity, the crews trained and methods found to combine them in teams taught to act in the elimination of every possible obstacle combination.

Hobart builds his 'siege train'

This was to be the Twentieth-Century equivalent of a medieval siege train, constructed to substitute machines for manpower and restore mobile, armoured dominance at every stage in an assault, even where the defences were strongest. With only 14 months to spare, Brooke searched for a man to spring a miracle—pitching his choice on Hobart who, at 58 years of age, still looked the only one with deep enough experience of armour in all its aspects, joined with ruthless energy capable of accomplishing so enormous a task in such a short time. But cutting a hole through the Atlantic Wall was but the last stage of Hobart's task: first he had to persuade and bulldoze the military and industrial machines to improve and construct the necessary equipment to his specifications at his speed: above all he demanded that each special vehicle should retain the ability to fight on its own should it be necessary, and then he had to drill ordinary tank crews in the spirit of dauntless improvisation which recognised no insuperable defence. Against all sorts of frustration Hobart succeeded in his task and was ready, early in 1944, to show a wide range of armoured hardware to General Eisenhower, and to his own brother-in-law, General Montgomery, when they came home to take charge of the invasion forces.

There was a brigade each of DD Shermans and Crab Flail Shermans, and another of Churchill AVREs armed with the Petard demolition projectile, a regiment of Crocodiles and a brigade of Grant CDLs, the latter never, in the event, put to use in their intended role of illuminating the battlefield in order to continue an advance in the dark. Other devices with animal names— 'Hobo's Menagerie' or 'The Funnies' as they came to be known—followed in the months to come, but the combination of DD, Flail, and AVRE were the basic elements of the beach assault team which worked

British Churchill: Tough but still under-gunned

British Cromwell: No match for the Panther

Central Press

American Shermans on an exercise: through standardisation on this type the Allies achieved the quantity they needed to overcome the quality of Germany's armoured defences

Associated Press

Shermans of a British armoured regiment halted 'somewhere in England' during their journey to an assembly area. The white star was the main Allied ground-air recognition sign

ahead of the infantry on June 6.

Montgomery grasped the purpose and significance of specialised armour at once, calling for the necessity of armour to spearhead the assault. Simultaneously, he insisted that the Americans should be offered a half share of everything the British had made, getting Hobart to demonstrate each device to his allies. But, while Eisenhower fell heavily for the DDs, and demanded a brigade's worth, he left the choice of the other items to General Bradley, and he passed it to his staff who, for various reasons, mostly thin, rejected the devices. The terrible outcome of this omission will appear later.

Specialised armour promised to restore balance to Allied armour on the beaches against mines and obstacles. In so doing it might open the way for conventional vehicles to press quickly inland and engage their greater numbers in open battle with the technically superior German armour and anti-tank guns. There was nothing to choose between the determination and gallantry of the men of either side – there never had been – so it remained to be seen if the heavier losses inflicted by a qualitatively superior foe on a numerically superior one might eventually undermine the élan of the latter. Here dwelt a deadly but imponderable threat, hidden behind the soaring morale of the confident British and Americans. In the end a single Tiger which had destroyed a squadron of Allied tanks might be overwhelmed, but would the survivors of that sort of Pyrrhic victory be so ready to stalk the next Tiger when it appeared? And could they go on doing so until the last Tiger had been shot – that is, when no more could reach the battle-front down ramshackle roads and railways from the German interior?

Indeed, the likelihood of the Germans being able to sustain the routes carrying reinforcements and, above all, the fuel and ammunition to nurture a mobile battle, hung in doubt. Here was the crux of the battle – since half-replenished fuel stocks in mechanical war can be almost as crippling as no stocks at all, for planning gets clogged by imponderables. In the ability of the Allied air forces to disrupt fuel supplies resided an indirect threat infinitely more potent than their erratic claims to be able to knock out armour with unstable rockets and bombs.

In 1940 the balance of armour could be reduced to comparatively simple terms and almost in splendid isolation, with the other combat elements playing walking-on parts after the tank heroes had trodden the centre of the stage. Now, in 1944, armour still filled a vital role but merged tightly with every other fighting asset of each army. Yet both sides came to grips again acutely aware that aerial supremacy tipped the scales most profoundly, but not irrevocably, while destruction or neutralisation of armour most certainly would be decisive in the final analysis.

Updating the Armour

The Pershing T-25 E1. The best and most 'modern' American tank of the war, the Pershing had a low silhouette and armour well angled for maximum deflection. One Pershing survived 13 consecutive hits from a German 75-mm tank gun at 1,200 yards without one complete penetration. Moreover, its 90-mm gun enabled it to outshoot its main rival, the German Tiger Mark VI. *Crew:* Five. *Length:* 20 feet, 9 inches. *Weight:* 34·7 tons. *Range:* 75 miles. *Top speed:* 20 mph. *Armament:* One 90-mm gun, one ·50-inch and one ·30-inch machine-gun. *Armour:* 89-mm

John Batchelor

Below: The Joseph Stalin 3, an improved version of the JS series with a redesigned turret and glacis plate for better shot deflection, was first seen in 1945. It had the same main armament as its predecessors, a 122-mm gun, but heavier armour

Bottom: The Maus, the last German leviathan, appeared in early 1945. Only two prototypes were produced. Maus had a giant 128-mm gun with a co-axially mounted 75-mm gun, but its weight and length-width ratio made it slow and hard to handle

Below: The Pershing (details given above) was developed to replace the M6, whose weight posed grave transport problems: the Americans found it easier to ship two medium tanks of 35 tons each than one heavy tank of 65 tons

Bottom: The Tortoise, a British heavy tank produced at the end of the war, was developed only as an experimental prototype. Like the German Maus, it never saw action and only five models were ever built

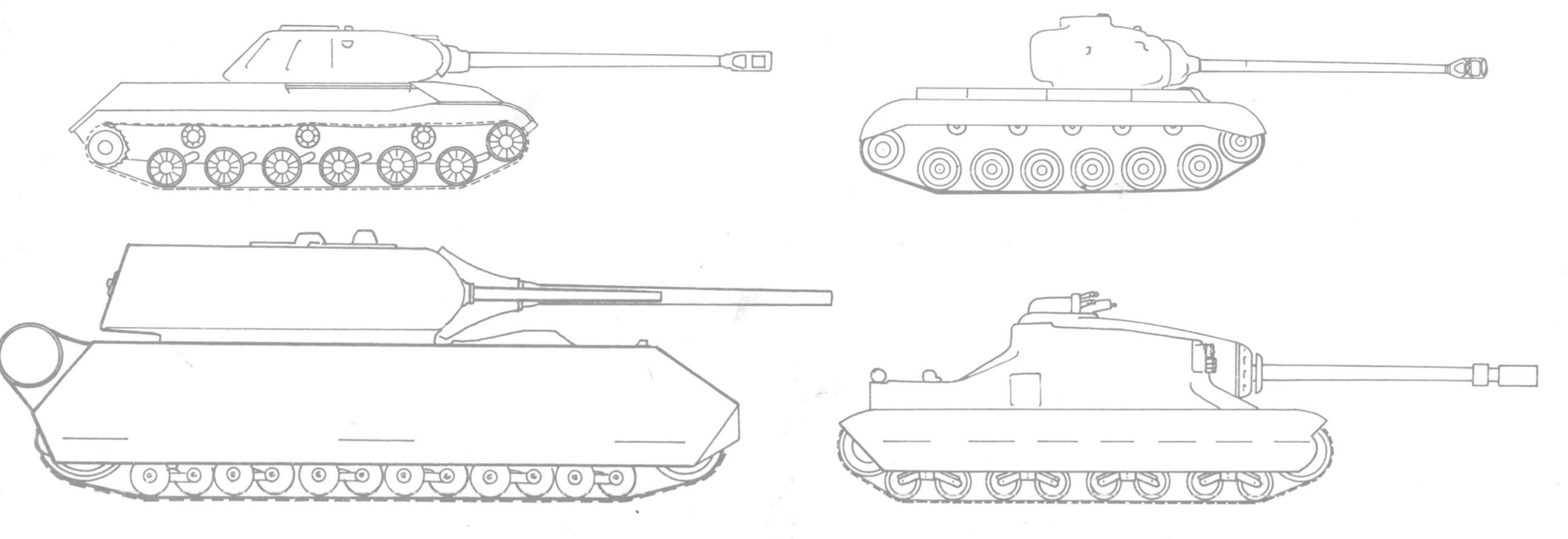

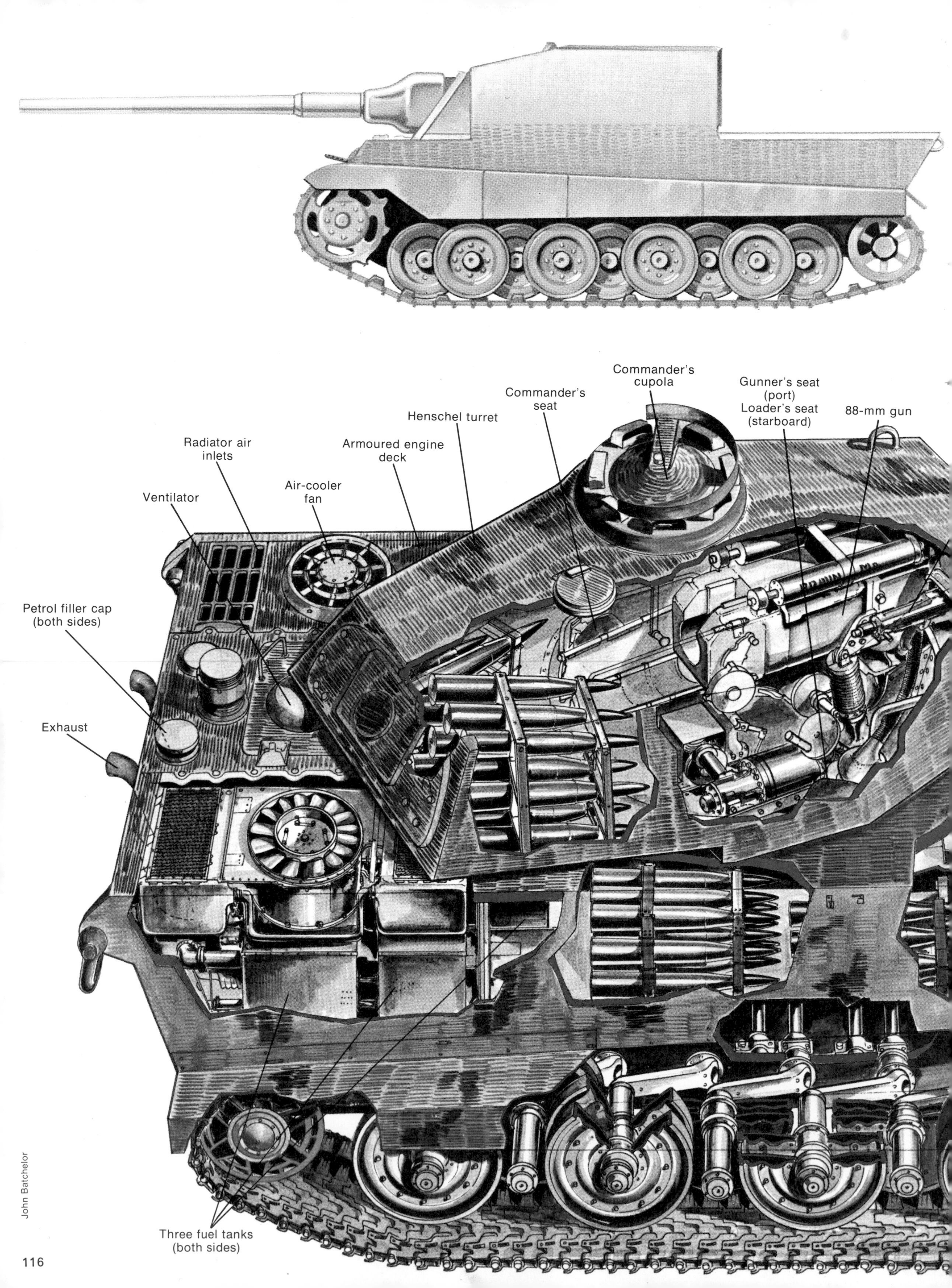
Commander's cupola
Gunner's seat (port)
Loader's seat (starboard)
Commander's seat
88-mm gun
Henschel turret
Radiator air inlets
Armoured engine deck
Air-cooler fan
Ventilator
Petrol filler cap (both sides)
Exhaust
Three fuel tanks (both sides)
John Batchelor

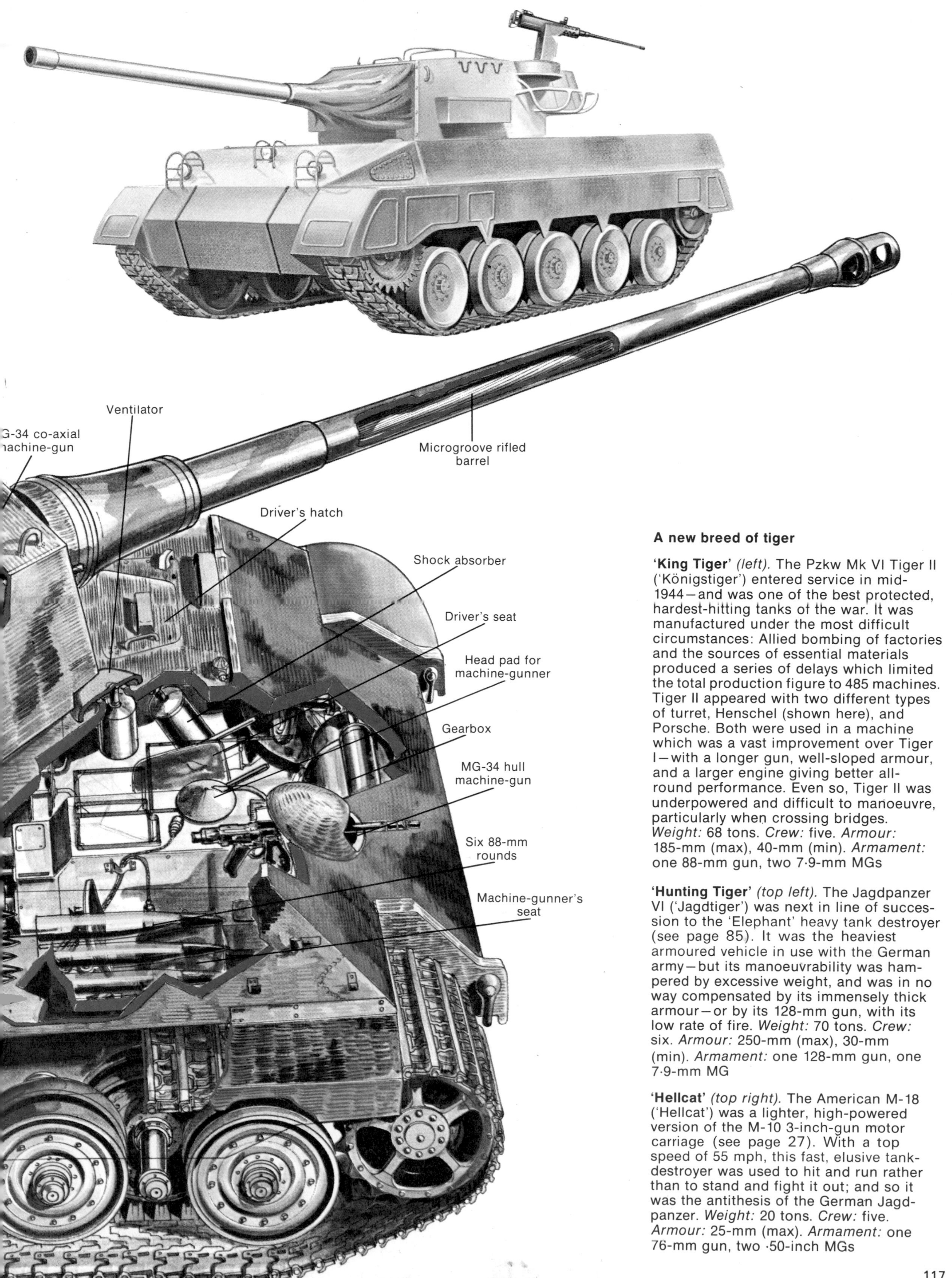

A new breed of tiger

'King Tiger' *(left).* The Pzkw Mk VI Tiger II ('Königstiger') entered service in mid-1944—and was one of the best protected, hardest-hitting tanks of the war. It was manufactured under the most difficult circumstances: Allied bombing of factories and the sources of essential materials produced a series of delays which limited the total production figure to 485 machines. Tiger II appeared with two different types of turret, Henschel (shown here), and Porsche. Both were used in a machine which was a vast improvement over Tiger I—with a longer gun, well-sloped armour, and a larger engine giving better all-round performance. Even so, Tiger II was underpowered and difficult to manoeuvre, particularly when crossing bridges. *Weight:* 68 tons. *Crew:* five. *Armour:* 185-mm (max), 40-mm (min). *Armament:* one 88-mm gun, two 7·9-mm MGs

'Hunting Tiger' *(top left).* The Jagdpanzer VI ('Jagdtiger') was next in line of succession to the 'Elephant' heavy tank destroyer (see page 85). It was the heaviest armoured vehicle in use with the German army—but its manoeuvrability was hampered by excessive weight, and was in no way compensated by its immensely thick armour—or by its 128-mm gun, with its low rate of fire. *Weight:* 70 tons. *Crew:* six. *Armour:* 250-mm (max), 30-mm (min). *Armament:* one 128-mm gun, one 7·9-mm MG

'Hellcat' *(top right).* The American M-18 ('Hellcat') was a lighter, high-powered version of the M-10 3-inch-gun motor carriage (see page 27). With a top speed of 55 mph, this fast, elusive tank-destroyer was used to hit and run rather than to stand and fight it out; and so it was the antithesis of the German Jagdpanzer. *Weight:* 20 tons. *Crew:* five. *Armour:* 25-mm (max). *Armament:* one 76-mm gun, two ·50-inch MGs

The Allied Juggernaut

After the earlier designs of the Grant and Lee tanks—which had themselves performed invaluable services with 8th Army in early 1942—the main American and Empire battle tank came to be the Sherman. Its mass delivery to the Allied armies in North Africa and southern Europe was the result of an unprecedented feat of production. In 1941, American factories turned out 14,000 Shermans; in 1943, this rose to 21,000. And these numbers alone, matched by the virtues of mechanical reliability, gave the Sherman a very significant counter to the German gun and armour superiority. Solidly armoured, formidably armed, this model's most extraordinary feature was its Chrysler engine, built up from five 25-hp truck engines. *Max speed:* 23 mph. *Range:* 80 miles in average conditions. *Crew:* five. *Weight:* 71,900 lb. *Engine:* Chrysler model A57 (30-cylinder, 460-BHP). *Armament:* one 75-mm M3 gun, one ·30-inch machine-gun in hull, one ·50-inch machine-gun on flexible mounting

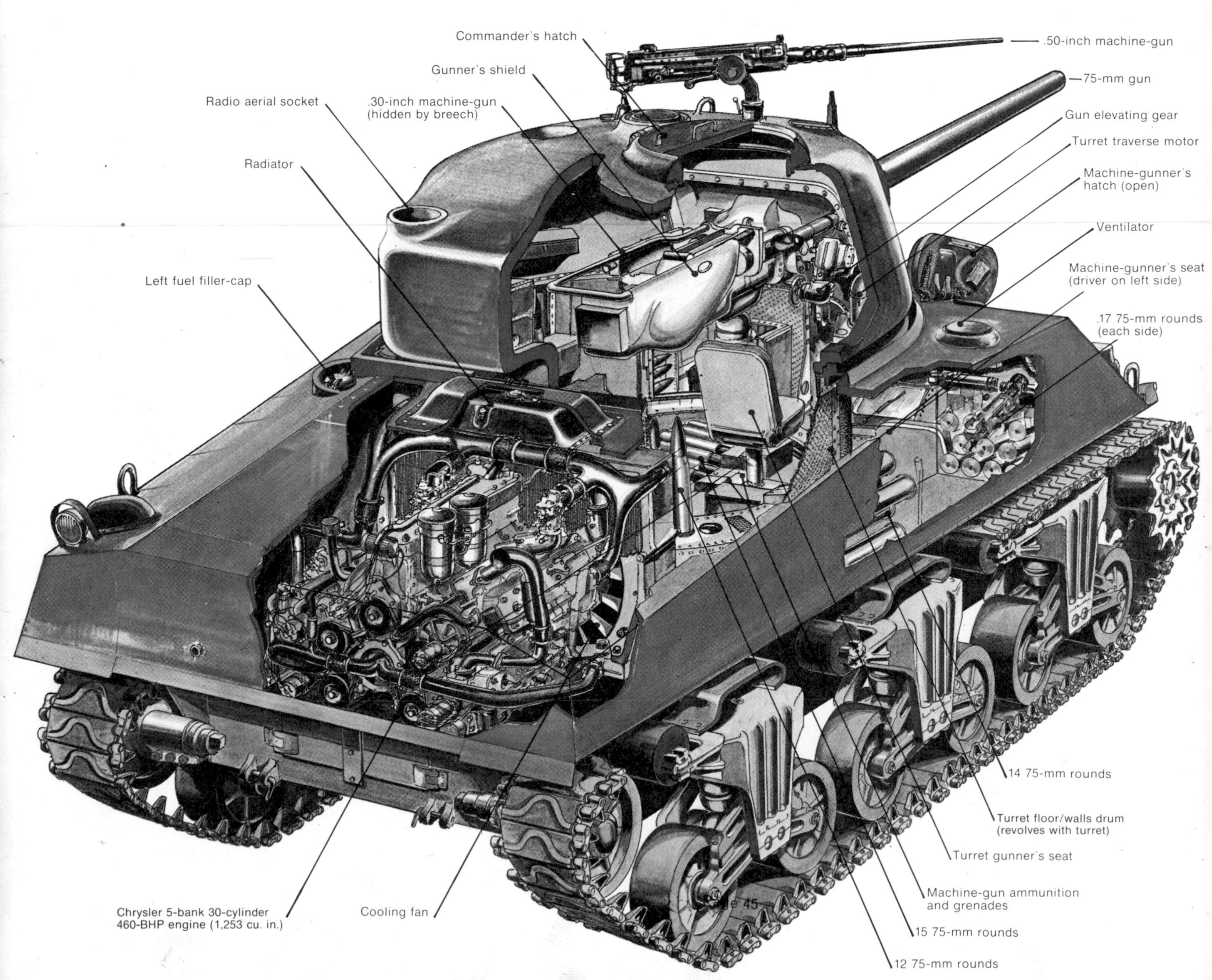

THE V-1

Germany and Britain, June 1943/July 1944 *John Vader*

In late 1943 the rumours of a German 'secret weapon' became a reality. RAF photographs and spy reports clearly revealed the existence of launching ramps on the Channel coast aimed at London – and German plans to launch a flying-bomb blitz against England. London's 'Baby Blitz' duly began in June 1944, one week after D-Day, and casualties in the capital were serious – but had the 'doodlebugs' been launched against England six months earlier, D-Day might have had to be postponed indefinitely. *Above:* AA guns on the British south coast send up a barrage against an incoming V-1

During the war there were always threatening rumours of 'secret weapons' that were about to be used, some dreamed up by inventive pranksters and others based on news of factual weapons and equipment that did eventually appear in one camp or the other. Even the most far-fetched rumours suggested a new kind of violence to add to the psychological strain on both civilians and servicemen.

As the German march of victory stumbled to a halt, Hitler provided more funds, raw materials, and manpower for his scientists, who had made remarkable advances in the development of a variety of secret projects – jet- and rocket-propelled aircraft, improved gun sights, air-to-air rockets, giant mortars, and two particularly frightening weapons: a winged but pilotless jet-propelled flying bomb that would carry almost a ton of high explosive to a target 150 miles away, and a titanic wingless rocket.

To professional soldiers these two weapons offered certain possibilities in strategic warfare. To Hitler they were Reprisal Weapons – *Vergeltungswaffen*; V-1 and V-2 – and to satisfy his mad desire to smash London they were designed to encompass the city within their flight range.

Some information about German weapon development was known before the war, and in the autumn of 1939 references to long-range weapons of various kinds began to appear in British Intelligence reports. In the spring of 1943 General Ismay sent the Prime Minister a memorandum on the subject:

'The Chiefs-of-Staff feel that you should be made aware of reports of German experiments with long-range rockets. The fact that five reports have been received since the end of 1942 indicates a foundation of fact even if details are inaccurate . . . no time should be lost in establishing the facts and in devising countermeasures . . . suggest you should appoint one man . . . Mr Duncan Sandys to direct investigations. It is not considered desirable to inform the public at this stage, when the evidence is so intangible.'

Churchill soon received reports from Sandys, who had received additional information which confirmed that development work on heavy rockets, jet-propelled aircraft, and airborne rocket torpedoes was being carried out around Peenemünde, on the German Baltic coast, and that experimental establishments appeared to be in the coastal region of north-west France. Aerial photographs showed that the Germans were pressing on as quickly as possible and that firings were taking place at Peenemünde. Sandys' report to the Prime Minister on June 28, 1943, indicated that more was being discovered about the large rockets than about flying bombs or the very long-range guns that were also under construction: 'It is desirable that the projected bombing attack upon this establishment should be proceeded with as soon as possible,' he advised the Prime Minister. The Home Office prepared plans to evacuate schoolchildren

Fox Photos

Hitler orders: 'Concentrate on London!'

and pregnant mothers, and more Morrison table shelters were moved into London.

Like many other opportunities that might have enabled Germany to win the war, but came too late, the flying bomb was one of the most spectacular and, had it been developed early enough and produced in large numbers, should certainly have held up the invasion for many months. Fortunately there were enough cloudless days for aircraft to photograph Peenemünde on their routine reconnaissance flights to Baltic ports. Fortunately too there were eagle-eyed, intelligent photographic interpreters such as WAAF Flight-Officer Constance Babington Smith, who spotted on the prints a tiny aircraft on a ramp and a set of rails ending pointlessly at the sea. And most fortunately there were do-it-yourself agents in France like Michel Hollard who, when he heard that the Germans were using large quantities of concrete in a job of unusual construction near Rouen, went there and worked on the site himself, observing a ski-shaped building and also a ramp: his compass indicated that the ramp stretched forward in the general direction of London. With other agents, Hollard bicycled around northern France and discovered many more of the mysterious sites and actually got a plan of the Bois Carré site.

Collecting the evidence

Naturally this information impressed the Air Ministry. On the night of August 17, 1943, Pathfinder aircraft dropped marker flares at aiming points for nearly 600 RAF bombers that raided Peenemünde. Many scientists and technicians, including the chief scientist in charge, General von Chamier-Glisezenski, were killed and dozens of assembly shops and laboratories were destroyed. German night-fighters caught up with the bombers as they flew home and shot down 41. However, as a result of the raid the Germans concentrated their main rocket factory in the Harz Mountains and carried out firing experiments in Poland. In September 1943, the head of the Air Ministry's Scientific Intelligence Branch, Dr R. V. Jones, reported that 'although Hitler would press the rockets into service at the earliest possible moment, that moment is probably still some months ahead. It is probable that the German Air Force has also been developing a pilotless aircraft for long-range bombardment in competition with the rocket, and it is very possible that the aircraft will arrive first'. And from Mr Sandys: 'There is evidence that the enemy is considering using pilotless aircraft as a means of delivering bombs on London. The countermeasures should be the same as for the long-range rocket, namely, the destruction by bombing of the sources of manufacture and of the sites or airfields from which they are launched.'

The politicans were vague about what was being prepared on sites that varied in shape and construction; but by December 14 Air Marshal Bottomley, the Deputy Chief of the Air Staff, reported: 'Evidence is accumulating that the "ski sites" are designed to launch pilotless aircraft . . . 69 confirmed by photographic reconnaissance . . . launching points on the sites in the Pas-de-Calais and Somme-Seine areas are oriented on London and those on some of the sites in the Cherbourg area on Bristol.'

Lord Cherwell informed Churchill that in his view the bombardment would not begin before April 1944. Not more than 100 missiles a day would be dispatched, of which about 25 would get within 10 miles of the aiming point, and as this would produce 50 to 100 casualties he deprecated evacuation moves. He discounted the probability of the use of large rockets because of the high cost of man-hours that would be consumed in building them. He must also have discounted Hitler's madness and desperation.

In December 1943 the strange ski sites were heavily attacked when bombers dropped 3,000 tons of bombs among them. Between January and June 12, 1944, another 2,000 tons had been dropped in a variety of attacks by aircraft which included high-level bombers, rocket-firing Hurricanes, and Spitfires equipped with 500-pound bombs. Many of these sorties were wasted, as the Germans were quick to realise that obvious sites would be easily identified: instead, they built modified sites which were carefully camouflaged, and pre-fabricated buildings which could be erected when the sites became operational.

A special German army unit, the 155th Flakregiment (W), was formed and trained to handle the flying bomb, which was primarily a development of the Argus (engines) and Fieseler (aircraft) companies, sponsored by the German Air Ministry. The FZG-76 (known as the V-1, 'doodle-bug', 'buzz-bomb', or 'cherry stone') was 25 feet long with a wing span of 16 feet, and weighed about 2 tons with a full load of fuel and a warhead of about 2,000 pounds. It could be launched from a catapult ramp or from a modified Heinkel 111 bomber. The pulse-jet power unit incorporated an Argus duct; the fuel was low-grade aviation spirit. A Colonel Wachtel was given command of the new unit, which came under the administration of Lieutenant-General Erich Heinemann's 66th Corps, formed as a special V-weapons branch.

The first V-bomb barrage

After many delays caused by the Allied bombing, Wachtel reported to Heinemann at the end of May 1944 that there were over 50 sites almost ready for launching flying bombs. On D-Day, June 6, Heinemann ordered Wachtel to prepare for an immediate offensive with the V-1. Although there were 70 to 80 modified sites structurally ready north and east of the Seine, only 55 were fitted with launching rails. There was a shortage of safety equipment and the men of the Flakregiment needed further training. And although Wachtel was ordered to start the offensive on June 12, none could be fired until the following day. At midnight the German heavy guns on the French coast shelled Maidstone and Folkestone and a spotter plane was ordered to fly to London to observe the blasts of the first flying bombs to crash on the city.

At 0415 hours on the morning of June 13, the shelling stopped; the spotter plane had already been shot down in flames near Barking. A few minutes later a member of the Royal Observation Corps stationed in Kent heard a peculiar 'swishing sound' and, looking up, saw the bright yellow glow at the rear of an aircraft he identified as a flying bomb. He immediately alerted the defences by telephone, using their code-word, 'Diver'.

The first flying bomb to cross the English coast flew on until the Argus cut-out made its pulsating bangs, and when these stopped the missile glided down in silence until it exploded at the village of Swanscombe, between Dartford and Gravesend, 20 miles east of the Tower Bridge. A second V-1 fell at Cuckfield, a third at Bethnal Green in Greater London, a fourth at Sevenoaks. The only casualties were six people killed at Bethnal Green.

Of ten missiles launched that day, these were the only four that managed to get across the Channel. Of the other six, four crashed on take-off and two disappeared into the sea. If the 70 or 80 sites had been operational then south-east England and London could have been smitten with at least 400 tons of bombs on the first day.

Then there was a respite for three days while the embarrassed Heinemann ordered the 55 sites to be properly tested and made fully operational under their elaborate camouflage. Hitler's Reprisal Weapons were too late to interfere with Operation Overlord, but the threat to London was enormous and the defence plans for the city were rapidly reviewed.

Coping with the V-1s

With such little information available it was very difficult to know how to cope with a flying bomb that no one had seen fly; its speed and flying height were unknown. Apart from knocking them to pieces on the ground at their bases the only way to stop these winged missiles was to shoot them down with fighters and anti-aircraft guns, and to string barrage balloons across the courses they would take as they headed for London. Shooting them down over London only meant that they exploded anyway and the mixture of anti-aircraft fire and fighter aircraft was too dangerous and inhibiting for the pilots. The planning of the defences required new ideas and methods.

Attacking them at their bases, the RAF and USAAF had dropped very few bombs on the modified sites – they continued to attack what they still believed to be supply sites but which had actually been abandoned. The modified sites where the 155th Flakregiment operated were ignored at this period in June, apart from aerial reconnaissance of the main areas around Bois Carré, Nucourt, and Saint-Leu-d'Esserent.

In Britain, the defence against the flying

By the end of June, 2,000 V-1s had been launched on England . . .

bombs was placed in charge of a capable Air Marshal, R. M. (later, Sir Roderic) Hill, a Battle of Britain fighter pilot. As commander of the Air Defence of Great Britain he controlled the movements of the Anti-Aircraft Command (whose head was Lieutenant-General Sir Frederick Pile) and Air Vice-Marshal W. C. C. Gell's Balloon Command. When the operational height of the V-1 was found to be between 2,000 and 3,000 feet, the gunners were in a difficult position: the height was too low for the heavy guns and too high for the light guns. The missiles' speeds were high: from 340 mph crossing the coast to over 400 mph as they approached London. Yet there were several aircraft that could catch it and pass it, particularly if they had some height so they could pick up speed quickly in a dive: the Spitfire XIV, Mustang III, Tempest V, and the Mosquito night-fighter were all fast enough—but they could not chase a V-1 too far over England before running into the areas allocated to the gunners.

No other target but London

The first real test of the existing defences came on June 15, when Heinemann again ordered Colonel Wachtel to re-commence the attack. The catapults at 55 sites flew off 244 missiles against London within 24 hours. Of these, 144 crossed the coast of south-east England and 73 fell in the Greater London area, two-thirds of them exploding south of the Thames. Some 100 missiles failed to cross the Channel: 45 of them crashed soon after launching, wrecking nine sites; and in a French village where one crashed ten civilians were killed.

Heinemann was at Wachtel's HQ bunker when the catapulting began, and stayed to listen to the spotter aircraft pilot's radio report that the glow in the target area was 'brighter than he had ever seen after conventional air attacks by the IX Air Corps'. The German High Command announced the attack over the radio, saying that 'southern England and the London area were bombarded with very high-explosive missiles of novel design during last night and this morning'. On Dr Goebbels' order the word 'revenge' was not used.

On June 17 the British Chiefs-of-Staff and Tedder, Hill, and Pile attended a meeting with Churchill to discuss the new defence requirements: these necessarily varied from the earlier plan, when only a few ski sites were regarded as points of enemy activity. Hill and Pile were directed to counter the attack with reinforcement of the defences and effective deployment of the guns, aircraft, and balloons, and to General Eisenhower was sent a request 'for all possible measures to neutralise the supply and launching sites subject to no interference with the essential requirements of the Battle of France'.

Also on June 17 Hitler flew to northern France to congratulate Heinemann and Wachtel. He forbade the regiment to aim the 'cherry stone', as he called the missile, at any other target but London and readily agreed to order an immediate increase in the production of the weapon. The following day a flying bomb destroyed the Guards Chapel of Wellington Barracks, a few hundred yards from Buckingham Palace. It was hit during a morning service and 121 men, women, and children were killed and 68 injured. Also on this day the 500th V-1 left its launching ramp.

Eisenhower readily ordered that the V-weapon bases (code-named 'Crossbow') should be second only in priority to 'the urgent requirements of battle'. However, the heavy air offensive against the German oil industry did not slacken to any degree because of V-site attacks which were, in most cases, quite useless, since the old supply sites were again the target. Fortunately, Nucourt and Saint-Leu-d'Esserent were identified as V-1 store depots and heavily attacked by the US 8th Air Force during the last week in June. In the first week of July the RAF made two attacks on the heavily defended mushroom caves of Saint-Leu-d'Esserent. In the first attack 617 Squadron dropped the 12,000-pound 'Tallboy' bombs: but the limestone roof of the caves held.

Much to Hitler's chagrin, Eisenhower did not order an invasion of the Dieppe area in order to chase through the Pas-de-Calais after V-1 bases—even if it were possible to mount such an invasion at short notice. The Germans did, however, benefit greatly from the deployment of Allied bombers from other activities more closely connected to the battle being fought on the ground. The Führer again underestimated the British determination to put up with hardship and refusal to be coerced into making a rash move. Hitler was jubilant that England was under fire again and reported to be suffering more than it did during the Blitz. He described how the V-1 attacks were 'tying down hundreds of enemy aircraft . . . and bringing vital relief to the Fatherland and to the battlefields in the West'. He also seemed to be impressed by the economy of the V-1: 'It needs no fuel for a return flight!' he boasted.

By June 29, 2,000 flying bombs had been launched against England.

Meanwhile the defenders south of London changed their formation when they found that both the guns and the fighters were restricted. The solution was to place the guns in a belt along the coast from Newhaven to St Margaret's Bay. They would have an unrestricted field of fire and their shells could explode harmlessly out to sea instead of over towns and villages. New proximity-fuse shells would help to overcome the deficiency of the heavy guns when firing at the low-flying missiles, and radar experts decided that their equipment would work better on the coast than inland.

This positioning too gave the fighters a better chance to catch their quarry on the run from the coast to the North Downs where the balloons hung their wire tentacles, floating in thick bunches between Limpsfield and Cobham. Some 370 flying bombs out of an estimated 1,000 launched had reached London up to June 23. But by June 28 nearly 800 guns of all calibre were in readiness and 1,000 balloons were elevated. The fighter pilots found that it was too dangerous to shoot down a V-1 from too close behind and that the safe distance was not less than 200 yards. The best method was to allow the missile to fly past on one side, then fire a deflection shot once it was far enough away. Some pilots, particularly if out of ammunition or with jammed guns, placed a wing tip under the wing tip of the V-1, tumbling it off course by quickly banking away. Another simple method of spoiling its flight was to fly in front of it and allow the slipstream to unbalance it so much that it would spin out of control.

120 flying bombs a day

While the Germans maintained their launching rate of 100 a day the continuation of V-site bombing was an essential part of the defence. Towards the end of June, over 40% of the Allied bomber effort from Britain was directed against Crossbow targets—despite objections from some Allied commanders who wanted more strategic air operations to be flown over Germany. Despite the bombing of the V-sites and supply centres, an average of almost 120 flying bombs a day were launched in the first week of July. After the first two weeks of bombing, some 1,769 people had been killed and in the Strand the Air Ministry itself was hit and 198 people killed. On July 1 a flying bomb crashed in Chelsea, killing 124; four days later the total death roll was 2,500. Reprisals against German towns and villages were considered but such reprisals were not likely to ease the situation. Moreover, Eisenhower was opposed to this kind of retaliation.

By July 19 there were 1,600 guns and a couple of hundred rocket-projectiles in the anti-aircraft belt and there were hundreds more balloons holding up cable. The gunners and fighter pilots were accounting for more and more flying bombs: by the end of the month the figures were beginning to show a marked upward trend.

Hitler's Reprisal Weapons were missiles of terror aimed at London, where some war production fell because of time lost during raids and the loss of killed and injured workers. Moreover, the Allied air forces were distracted from their main objectives in tactical support of the armies. But it could have been much worse, as General Eisenhower suggested in *Crusade in Europe*: 'It seemed likely that if the German had succeeded in perfecting and using these new weapons six months earlier than he did, our invasion of Europe would have proved exceedingly difficult, perhaps impossible. I feel sure that if they had succeeded in using these weapons over a six-month period, and particularly if they had made the Portsmouth-Southampton area one of their principal targets, "Overlord" may have been written off.'

Birth of the missile age: 'Doodle-bug' and rocket-bomb

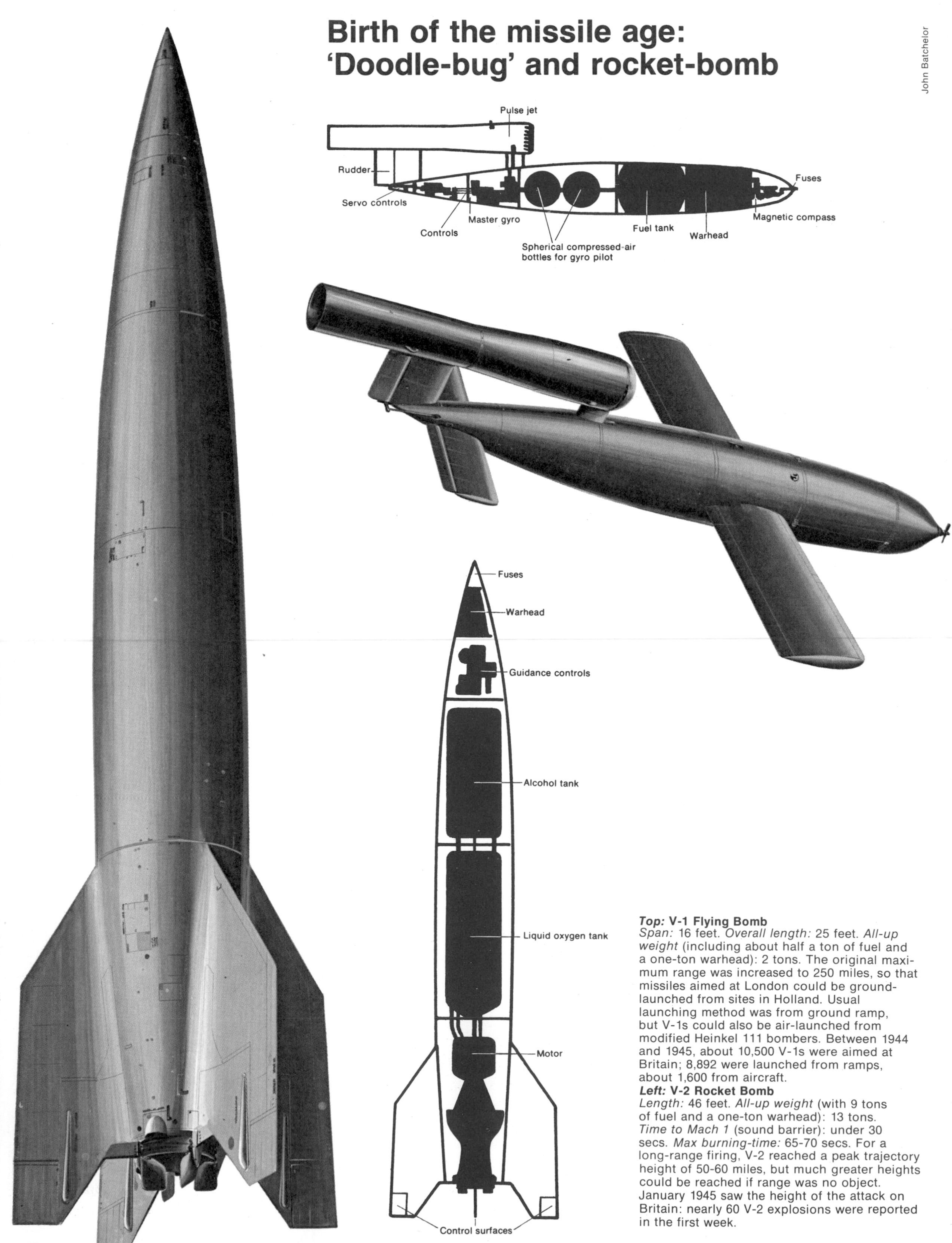

John Batchelor

***Top:* V-1 Flying Bomb**
Span: 16 feet. *Overall length:* 25 feet. *All-up weight* (including about half a ton of fuel and a one-ton warhead): 2 tons. The original maximum range was increased to 250 miles, so that missiles aimed at London could be ground-launched from sites in Holland. Usual launching method was from ground ramp, but V-1s could also be air-launched from modified Heinkel 111 bombers. Between 1944 and 1945, about 10,500 V-1s were aimed at Britain; 8,892 were launched from ramps, about 1,600 from aircraft.
***Left:* V-2 Rocket Bomb**
Length: 46 feet. *All-up weight* (with 9 tons of fuel and a one-ton warhead): 13 tons. *Time to Mach 1* (sound barrier): under 30 secs. *Max burning-time:* 65-70 secs. For a long-range firing, V-2 reached a peak trajectory height of 50-60 miles, but much greater heights could be reached if range was no object. January 1945 saw the height of the attack on Britain: nearly 60 V-2 explosions were reported in the first week.

Bibliothek für Zeitgeschichte

V-1 could be carried to the launching ramp on a simple trolley due to its convenient size (for scale see man)

Imperial War Museum

But V-2 was a far bigger affair: a special vehicle, the *Meillerwagen,* was devised to carry it to the launching pad

Imperial War Museum

Here the *Meillerwagen* has erected a V-2 halfway to its launching position

FIGHTING THE FLYING-BOMB MENACE

Flying straight and level—as was usually the case when it crossed the coast—V-1 was a small, fast-moving target for the AA guns and the fighters of the RAF. Once contact was made by the latter, there was a choice between tipping the missile over, or blowing it up with gunfire. Both were effective—but there was no possible way of stopping the deadly, invisible plunge of the V-2 rockets

1. Target sighted: the ominous, flying-dagger shape of the V-1
2. Interception: a Spitfire closes in on its target
3. The hard way: a Spitfire tips over a V-1 with its wing-tip
4. Orthodox: camera-gun film shows destruction by gunfire
5. When the auto-pilot failed: a crashing V-1's track
6. But many got through: a V-1 bomb site in London

1

Imperial War Museum

2

Imperial War Museum

3

4

Imperial War Museum

5

Imperial War Museum

US Air Force

6

Mirrorpic

BATTLE OF THE BULGE: THE LAST GASP

Belgium, December 1944

Peter Elstob

Few of the British troops preparing to celebrate Christmas 1944 in Brussels attached much importance to what seemed like a minor German counteroffensive which the Americans would extinguish quickly. But soon it was realised that the Germans were driving hard for Brussels, and that little stood in their way except one brigade—hastily re-equipped with the tanks it had turned in for scrap. Peter Elstob—whose unit was part of this 'death-or-glory' brigade—describes the skirmish which halted the last desperate German thrust. *Right:* Men of 5th Bde Guards Armd. Div. watch for German paratroops in a battle-weary Sherman tank rescued from the scrap heap

After six months of continual use the tanks of the British 29th Armoured Brigade needed replacing, and as there was a lull between offensives on 21st Army Group's front in early December 1944, the three armoured regiments of the brigade, the 23rd Hussars, the 3rd Royal Tank Regiment, and the 2nd Fife and Forfar Yeomanry, were ordered to drive to Armoured Replacement Group in Brussels and turn their Shermans in for scrap. They were to be re-equipped with the new, heavier-armoured Comets, low-slung, fast, armed with a high-velocity 77-mm gun and said to be a match for the Germans' second best Panzer—or anyway their third best.

But the Comets had not yet arrived and the tankmen happily went into civilian billets around Ypres and started to make preparations for an unexpected merry Christmas. Leave was generous and two days after coming out of the line many of these men were watching the exciting performance by Errol Flynn as Robin Hood when a V-2, part of the opening of the Ardennes offensive, landed on the cinema. It killed twice as many British servicemen as were going to die in the Battle of the Bulge.

On that same day Field-Marshal Montgomery, having completed plans for his next offensive, the battle of the Rhineland, was playing a round of golf with Dai Rees at the Eindhoven Golf Club. He too was looking forward to Christmas, having got permission from his commanding officer to spend it in England. A message brought out to him on the fairway about the surprise German attack put paid to the golf game and the leave. Within minutes he was flying to his TAC HQ reflecting, among other things, that the only available reserve in 21st Army Group was 30th Corps' 29th Armoured Brigade—and they had no tanks.

No one in the three armoured regiments took much notice of what was happening some 150 miles away on the US 1st Army front. The only information came from two-day-old situation reports and the BBC news, and anyway the Intelligence experts had said so often that the Germans had very little armour left that it seemed that this could only be a local counteroffensive with which the Americans would quickly deal. The important matter of the moment was to get hold of sufficient food and liquor for the coming festivities.

This air of detachment was shattered in the early hours of Wednesday, December 20, by telephone calls to duty officers ordering them to see that their regiments moved immediately to the International Exhibition grounds in Brussels where they were to sort out their old tanks, put back their wireless sets, get the engines running, draw fuel, rations, and ammunition, and move as fast as possible to battle positions along the Meuse. Their task was to 'deny the enemy the river crossings' from Namur southwards for

US Army

about 30 miles, to Givet in France.

The 29th Armoured Brigade's motor battalion, the 8th Rifle Brigade, which had only just pulled out of the mud and cold of the front line in Holland, was sent on ahead and ordered to hold the bridges with its armoured cars and half-tracks until the tanks came up to it. No one knew how far the German armour had advanced and it must be prepared to run into a hostile column coming the other way. As this was in the American zone no one had any maps, so school atlases were in great demand.

A motley collection of defenders

The motor battalion moved through an alarmed and despondent Brussels—by this time the full menace of the great German attack had made itself felt—and, passing through hastily thrown up road blocks manned by a strange collection of rear area troops, arrived at the Meuse about noon the following day. The bridges were being stoutly held by 'R' Force, a scratch collection of sappers and elderly tank men in worn-out Shermans and veteran armoured cars. There was as yet no sign of the advancing German XLVII Panzer Corps.

At that moment its three Panzer divisions were driving hard for this section of the Meuse, the only part of the 90-mile-long German attack line that was still moving westward, and although great American strength was bearing down towards both flanks of this penetration, nothing yet lay between the point and the Meuse. Leading this attack was a battle group of the Wehrmacht's crack II Panzer Division, and as the British reached their battle positions the Panzers forced a crossing of the next river east, the Ourthe, giving them a practically unopposed run to the Meuse bridge at Dinant.

In Dinant the officer commanding G Company of the Rifle Brigade, Major Noel Bell, MC, co-ordinated the existing defences. A large detachment of the US Air Service Corps—officially non-combatants—and a company of American Military Police put themselves at his disposal, and there was a single platoon of American infantry under an enormous sergeant who was grimly determined 'to do a Horatio' on Dinant bridge. There was also a small force of British sappers who had mined the bridge and were standing by their plungers ready to blow it as soon as the Germans appeared in force on the other side.

Finally, the leader of the local resistance, Captain Jacques de Villenfagne, turned up and in those chaotic and suspicious times nearly got himself taken into custody by asking for supplies of hand grenades and offering to lead night patrols of officers—the more senior the better—forward to find the enemy. His *bona fides* were quickly established and for the next four critical days he moved about the woods and fields he knew so well, keeping tabs on the movement and disposition of the German tanks and guns, calling down artillery concentrations and afterwards happily counting dead Germans.

Just as the shortest day of the year was ending the leading squadron of the 3rd Royal Tank Regiment arrived in Dinant. Overall command passed into the hands of Colonel A. W. Brown, DSO, MC: now the bridge was only to be blown on his personal order. Shortly afterwards the rest of the tanks arrived here—as elsewhere—and by 2000 hours Brigadier R. Harvey, DSO, was able to report to General Horrocks that 29th Armoured Brigade were 'complete on the river line'; the 2nd Fife and Forfar at Namur, the 3rd Royal Tanks at Dinant, and the 23rd Hussars at Givet—about 36 hours after receiving orders 100 miles away. General Horrocks was pleased—although his own reaction to the news of a German army advancing towards Brussels had been to suggest that they were allowed to come on so that he could fight the Battle of Waterloo over again.

Most of Dinant, a small town of narrow streets, is squeezed along the narrow strip of comparatively flat land on the east bank of the Meuse, between the river and steep bluffs. The main approach along which the Germans would come enters Dinant from the south and runs alongside the river—at one point passing through an opening cut out of solid rock. Here a check point was set up and a little further on a necklace of Hawkins mines was placed ready to be pulled quickly across the road should any vehicle refuse to stop. About midnight on December 23 a jeep with US markings crashed through the check point and was blown to bits by the mines, and as the dead occupants wore American greatcoats it was feared that one of war's tragic mistakes had been made; but underneath were found SS uniforms—the men were part of Skorzeny's 'Operation Greif'.

A 'death or glory' operation

Captured German orders for this offensive had stressed the importance of night fighting, so after the first night, when the defence had been concentrated around the bridge, a squadron moved across the river and one tank was put out to cover each approach road. If the Germans attacked in strength, the bridge would be blown and tanks on the wrong side of the river were to hold up the enemy as long as possible and then to place themselves in such a position as to form a road block when they were knocked out. None was to come back.

This was wryly called a 'death or glory' operation but as is so often the case when the worst is expected, nothing happened during the whole of that first night of waiting. Orders were unchanged for the night of December 23/24 but lack of sleep began to tell—so that when the point of the leading German armoured column, probing forward to test resistance, did advance up a road towards a hull-down Sherman, its exhausted crew was fast asleep. They were awakened by the noise of straining engines and clanking tracks, and in the confusion the startled sergeant tank commander shouted the order to fire. The equally confused gunner hastily aimed at the lead vehicle, but neglected to bring down the range on his sight, so his high-explosive shell hit a truck further down the German column—which was evidently full of ammunition: the resulting explosion set fire to another truck full of fuel—and successfully stopped the advance.

The Sherman's crew, now a little better organised, then methodically worked down the line, destroying a Mark IV, a half-track, and a scout car before a German self-propelled gun, determinedly pushing past the blazing wreckage, opened fire and forced the Sherman back.

Radio crackled busily on both sides. 'Heavy armoured resistance', the Germans reported; 'We tore him apart!' was the modest British claim, and it was all a great boost for morale, in addition putting the rest of the tank crews on their toes. Quarter of an hour later, another Mark IV was destroyed on a different approach, followed by the destruction of two Panthers moving along yet another back road. The Germans were now fired at whenever they moved, and British artillery west of the Meuse, firing their mediums at maximum range, did such great damage that the II Panzer Division stopped where they were. They had advanced further than anyone else in Army Group B—some 60 miles in eight days and to within sight of the Meuse (just as they had got within sight of Dunkirk in 1940 *and* of the towers of the Kremlin in 1941)—but once again they were to be disappointed.

Almost another Waterloo

Had II Panzer not been held for two critical days at the very outset of the offensive by the US 28th Infantry Division, and then further delayed by the illogical refusal of the defenders of Bastogne to surrender, they would have reached Dinant earlier and would most certainly have formed a bridgehead through which the rest of XLVII Panzer Corps armour would have poured—and General Horrocks might well have had his Battle of Waterloo. As it was, the delays used up their ration of fuel and they found none to capture; the steam thus went out of their advance, and when they were met by the fire of a few British tanks and guns they most uncharacteristically hesitated for a fatal day: fatal because during that day there moved swiftly down from the north the US 2nd Armoured Division of 14,000 men, 3,000 vehicles, and 390 tanks—about a third as many tanks as the Germans were able to commit in all three armies that launched their offensive.

This mighty force swept from north to south between the thin line of British and the weary Germans, and very soon afterwards cab ranks of Lightnings came over and strafed everything that moved—including C Squadron, Third Royal Tank Regiment, who luckily incurred only one casualty.

The British from the Rifle Brigade and the Tanks had a grandstand view of this attack. After the aircraft had reduced almost everything to rubble at least 50 American tanks moved slowly forward as though on parade, their machine-guns blazing continuously against absolutely no opposition. 'There's no doubt,' said one of the British tank commanders wistfully, 'that if you've got the ammunition, that's the way to use it.'

The battered II Panzer Division was ordered to escape and, abandoning its vehicles—many were found undamaged but without a drop of petrol in their tanks—made its way back on foot. But not all, for in the area where the point of the German advance was broken it lost 1,100 prisoners and left behind 900 dead. After the battle was over and the fighting had moved on, the indefatigable Captain de Villenfagne 'went carefully over the battlefield. It was a great cemetery of destroyed vehicles and abandoned equipment half-buried in the snow. I counted 840 vehicles including 40 tanks'. It was a humiliating end to an advance that was to change the whole war on the Western Front.

During the Battle of the Bulge, the Americans lost a total of 733 tanks and tank destroyers. Many of these of course fell to German armour, but many also were destroyed by infantry and artillery anti-tank weapons. A good anti-tank weapon needed three essentials: a high muzzle velocity for good penetration, low silhouette for concealment, and accuracy. Here we show some of the most successful German anti-tank guns

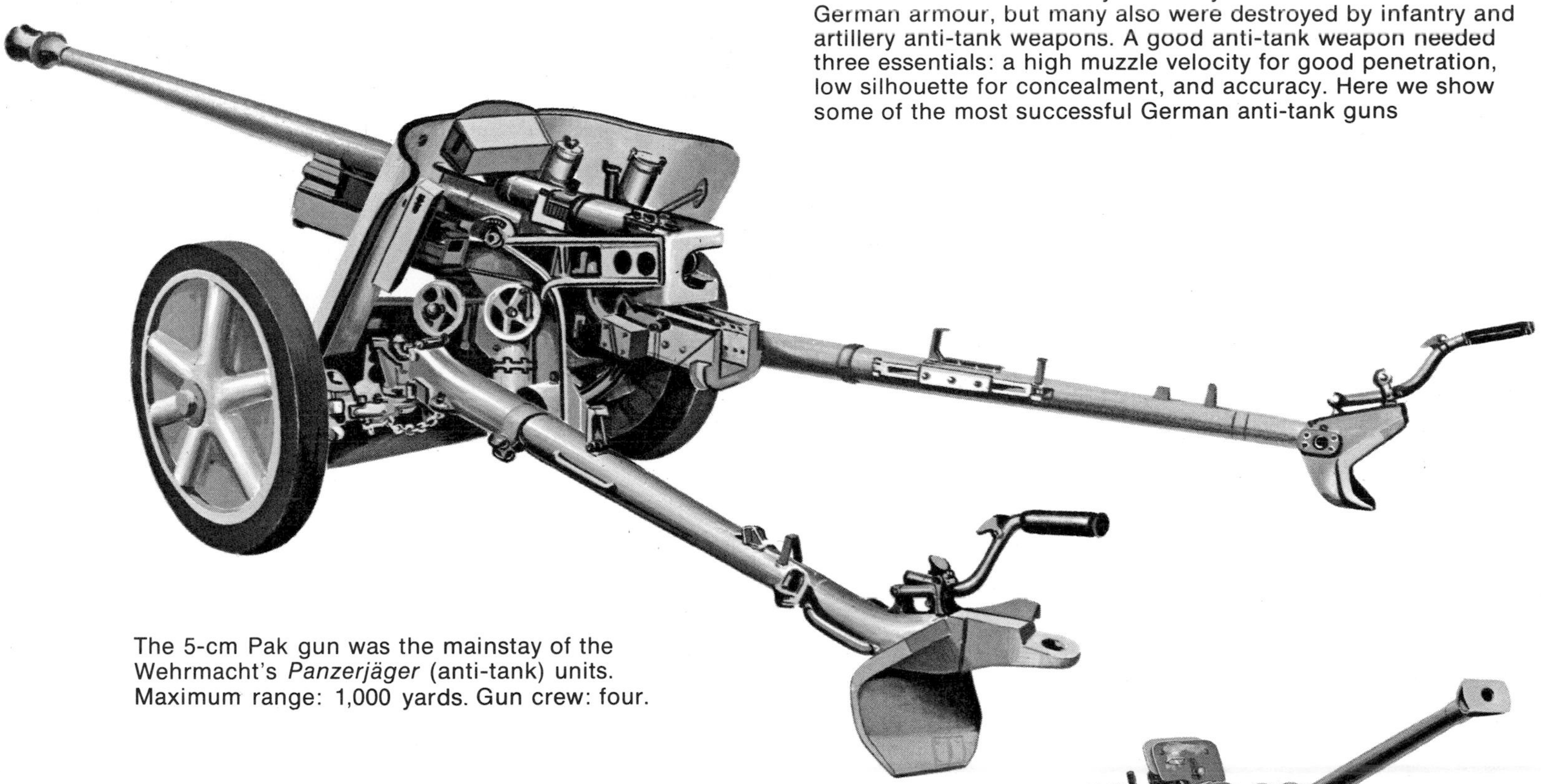

The 5-cm Pak gun was the mainstay of the Wehrmacht's *Panzerjäger* (anti-tank) units. Maximum range: 1,000 yards. Gun crew: four.

PZB 41 (The 'Squeeze' gun): *Bore:* A continuous taper from 28-mm at the breech to 20-mm at the muzzle. *Weight:* 501 lb. *Muzzle velocity:* 4,600 feet per second. *Penetration:* 72-mm of armour at 400 yards, and 49-mm at 800. *Crew:* Two or three. The taper imposed a great strain, but each barrel had a life of 500 rounds

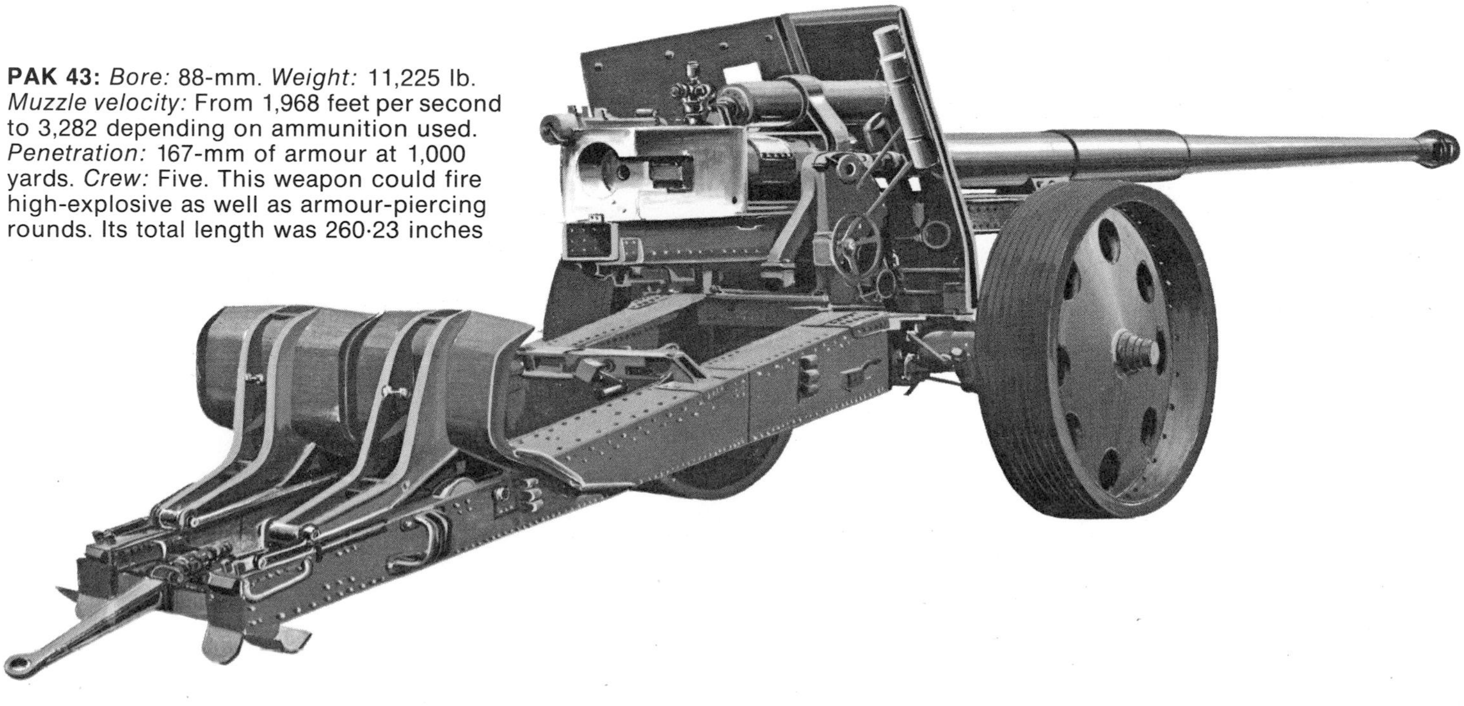

PAK 43: *Bore:* 88-mm. *Weight:* 11,225 lb. *Muzzle velocity:* From 1,968 feet per second to 3,282 depending on ammunition used. *Penetration:* 167-mm of armour at 1,000 yards. *Crew:* Five. This weapon could fire high-explosive as well as armour-piercing rounds. Its total length was 260·23 inches

John Batchelor

British 'Wasp'
The Wasp, a flame-throwing Bren-gun carrier, assisted the infantry attacks across the canals of the Scheldt region. *Crew:* two. *Range:* 117 miles. *Speed:* 20 mph. *Range of flamethrower:* 50/60 yards

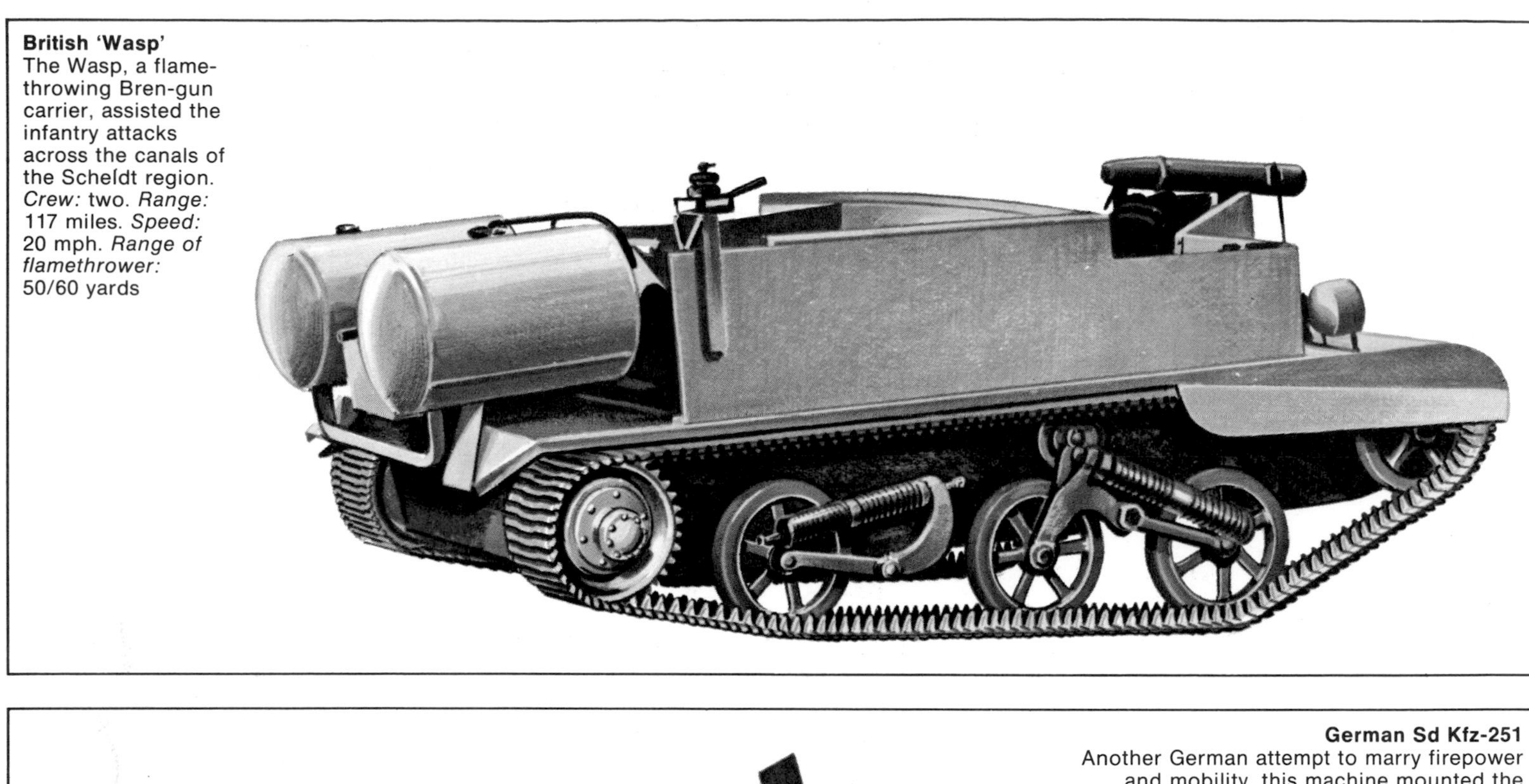

German Sd Kfz-251
Another German attempt to marry firepower and mobility, this machine mounted the hitting-power of a Nebelwerfer rocket-mortar on a half-track hull. *Crew:* three or four. *Range:* 187 miles. *Speed:* 31 mph. *Armament:* six Wurfrahmen rockets, two 7·92-mm machine-guns

US 'Weasel'
The M-29C light carrier proved of great use during the campaign in the flat, soft polder country. It was an amphibian machine, with a remarkably light ground pressure —2 lbs per square foot, which was lighter than the pressure of a man's foot

SCIENCE AT WAR

Germany's Wartime Technology
H. W. Koch

Technical superiority bedevilled by administrative muddle—this too often was the story of Germany's scientific achievements during the war. Possessing a lead in many fields anyway, and very often gaining a lead where they at first had none, German technologists frequently saw their achievements come to nothing through inter-service rivalries and an utter lack of vision at the top

Braun **Messerschmitt** **Heinkel**

It is, unfortunately, still a popular myth that, however preferable it may be to live in a democracy, totalitarian states are the ones which really 'get things done', as opposed to a permanent policy of 'muddling through' in democratic states. The war years should have done a great deal to disprove this myth. A simple comparison of the degree of military and political co-ordination throws into sharp relief the fact that the Axis lacked the thorough co-ordination of the Allies. On the domestic scene detailed studies of pre-war Germany between 1933 and 1939 demonstrate that Nazi social policy was no more than an *ad hoc* improvisation, rather than the product of clearly formulated aims.

The most glaring example—despite considerable achievements—of this lack of centralised effort is supplied by Germany's programme of technological and scientific development, a programme characterised not by organisation but by chaos.

This is even more surprising when one considers that the lack of a central organisation to manage weapon development had already been responsible for a considerable amount of havoc in Germany's First World War effort. The various branches of the services and their sub-branches all employed their own experts who worked independently of one another and negotiated directly with industry outside. With the rapidly growing importance of the rôle of science and technology, particularly in the later stages of the war, the results of this proliferation of effort were disastrous.

However, in the process of reorganising the new *Reichswehr,* some allowances *were* made for lessons learned this way. In 1928, for example, the army organised its *Heereswaffenamt,* the Army Weapons Administration, responsible for planning, developing, testing, procuring, and managing army weapons, munitions, and related equipment. The navy organised a similar institution, as did the Luftwaffe after 1935. Each administration represented a link between the General Staff and industry and was headed by an officer who was himself a science or engineering graduate.

Initially their achievements were substantial. Standardisation was introduced at army as well as at industrial level, and this facilitated mass-production of weapons and ensured their uniformity. Tactical requirements demanded by the General Staff were translated by these offices into technical requirements which were then ultimately contracted out to industry. The 'product' was then tested by the service concerned.

This arrangement was very successful between army and industry, less so in the case of the Luftwaffe and the navy. In the Luftwaffe, requirements were subject to abrupt and frequent vacillations, stemming mainly from the two conflicting concepts of the use of air power. For there was a constant tug-of-war between those who advocated that the German air force should be primarily a strategic weapon and those who believed its major rôle to be tactical, a kind of extended artillery. The argument came to an end with the death of the proponent of the strategic rôle, General Wever, in 1936. After that date the German air force was meant to play primarily a tactical rôle, although Göring believed it could also fulfil a limited strategic function. The Luftwaffe's failure as a strategic weapon became apparent by its performance in the Battle of Britain.

The confusion within the German air force over its purpose was bound to have its repercussions upon Germany's aircraft industry itself. And as the Luftwaffe's requirements changed frequently as well as drastically, the net result was a vast number of prototypes built only to be abandoned. Some firms found themselves on the brink of financial disaster; others, like those of Willy Messerschmitt and Ernst Heinkel, were revolted by the chaos of officialdom and took development projects into their own hand, hoping that the ultimate 'product' would find favour in the eyes of Göring and General Udet, head of the Luftwaffe's construction programme.

Hence, although each branch of the service had now its own administration for planning and developing projects, there was still no superior office to co-ordinate the efforts of all three services at OKW level, the level of the German High Command. Personal rivalries between the service chiefs aggravated matters:

GERMANY'S EARLY MISSILES

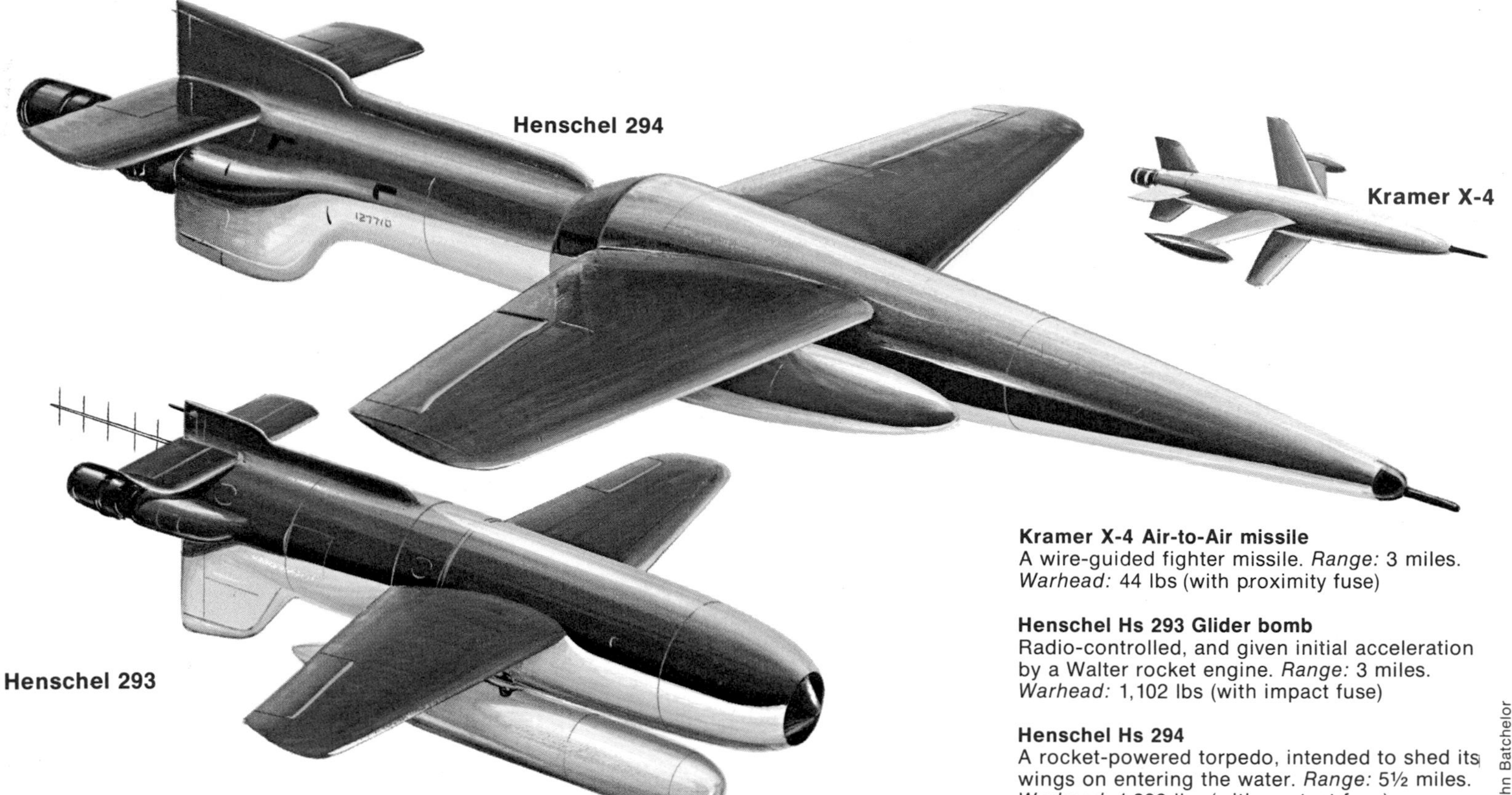

Kramer X-4 Air-to-Air missile
A wire-guided fighter missile. *Range:* 3 miles. *Warhead:* 44 lbs (with proximity fuse)

Henschel Hs 293 Glider bomb
Radio-controlled, and given initial acceleration by a Walter rocket engine. *Range:* 3 miles. *Warhead:* 1,102 lbs (with impact fuse)

Henschel Hs 294
A rocket-powered torpedo, intended to shed its wings on entering the water. *Range:* 5½ miles. *Warhead:* 1,390 lbs (with contact fuse)

each feared that a centre of co-ordination would restrict and interfere with his own domain. Nevertheless, in April 1940 Hitler directed the setting up of an organisation of this type—only to countermand the order on the same day it was issued. Industry feared direct intervention and supervision by the OKW, stressing the point that under its own initiative Germany's war industry (so long as specific requirements were laid down by the armed forces) would work much more energetically and productively. Hitler apparently accepted this argument.

Off to a bad start

Under practical conditions such as these Germany's war effort in the fields of technology and science was bound to start with a serious handicap. But added to this must be other, on the surface less directly relevant factors. The image of the studious but unworldly German professor had been proverbial before the First World War, and indeed the image had still some currency during the interwar years when in times of serious political upheavals, in the face of the dissolution of traditional loyalties, 'one's own subject' provided a much more compelling attraction than the flux of day-to-day politics.

Even Hitler's advent to power at first did very little to change this. Nazi Germany was not a fully totalitarian state, in the sense that those who detested Hitler and all he stood for, in place of opposing the regime openly and taking the risks attached to such opposition, could retreat into the privacy of their own lives and professions.

That the Nazi Party disliked this attitude was made obvious frequently by Hitler and his underlings in their diatribes against the 'intellectuals'. Anti-intellectualism was a pronounced feature of Nazi propaganda. Robert Ley, the head of the DAF (the German Labour Front, the Nazi substitute for trade unions), went on record as saying that 'I prefer a road-sweeper to an academic. A road-sweeper with one sweep of his brush clears hundreds of thousands of germs down the grid, while a scientist is proud when during his lifetime he has discovered a single germ.'

The significance which Hitler attached to scientists in general is illustrated by the appointment of Bernhard Rust, a suspended grammar-school teacher, as Minister of Science and Education. Throughout the war Rust never once submitted a report of the work of his ministry to Hitler, either personally or in writing, nor was he ever asked to do so. The last time that Hitler himself talked to one of Germany's leading scientists was in 1934, when Max Planck pleaded in vain for the reinstatement of his Jewish colleagues.

Hitler's anti-Semitism had—all individual suffering quite apart—catastrophic consequences in Germany's universities where, besides the departments of politics and social sciences, the natural sciences were most seriously affected by the purge of its Jewish members. Between November 1932 and July 1933 the number of university teachers had decreased by 7·5 %. By the end of 1935 a total of 1,684 German university teachers had been dismissed, the majority of them (about 62%) Germans of the Jewish faith. Hitler's purge deprived Germany of many of its most fertile scientific brains. The question has been asked—quite legitimately—how Germany could ever have been expected to harness the resources of atomic power, when the Nazi Party declared Einstein's theory of relativity as invalid because Einstein was a Jew.

Three types of research

Although Hitler's leadership principle was operative in most spheres of life in Germany, the one area in which it did not exist was in that of technological and scientific research. In peacetime there seemed no immediate need for it, but its absence was seriously felt during the war. Throughout its course German scientists and technologists operated, roughly speaking, in three broad groups, not side by side but completely independent of one another.

First, there was the research carried out at the universities of Germany, to which one can add the approximately 30 research institutes of the *Kaiser Wilhelm Gesellschaft* with its institutes for applied physics in Berlin-Dahlem and in Heidelberg. Within that sector there was some attempt at centralisation through the creation of the *Reichsforschungsrat,* the Reich's Research Council, which was organised according to fields of research such as physics and chemistry. It was subject directly to Rust's ministry, but possessed no powers whatsoever to give directives to any of the other bodies, or even to obtain access to and knowledge of their activities.

Second, there was the important sector of industrial research conducted in the laboratories of such industrial combines as Krupp, Röchling, I. G. Farben, AEG, Siemens, and Zeiss. Backed by much greater financial resources than the universities, their

Sturmtiger was a specialised Tiger hull packing a 15-inch mortar; the tank weighed 68 tons. Only 18 were built

The *Nebelwerfer* rocket mortar, apart from being used as static artillery, was often mounted on armoured half-tracks

Ullstein

equipment was bound to be much more advanced than that found for instance in Göttingen or Tübingen. Industrial research concentrated of course more on the *practical* rather than the *theoretical* aspect of a project; it enjoyed full sovereignty, it was not subject to any superior body, and worked by itself, for itself. Exchange of information between university scientists and scientists employed by German industry was actively discouraged – a feature which of course comes from the inherent competitive nature of private industry.

Third, there were the research establishments of the Wehrmacht, which, as we have seen, was divided into service branches, virtually independent of one another. During the course of the war, besides weapon development they acquired very large medical sections which carried out, among other things, research into spotted typhus and into human responses to high atmospheric pressures and sub-zero temperatures. The unfortunate human 'guinea pigs' were in the main concentration-camp inmates. The Wehrmacht's research establishments also operated with ample funds and relatively up-to-date equipment. When at the outbreak of war Hitler issued his famous 'secrecy order', according to which each individual was to know no more than would be absolutely necessary for the accomplishment of a specific task, the result was even greater insulation of each of the three research groups.

But apart from these, there was still a host of others, smaller ones like the research laboratories of the *Reichspost,* the German postal services. Its projects were not restricted merely to those affecting communications, but even included nuclear research, as well as research into the uses of infra-red rays.

Throughout the war, then, there was not one single German agency, let alone one individual, which controlled or even knew of the vast multitude of projects in hand. Knowledge of the full range of these was obtained only after the war by the victorious Allies.

How much the Third Reich thought of its scientists at the outbreak of war is shown by the large-scale call-up of thousands of Germany's leading experts in the field of ultra-high frequency, nuclear physics, chemistry, and engineering – to serve as ordinary soldiers. It was not by any means an uncommon experience for a company commander to have as his batman a private who in civilian life was a fully qualified DSc. Only in response to the turn of the tide of the war against Germany were over 10,000 of them released to serve their country in their professional capacity.

Under these circumstances the actual achievements of German technology and science are all the more remarkable; but these circumstances also account for none of these achievements having been in any way decisive so far as the outcome of the war was concerned.

The anti-tank gun problem

Without doubt the German army's greatest single problem during the war was to find a successful anti-tank weapon which could be used by the individual infantryman. This problem was not immediately apparent. As the German army swept through Poland, Norway, Belgium, the Netherlands and France, the Allied armour encountered could be dealt with by the conventional 37-mm anti-tank gun, though it was definitely inferior to the 47-mm gun taken over from the defunct Czech army.

The surprise came in the autumn of 1941 when Russia's T-34 tank made its first appearance. Against that tank the existing German anti-tank guns were totally inadequate (the German soldier referred to them as *Panzeranklopfgerät,* a device to 'knock on' rather than to 'knock out' a T-34). During the severe winter of 1941/42 the German infantryman in Russia had to rely on the 75-mm self-propelled assault gun or the 88-mm anti-aircraft gun where and whenever available. Frequently he had to rely on his own ingenuity and desperate courage by jumping on to a T-34 and putting it out of action by various means, like pushing a grenade down the tank's gun barrel or attaching a magnetic hollow charge to one of its more vulnerable parts (particularly below the rear of the turret).

During the course of 1942, and from then onwards, new and improved anti-tank guns came into use, culminating in the 88-mm PAK 43L/71. But the problem of providing the individual soldier with a satisfactory weapon – despite the introduction of recoilless weapons like the *Panzerfaust* – was only partially solved.

As the appearance of the T-34 revolutionised anti-tank weapons, it equally revolutionised German tank design. Thus the Panzer V, the Panther, shows an extremely close resemblance in body line to the T-34, while its close-fitting turret did not possess any of the T-34's vulnerable points. A product of the Henschel, Daimler-Benz, and MAN works, the Panther was to become one of Germany's most effective tanks, in spite of Panzer VI, the Tiger, which, though mounting an 88-mm gun against the Panther's 75-mm, was far too slow and cumbersome. In fact the Tiger II, the 'King Tiger' developed by Henschel and Ferdinand Porsche (inventor of the Volkswagen), except for a different size, different turret, and heavier gun, returned to the body line of the Panther.

The jet aircraft problem

In the field of German aviation the serious limitations of the conventional piston-engined aircraft had been recognised by aircraft and engine designers some years before the Second World War. The man to take the first practical step towards introducing jet-propelled aircraft was Professor Ernst Heinkel. On June 20, 1939, the He-176, the world's first jet-propelled aircraft, took to the air. Two weeks later, on July 3, 1939, the He-176 was flown at Peenemünde before a selected group of experts and officers, reaching a speed of approximately 510 mph. The experts were not impressed. General Udet, the First World War fighter ace, felt uneasy at Heinkel's new idea. He had had his misgivings at the introduction of fighter aircraft without an open cockpit—but now one without an airscrew as well was a little too much for him. Heinkel continued on his own initiative, at his own expense, and on April 5, 1941, the twin-engined He-280 was flown

But Heinkel had not been the only one in the field. Since 1938 Professor Willy Messerschmitt had been in the process of designing and constructing a twin-engined jet fighter—the aircraft which was to become the famous Me-262. As with most jet projects of the period, Heinkel's major obstacle was to find a jet engine sufficiently powerful to develop the necessary thrust. But before that had been developed Hitler, expecting a quick peace with Great Britain after the fall of France, ordered the cessation of work on all projects which would not be finished by the end of 1940. This order was cancelled later during the same year, but it still took until July 1942 to develop turbojets powerful enough for the Me-262, which flew under its own jet power for the first time during the same month.

General Udet had in the meantime committed suicide in 1941, but the German Air Ministry was still as conservatively minded as ever. Messerschmitt officials had to stress the Me-262's potentialities as a fighter time and again. Finally, by December 1942, the Air Ministry relented to the extent that it sanctioned a production rate of 20 Me-262s per month to be attained by 1944! Five months later, the General of the Fighters, General Adolf Galland, tested the aircraft himself and was immensely impressed. Here was the answer to the Allied air offensive. Galland persuaded Göring to inspect it. He was equally impressed. However, on Hitler's direct orders no priority was allocated to it, and when he finally did see its performance in December 1943 he ordered it to be developed as a bomber for retaliation against Great Britain. Only under the increasing blows of Bomber Command and the US 8th Air Force did Hitler at last sanction a fighter version in 1944.

Thus a combination of apathy, conservatism, and outright ignorance in Germany's Air Ministry, together with Hitler's typical preference for an offensive weapon when really a defensive one was required, ensured that an aircraft with a speed of 540 mph which could have been in service in 1943 came in only towards the end of 1944.

The Me-262 was not the only German jet operational by 1944. The Arado 234-B *Blitz,* designed by a team headed by Walter Blume, was the first operational jet bomber. During the closing months of the war *Kampfgeschwader* (Bomber Wing) 56 undertook in it, besides reconnaissance missions, the aerial attack upon Remagen bridge after it had fallen intact into American hands.

It was perhaps only fitting that the very man who put Germany's first jet into the air, Ernst Heinkel, was to design, develop, and produce Germany's last. This was the He-162, which, for economy's sake and to facilitate rapid mass production, had its single jet mounted on the fuselage behind the cockpit. The order for the design was given to Heinkel in September 1944; three months later the first prototype flew successfully, and by February 1945 the He-162 was on the production line.

In the final analysis it was one major factor which rendered the introduction of new aircraft and new types of armoured vehicles virtually useless by the summer of 1944: Germany's lack of fuel. Even when in full possession of the Rumanian oilfields at Ploesti, Germany still needed to meet nearly 40% of her fuel requirements with synthetic fuel. The process for extracting fuel from coal had been discovered in the 1920s by Professor Franz Fischer and his assistant Dr Hans Tropesch. The fuel was produced mainly by the Leuna-works at Magdeburg—but concentrated Allied air attacks from May 1944 onwards, together with the loss of the Rumanian oilfields in August 1944, brought about a situation by which in January 1945 only 31% of the Wehrmacht's fuel requirements could be met. In April 1944, some 195,000 tons of fuel had been used by the Luftwaffe alone. One year later only 11,000 tons were still available. On the other hand, in the production of synthetic rubber, *Buna,* Germany's chemical industries mastered the situation

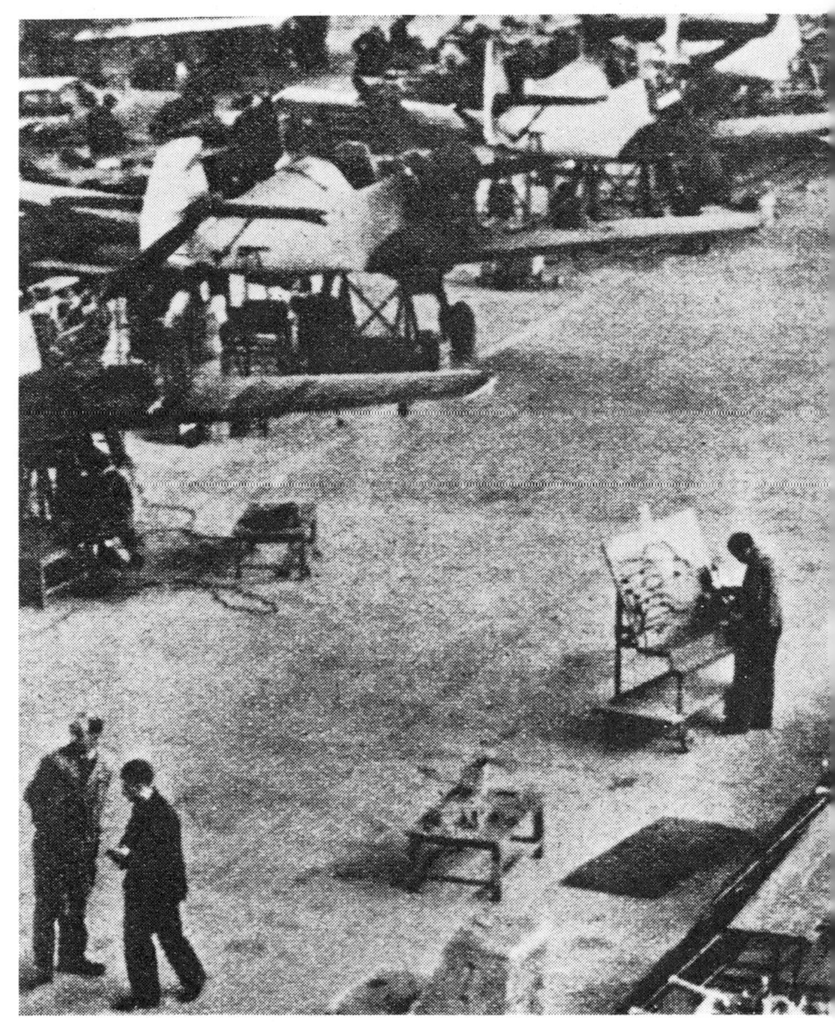

Me-109 fighters on the production line in one of Messerschmitt's aircraft factories. The decision to maintain full-scale

throughout the war, for production was generally in excess of actual consumption.

The U-boat problem

Of all three services, the German navy was worst prepared for a war of global dimensions. Its surface vessels—though some of them were spectacular like the pocket battleships or giants like the *Bismarck*—apart from a commerce-raiding rôle could not seriously challenge Britain's naval strength. That alone was sufficient for the emphasis of the German war effort at sea to lie on the submarine, the U-boat. This is why Germany's technological advances in the naval sphere were found almost exclusively in the further development of the submarine.

On September 1, 1939, Germany had 56 U-boats, 46 of which were in service. Only 22 of these were suitable for use in the Atlantic. In comparison with Germany's submarines of the First World War their operational radius had increased and the vulnerability to depth charges had been reduced. But their underwater speed was much the same as that of the boats of 1917/18, which made them almost stationary. Since a U-boat, because of the lack of oxygen, could run underwater only on electric power supplied from accumulator batteries, it had to surface regularly and sail under the power provided by diesel engines and during that time recharge its batteries. In other words, the submarine was not a submarine at all, but merely a diving boat.

In spite of the immense toll taken of Allied shipping—especially during 1942 up to May 1943—the perfection of radar equipment on Allied vessels and the virtually complete survey of the Atlantic by radar-equipped Allied aircraft left the U-boats with two alternatives: either to be spotted or picked up at night on the radar-screens of aircraft, or to exhaust their batteries below the surface.

Only a very drastic solution could resolve that dilemma. In the first place the 'diving' boat had to become truly a submarine, and in the second while underwater achieve speeds exceeding even those of the convoy protection vessels. To stay under water for a very long period was relatively the easiest step, through the introduction of the *schnorkel,* an invention which cannot, it seems, be attributed to anyone in particular. Ideas of that kind had been floating around in naval circles ever since the end of the First World

production of such trusted designs as the Me-109 meant that many revolutionary weapons were never given their chance

War. The *schnorkel,* essentially an air-pipe extended like the periscope above the surface of the sea, supplied the diesel engines with the necessary oxygen. Consequently, a U-boat could sail underwater with its *schnorkel* extended, close to the surface, under the power of its diesel engines and at the same time recharge its batteries. This did not eliminate location by Allied aircraft, but at least it limited this danger. Nor, of course, did it solve the problem of underwater speed. To meet this, a new type of boat was designed —the Type XXI U-boat, capable of diving to a depth of 430 yards and, with the aid of specially designed electric motors, of reaching an underwater speed of 17·5 knots. Although a total of 120 of these boats was built they came too late to see action.

Far more revolutionary was the introduction of the Walter combustion turbine by Professor Hellmut Walter. Walter had originally worked on the development of aircraft powerplants which would make them independent of the oxygen in the air. Using hydrogen peroxide as well as nitric acid as 'oxygen carriers' he produced liquid oxygen. In essence the Walter system was a closed-circuit turbine activated by the thermal energy produced by the decomposition of a high concentration of hydrogen peroxide. This resulted in the formation of hot gas which under considerable pressure was sufficient to drive the turbine.

The first four U-boats powered by the Walter turbine (Type XVII), each weighing 236 tons, were supplied to the German navy during 1944 and reached an underwater speed of 21 knots. Larger boats were immediately put into production (Type XXVIII) but not completed before the end of the war. Nevertheless the transition from 'diving boat' to real submarine had been made, based on conventional sources of power, before atomic energy had been harnessed for that purpose.

The radar problem

In the field of using radio waves to detect aircraft or vessels over long distances (radar), Great Britain and Germany stood at a similar stage of development at the outbreak of war. In 1938 Germany's *Freya* radar set, operating on the decimetre wave, could pick up a Junkers 52 at a distance of 90 miles. However, it was unable to locate precise heights, and so, to determine distance, height and direction, *Freya* was replaced by the *Würzburg* set, whose range was limited to less than 20 miles. The Luftwaffe, unlike the RAF, failed, until late in 1942, to develop a system of co-ordination which established direct connection between radar, central operational control, and the aircraft in the air—a failure which was one of the root causes of Germany's defeat in the Battle of Britain.

Britain's decisive advance in 1942—the ultra-high-frequency wave—made it possible to construct radar sets small enough to be fitted into aircraft and thus, among other uses, to scan the Atlantic day and night for submarines. From then onwards the Allies regained the initiative in the Battle of the Atlantic.

Only through the forced landing and capture of a British aircraft near Rotterdam early in 1943 did a British set, duly called *Rotterdamgerät,* fall into German hands. The Germans copied it under various names and equipped their night-fighters with it. And the usefulness of radar for artillery ranging in surface vessels was dramatically demonstrated by the *Bismarck's* destruction of the *Hood*—and at Christmas 1943, when at night, at a distance of 14 sea miles, the *Scharnhorst* was sunk by the Royal Navy.

During 1944, on the basis of research carried out by Dr Esau, who already in 1938 had discovered the 4.4-mm wave—a discovery dismissed at the time as unimportant by the German Air Ministry—the *Heidelberg* radar set was developed. With a range of 240 miles the *Heidelberg* set could detect the take-off of RAF bomber squadrons as far away as Norfolk.

The V-weapon problem

The weapons to strike public imagination most impressively, and which were also a serious portent for the future, were Germany's rockets—Hitler's *Vergeltungswaffen,* his weapons of retaliation. As early as October 1939 British intelligence received a rumour that at Peenemünde the German army was experimenting with rockets. The rumour, unverified, was filed away.

But in its substance the rumour was true. Since 1937, on the suggestion of Wernher von Braun and sanctioned in 1938 by the then-Chief of the OKW, General von Brauchitsch, the army under the auspices of the *Heereswaffenamt* had built a testing centre for rockets, with its own laboratories and plants for the production of liquid oxygen (as pioneered by Hellmut Walter). There, under the command of an artillery officer, Dr Walter Dornberger, the army pursued rocket projects which had their origins in the years before 1933. From Hitler's assumption of power onwards work had been progressing systematically. The first rocket aggregate, the A-1, designed by Dornberger, Braun, and others, was tested in the same year—though without the expected success. But a year later, in December 1934, the A-2 was tested and reached a height of nearly 8,000 feet.

In order to go on with the work on a larger scale, the army now needed its own base, one away from urban centres, and Peenemünde seemed an ideal choice. Once the war had started, Dornberger and Braun, like Messerschmitt, faced an OKW reluctant to allocate raw materials to a project which might never become operational. Inter-service rivalries, as usual, played a rôle too. The Luftwaffe (which also had its own testing base at Peenemünde) viewed the army's 'aerobatics' with grave suspicion. Only after the Battle of Britain did the army's rocket project obtain a special priority. After three previous failures, at long last, on October 3, 1942, the first A-4 made its 'maiden flight' along the Baltic coast over a distance of 100 miles. Four months later plans were ready for the mass production of the A-4. By then it had been sufficiently improved to reach a distance of 240 miles, at a speed of 3,270 mph.

In the meantime, what had been once dismissed as a rumour in Britain had been confirmed from foreign labour employed at Peenemünde and verified by aerial photographs. During the night of August 17/18, 1943, the RAF successfully attacked Peenemünde. The net effect was, first, that the entire rocket programme was thrown back for a number of months, and, second, that Hitler's attention shifted to an alternative developed under the auspices of the Luftwaffe—the Fi-103, a flying bomb designed and jointly built by the firms of Fieseler and Argus.

As in the mid-1930s the Luftwaffe had been reluctant to abandon the open cockpit and, later on, the airscrew, so it was now reluctant to abandon its wings. The Fi-103 was a catapult-launched, pilotless aircraft carrying an explosive charge, powered by rocket propulsion, partly remote-controlled. Direction and distance were preset by a small propeller at its nose which at a given speed and predetermined distance would make a specific number of revolutions. When the revolutions were completed, the engine would cut out and the Fi-103 would enter a steep dive toward its target. Hitler was quick to allocate to it the name *Vergeltungswaffe 1,* the V-1. While the A-4 project (which by then had been re-baptised as V-2) was recovering from the RAF attacks on Peenemünde, which had affected the Luftwaffe's base only in so far as it deprived it of some of its foreign labour, Hitler turned his eyes on the V-3, a peculiar weapon invented by Dr Cönders of the Röchling works.

'Busy Lizzie', one of the nicknames of the V-3, was a gun barrel consisting of individual sections, each 12 to 15 feet long, which could extend the barrel to a length of just under 500 feet. On the side of each individual section was a chamber containing an explosive charge which would be ignited automatically the moment the missile, 6-7 feet long and with a diameter of about 10 inches, had passed. As the missile, fired from the end of the barrel, passed successive explosive chambers, each explosion increasing its speed, it left the barrel with a muzzle velocity of 1,700 yards per second and a maximum range of over 100 miles. Two-thirds of the 'pipeline' was to be built into the ground at an angle of 40 to 50 degrees. Five such 'Busy Lizzies' were installed near Mimoyecques in the Pas de Calais to bombard London. But before installation was completed, the Allied air forces had destroyed them (although two shorter versions of this weapon were used against Antwerp and Luxembourg in January and February 1945).

Parallel to the installation of the V-3 went the building of launch sites for the V-1; and, as in the case of V-2 and V-3, Allied bombing seriously retarded their completion. Consequently the first V-1, scheduled to be launched on February 15, 1944, was delayed until June 16, 1944. The V-1, however, could be produced in large quantities, since each V-1 required only a total of 280 manhours as compared with 12,950 hours needed to produce a V-2. Ironically enough, both were cheaper to produce than a conventional fighter aircraft of the type FW-190D, which cost about 500,000 RM each (the V-2 cost only 38,000 RM).

In the meantime the V-2 programme had recovered from its setback. An alternative test site had been selected in Poland, development work was carried out in Upper Austria, while a 'production line' was established in underground tunnels in the Harz mountains. Apart from carrying a larger explosive charge than the V-1, the V-2 had also the advantage of being mobile. Its launch pad could be set up almost everywhere, rocket and pad transported by a special carrier vehicle. It is in this context that the *Reichspost*'s research into infra-red rays proved its worth. With the skies dominated by the Allies during the day, the conspicuous V-2 could only be moved during night-time. The carriers often had to make their way through difficult terrain to sites away from busy town or village centres. To aid drivers in their arduous task their vehicles were equipped with infra-red light equipment.

When, on September 8, 1944, the first V-2 was launched against London, Dornberger and Braun were already working on another project. This was the A-9, a slightly larger version of the V-2 which could reach a distance of 360 miles. This rocket was to carry a pilot in a separable nose-cone and he was to guide it across the Atlantic to the USA. To help provide the necessary power, a three-stage rocket was to be joined to the A-9. Before reaching the target, the pilot in his nose-cone was to blast himself free and then descend by parachute. But this and similar projects were still very much on the drawing board by the spring of 1945.

More immediately feasible seemed to be the *Laffarenz-Projekt*. A U-boat, Type XXI, was to tow three V-2s, each in a special container, across the Atlantic. The containers were provided with special ballast cells, so that at a suitable point off the American coast the cells would be flooded, moving each container into a vertical or angular position and held there by special stabilisers. The rocket fuel would then be pumped from the U-boat into the missiles: then the missiles would be fired. Some of these containers were in fact built at the Baltic port of Elbing late in 1944.

The argument is often encountered in memoirs, such as General Eisenhower's, that had the Germans brought to bear the full brunt of their V-weapons upon Britain three months earlier, the invasion might well not have taken place and that they might even have changed the course of the war. In retrospect all that the historian can say is that we are fortunate that this was not the case, because these three months made the crucial difference which preserved Germany, and with it Europe, from the first experience of the Atom Bomb—at a time when Germany was nowhere near capable of producing it.

When in 1938 Professor Dr Otto Hahn and his collaborator Dr Fritz Strassmann bombarded uranium atoms with neutrons, the uranium atoms divided into lighter barium atoms. At the same time part of the original mass changed into energy—atomic energy. The implications of this led Albert Einstein to conclude, rightly, that the energy produced could be contained and released in a bomb of hitherto unknown destructive power. Of that possibility he informed President Roosevelt.

Hahn's experiment caused enough headlines outside Germany for the *Heereswaffenamt* to ask a number of German physicists to investigate the aspects of atomic power. But with the exception of one man, Germany's physicists did not realise the possibility of building an atomic bomb. This exception was Baron von Ardenne, who had spent only two years as a student at a university. Those two years, however, had been sufficient for him to make a name for himself by inventions in various fields. The laboratory in which he worked belonged to the *Reichspost,* and when he tried to draw attention to the potential inherent in Hahn's discovery his views were dismissed as those of a dilettante. Carl-Friedrich von Weizsäcker of the Kaiser Wilhelm Institute for Physics at Berlin-Dahlem, together with Professor Werner Heisenberg, was of the opinion that it was impossible to build an atomic bomb.

Both Heisenberg and Weizsäcker and their staff, who through 1940 and 1941 had brooded over problems concerning the nature of atomic energy, were shocked when, late in 1941, calculations showed just what precise amount of uranium, U-235, was necessary to build a bomb. Heisenberg immediately visited the Danish physicist Niels Bohr, a sort of 'father figure' to many of Europe's physicists, and suggested that through Bohr's mediation America's physicists—most of them previous colleagues of Heisenberg's, forced into emigration—and Germany's should refrain from building an atomic bomb. Bohr was shocked not by Heisenberg's suggestion, but by the suspicion that the Germans could and would produce an atomic bomb, about which he immediately informed the Americans after he had succeeded in escaping from German-occupied Denmark.

While in the USA a major effort was put behind the atomic project, in Germany the whole affair was treated lethargically. Germany's physicists knew that they could build an atomic reactor and with it, ultimately, bombs. But 1941 and 1942 were still years of great military successes for the Germans, and so projects like the V-1 and the V-2 received priorities simply because they were likely to be operational within a specified period, while Germany's physicists at their most optimistic estimated the time it would take to produce an atomic bomb to be three to four years. That this estimate was more than optimistic is borne out by the American experience, where it took just about that time, but with the mobilisation and concentration of resources of a magnitude which Germany did not possess. So far as the German scientists were concerned, a 'race' for the atomic bomb was just not on.

No match for the Manhattan Project

German scientists concentrated their effort on building a uranium pile which could supply data on the behaviour of neutrons when liberated in a chain reaction. As an atomic chain reaction was bound to release tremendous energies, the reaction in an atomic reactor had to be braked and the energies contained. Now, the 'braking substance' with which the uranium is surrounded can be 'heavy' water or pure carbon (graphite), but in 1940 Professor Bothe of Heidelberg tested graphite for its suitability and concluded, wrongly, that it was unsuitable. This left the Germans dependent on 'heavy' water, which was produced only by the Vemork Plant near Rjukan in Norway.

In February 1943, however, the Vemork Plant was put out of action by Norwegian Commandos sent from Britain, and it took several months before production could be resumed. Added to this came the growing impact of the Allied air offensive, which forced the evacuation of the research centres. More important, with the bombing of the Degussa works at Frankfurt/Main, Germany's uranium production came to a dead halt.

Göring, who in the meantime had realised the importance of atomic power, appointed his own plenipotentiary for nuclear physics, Professor Walter Gerlach. It was a measure of little consequence. At Berlin-Dahlem, Dr Karl Wirtz, one of the few scientists who had remained behind in the bombed capital, still continued to build an atomic reactor—which was ready for its first test when the first Russian tanks rumbled toward Berlin. The test was abandoned, the reactor dismantled and transferred to south-western Germany, to Haigerloch in Württemberg, where most of Germany's nuclear scientists were now concentrated. Though reassembled, the reactor was never tested. The Americans were there first and, much to their surprise, found that their fear of an imminent German atomic bomb was without any foundation.

Without the driving force of a single agency behind them, and themselves more interested in theoretical aspects than in their practical application, Germany's nuclear scientists could not match the purposeful organisation and dynamic drive of the Manhattan Project. But then the lack of organisation and purposeful direction was—with the exception of the actual production of armaments under Speer during the last two years of the war—the most significant characteristic of Germany's technological and scientific war effort.

Chemical Warfare

Technology, 1940/1945

The wartime use of gas and other chemical weapons has never been considered 'civilised', and successive conventions have tried—unsuccessfully—to ban even so much as their manufacture. The use of mustard gas during the First World War (*below*) gave rise to widespread fears of this weapon during the inter-war period; but although both sides stockpiled large numbers of chemical weapons, they were never used, probably through fear of retaliation. **Brian Ford** describes the development of chemical weapons, from the early 'choking' gases to, most terrible of all, the 'nerve' gases

Imperial War Museum

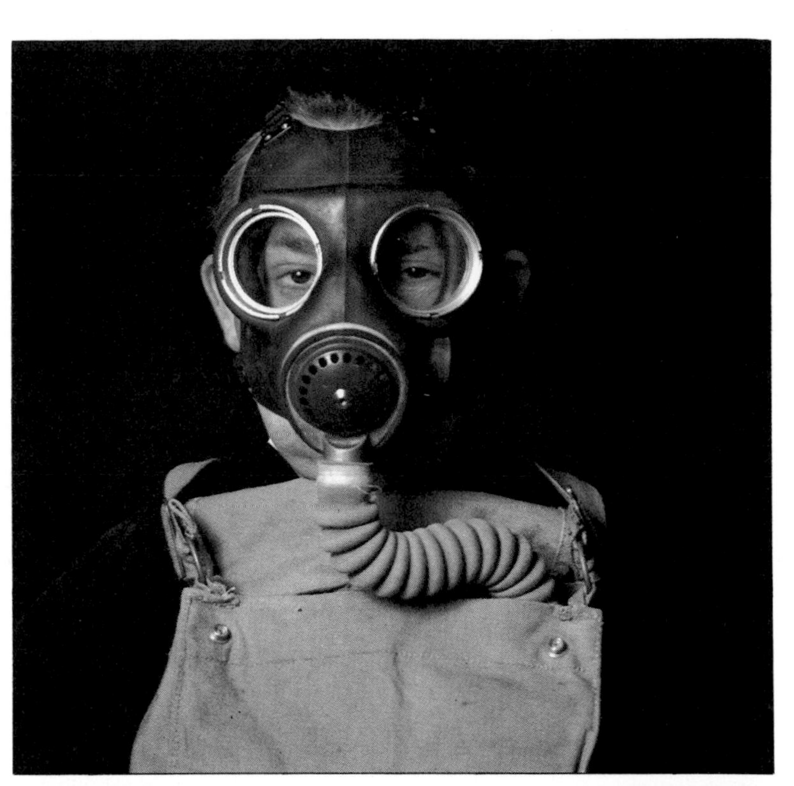

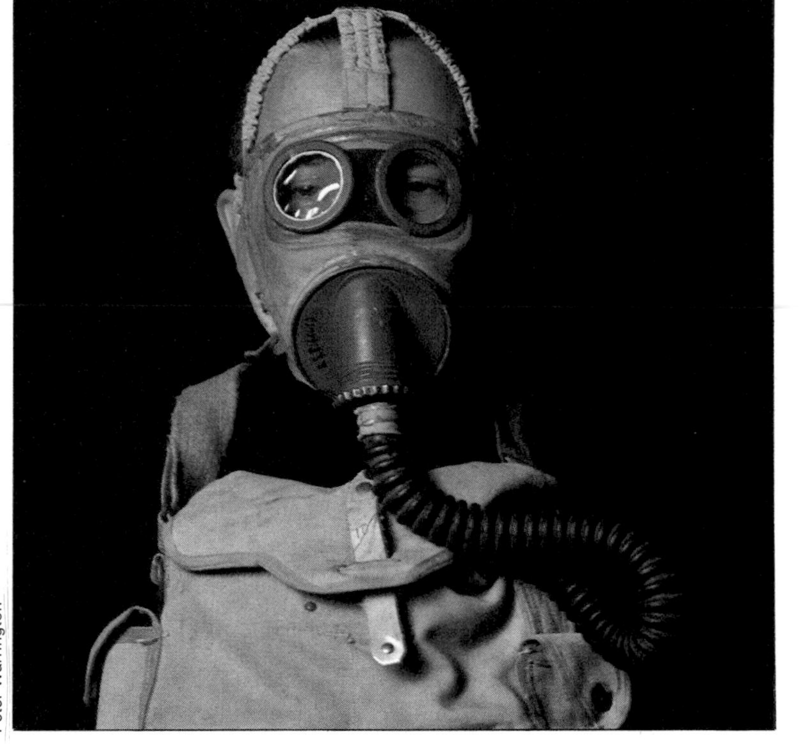

Peter Warrington

The basic pattern of the gas-masks of the Second World War was that of a close-fitting face-mask unit, containing the outlet valve, connected by a flexible hose to a respirator. The latter unit contained the air inlet holes, the anti-gas filters, and the inlet valve. The cycle as indicated on the diagram at top left is as follows:
1. Air is drawn through the inlet holes and passes through four filters separated by grids;
2. The indrawn air then passes upwards through the main anti-toxic filter of carbon granules sandwiched between two cotton pads, and passes on up the flexible tube through the inlet valve (which closes when the wearer breathes out);
3. The indrawn air is then channelled straight to the wearer's nostrils and mouth where it is breathed in;
4. When the wearer breathes out, the foul air passes straight through the outlet valve (which closes when the wearer breathes in) through the ring of holes in the gas-mask's 'snout'.
The British mask (*top right*) and the French (*below right*) both used this system—but both were rendered obsolete on the introduction of nerve gases which work through contact with the skin—and which do not have to be inhaled to be deadly

A First World War legacy which would not be needed . . .

By 1939, Britain was looking nervously to her anti-gas defences . . .

The history of poison gases is an interesting and almost prophetic one, in that this method of warfare has never been considered morally acceptable. One of the earliest decisions to use sulphur dioxide, produced by burning flowers of sulphur up-wind, was taken by Lord Dundonald in the 1855 Crimean campaign. The suggestion, however, was vetoed by the British government as being inhumane. A similar decision was reached when, in 1862, it was proposed that 'noxious gases' be used in the American Civil War; it had been requested that chlorine shells be used in battle, but the government declined to permit the step.

In 1899, at The Hague International Peace Conference, a resolution was put forward to ban such gases in warfare. But America, not yet convinced that the use of gas was demonstrably inhumane, did not support the proposition – nor did Britain, at least in the vote: she felt that the proposition was right, but her vote depended on unanimity within the other countries represented and America, of course, precluded that possibility.

It was Germany that first used the gas chlorine in the First World War, on the Russian front in Poland in 1915. Mustard gas was introduced by the Germans in 1917, and by the end of the war 50% of the German shells were filled with such materials; the British by then were prepared to load 25% of their shells with gas chemicals. Mustard gas was first used at Ypres: the French called it 'Ypérite' for a time.

It is important, before we examine the gases available for use in the Second World War, to emphasise one fact: not all of them were gases in the true sense. Many were in fact minute solid particles, suspended as an aerosol in the atmosphere. None the less, they did exert their effects as a gas – although, because of their nature, they were not removed from the air by the normal adsorbent elements in gas-masks.

There are several major types of gas used in wartime, of which 'choking gases' are the most common. They affect the respiratory system and are irritants. As a result, since their point of attack is the soft, unprotected lining of the lungs, they may produce extensive damage and cause death. They produce an initial response of coughing, as the lung involuntarily tries to expel the irritant, and then as fluid accumulates in the lung tissue to attempt to wash away the gas, oedema, or watery swelling, occurs, and death, virtually from suffocation, results.

Chlorine (which was, as we have seen, first used in the First World War) is now an obsolete combat gas. It is a dense, yellowish-green vapour which when propelled by a light breeze rolls along the ground in dense, choking clouds, filling crevices and trenches where men may be hiding. It damages the tiny bloodvessels in the lungs and causes oedema; the lung tissue swells into a spongy, wet mass and air exchange becomes virtually impossible. Diphosgene is a similar choking gas obtained in the form of a clear, volatile liquid. Its effects are often delayed for some hours, but it is moderately persistent in its action. Carbonyl chloride, a closely related phosgene, is more immediate in its effect, and it passes off quicker; but both phosgene and diphosgene produce the same characteristic odour of freshly cut grass or hay.

Tear-gas compounds produce a similar irritation, though in most cases it is confined to the eyes and the upper respiratory tract. The tear gases are not persistent, and the effects are generally gone a short while after the victim leaves the contaminated area. Much of the use of tear-gas in the war was, naturally enough, in civil disturbances. Another compound, Adamsite, acts initially as a tear-gas but produces more severe effects. This yellowish-green solid acts within a minute or so to produce irritation of the eyes and respiratory passages, coughing, blinding headache, violent spasms and pains across the chest with difficulty in breathing, nausea, and vomiting. The gas persists for less than 10 minutes in the air, and is therefore classed as 'non-persistent'.

Blister gases are capable of producing agonising surface effects. Technically known as *vesicants,* they attack any part of the skin which they contact, producing burns, destruction of the tissues, and painful, raw ulcers. More general systemic effects may also become apparent. 'Distilled mustard' is a straw-coloured liquid (colourless when pure) with an odour rather like garlic. It is highly persistent when liberated as vapour and may produce delayed effects for over a day after release. Methyl *bis*-amine hydrochloride – nitrogen mustard, as it became known – is a dark-coloured liquid which produces burning and blistering of the skin. The gas is persistent, often for over 12 hours. A more quick-acting gas is Lewisite, an oily fluid which in addition to the effects of nitrogen mustard also produces pulmonary oedema (rather like the choking gases) and pneumonia. It has a musty odour which may vary somewhat from specimen to specimen, but is said to be quite characteristic.

Painless, but deadly

Most severe of all in their lethal effects are carbon monoxide, cyanide, and cyanogen chloride. Apart from a slight 'gassy' or metallic odour, they are – when pure – odourless in practice. All interfere with the uptake of oxygen by the haemoglobin in the blood – thus a form of 'physiological suffocation' takes place. The poison forms a kind of loosely bonded compound with the haemoglobin, by becoming attached in the blood molecule at the site normally occupied by the oxygen. As a result, oxygen can no longer be carried. The effects are, in the main, irreversible and, unless the victim can be removed to fresh, uncontaminated air and allowed to conserve what oxygen capacity he may have remaining, death is certain. These gases are non-persistent, however, since they are low in density and tend rapidly to leave the place of release. Hydrogen cyanide, of course, is the same gas which the state authorities in the United States have used for legal execution in peacetime. Death is rapid, sure, and relatively painless.

Nerve gases (one of the first to be developed was the German discovery, Tabun) are among the most unpleasant of these agents. They act by destroying the enzyme cholinesterase. Normally acetyl choline is produced at the nerve endings during their normal message-carrying functions, and cholinesterase is the material which leads to the breakdown of the compound; otherwise the acetyl choline would tend to accumulate in harmful amounts.

These gases, by damaging the enzyme, cause large amounts of the acetyl choline to accumulate in the nerves; they are no longer able to transmit messages effectively and therefore bodily functions become uncoordinated and spasmodic, and the nerves themselves are damaged by the toxic accumulations that result. Tabun, a pale brownish liquid, is fairly persistent, and is generally quite odourless when pure. On inhalation, nausea, vomiting, and diarrhoea occur, muscular twitching and convulsions ensue rapidly, and there are systemic effects on the blood system. Even the smallest traces have an effect on the eyes, making the pupil contract which hinders clear sight and makes the victim uncertain and, in war, unable to fight effectively. Large doses in any degree produce potentially fatal results.

Sarin is a similar material, but it tends to be less persistent. Soman, however, is the most lethal of all the nerve gases. It has a fruity smell (Sabun tends to have this characteristic when impure) and in most respects its behaviour is the same – but it is far more severe in its effects, and they are swifter. Often within seconds of inhalation the victim is in a state of convulsive collapse which may prove fatal.

The effects of these poison gases have been codified, since the war, by American strategic experts, since many of these materials are still held for possible use today. The US Army Technical Manual TM 3-215 lists the following sequential effects of the nerve gases:

- running nose
- a tightness of the chest which interferes with breathing
- pinpointing (severe contraction) of the pupil of the eye resulting in distorted vision
- severe difficulty in breathing
- salivation and heavy perspiration
- nausea and vomiting
- painful cramps, accompanied by involuntary urination and defecation
- twitching of the muscles, jerky and uncoordinated movements of the limbs, a staggering gait
- coma
- convulsion, cessation of breathing altogether, and death.

When a nerve gas is absorbed through the skin the effects come on rapidly and death may occur within one or two minutes. With smaller doses coma and death may be delayed for over an hour, as the effects listed occur in that order; should the gas contact the naked membrane of the eye or be inhaled, death comes within about 10 to 15 minutes.

Before the Second World War, phosgene was always considered to be the most lethal of all war gases. However, the danger of death from Sarin is more than 30 times as great. One-tenth of a milligram of this gas (equivalent to a particle about the size of a large grain of sand) is enough to kill a child, and three-quarters of a milligram will kill a healthy adult. Even so, it has been calculated that over 250 tons of the material would have to be distributed to reach a lethal concentration, to an average depth of some 50 feet, covering a city the size of Paris.

Another of the 'blood gases'—so-called since the effect is primarily exerted through dispersion through the bloodstream, rather like the cyanide compounds discussed earlier—is Arsine, a colourless gas with a smell somewhat like garlic. Arsine is an inflammable gas, though it would take a high concentration to provoke any risk of an explosion; and it is very poisonous indeed. Its action in the body is to interfere with the normal metabolic transport system of the red blood cells. Arsine tends to accumulate in the liver, where it also causes severe and often irreversible damage, and is excreted to some extent by the kidneys, although they too soon become damaged, and death may occur. Arsine is one of the most long-term of the war gases, in the sense that the onset of symptoms may be greatly delayed. There have been instances where an accidental exposure to the gas has produced severe handicap and death well over a week after the incident. In the field, however, the gas is classed as 'non-persistent' since it rapidly diffuses into the air in concentrations too low to cause damage.

Experiments on prisoners

The Second World War gave rise to these nerve gases and, together with the materials which had been developed from earlier knowledge, both sides in the war effort stockpiled a considerable amount of gases. The Germans (who discovered the gases of the Tabun/Sarin series) produced a number of nerve-gas weapons, and by the end of the war they had stockpiled over 7,000 tons of Sarin alone—enough, as we have calculated earlier, to kill the population of some 30 cities the size of Paris. The Americans, too, had considerable reserves of sophisticated war-gas materials, and devoted much effort, both during and after the war, to improving their knowledge of the subject. In many ways, then, the period was an important one for the development of poisons that could be used in war, and many of these agents have since been used for other purposes—for experimental work in the laboratory, for example, and also in medicine. Mustard gas has given rise to the techniques by which human chromosomes have been studied in the laboratory, and newer hallucinogenic materials developed from war gases are used in psychiatry. It will be remembered that the Germans used poisons of this sort in a series of fatal experiments on prisoners.

Yet, although these agents were so intensively studied and produced in sizeable quantities, they were never released for widespread use in the war, and never became part of the conventional armoury. Why should this be?

Almost certainly the reason lay in the mutual deterrent balance that both sides were led to observe because of occasional Intelligence reports about the secret developments that were going on in the enemy's chemical laboratories. Indeed so well have the secrets of this research been kept that even today there is only scant information about the research that went on. What *is* certain is that war gases (whose effects, as we have seen, are terrifyingly widespread and severe) were ready for use—but neither side was in a position to risk reprisal by an opponent using similar, or perhaps even more severe, gases in retaliation. The possible consequences of the use of poisonous gases are incalculable; but had they been sanctioned for use the effect on 'civilisation' and the policy of chemical warfare might have been very different indeed.

US Air Force

Sophisticated incineration: the 'splash' of napalm

More chemical horrors: napalm and phosphorus

US Army

Fragments shoot skywards from a phosphorus grenade

In one respect, however, the chemical industry did provide an important tactical innovation: the production of chemical (as opposed to gas) grenades. One of the most widespread of these was the phosphorus bomb, which contained an explosive charge and a quantity of white elemental phosphorus. These bombs were used as incendiaries by both sides in air attacks on large cities, and with devastating results. As the charge burst, fragments of the white phosphorus would be scattered over a wide range at speed, and the particles spontaneously ignited on contact with the air. They had a marked tendency to adhere to naked skin, where they would continue to burn and cause painful flesh wounds which took a great deal of time to heal effectively. Thus the direct incendiary effect was supplemented by an anti-personnel one as well. Large tonnages of phosphorus were produced by the leading chemical manufacturers in Germany, America, and Britain, and were used as the normal incendiary bomb throughout the war.

The advent of Napalm

An even more effective incendiary arrived on the scene as the war progressed. The 'Molotov cocktail', of course, has been a traditional weapon for some time, but petrol (the inflammable ingredient of this hand-made 'bottle' grenade) is not usually an effective incendiary material, as it disperses and evaporates too rapidly. However, research was directed to overcoming this problem, and it was determined to find a means of forming the petrol into a 'gel', a jelly-like substance. Eventually a formula, made from palmitic and naphthalenic acids, was perfected. It has the effect of converting the petrol into a viscous jelly, the basis of a high-efficiency incendiary material which burns fiercely for longer than ordinary petrol. On contact with organic materials it continues to burn with a violent, intense flame and its detonation near personnel results in their becoming human torches.

This gelled petrol was called Napalm and it is still used by American forces today. In the war it was used widely by all the Allies against soldiers entrenched on the battlefields, and also against civilian populations in large towns and cities.

The chemical industry thus played an important part in developing weapons of unprecedented lethality. Much of the effort was devoted to the production of explosives for high-blast bombs, but the crucial development work was, without doubt, centred on the poisonous war gases which, as it happened, were never used. Their discovery, however, was one of the most far-reaching and significant chemical developments of the entire war.

Brian J.Ford **Rocket Technology, 1930/1945**

THE ROCKET RACE

From the Chinese official Wan Hu, who incinerated himself during the first recorded attempt at manned rocket flight in 1520, to the equally inventive and more successful Werner von Braun, rocketry has played an increasingly important part in man's attempts to propel his weapons, and himself, through the air. It was not until the Second World War, however, that the full potential of rockets became apparent. Every major belligerent power made some advances in this field, but it was the Germans who made the greatest progress

Ancestor of the *Katyusha* and *Nebelwerfer*: a Mongolian rocket battery of the late 13th Century, developed by the Chinese

Camera Press

A British Z-Battery in action. These rockets were intended to supplement the anti-aircraft barrage

The war was in many ways responsible for a dramatic change in rocket technology. In the 1930s the subject was, if not ignored, certainly widely misunderstood and underestimated by the majority of informed opinion; developments took place in irregular, uncoordinated leaps and the whole subject was more the province of the eccentric inventor than the serious scientific investigator. Today of course the scene is very different indeed. The rocket is part (in some senses a mainstay) of our civilisation, and the technology of rocket development and design has become one of the foremost branches of scientific advance.

It is easy to imagine that progress would have been inevitable even without the stimulus of the wartime effort—but there is evidence to the contrary. In the first place, rockets were first used in war many centuries ago (they were well documented in the 13th Century—and rockets for less warlike purposes date back certainly well over 1,000 years), but without any startling progress in principle being made for literally centuries on end. And secondly it is worth noting that the German A-4 (the V-2 rocket) was still used by the USA as its most successful space vehicle for research as late as 1952—the American scientists had to use one of their former enemy's weapons for their own research!

So we can see the importance to the history of rocketry of the Second World War. Earlier rockets had been no more than simple 'fire-propelled' charges or flimsy, experimental rigs designed to test an idea. It is believed that the first recorded use of rockets in war was in 1232, when the Chinese fired propelled arrows at invading Mongols. Roger Bacon gave a good formula for the propellant gunpowder in the early part of the 13th Century and the Paduans (1379) and the Venetians (1380) used rockets extensively in war. Indeed it was as long ago as 1520 (or thereabouts) that a Chinese government official named Wan Hu built an apparatus made of kites, fitted with a saddle and with a battery of rockets at the rear—truly the first rocket vehicle. Mr Wan, sadly, was blown to fiery pieces in the attempted launch.

In 1802 a British officer, Colonel William Congreve, began to study the use of rockets in war and a few years later the first Rocket

Troop—175 men in all—was formed. By 1815 the Americans had followed suit with the formation of ten rocket batteries; and later William Congreve was knighted for his enterprise. His book on rocketry published in 1814 was the first work of any detail on this subject. Then, following the use of rockets in ship rescue (they were used to secure a line aboard a stranded vessel) the Frenchman Le Prieur produced a rocket that could be fired from an aircraft—the first air-to-ground missile. The Horace Farman F40P biplane was later fitted with racks of five of these rockets on each side of the fuselage.

The father of the rocket, in its theory at least, was the Russian Tsiolkovsky who—in 1903—had designed a hypothetical liquid-fuelled rocket powered by liquid oxygen and liquid hydrogen. He also expounded the principles of the multi-stage rocket. Later, in America, the physicist Robert H. Goddard made several experimental liquid-fuel rockets, many of which flew in the late 1920s to heights of several hundred feet. By the time he died in 1945, Goddard had done sterling work in the field, but he was still largely unrecognised and had (due to unsympathetic treatment by the US government) been unable to take his ideas past the prototype stage. Not until 1959 was he posthumously honoured by Congress.

Though it is not widely realised, the Russians made similar progress at about the same time. In 1929 a petrol-and-air motor was tested by the Russian designer Tsander, and by 1935 a 10-foot rocket (very like the V-2 in appearance) fuelled by paraffin and nitric acid, had been developed and successfully fired. However, it was the Russian *Katyusha* rocket, a solid fuel device, which came to prominence in the war, rather than their larger missiles. The standard model was 5 inches across, 6 feet in length, and weighed just over 90 pounds—half of that was the warhead. The rocket was feared by the Germans, and it was used with devastating effect during the war years.

Japan: time was too short

The Japanese had carried out piecemeal development, like the West, before the war but not on a significant scale. However, on the stimulus of the war conflict, greater efforts were made in the field. Support arms in the form of short-range rockets were hurriedly produced for limited use. The range was between 100 and 150 yards, and the size of the rockets varied greatly, from 10-pound 3-inchers up to 1,500-pound rockets nearer 18 inches in diameter.

However, the pressure of increased US air attacks was predicted by the Japanese, who then set up a development section at the Naval Technical Research Unit. Solid-fuel rockets were developed for surface-to-air deployment, in the 10- to 55-pound range, and at the same time the first of the *Funryu* missiles was produced, the case being made by the Yokosuka Dockyard, the engines by Mitsubishi. *Funryu* 1 was only experimental. It was designed as a means of attack against warships and had a control guidance system; but the rocket—solid fuelled—was not successful and was abandoned without any flight tests. *Funryu* 2 was more successful. It was produced with modifications learned from the earlier prototype and became a perfectly practical guided missile.

Time was too short, however, with the war nearing its end, for large-scale production to start. However, a liquid-fuelled *Funryu* 3 was produced (again as an unsuccessful prototype), and like the *Funryu* 2 on which it was based it was theoretically capable of reaching an altitude of about 3 miles. *Funryu* 4, the climax of the series, was more successful than the *Funryu* 2. A liquid-fuelled guided missile, it was capable of reaching altitudes of 20 miles although it was never produced on a large scale.

The Japanese also developed air-to-surface missiles which were, in effect, rocket-powered bombs. The framework of these devices was produced by the Kawakasi Aircraft Company and was made of wood, and a Mitsubishi peroxide motor specially designed for the purpose gave them a range of some 3 miles (increased in later modifications to over 5). The maximum thrust developed was in the region of 550 pounds and the rocket motor fired for 75 seconds to accelerate the rocket along its predetermined trajectory. A Mk 3 version of these weapons was also designed, with an audiosensory system intended to 'home' on the shock waves of Allied gun batteries—but the project was cancelled in the early part of 1945.

It was in the same year that the *Ohka* kamikaze rocket plane (also known as the *Madurai*) appeared. This had been conceived in 1943, and was developed during 1944; it was first used in battle in April 1945. The device was a 2,645-pound bomb (which took up more than half of the entire weight) housed in a wooden winged casing equipped with three rocket motors capable of delivering 1,700 pounds of thrust. The overall length was some 20 feet, with fins being just over 16 feet from tip to tip. The device was carried by a mother plane until within 50 miles of the target. Then, with a pilot securely strapped in position, it would be released and allowed to glide at less than 250 mph towards the target—it was, because of its speed, an easy target throughout the glide phase. The pilot then ignited the rockets, which burned for 10 seconds, accelerating the device to over 600 mph, as he tried to keep it aimed at the target vessel; it was capable of causing considerable damage. The pilot, who was of course sacrificed in the attempt, gave rise to the two nicknames of the device used by the Allies: the British often referred to it as 'the suicide plane'; the Americans gave it a Japanese word, *'Baka'*. It means, literally, 'fool'.

Britain: advisers to the USA

Work in Britain during the years immediately before the war was far greater than is generally realised—indeed the USA sent specialists to learn British rocketry techniques as part of the American effort later in the war. British research and development first produced a 2-inch rocket propelled by cordite. Both the inner and outer surfaces of the charge burned during firing, which kept the exposed surface area relatively constant and prevented the risk of premature explosion; the warhead itself was protected from the heat by a special compound of sodium silicate and ground aluminium. Tests were highly encouraging, and by late 1940 a large 3-inch version—which could be fired in volleys of up to 128 from a pad known as a 'projector'—was brought into service. But of course there were many problems to overcome and the organisation of such a rocket battery had to be developed experimentally with virtually no previous tactical experience to go on. Accordingly, on May 20, 1940, in the back room of a public house at Aberporth in Wales, a meeting was convened under the command of the Ordnance Director, and it was decided at that discussion that the rockets should, in principle, be used as a routine measure against aircraft. Within weeks the Greenwich firm of G. A. Harbey had been appointed to the task of mass-producing the 'projectors', and by September over 1,000 had been manufactured.

The following month, Duncan Sandys (then a major) took control of the experimental battery and organised a rocket section to defend Cardiff with the 3-inch rocket, and the first German plane was brought down on April 7, 1941. By the end of 1941 there were three such batteries (known as 'Z' batteries) in existence, one at Aberporth for training (where there is still a missile testing range) and the other two in operation around Cardiff. Later, pioneer radar, radio-command, and order-of-battle prediction apparatus was assembled on the nearby Penarth golf course, and the UP-3, as the rocket became known, was intensively studied and modified, eventually emerging as a 6-foot rocket with a lethal radius of nearly 70 feet. Within a year—by December 1942—there were 91 batteries in existence, despite persistent enemy raids which twice razed the factory producing the rocket fuses.

At about this time, the British produced the first of their air-to-surface missiles, a modification of the 3-inch rocket, nearly 6 feet in length and capable of a speed of 1,000 mph. By 1942 they had been developed to operational stage, and although their use was confined to naval warfare (particularly against submarines) they were a very successful development. In 1943 the army, which had been investigating the potential of a 5-inch rocket, 6 feet in length, decided to turn the idea down as impracticable and in the tactical sense superfluous. However, realising that it could be used to back up assaults from amphibious craft, the navy acquired the interest instead and began production of the six-unit 'Mattress' projectors for use at sea. They were used, with devastating effect—particularly on the morale of the enemy forces—in the landings on Sicily and Italy which followed. Further trials at Sennybridge, also in Wales, encouraged the army to change its mind during the following year, and a 'Land Mattress' went into production which was used by the Canadians when they fought for the Rhine and Scheldt rivers.

It was towards the close of the war that the most enterprising rocket was developed: the so-called 'Stooge'. This was designed specifically to attack enemy aircraft, particularly (as it happened) the Japanese suicide squads, and was a 740-pound, 10-foot-long, radio-guided missile with a range of some 8 or 9 miles. It had a top speed of 500 mph and carried a 220-pound warhead.

An English scientist, Dr Lubbock, also did some experimental work on liquid-fuel rockets but it came to nothing in practice; however, the British were left with such a fund of knowledge and so wide an experience of solid-fuel devices that after the Pearl Harbor attack the Americans sent specialists to study British techniques. Subsequently a British pilot plant for production of fuel was sent to the USA to help with American developmental research.

America: one step behind Germany

Quite apart from their co-operation with the British later in the war, the Americans had of course carried out much original development in the earlier years and, although they did not make such

1. Explosive warhead
2. Guidance systems
3. Gyros
4. Helium (to prevent oxygen and alcohol from exploding)
5. Oxygen tank
6. Refrigeration tanks
7. Alcohol tank
8. Oxygen feed pipe
9. Alcohol feed pipe
10. Hydrogen peroxide tank
11. Steam generator
12. Pump (driven by turbine)
13. Steam turbine
14. Steam outlet pipe
15. Fuel injectors
16. Igniter
17. Fuel coolant (alcohol, which is heated and mixed with oxygen)
18. Combustion chamber

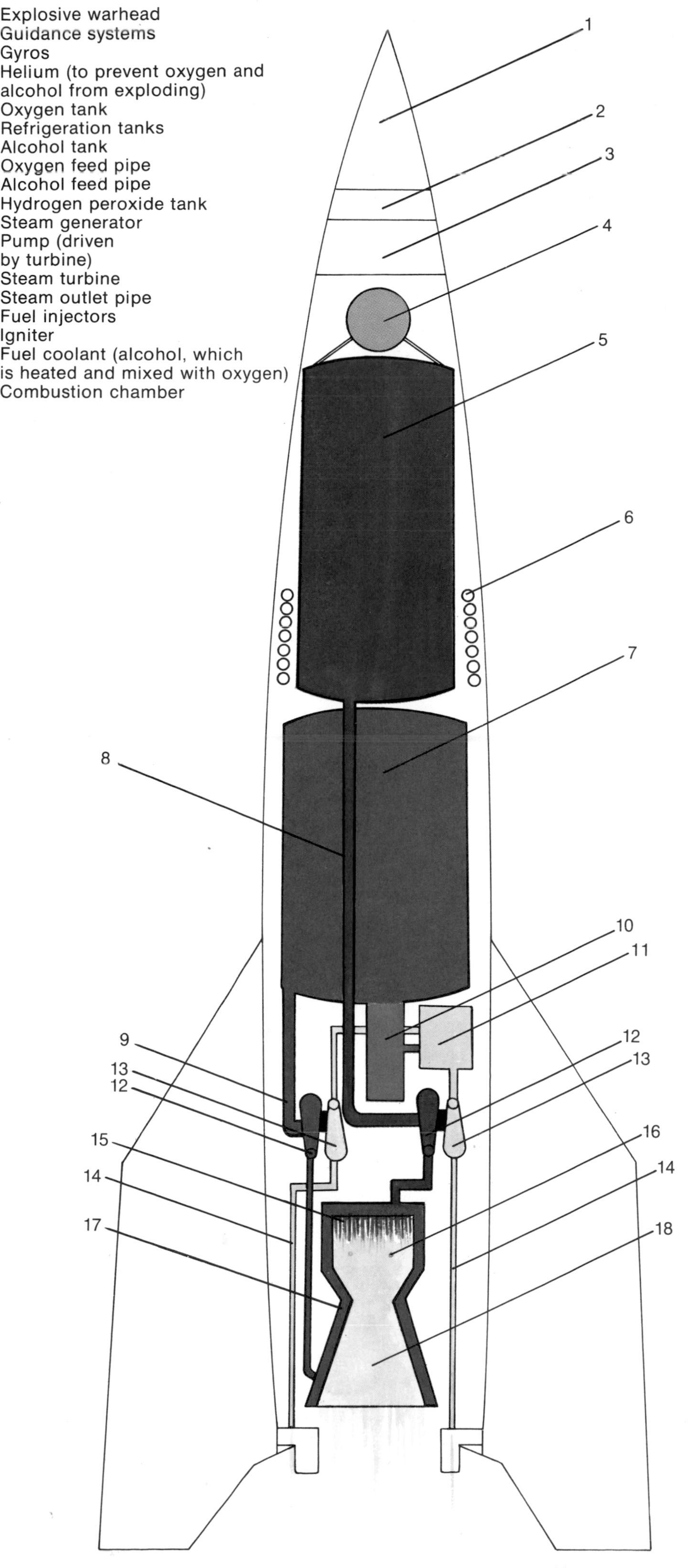

BOTH ENDS OF THE SCALE

In the notorious German A-4 'V-2', shown in cutaway at left, the rocket war reached its technical zenith; but at the other end of the scale were rocket weapons which either saw longer service or which were equally important in the fields for which they were designed. Some of these are shown below

The Russian *Katyusha* missile was invariably used in mass. The full salvo did have an unavoidable 'scatter', and a considerable part of its effect was on the morale of both Soviet and enemy troops; but *Katyusha* salvoes amounted to a vast concentration of firepower

The British developed the 2-inch AA rocket to supplement their anti-aircraft gun barrage, and the rockets were intended for use against low-flying bombers. Like the *Katyushas,* the British 2-inchers were fired from batteries known as 'projectors'

Developed as an air-to-surface weapon, the US 4·5-inch missile was soon pressed into service as a ground-to-ground missile, fired from tanks, trucks, jeeps; and it was also used by the US Navy in pre-landing softening-up bombardments

The British 3-inch followed the 2-inch into service, and by the end of 1940 3-inch batteries were being used alongside the heavy gun defences in the UK. The rockets were fired from batteries of twin-barrelled launchers in salvoes of 128

The US 'Mousetrap' was introduced late in 1942 after the US Navy had asked for an anti-submarine bomb similar to the British 'Hedgehog'. For this sub-chaser role they were grouped in batteries of four, and scored many kills against both Japanese and German submarines

The British 'Stooge' rocket was a winged missile introduced to combat the Kamikaze menace. It had a power plant of four rockets, was guided by radio control, and had a range of 8 miles

Russian 92·5-lb *Katyusha*

British 2-inch Anti-aircraft

US 4·5-inch Anti-aircraft

British 3-inch Air-to-Surface

US 'Mousetrap' Anti-submarine rocket bomb

British 'Stooge' 740-lb Anti-Kamikaze

Camera Press

impressive practical strides as the German rocketry teams, they did much work in a greater range of devices than is generally realised. For instance, it is perhaps surprising to realise that by the end of the war the US Navy alone had over 1,200 factories engaged in rocket production in different ways.

Almost certainly the first really successful American missile was one of the smallest: the bazooka. It was in December 1940 that development began, largely to find an answer to the insurmountable problem of recoil when an armour-piercing shell was fired from a portable gun; so fierce was the equal-and-opposite recoil that it seemed impossible to design an anti-tank weapon which could be used by the individual soldier on the battlefield. But of course a rocket-propelled missile would overcome all these problems, since the motive force is generated during flight and is not due to the massive reaction of an exploding cartridge. As a result the 3½-pound, 1-foot, 9-inch rocket was developed and this, fired from a 7-inch tube, was capable of being carried by a soldier and fired from shoulder-height in battle. It is said, incidentally, that the device derived its title from a sardonic description applied by an unimpressed major who witnessed the first demonstrations of the prototype. 'Recoilless gun?' he is reputed to have said. 'It looks more like Bob Burns' Bazooka to me!' – so the name was born and it has stuck ever since.

The bazooka in war was a formidable weapon: it could knock out a tank at over 200 yards and was effective against stationary targets (emplacements, etc) at up to 750 yards.

Subsequently (and after a period of Air Corps opposition which was only overcome by witnessing the results of British experience in the field) similar but slightly enlarged rockets were developed for use in aircraft. One of the most popular was a series of devices 4½ inches in diameter, some of them with a range of several miles, and a slightly smaller rocket (3¼ inches in diameter) was also developed as a test vehicle for proximity-fuse experiments. Later a larger version – $7\frac{1}{5}$ inches in diameter – was used for heavy bombardment on land. Then 20-tube 'Whizz-Bang' launchers, and 24-tube 'Grand Slam' launchers were fitted to tanks, and later a 120-tube launcher – the 'Woofus' – was fitted to landing craft. These missiles had a range of only a few hundred yards and a speed less than 125 mph but they did prove effective for their specialised purposes.

Two other Air Corps developments in 1943 were less successful. The first of these was a 'hydrobomb', a kind of rocket torpedo which would propel itself through the air and then through water to its target by means of conventional rockets – but this idea was soon abandoned as impracticable. Another plan was for a rocket-assisted bomb which – because of the boost in speed it received in flight – would penetrate heavy armour. This idea, too, was dropped; however, the experience gained in its development was used in a navy project. At the time too many enemy submarines were escaping because the pilot overshot his target: by the time the attacking aircraft had sighted the submarine and released its bombs, they were usually too late to land, and so overshot the submarine harmlessly. The navy therefore decided to develop a retrorocket which would slow a bomb and allow it to fall straight down on to the target – this was, in many ways, the same principle the Air Corps had already developed, and after modifications the idea became

Imperial War Museum

National Archives

Far left: A British 3-inch rocket streaks away from a Hawker Typhoon. Around the target—a goods train—other rocket bursts can be seen. These rockets were far from accurate but those which found their way to the target inflicted spectacular damage
Top left: It was the Japanese who developed the biggest operational anti-shipping missile of the war: the Kamikaze Ohka, carried within range of the target by a mother plane and then released to become a piloted stand-off bomb; it was powered by three rocket engines
Top right: America's 'Tiny Tim'—10 feet long and 11·75 inches in diameter—packed the punch of a 12-inch naval shell. It was primarily created for use against pillboxes and bunkers in the invasion of the Japanese home islands.
Bottom right: The US 'Bat' was a radar-guided air-to-surface missile, 12 feet long with a 1,000-lb payload. In April 1945 a Bat sank a Japanese destroyer 20 miles from its launch point—its maximum range
Bottom left: British aircraft used rockets against shipping with devastating effect. Here a Beaufighter on an anti-shipping strike unleashes a full salvo of eight 90-lb missiles

Camera Press

National Archives

reality. The last submarine to be sunk in the war, on April 30, 1945, in the Bay of Biscay, was destroyed by one of these weapons.

The USA also developed, during the later years of the war, what proved to be the largest airborne rocket (fired from an aircraft in flight) used in battle. This weapon—as is often the case—was incongruously dubbed 'Tiny Tim' and was a 10-foot missile carrying 150 pounds of TNT, and designed for attacks on bunkers. It was fired by a length of cord which triggered the ignition sequence when the rocket had fallen a few yards below the aircraft that released it. It was a crude method of firing: too crude in some ways, as the first test—in 1944—resulted in the rocket demolishing the mother-plane entirely. The crew was killed.

Air-to-surface missiles also made an appearance in the American war effort; one, the 'Gargoyle', was developed from a glide-bomb and was fitted with liquid-fuel motors when it went into production in 1944; but it missed the war, and ended up as a postwar test vehicle. The 'Bat' was a long-range radar-guided weapon nearly 12 feet in length and capable of speeds of 3,000 mph. It had a range of 20 miles, but also arrived too late to make any significant impact on the progress of the war.

It is not generally known that the French, during the period of occupation, also made some small progress in rocketry by the development of liquid-fuel prototype rockets at a secret base in Lyons. This was given the title of *Service Central des Marchés et de Surveillance des Approvisionnements* (literally: Central Service for Markets and the Control of Supplies) and developed a perfectly workable LOX (liquid-oxygen) petrol-ether motor which was fired experimentally in 1941. During the tests one of the rockets disappeared and was never found; it apparently flew some 20 miles from Le Renardiere and landed—but the occupying troops do not seem to have made any record of finding it. It was probably just as well.

Germany: supreme in the field

There can be no doubt, however, that the major advances in rocketry were made in Germany. The German scientists and technicians were supreme in their field, and set the pattern that postwar missile development—including the modern drama of space exploration—has followed. And yet much of the German effort in the field was prewar; it was anticipatory—unlike the other developments we have considered—and was designed to fit the nation for its envisaged rôle: as a leading world power, with force to back its arguments.

We must not interpret this widely-held view too literally, however. The gist of it is accurate, certainly, but Germany did have a heritage of rocket development in the early 1930s which was carried out for its own sake by earnest and well-intentioned pioneers, and it is arguable that this in itself engendered the right climate of opinion which in turn gave impetus to the later development of rockets as machines of aggression. Early in 1931 the first of the modern era of liquid-fuel rockets was launched from a base near Dessau. It had been made by an enthusiast, Herr J. Winkler, with financial support from Herr H. Huckel; and the so-called Huckel-Winkler 1 flew, on March 14, 1931, to an altitude of perhaps 1,000 feet.

In May of the same year the first Repulsor rockets were fired to heights of several thousand feet, and simpler solid-fuel rockets

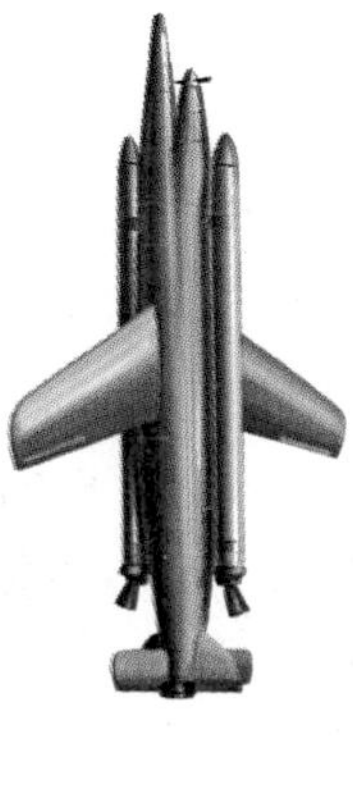

Rheinmetall Rheinbote ('Rhine Messenger')
A four-stage ground-to-ground missile, based on experience gained with the two-stage *Rheintochter*. The first and second stages separated from the missile 6 miles after launch, while the third and fourth stages remained attached to the warhead. Tests were so successful that at least 220 *Rheinbote* missiles were fired against Antwerp in November 1944; but the missile's chief weakness was its very light warhead.
Range: 136 miles.
Warhead: 88 lbs

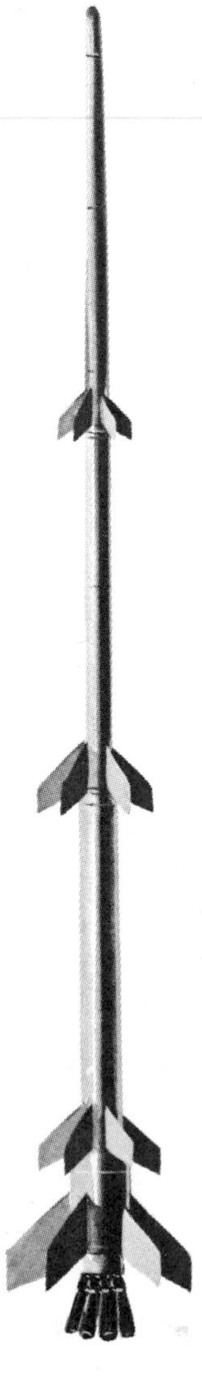

A4 ('V-2')
First test flights in the summer of 1942 were failures, but in October of that year came the first successful flight. Once full-scale production had been ordered, the completion-time was cut down from 19,000 man-hours in 1943 to 4,000 man-hours in early 1945. This was all the more notable as each A4 contained some 30,000 parts—and the bulk of the workers at the Nordhausen production plant were semi-skilled slave workers: Poles, Czechs, and Russians. The first operational firing of an A4 came on September 8, 1944, and by the end of the war some 5,000 had been fired. Of these, 1,115 came down over England, and 2,050 over Brussels, Antwerp, and Liége. In addition to the normal land-based rôle, there was a project to use A4s against America. Type XXI U-boats were to tow three containers apiece to within range of the US seaboard, each container carrying an A4; but the project came to nothing.

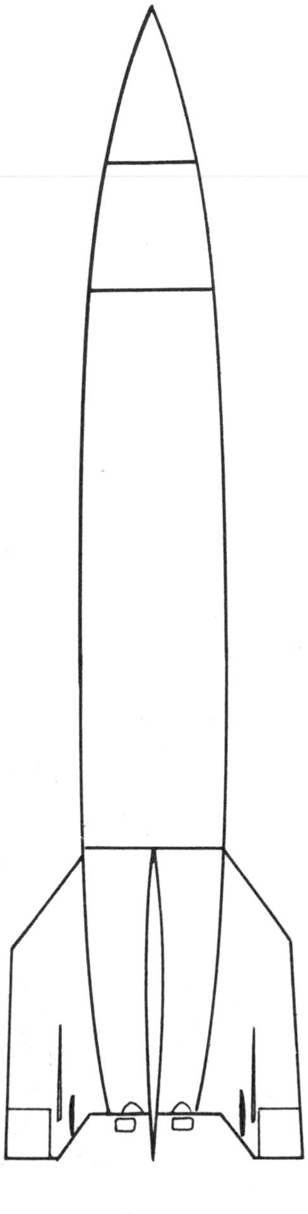

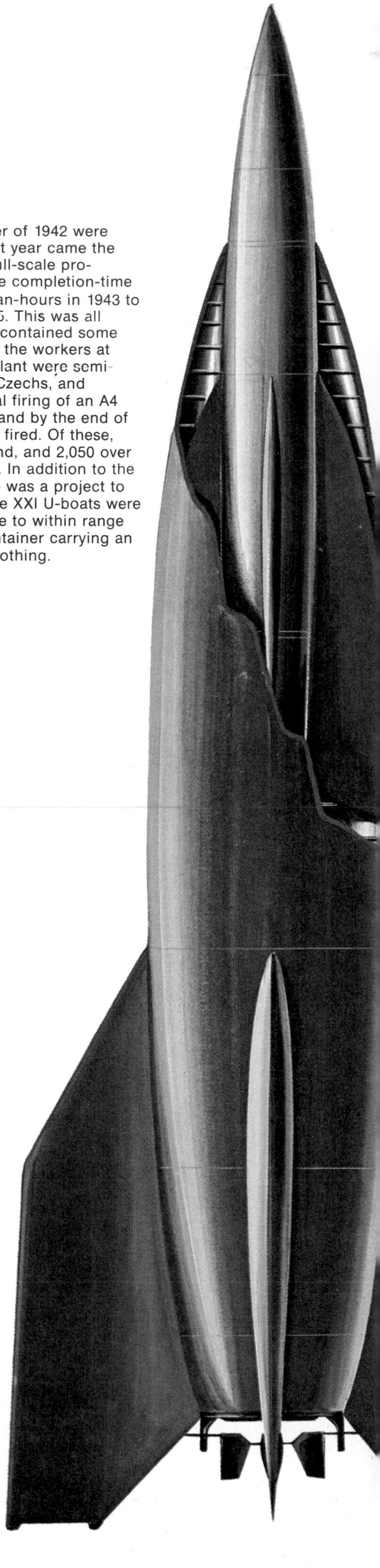

Konrad *Enzian*
Designed in 1944 by Dr Konrad of Messerschmitts, the *Enzian* was basically an unmanned development of the Me-163 *Komet* rocket fighter, intended for an AA rôle. Some 60 *Enzians* were completed, of which 38 were flight-tested. Although series production began in late 1944, none of these highly powerful missiles ever saw service.
Warhead: 600 lbs (with proximity fuse)

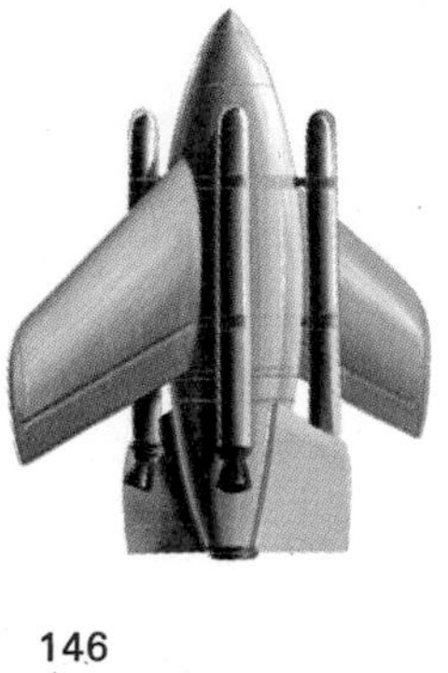

Henschel Hs 117 *Schmetterling* ('Butterfly')
Developed from the Hs 293 glider bomb, the *Schmetterling* was a subsonic AA missile with swept-back wings and a cruciform tail. When first submitted in 1941, the design was rejected, only to be resurrected in 1943 too late to attain full-scale service. It was the most advanced German missile of the war, radio-controlled, with the altitude range to combat high-flying bomber formations.
Range: 3,300 feet.
Warhead: 50 lbs

From the Reich's rocket armoury

A4-B (Below)
It was practically impossible to enlarge the A4, or to use more powerful fuels to extend its range; and so the Peenemünde team decided to perfect a winged A4, which would use the speed of the missile after power cut-off for a prolonged glide. The result was the A4-B, which had reached test-flight stage by January 1945

A9/A10 (Left)
As a result of the A4-B tests, the two-stage A9/A10 – a projected rocket to bombard the USA from Germany – was rushed ahead: too late to reach prototype stage. The A10 booster was to separate at 110 miles; it was to be recoverable, and special parachutes had to be designed to cope with the thin air of the stratosphere. The A9 second stage, a streamlined winged version of the A4, would then continue under its own power to an altitude of some 217 miles. It would then descend to 28 miles, where the air would be dense enough for the wing controls to guide it on the final glide-path to the target. Range was estimated at about 3,000 miles; the warhead was the standard A4 weight of 2,145 lbs

C-2 *Wasserfall* ('Waterfall')
Very similar in basic design to the A-4 (V-2) rocket, *Wasserfall* was shorter, with four stub wings. Like *Schmetterling,* it was intended as an AA missile to break up the high-flying US day bomber formations; but only 45 firings had been made by the end of the war, of which only 12 were successful. *Range:* 31 miles. *Warhead:* 550 lbs

Rheintochter R1 ('Rhine Daughter')
A two-stage flak rocket launched from an inclined ramp, *Rheintochter* was designed for use with the *Rheinland* system: two radar plots, one following the target and the other guiding the missile, both of them correlated by a ground controller. The booster unit separated from the main missile just over 1 mile from the launch point. *Altitude:* 20,000 feet. *Warhead:* 250 lbs (with proximity fuse)

John Batchelor

were carrying mail on an experimental basis in the same year. Indeed in 1933 a largely unsuccessful rocket was built in Magdeburg as an experimental forerunner of a manned projectile! But in Germany, as in other parts of the world, the slump of the following years put a brake on progress in the field.

However, by the beginning of the war there had been several new developments – and these were directly orientated towards weaponry. The first of the 'A' series (which culminated in the V-2 rocket) was developed about 1933; the A-2 flew to 6,500 feet at the end of 1934, and by 1937 the A-3, a large rocket of 1,650 pounds and standing 21 feet tall, had been flown. Its LOX/ethanol motor was virtually the experimental prototype for the A-4 – the V-2 rocket as it came to be called.

Subsequently an A-5 was built, a smaller version of the A-3 and with a much improved guidance system, and by 1939 it had been successfully flown in test flights over the Baltic. Many of the rockets were recovered by parachute and flown again. Most of this work was carried out at Peenemünde, under the direction of Germany's two leading rocket scientists, a Captain Dornberger and Wernher von Braun (who now commands America's side of the 'space race'). There were, however, other workers in the field: Hellmut Walter had set up his own *Kommanditgesellschaft,* a firm to produce rockets for assisted take-offs in aircraft, and the Bavarian *Bayrische Motoren Werke* was engaged in rocket development work in Munich.

As we can see, then, Germany had something of a national heritage of rocket expertise before the declaration of war in 1939, and further developments were clearly possible. One of the first devices to materialise was the V-1, a winged missile propelled by a petrol-fuel pulse-jet developed in the late 1930s by *Argus Motoren Gesellschaft* from an idea by the Munich engineer Paul Schmidt. It was a principle of almost captivating simplicity. The motor was, in essence, a tube several feet long, closed at its front end by a series of hinged flaps which could only open inwards. In the middle of the tube was a series of perforated fuel-delivery tubes.

As the motor moved at high speed through the air the power was produced in a series of pulses: the shutters at the front end, forced open by the slipstream, admitted a column of air to the combustion chamber, drawing with it a spray of fuel. The mixture was ignited by an electrically heated filament and it burned rapidly, the back-pressure forcing the shutters closed and so propelling the machine forward by the jet of exhaust gases leaving the rear of the motor. Then, because of lack of air, the burning gases were temporarily extinguished and the slipstream was once again sufficient to open the one-way shutters and so another blast of air was admitted to continue the cycle.

This motor is extremely simple to manufacture, almost foolproof to run, and cheap to produce on a large scale – indeed it has only one practical disadvantage, and that is of course that the device needs to be rapidly moving forward before the motor will start at all. A spontaneous takeoff is therefore impossible, and the Germans had to launch the machine at speed from specially designed ramps or from aircraft. The ramps that were built were visible to aerial reconnaissance, however, and many were destroyed by Allied bombing.

As we have seen, the V-1 had much to commend it. But it also had many disadvantages, and these prevented it from becoming the serious threat to the Allies which Hitler had envisaged. For one thing, it was too slow and could be shot down by anti-aircraft gun emplacements or ignominiously tipped over in flight by a judicious nudge from a fighter aircraft and sent to a premature end in the English Channel. The guidance system, too, was unreliable, and of the 5,000-odd V-1s fired at Antwerp only 211 ever detonated on the target. Moreover, less than one-fifth of the V-1s fired at the British Isles are believed to have actually exploded anywhere in the target area.

A little known four-stage rocket was developed in 1944 and tested in Poland. This was the *Rheinbote,* of which little was ever heard in the West; it was a solid-fuel unguided missile, merely aimed at the target. It was not a success: some 60 *Rheinbote* missiles were fired at Antwerp in January 1945, but virtually no damage of any kind resulted.

The only rocket offensive

The A4 rocket – or the V-2, as we shall call it – was first given a completely successful test flight on October 3, 1942, and after several delays production of the missile went ahead near Peenemünde. After heavy Allied bombing in August 1943, the assembly line was moved to Nordhausen in the Harz Mountains and towards the end of the war 900 missiles per month were being produced. The V-2 offensive started on September 6, 1944, when two were fired towards Paris. They both failed in flight. Two days later the assault against southern England started but here too there were many problems: the payload was too small, the development time had not been sufficient to eliminate all the teething troubles of the rocket's many mechanisms, the control system sometimes failed suddenly or – because of design weaknesses – the missile would occasionally explode violently on the pad or during its descent. Roughly 4,000 were fired against England in the seven-month offensive, but less than 1,500 reached England at all. Even so they caused much damage and claimed 2,500 lives – although the great speed of the rocket at impact (it landed at over 3,500 mph five minutes after the launch) meant that it dug itself in before detonation and it expended most of its energy on producing no more than a deep hole.

Though the V-1 and – more particularly – the V-2 were giant examples of ground-to-ground missiles, there were also smaller versions in existence. A smoke-rocket, designed to produce cover for advancing assault troops in 1941, proved so accurate that it was modified for bombardment a little later, and the Germans also developed a copy of the American bazooka after its effectiveness had been demonstrated in battle. Later a two-stage anti-tank rocket 2½ feet long was developed; it was guided by impulses sent along wires which unspooled from the wingtips as the missile flew. Underwater missiles were launched with complete success in the latter part of 1943, but (because of fears about the impairment of submarine manoeuvrability that might result) this enterprising idea never became a production-line reality.

A range of surface-to-air and air-to-surface missiles was also developed in Germany during the war years. The *Feuerlilie* F-25, which first flew in 1943, and the F-55, which followed a year later, were both surface-to-air missiles using sophisticated gyro-control and servomechanisms for direction and stability. The latter missile flew faster than the speed of sound, and both were about 16 feet long. The unsuccessful *Enzian,* developed at about the same time, was a solid-fuel plastic wood device but it was cancelled when only 25 of the rockets had been produced. The aircraft-like *Hecht,* a peroxide-powered rocket only 8 feet long, was only developed to the prototype stage, and 80 *Rheintochters* – of which only 18 were successful – were produced experimentally too. These were 3,500-pound rockets over 16 feet in length and capable of near-sonic speeds. The *Schmetterling* Hs-117 was 12 feet long and took the form of a midwing monoplane. It was fired from a pad with some success, and began to be known as the V-3, but it never entered large-scale production. The 6-foot *Taifun* barrage rocket which could reach over 2,000 mph was still in trial stage at the end of the war, although both liquid- and solid-fuel motors for it were in production by 1945. Last in this category was the *Wasserfall* missile, virtually a smaller model of the V-2, which was intended to have an infra-red homing device for the final 'kill'. Over a dozen of them were successfully fired.

Rockets designed for firing from aircraft were just as varied. The BV series were unsuccessful attempts to make an anti-ship missile that would drop to within 10 feet above the sea and then level off and fly to the target. But the task was too difficult in practice and the idea was abandoned. Several Hs rockets were also designed: winged missiles between 12 and 20 feet long with a range varying between 4 and 10 miles. They were liquid-fuelled, but not a success in practice and many modifications throughout the series were carried out. The X-4 was a 6⅔-foot-long rocket guided by signals sent along a wire unspooled from the wing-tips (rather like the X-7 anti-tank rocket, which was intended for land use) and said to be in an advanced state of production at the war's end; these were descended from the so-called X-1, the SD-1400, a 15-foot rocket with four wings and a tail unit containing automatic guidance apparatus.

However, despite the variety and the undoubted technical skill embodied in all these devices, the war was already moving to its inexorable end. Early in 1945 contradictory directives from different authorities were arriving at Peenemünde and the aura of the chaos inevitable in defeat led to the halting of research and development. Within weeks Braun and his colleagues had moved south, to the Harz Mountains, in an effort to make contact with the advancing American troops. This they succeeded in doing, early in May 1945, when in the town of Reutte they finally surrendered to a counter-Intelligence officer, Charles L. Stewart. It is interesting, with the benefit of hindsight, to recall the difficulty that Stewart had in convincing the authorities that these rocket technicians were of any importance at all, and indeed Dornberger, who was turned over to the British, spent two years in a POW camp in England before being released and joining the others in the USA. In fact, as we can now see, these scientists have probably done more than any other wartime team to alter the face of modern civilisation.

The first guided-missile attack in history was launched in 1943, when Dornier aircraft attacked Royal Navy ships with powered bombs. The effect was hardly spectacular, but had these German guided missiles been ready a little earlier—say in time for the Malta convoy actions—they might well have influenced the course of the war. *Flight-Lieutenant Alfred Price*

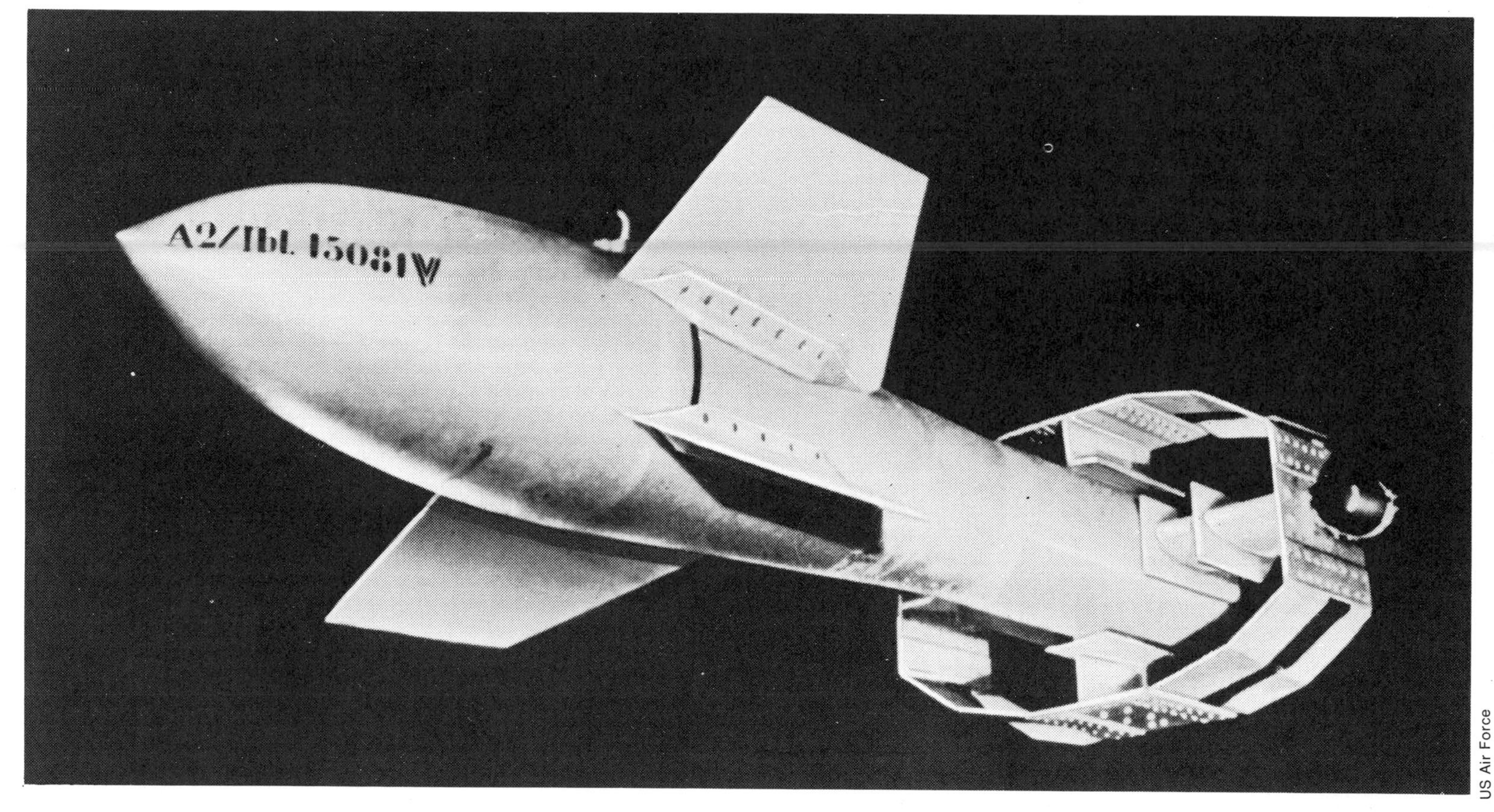

US Air Force

From the beginning of the war the Germans had concerned themselves with the problem of increasing the effectiveness of their aircraft against armoured warships; and at first there were only two air-launched weapons which could be used: the bomb and the torpedo.

If released from an aircraft flying horizontally, bombs needed to be dropped from an altitude of at least 10,000 feet. Otherwise they would not reach a sufficiently high speed to punch their way through the heavy layer of deck armour on a modern battleship. But a bomb released from such an altitude took about 25 seconds to reach the surface, during which time a warship speeding at 30 knots in open water covered 425 yards. Since ships under air attack almost invariably weaved all over the place, the chance of a hit with a bomb dropped from high level was slim indeed. One answer to this problem was the dive attack, in which the bomber dived towards the target at an angle of 60 degrees and a speed of 400 mph, and let go of the bomb when at an altitude of 3,000 feet. In this way the bombs were given a good start, and took five seconds to reach the surface, during which time a 30-knot battleship moved only one-third of its own length. But the dive-bombing aircraft were most vulnerable to AA fire during the time of the pull-out. Moreover, the diving attack could not be performed by the heaviest aircraft, and these were the only ones with the range necessary for long oversea flights.

The air-launched torpedo was also a very difficult weapon to use against ships manoeuvring at sea. It had to be released at exactly the right speed and altitude, otherwise there was a likelihood of the weapon suffering damage upon impact. This was also a danger if there was a sea running. Moreover the dropping aircraft could not help but fly very close to the target ship, and was vulnerable to AA fire from both it and its escorts. Once it had been released and was running true, the 40-knot torpedo was only marginally faster than the 30-knot warship, hence the favourite naval tactic of 'combing' the torpedoes—that is to say, turning away and trying to outrun them. Even when one of the relatively small aerial torpedoes did hit a modern battleship it usually caused little more than local damage, so unless there was a number of hits the ship was unlikely to sink.

The long-term answer to the problem lay in an air-launched weapon that could be

Alfred Price

◁ Fritz-X was used against heavily armoured targets such as warships
▽ Trial installation of a Fritz-X under the fuselage of a Heinkel He 177

△ Hs-293 was the world's first guided missile, with a 1,100-pound warhead
▽ A captured Henschel Hs-293 guided missile being examined

Imperial War Museum

controlled from the parent aircraft during its flight to the target. In this way the aircraft could stay out of range of the AA fire, but still counter the ship's evasive weave. Technically the problem of radio controlling such a weapon was not great, and two German firms—the Henschel and Ruhrstahl companies—each produced a guided anti-shipping weapon.

The Henschel Hs-293 glider bomb was in fact a miniature aircraft, with a wing span of 10 feet. In the nose was fitted a 1,100-pound warhead, and after release the rocket motor under the fuselage accelerated the weapon to a speed of 370 mph in twelve seconds. Then the motor cut, leaving the missile to coast on in a shallow dive to the target. At the rear of the weapon was a bright flare, to enable the bomb aimer in the parent aircraft to follow its progress in flight. The man operated a small 'joy-stick' controller, the movement of which fed the appropriate up-down/left-right impulses to a radio transmitter which in turn radiated them to the missile. Thus the bomb aimer had merely to superimpose the missile's tracking flare on the target, and hold it there until it impacted. The warhead had little penetrating capability, and the glider bomb was intended mainly for use against freighters and the more lightly armoured warships.

The second of the German anti-shipping weapons, the Ruhrstahl Fritz-X guided bomb, was intended for use against heavily armoured targets. In appearance it looked like an ordinary bomb, except for the four stabilising wings mounted half way along its body. Like the glider bomb, the Fritz-X was radio-controlled by means of a 'joy-stick' controller in the parent aircraft, and also it carried a bright tracking flare in the tail. The 3,300-pound bomb had no power unit; released from altitudes between 16,000 and 20,000 feet, it accelerated under the force of gravity to reach a speed close to that of sound. Fritz-X was aimed using the normal aircraft bombsight, and during the latter part of the flight the bomb aimer corrected the weapon so as to hold the tracking flare over the target.

In July 1943, even as the British specialist 617 Squadron was re-forming after its attack on the Ruhr dams, the Luftwaffe was forming two special units of its own to use the new guided weapons in action. The units were the II and III Gruppen of *Kampfgeschwader* 100, both equipped with the Dornier Do-217 medium bomber; the former unit was to use the Hs-293 glider

Alfred Price

Alfred Price

Major Bernhard Jope: he led KG-100 on the raid which sank the battleship *Roma* with a Fritz-X

bomb, the latter the Fritz-X. The Dorniers would carry two Hs-293s, one under each outer wing panel, or else a single Fritz-X on the wing between the starboard motor and the fuselage.

By August 1943 the missile-carrying units were trained and ready, and now they moved from their training airfields in Germany to the south of France. In command was Major Bernhard Jope, who had earlier led a successful career flying anti-shipping strikes with Condor four-engined bombers over the Atlantic.

The first guided-missile attack in history was launched on August 25, 1943. That afternoon twelve Dornier 217s of II Gruppe attacked Royal Navy escort vessels off the north-western tip of Spain with glider bombs. Many of the missiles failed to function properly, and only superficial damage was caused to one of the corvettes. In a more successful attack three days later the corvette *Egret* was sunk and the destroyer *Athabaskan* was damaged.

Fritz-X in action

Next it was the turn of Jope's other unit, III Gruppe, with the Fritz-X guided bombs. Early on the morning of September 9 the Italian battle fleet set sail from La Spezia for its final sortie: it was bound for Malta, to surrender under the terms of the armistice which came into effect that day. As the ships neared the narrow straits which separate Corsica and Sardinia, Major Jope, personally leading a formation of eleven Dorniers, attacked. The action invites comparison with those of the Royal Navy against French warships in 1940, for the Germans were attacking men who had only the previous day been their allies.

Two of the guided bombs struck the flagship, the modern 42,000-ton battleship *Roma*. One hit, near the after mast, penetrated the deck armour and damaged the starboard steam turbines to reduce the speed of the ship to 16 knots. A few minutes later the second missile struck *Roma* on the port side near her bridge, to bring the remaining turbines to a standstill. *Roma* wallowed helplessly, while below decks men struggled to control a serious fire the bombs had started. Twenty minutes after the first hit the flames reached the ammunition magazine, which exploded violently. *Roma* broke into two, folded up like a jack-knife, and sank with most of her crew. Shortly afterwards *Roma*'s sister ship, *Italia*, was hit by a Fritz-X on the bow. The battleship suffered some damage, and shipped 800 tons of water, but was able to reach Malta under her own steam.

On the same day as the Italian fleet sailed, Allied forces landed at Salerno near Naples. Here was a large concentration of shipping, just the sort of target for which the German guided weapons had been designed. Jope's men pressed home their attacks, and in the week that followed they scored hits with Fritz-X bombs on the battleship HMS *Warspite*, and the cruisers HMS *Uganda* and USS *Savannah*, causing serious damage to all three.

Some idea of the power of the Fritz-X may be gained from the damage suffered by *Warspite* when she was hit by a salvo of three of these weapons. One bomb scored a direct hit which penetrated six decks to explode on, and blow a hole through, the ship's double bottom; the other two bombs gashed the side compartments. One boiler room was demolished, and four of her other five were flooded. Fortunately there was no fire, or the consequences could well have been disastrous. As it was all steam was lost, the ship would not steer, and her radar and armament ceased to function. *Warspite* took on 5,000 tons of water, which lowered her freeboard by 5 feet. Perhaps miraculously, considering the damage suffered, only nine men were killed and 14 wounded. The battleship was towed back to Malta for temporary repairs, and did not see action again until June 1944.

The Salerno landings marked the high-water mark in the fortunes of *Kampfgeschwader* 100. The losses the Allies had suffered there taught them the utter folly of allowing shipping within range of Jope's Dorniers without continuous fighter cover at all levels. Accordingly the next landing at Anzio in January 1944 enjoyed lavish fighter protection and the missile-carrying aircraft suffered heavily. In spite of double the Salerno effort, with attacks by both Dornier Do-217s and the latest Heinkel He-177s with glider bombs, the only major German success was the sinking of the cruiser HMS *Spartan*. The Anzio operation underlined the tenet that the effectiveness of an air-launched weapon is not one ounce better than the ability of the parent aircraft to get it to within launching range of the target.

By the early part of 1944 the Allies had taken the technical, as well as the operational, measure of the German guided missiles. The radio control system fitted to the weapons was a simple one, and easily jammed. Two types of radio-countermeasures transmitter were built. One blotted out the parent aircraft's transmissions altogether; the other, more subtly, radiated a full up, down, left, or right signal on the German control frequency—to produce an effect similar to that of swinging the steering wheel of a car hard over while travelling at speed along a straight road.

When the Allies landed at Normandy in June 1944 the German guided-missile-equipped units smashed themselves bravely but in vain against the almost impenetrable barrier of covering fighters. On the rare occasions when the German bombers did get through, the ship's own radio jammers effectively shielded them from the weapons.

If the German guided missiles could have been ready a little earlier—say in time for the Malta convoy actions—or if the Luftwaffe could have achieved even a temporary air superiority over one of the Allied invasion fleets after Salerno, these weapons might well have had an important effect upon the course of the war. But as it was, the long-term effect of the world's first guided missiles was negligible.

MANHATTAN PROJECT

Ronald Clark

Europe and America, December 1938/July 1945. The world's first nuclear bomb, exploded at Alamogordo on July 16, 1945, had a complex history. First came the sensational discovery of nuclear fission in Germany in December 1938; British research then showed that the manufacture of a nuclear weapon was almost certainly possible; and American technological, scientific, and industrial effort—all combined in the Manhattan Project—actually built the bomb. Finally came the nerve-racking initial test, carried out in the wastes of the New Mexico desert, which announced that the nuclear age, for better or for worse, had arrived.

The first atomic bomb, set off in a test explosion at Alamogordo in the New Mexico desert on the morning of July 16, 1945, was made possible by a long series of scientific discoveries and advances. The first was in 1895 when the Frenchman, Henri Becquerel, discovered radioactivity. However, for the greater part of the following half-century the feasibility of using the energy locked within the atom was hardly considered seriously. It was only in December 1938 that the German chemist Otto Hahn discovered, in the Kaiser Wilhelm Institute, Berlin, what was soon called the fission process; and it was only with the description of Hahn's experiments the following month that physicists throughout the world began to speculate on whether it would be possible to make an atomic bomb.

The critical importance of Hahn's work in leading to nuclear weapons—the word 'nuclear' has largely replaced 'atomic' because the weapons depend on splitting the heart or nucleus of the atom—can be simply explained. During the first decades of the century it was discovered that all atoms consist of a nucleus containing one or more positively-charged particles called protons and (with the exception of normal hydrogen) one or more uncharged particles called neutrons; that circling this positively-charged atomic nucleus there is a cloud of negatively-charged électrons, equal in number to the protons; and that the differences between one element and another are accounted for solely by the number of protons and neutrons which their nuclei contain.

In 1919 Rutherford succeeded in 'splitting the atom' by using the particles thrown out by the radioactive substance radium to bombard nitrogen atoms; about one in every million of the particles thrown out by the radium penetrated a nitrogen nucleus and transmuted it into the nucleus of an oxygen atom. In 1932 Cockcroft and Walton used streams of hydrogen protons which had been artificially speeded-up by high voltages to bombard lithium and change it into a different substance. In both these cases the atomic nuclei were 'light'—they contained only a few particles—and in both cases the number of 'hits' scored was very slight, with the result that the energy released when a nuclear transformation took place was far less than that needed to create it. In other words, more had to be poured into the nuclear stockpot than could be got out of it.

It was the chance of radically altering this situation which made Hahn's experiments of December 1938 so vitally important. What he did was bombard with neutrons the heavy metal uranium whose nuclei each contained 92 protons. What he discovered was that the heavy uranium nuclei split apart into those of two other substances, barium and krypton.

This was the key to the bomb. For it was known that the energy contained in a uranium nucleus was much more than twice that contained in the two new nuclei—so the energy release was comparatively great. More important was the possibility that each 'fission' of a nucleus released one or more neutrons; for if this were so, then these newly-released neutrons might split more uranium nuclei, which would in turn release more energy and more neutrons—thus starting off a chain reaction.

Prompt and sensational response

The response to Hahn's experiment was prompt, world-wide and, in the scientific world, sensational. In Copenhagen one of his former collaborators, the physicist Lise Meitner who had worked in Berlin until being forced to flee the anti-Jewish laws, worked out with her nephew Otto Frisch the theoretical implications of what they christened 'nuclear fission'. In Washington the Danish physicist Niels Bohr described to the Fifth Conference on Theoretical Physics this startling theory, which he had been told about by Frisch and Meitner before leaving Copenhagen. Workers in Columbia University, in the Carnegie Institution of Washington, in the Johns Hopkins University, and in the University of California—all repeated Hahn's experiments. So did others in Warsaw and in the Leningrad Physico-Technical Institute.

Meanwhile, a team of French physicists in Paris, working in the Collège de France and headed by Frederic Joliot-Curie, proved that when nuclear fission took place a number of neutrons were in fact released. Hans Halban, the man in charge of the experiments, thought this so important that he rushed the report of the experiment to Le Bourget airport so that it would appear in the first possible number of *Nature*. And a few weeks later the same French team showed that the number of released neutrons was three or four—thus making a chain-reaction theoretically possible.

By the spring of 1939 it therefore seemed that a nuclear weapon might conceivably be constructed within the foreseeable future. But it was still a very big 'might'. The answers to many complex questions inherent in the starting of a chain-reaction were still unknown. The possibility of a 'pop' rather than a 'bang' was very real and continued to haunt the nuclear weapon enterprise until the first test on the morning of July 16, 1945.

The technological problems were seen to be immense. And these difficulties were soon increased when it was realised that only one particular kind of uranium was really fissile. This metal, like many other elements, exists in the form of different isotopes—varieties which are chemically identical and are different only in the number of neutrons which their nuclei contain. There were, it was discovered, three main isotopes of uranium mixed up in the natural metal. More than 99% of it consisted of atoms which had 146 neutrons locked within each nucleus. Of the other two isotopes, one had 142 neutrons in each nucleus and the remaining one had 143. It was this last—which on account of its 143 neutrons plus 92 protons was known as Uranium 235—that was essential for the fission process. But of pure uranium only 0·7% was of this variety; and since it was chemically identical with the other 99·3%, the chances of separating it appeared immense if not insuperable.

'This new phenomenon . . .'

Throughout the summer of 1939, as Europe prepared for war, obstacles to the making of a nuclear weapon thus continued to appear formidable. However, in the United States, in France, and in Britain, further steps were taken along the road that was to lead to the bomb.

In the United States Enrico Fermi—who had repeated Hahn's experiments in Columbia University within a few days of their publication—joined with Leo Szilard and Paul Wigner, two other refugee scientists, in persuading Einstein to write a letter to President Roosevelt. 'This new phenomenon,' Einstein wrote of nuclear fission, 'could also lead to the construction of bombs, and it is conceivable—though much less certain—that extremely powerful bombs of a new type may thus be constructed. A single bomb of this type, carried by boat and exploded in a port, might very well destroy the whole port together with some of the surrounding territory.' It was essential, Einstein added, that Roosevelt should appoint someone to ensure that adequate supplies of uranium were available if necessary, and that research on its potentialities be speeded up.

In France, where the physicists were interested in the possibilities of using nuclear energy either in a bomb or for the production of power, research was pushed ahead with the support of the Centre Nationale de la Recherche Scientifique. What is more, the French team now lodged five patents, of which the third covered the construction of a uranium bomb, and discussed with M Sengier, a Director of the Belgian Union Minière which controlled the vast uranium deposits of the Belgian Congo, the possibility of testing a uranium bomb in the Sahara.

By this time, however, M Sengier had already become involved with the British. For it was in Britain, with her crowded cities, and notably her capital, inherently vulnerable to attack from the air, that research on the possibility of a nuclear weapon had first been brought under the wing of the service authorities. In Bristol, London, Cambridge, Manchester, and Oxford Universities, physicists independently considered nuclear fission. A number of them wrote to Sir Henry Tizard, scientist and Rector of Imperial College, who, as chairman of the Air Ministry's Committee for the Scientific Survey of Air Defence, had been largely responsible for sponsoring the secret chain of radar stations which was protecting Britain by the time war broke out. And in the spring of 1939 Tizard was given, through the Minister for the Co-Ordination of Defence, Lord Chatfield, the task of investigating the whole question of using nuclear energy in a weapon. One of his first actions was to consult Sengier on uranium supplies.

Although nuclear research was now brought under the British Air Ministry, supplies of uranium for experiments obtained through the Ministry's Director of Scientific Research, and the work of the various scientists very loosely co-ordinated under Tizard's committee, Tizard himself was sceptical of success. So were many other scientists, notably Professor Lindemann, later Lord Cherwell and Winston Churchill's wartime adviser. And on Lindemann's suggestion Churchill wrote to the Secretary of State for Air, Sir Kingsley Wood: 'It is essential to realise that there is no danger that this discovery,' he said of nuclear fission, 'however great its scientific interest, and perhaps ultimately its practical importance, will lead to results capable of being put into operation on a large scale for several years.'

There were good reasons for this scepticism. Quite apart from the 'pop' or 'bang' problem, it was thought that the amount of Uranium 235 which would be required to make a bomb—the 'critical mass' as it is called—would run into hundredweights or even tons; and there was the apparently insuperable difficulty of separating this from the other chemically identical isotopes.

Rough blueprint for a bomb

This situation was dramatically altered in March 1940. On the 19th two memoranda arrived on Tizard's desk. Both of them were signed by the Otto Frisch who had helped to formulate the fission theory and who was now in England, and by Professor Rudolf Peierls, a young Berliner, recently naturalised and now working in Birmingham University. One memorandum, headed 'On the construction of a "super-bomb" based on a nuclear reaction in uranium', was highly technical. The second, headed 'Memorandum on the properties of a radioactive "super-bomb"', contained not only a rough theoretical blueprint for the bomb, but also hinted in simple terms at those questions of strategy and morality which have since exercised the civilised world.

The Frisch-Peierls memoranda were crucial for two reasons. In the first place the calculations of the two men appeared to leave little room for the 'pop' theory of a nuclear explosion. 'The energy liberated in the explosion of such a super-bomb is about the same as that produced by the explosion of 1,000 tons of dynamite,' they wrote. 'This energy is liberated in a small volume, in which it will, for an instant, produce a temperature comparable to that in the interior of the sun. The blast from such an explosion would destroy life in a wide area. The size of this area is difficult to estimate, but it will probably cover the centre of a big city.'

This was important enough. But the startling thing about the Frisch-Peierls calculations was that they showed the 'critical mass' of the uranium required to produce a self-sustaining chain-reaction to be a matter not of tons or hundredweights, but of pounds. To produce hundreds of pounds of the required uranium isotope, by methods which had not yet been worked out but which would be fantastically complicated and expensive, was beyond the realms of possibility. But a pound or so was a different proposition. What is more, if it was different for the British, it would be different for the Germans, in whose country nuclear fission had been discovered.

It was with this in mind that Tizard shortly afterwards set up a small group 'to examine the whole problem, to co-ordinate work in progress and to report, as soon as possible, whether the possibilities of producing atomic bombs during this war, and their military effect, were sufficient to justify the necessary diversion of effort for the purpose'. Its name was the Maud Committee, its chairman was Professor—later Sir George—Thomson, and it met for the first time in the rooms of the Royal Society in Burlington House, in mid-April, while the German offensive against Norway was pushing all before it.

There had been something curiously dramatic about the discovery of nuclear fission just as Europe was preparing for war, and the same quality pervaded the meeting of the handful of quiet men in Burlington House as the Wehrmacht began to overrun Europe. They had, moreover, a dramatic visitor. This was M Allier, a Frenchman whose actions were to have unexpected, and potentially very grave, repercussions on the building of the bomb in the USA.

The French team in Paris had been almost as interested in the use of nuclear fission for the production of 'peacetime' energy as for making a bomb. This would require a 'moderator' which would slow down the neutrons released by fission—which would, in a not too inaccurate sense, 'control' the nuclear fire which would otherwise burn itself out in a massive explosion. The most likely material for a moderator was 'heavy water'—a mixture of oxygen and the heavy isotope of hydrogen which reduces the speed of neutrons but rarely absorbs them. The only source of heavy water was the Norsk Hydro Company in Norway, and Allier, acting on behalf of the French government, had only recently travelled to Norway, bought the entire stock of 400 pounds of heavy water, flown it to Britain from beneath the noses of the Germans, and then transported it down the length of Britain from Scotland and across the Channel to France. This, however, was only the first stage in an adventurous journey for the rare material which was subsequently to be brought to England, insured for £10,000, lodged in the vaults of Windsor Castle, taken to the Cavendish Laboratory, moved across the Atlantic to Canada, and finally returned to Britain.

Now, in mid-April, Allier did three things. He told the British of the work on the bomb being done by the French team. He stressed French fears that the Germans were also working on a nuclear weapon. And on behalf of the French Arms Ministry he proposed long-term nuclear co-operation between the two countries.

The British now settled down to discover how nuclear theory could be translated into nuclear practice. Before they had got very far they were joined by two members of the French team, Halban and Kowarski, who succeeded in bringing with them the vital stocks of heavy water, and who were shortly afterwards working with British scientists at the Cavendish Laboratory in Cambridge.

With the setting-up of the Maud Committee the British nuclear effort was put on a workmanlike if still small basis. Moreover it was no longer merely an academic effort. Imperial Chemical Industries and Metropolitan-Vickers were the most important but by no means the only firms brought in to help tackle the immense chemical and engineering problems. These were largely concerned with separating the rare Uranium 235 isotope. The most favoured method was by gaseous diffusion, which involved passing the uranium—in the form of the gas uranium hexafluoride—through vast numbers of membranes or barriers. The Uranium 235 atoms, being slightly lighter, would pass through the barriers more easily than the others; a 'filtering' effect would take place and eventually all the lighter atoms would be separated. At least, that was the theory. But the gas was dangerously corrosive: the holes in the barriers would have to be only a few ten-thousandths of an inch across, there would have to be some 160,000 holes per square inch, the barriers containing them would have to be made not in thousands but in millions of square feet—and the whole production carried out to the most exacting standards.

This was merely one of a multitude of industrial headaches which began as British teams in Liverpool, Birmingham, Oxford, and Cambridge Universities tried to fill in the vast number of gaps in what was known as 'the uranium problem'. At an early stage it had been appreciated that the bomb itself would have to consist of two pieces of Uranium 235, each smaller than the critical mass, which could be quickly brought together to produce more than the explosive amount. Much of the theory involved in this operation was tackled by Peierls in Birmingham and Frisch in Liverpool, where the team was under the direction of Professor Chadwick who had verified the existence of the neutron only eight years previously. In Birmingham, also, a team under Professor Haworth worked with ICI on the ways of obtaining pure uranium.

Second string to the nuclear bow

In the Clarendon Laboratory at Oxford, Francis (later Sir Francis) Simon worked out the main features of a £4,000,000 isotope separation plant which would have a daily output of a kilo of Uranium 235, 99% pure. And in the Cavendish at Cambridge two important developments took place. First of all the French team, consisting of Halban and Kowarski, finally proved beyond all reasonable doubt that a slow chain-reaction could be produced in a mixture of uranium oxide and heavy water. At the first glance this appeared to have no relevance to a bomb, although it did imply that nuclear power—the 'boiler' instead of the 'bomb' as it became known—was a possibility in the not too remote future.

However, this French work did, in effect, help provide what was to be a second string to the nuclear bow—and one that was to destroy Nagasaki. It had already been calculated that a chain-reaction of the sort which Halban and Kowarski had now shown to be practicable would produce, as the result of a series of nuclear transformations, an element which did not occur at all in nature. Just as Uranium had been named after the planet Uranus, and a transitory element formed by its breakdown had been christened Neptunium after the planet whose orbit lay next to Uranus, so was the new element now named 'Plutonium' after Pluto, the next planet.

In Britain, plutonium was quickly seen to be of great importance. For two members of the Cavendish team, Professor Norman Feather and the Swiss scientist Dr Egon Bretscher, now calculated that plutonium would be fissile, like the isotope Uranium 235. It was therefore a potential nuclear explosive. Moreover, it would be chemically different from the uranium which would be helping to produce it in the nuclear 'pile' – the word used to describe the assembly in which a slow chain-reaction takes place and which was soon to be replaced by the word 'reactor'.

All at once it seemed that it might be possible to bypass the massive problems of isotope-separation. This method of producing an alternative nuclear explosive would, however, demand large quantities of the scarce heavy water; there was no certainty that plutonium would, as prophesied, prove fissile; and as far as the British were concerned the main importance of the moderated chain-reaction lay in the possible production of postwar power. Yet it was plutonium which was to provide the fissile heart of the test explosion at Alamogordo and of the weapon which destroyed Nagasaki. Only the Hiroshima bomb was a uranium-bomb.

This new 'Element 94' – in whose nucleus there existed 94 positively charged protons – was also christened plutonium in the United States, quite independently of the British. There, across the Atlantic, President Roosevelt had responded to Einstein's letter by setting up an Advisory Committee on Uranium under Dr L. Briggs, Director of the National Bureau of Standards. Small American teams were investigating various ways of separating uranium isotopes, while in Columbia University Enrico Fermi was working on parallel lines to the French team – although far less optimistic of success. A special committee of the National Academy of Sciences issued reports describing the US work in May 1940 and in July 1941. But the emphasis in both was on the possibilities of postwar power and neither of them, according to an official American statement after the war, 'indicated that uranium would be likely to be of decisive importance in the present war'.

This was natural enough. The United States was still determinedly neutral; there was no pressure for survival such as spurred on a Britain which believed itself to be threatened with a German nuclear weapon; and there seemed little point in pursuing with anything more than academic interest what all but a few US scientists believed to be only a remote possibility. Later, once the Americans decided that a nuclear weapon was seriously 'on', their intellectual enthusiasm equalled that of the British and their industrial concentration and effort far surpassed it. But in the first half of 1941 it was still the British who were setting the pace.

Only the US could do it . . .

It was this pace, the crucial report of the Maud Committee which came in the mid-summer of 1941, and the effect of Anglo-US co-operation between the spring of 1940 and the autumn of 1941, which finally induced the US to expend a total of some $2,000,000,000 on what was still a great nuclear gamble. It was as well they took the chance. For as the British teams saw more clearly the purely technological problems of making a nuclear weapon they began to wonder whether the job was within the powers of a wartime Britain already industrially stretched to breaking-point. In fact, in the early 1940s only the United States *could* have made the bomb.

The Anglo-US co-operation which opened American eyes had begun with Sir Henry Tizard's mission to the United States in the autumn of 1940. His all-embracing brief was 'to tell them what they want to know, to give them all the assistance I can on behalf of the British government to enable the armed forces of the USA to reach the highest level of technical efficiency'. From then on, the Americans were sent copies of the Maud Committee reports, while two Americans, visiting Britain in connection with radar, sat in at various times on committee meetings.

The Americans were therefore well prepared for the Maud report of July 1941. They were less prepared for its contents. For the long report, with its detailed appendices, had one key sentence which put the Committee's work far in advance of anything else that had been achieved in the nuclear world. 'We have now reached the conclusion,' this went, 'that it will be possible to make an effective uranium bomb which, containing some 25 pounds of active material, would be equivalent as regards destructive effect to 1,800 tons of TNT and would also release large quantities of radioactive substances, which would make places near to where the bomb exploded dangerous to human life for a long period.'

It was estimated that the material for the first bomb could be ready by the end of 1943, and that while the isotope-separation plant would cost £5,000,000, 'the destructive effect, both material and moral, is so great that every effort should be made to produce bombs of this kind'. The following month Churchill, acting on the advice of his scientific adviser, Lord Cherwell (the former Professor Lindemann), ordered that plans for making uranium bombs should go ahead and a special organisation, code-named 'Tube Alloys', was set up to carry out the work.

The Americans were informed of this, and on October 11, 1941, President Roosevelt sent a personal letter to Churchill 'suggesting that any extended efforts on this important matter might usefully be co-ordinated or even jointly conducted'. On October 27 Professor Harold Urey – the discoverer of heavy water – and Professor George Pegram arrived in Britain to make a personal inspection of the British work. Even before they had returned to the United States, the National Academy of Sciences Committee reported that a fission bomb of 'superlatively destructive power' was now possible. On December 6 Dr Vannevar Bush, Director of the US Office of Scientific Research and Development, having considered the Maud Report, the National Academy Report, and others from Pegram and Urey, decided that an all-out attempt must be made to construct a nuclear weapon, and a new committee containing the cream of US physicists was set up to handle the work. The following day the Japanese catapulted the Americans into the war.

Staggering news

During the first half of 1942 the British continued their efforts to find the best sort of membrane or 'barrier' for isotope-separation; and a pilot-plant for separation was set up at a Ministry of Supply poison gas factory at Rhydymwyn in North Wales. But when a group of British scientists from the Tube Alloys project returned from a visit to the United States in April 1942, they had staggering news to report. Although the US project had only been started seriously a few months earlier, American resources, both industrial and academic, were already on a vastly greater scale than those in Britain.

It was quickly seen that if a bomb was to be made with the minimum delay – and the threat of a German atomic weapon was still the main spur – then the US offered immensely greater chances than Britain, or even than Canada. The French team, whose work on slow neutrons had helped show the way to the production of a second nuclear explosive, was eventually moved to Canada where their work, under the direction of Sir John Cockcroft, led the way to postwar British nuclear power. But it soon became clear that only the Americans could make the bomb, and this was formally agreed between Roosevelt and Churchill in June 1942.

Construction of the huge factories and laboratories which the Americans quickly appreciated were necessary was put in the hands of the US Army, and was soon in charge of General Groves, a brilliant engineer officer who became totally responsible for the enterprise, known as the Manhattan Project.

The size and complexity of this enterprise were partly the result of a brave decision taken by the American scientists forming the committee which had overall direction of the work. By the early summer of 1942 it had been decided that there were five possible ways of making a nuclear explosive:

- It might be possible to produce Uranium 235 by the gaseous-diffusion method on which the British had been working for more than a year;
- It might be possible to make it by electromagnetic-separation – for when uranium in gaseous form is passed through a magnetic field of constant intensity the Uranium 235 takes a more curved path than the other isotopes and can therefore be collected separately from it;
- It might be possible to produce Uranium 235 by use of the centrifuge, a method analogous to that by which cream is separated from milk. In addition, there was the chance of producing plutonium in a nuclear pile;
- By using heavy water as a moderator, as the French team in Cambridge had shown to be theoretically possible;
- By using graphite instead of the heavy water.

Each of these five alternatives presented immense industrial difficulties. What is more, the main problem was not to discover which of the methods would work best; it was, rather, to discover if any of them would work at all. For no one had yet separated Uranium 235 on the industrial scale that would be needed; and no one had yet proved, in practice, that a nuclear chain-reaction would be self-supporting, let alone produce plutonium.

Ideally, the solution would have been first to try the most likely method, then to try the next most likely, and so on. But the Germans were thought to be hot on the track of the bomb and no time was to be lost. Only the Americans were able to provide the strategically correct answer – intense and simultaneous concentration on *all* five methods. Within a year the centrifuge method of separating Uran-

The heart of nuclear power

When an uncharged neutron particle hits the nucleus of a Uranium atom, there occurs a burst of atomic energy; two new substances (Barium and Krypton) are created, and one or two fresh neutrons are released—some of which find other nuclear targets, and repeat the process. Each splitting or 'fission' causes more: this is the chain-reaction *(right)*.

A rapid chain-reaction becomes a nuclear explosion; a slow reaction (controlled by a nuclear 'pile', which cuts down the output of neutrons and therefore the speed of the chain reaction) is a source of usable energy.

But, like many other elements, Uranium has several 'isotopes'—varieties which, although chemically identical, have different numbers of neutrons in their atoms. For the pioneers of the 1940s, one Uranium isotope topped the bill: U-235, which has 143 neutrons and 92 positively-charged protons in its atomic nucleus. Its 'energy-factor' was therefore the highest, and so it was an essential ingredient for the development of nuclear power, beneficent or otherwise.

The problems, however, were immense, for U-235 only makes up 0·7% of pure Uranium, and has to be separated from 99·3% of chemically identical substance. The method finally selected was the gas-diffusion process *(right)* in which Uranium, in the form of the gas Uranium Hexafluoride, is passed through a long series of porous screens. This filtering action, repeated often enough, weeds out the heavier atoms and results in a deposit of pure U-235.

Below: Part of the nuclear plant built at Oak Ridge, Tennessee. There the Americans built the first gas-diffusion plant for the separation of Uranium isotopes on an industrial scale.

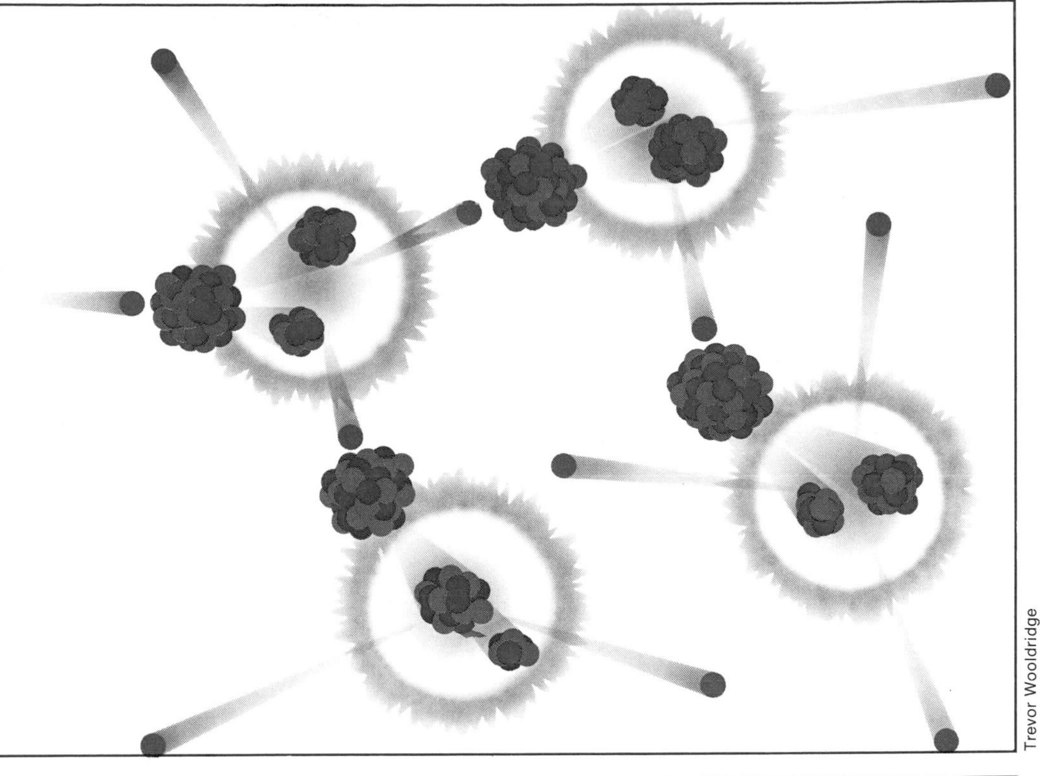

Trevor Wooldridge

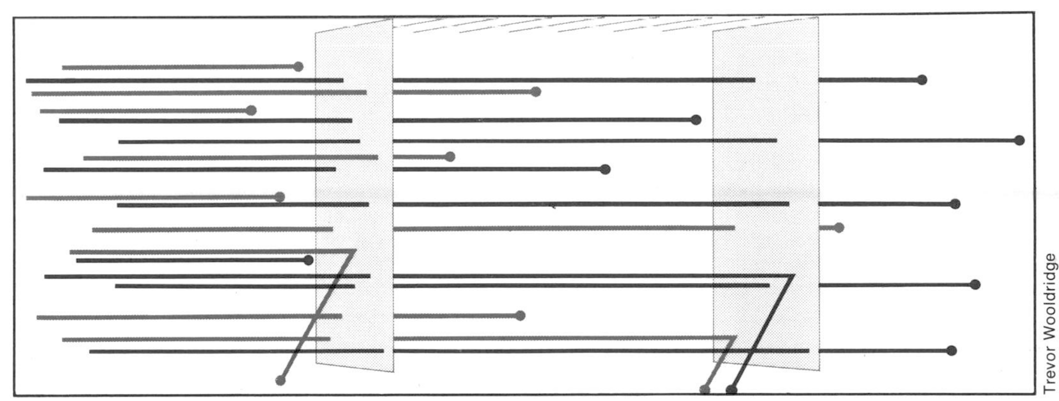

Trevor Wooldridge

US Army

ium 235 and the possibility of using heavy water as a moderator had both been dropped; but this still left three methods; and their fantastic industrial demands were to absorb an increasing amount of America's wartime efforts.

The work would not have started so quickly had it not been for M Sengier, the Belgian who three years earlier had been buttonholed by both the British and the French authorities for his supplies of Congo uranium. 'In August 1940,' he explained later, 'I instructed our people in Africa to ship discreetly to New York, under some kind of name, an existing stock of rich ore (about 65% of uranium oxide). The tonnage of 1,140 metric tons was shipped from Africa in 2,000 steel drums. The shipments left Lobito Bay in September and October 1940, arriving in New York in November and December 1940. These were stored in a warehouse in Staten Island, New York.' When the Americans needed uranium for the start of the Manhattan Project, quickly and in quantity, it had merely to be collected.

In the University of California Professor E. O. Lawrence developed the electromagnetic-separation process. In New York's Columbia University, SAM (for Substitute Alloy Materials) tackled under Dr Harold Urey the theoretical problems of separating Uranium 235 by gaseous diffusion. Both methods were finally put into operation at Oak Ridge, a huge factory complex built in the wilds of Tennessee. In the University of Chicago a group including Enrico Fermi and Leo Szilard—who had helped to alert Roosevelt to nuclear possibilities in 1939—worked on the construction of the world's first nuclear 'pile', while far away near the west coast, at Hanford, a small village on the banks of the Columbia river in the State of Washington, preparations were made to produce plutonium. To produce it, that is, *if* the Chicago experiment was successful.

The critical experiment

For on a score of occasions the shortage of time forced the Americans to assume that some particular operation would be successful and to spend millions of dollars on that assumption. Thus a massive and revolutionary powerplant for the gaseous-diffusion plant at Oak Ridge had to be built *before* the design of the barriers had been settled. When it came to mobilising short-supply scientists or technicians these often had to be mobilised for half a dozen jobs only one of which might eventually turn out to be essential to the bomb. And long before the industrial problems had been solved Robert Oppenheimer had been put in charge of a laboratory at Los Alamos, a lonely spot in the wilds of New Mexico where physicists would work out how best to bring together the two sub-critical masses of fissile material that would combine to create a nuclear explosion.

A great deal rested on Fermi's attempt in Chicago to create a self-sustaining chain-reaction. For this would not only be a confirmation of the Cambridge calculations: it would be the first practical proof that nuclear fission could, in fact, produce a new sort of energy, whether or not this was to be used in a bomb or a 'boiler'.

The critical experiment started on November 7, 1942, when Fermi's team began assembling a structure of uranium and graphite in the squash court beneath the university football stadium. There were some 40,000 blocks of graphite, weighing 500 tons in all and of a purity which had never before been attained on a commercial scale. Carefully spaced between them, in a structure which was about 24 feet across and about 50 layers high, was distributed 50 tons of uranium.

By the morning of December 2, the pile of uranium and graphite blocks was complete, its activity restrained only by the cadmium control rods which penetrated vertically down into its heart. These control rods absorbed the neutrons spontaneously released inside the pile and prevented the starting of a nuclear fire.

At 9.45 am Fermi ordered that the first of the control rods should be withdrawn. As the first of them came out, the recording instruments around the squash court showed how the number of released neutrons suddenly increased. The numbers would grow for a certain time and would then level off. At each stage Fermi watched the information on the dials of the instruments and made calculations with his small slide-rule. Around him were the other members of the team, each of whom realised that the world might be on the edge of a new age.

Throughout that morning the rods were slowly withdrawn. The increase in the neutron count, the levelling off, was going according to plan. And with each move the pile grew nearer to what was hoped would be the critical stage.

Tension was relieved by a break for lunch. At 2 pm work was resumed. After the withdrawal of each few inches of cadmium the trace marked on a wall-graph showed how the neutron count increased and then levelled off as a horizontal line.

It was just before 3.30 pm when Fermi gave the final order. The remaining cadmium control rod was withdrawn a few more inches. The neutron count increased. Then the line on the graph, drawn as the neutron count was given minute by minute, continued its straight upward course instead of levelling off. The chain-reaction was self-sustaining and the nuclear fire was burning.

Arthur Compton, in charge of the laboratory, returned to his office and telephoned James Conant, his opposite number in Harvard. 'The Italian navigator has just landed in the New World', he announced.

Practical results at last

If the Manhattan Project needed any further impetus, it was given by this demonstration in the Chicago University squash court; theoretical nuclear physics could be justified by practical results.

The Americans now pressed on with even more determination, and the following year, 1943, saw their plans entering a fresh stage. For at Oak Ridge the first gaseous-diffusion plant in the world for the separation of uranium isotopes on an industrial scale began operating; and in February 1943 work was begun, in another part of the huge plant, on a pilot-size graphite pile—a scaled-up version of the primitive nuclear reactor which had become critical for a short while in the Chicago squash court only two months previously.

It is typical of the whole Manhattan Project that while this pilot-scale reactor was still being built at Oak Ridge—it was not finished until November—work had begun at Hanford. Here, throughout 1943, tens of thousands of workers prepared the 1,000-square-mile site for the building of three full-scale nuclear reactors, each of which would release 25,000 kilowatt-hours of heat for each gram of plutonium which it produced—one reason for siting the project on the banks of the great Columbia river which could carry away and disperse this heat.

Preparations were also started for tackling the enormous and complex chemical problems inherent in separating the plutonium from the uranium once it had been formed in the reactors—preparations which finally produced the massive separation plant, huge windowless concrete blocks 800 feet long and 80 feet high, with walls up to 8 feet thick, and so sealed that the radioactive material inside them could only be handled at long range, by men who checked the separation process through complicated optical systems.

As the United States thus continued throughout 1943 to prepare the first quantities of both kinds of nuclear explosive, three events of a different sort took place.

Fears that the Germans might be well advanced in manufacture of a nuclear weapon were still strong, particularly as Intelligence agents reported increased activity at the heavy water plant at Rjukan in central Norway. Plans to destroy the plant were therefore put into operation—first with a disastrous sabotage attack and then with a successful bombing raid. A development of a different kind came with the escape from Denmark of Niels Bohr, possibly the most eminent of all living nuclear physicists. Bohr came first to London, where he was interviewed by the British Tube Alloys experts, and was then flown on to the United States where he was able to advise the Americans on a multitude of theoretical points which they were still trying to solve.

The balance swings to the US

It was natural that Bohr should give most of his advice in the United States since the British nuclear effort had been steadily diminishing in comparative importance throughout 1942 and 1943. Wartime Britain, desperately hard-pushed for men and materials, and well within the range of German bombers, was no place to build a nuclear weapon. By the end of 1943 the majority of British scientists previously engaged on the work had been integrated into the American teams—a number of them at Los Alamos where the crucial stage of the whole gigantic operation was now in progress. This move followed the signing of the secret Quebec Agreement (dealt with elsewhere) under which 'the British Government recognise that any post-war advantages of an industrial or commercial character shall be dealt with as between the United States and Great Britain on terms to be specified by the President of the United States to the Prime Minister of Great Britain'.

The problems which had to be solved in 1944 under Robert Oppenheimer's direction at Los Alamos, the new laboratory-town built on a high table-land 34 miles north of Santa Fe in New Mexico, were of a different kind from those which had so far been tackled. The first had been mainly theoretical, and they had been followed by what were largely industrial and technological difficulties of a size and complexity which had never been previously faced anywhere in the world. What Oppenheimer and his colleagues had to tackle involved both theory and practice. For no one yet knew exactly what the critical mass either of uranium or plutonium really was. There were still enormous queries hanging over the characteristics of fast neutrons—those which had not been slowed down by the moderator

Eye-witness at Alamogordo

We arrived about three o'clock in the morning at a spot 20 miles from the hundred-foot tower on which the bomb was mounted. Here we were met by a car containing a radio receiver. Round this we assembled, listening for the signal from the firing point which would tell us when to expect the explosion. We were provided with a strip of very dark glass to protect our eyes. This glass is so dark that at mid-day it makes the sun look like a little undeveloped dull green potato. Through this glass I was unable to see the light which was set on the tower to show us where to look. Remember, it was still dark. I therefore fixed my eyes on this light ten seconds before the explosion was due to occur. Then I raised the dark glass to my eyes two seconds before, keeping them fixed on the spot where I had last seen the light. At exactly the expected moment, I saw through the dark glass a brilliant ball of fire which was far brighter than the sun. In a second or two it died down to a brightness which seemed to be about that of the sun, so, realising that it must be lighting up the countryside, I looked behind me and saw the scrub-covered hills, 22 miles from the bomb, lighted up as though by a mid-day sun. Then I turned round and looked directly at the ball of fire. I saw it expand slowly, and begin to rise, growing fainter as it rose. Later it developed into a huge mushroom-shaped cloud, and soon reached a height of forty thousand feet. Though the sequence of events was exactly what we had calculated beforehand in our more optimistic moments, the whole effect was so staggering that I found it difficult to believe.

(Sir Geoffrey Taylor: from *Voices From Britain*, edited by Henning Krabbe, (published by Allen & Unwin))

Otto Hahn

Robert Oppenheimer

Sir Henry Tizard

Sir James Chadwick

Enrico Fermi

General Groves

Albert Einstein

Otto Frisch

Niels Bohr

US Army

of a nuclear pile or reactor. The method of getting the greatest practical effect from a nuclear explosion was still a matter of both calculation and dispute.

But in addition the men at Los Alamos had to decide how the plutonium and/or the Uranium 235 could be shaped into the requirements of a weapon, exactly how the explosion itself could best be initiated, and how the whole contrivance could be built to provide a weapon which could be accurately dropped by an aircraft. The greater part of this work had to be done, moreover, before appreciable amounts of either plutonium of Uranium 235 were available.

One of the main difficulties in this stage of building the world's first nuclear bombs was that of bringing the two subcritical masses of the fissile material together. For unless the two parts were assembled in a few millionths of a second there was the danger of a premature explosion – the 'pop' instead of a 'bang' that continued to haunt the enterprise. At first, the disarmingly simple cannon method of assembly was chosen. This consisted, in essence, of putting one of the subcritical masses as a target at one end of a cannon-like device and firing the second sub-critical mass at it from the other. But when a great deal of work had been carried out on this, the first deliveries of plutonium were found to contain an impurity – an impurity which demanded an even quicker method of assembly if premature detonation was to be avoided.

New theory at Los Alamos

It was at this stage that the Los Alamos workers reconsidered the idea of 'imploding' rather than 'exploding' the weapon. This method involved the use of two hemispheres of fissile material which were set a certain distance apart at the centre of a sphere some $4\frac{1}{2}$ feet across. Surrounding the fissile material was a complex spherical assembly of explosive charges which were wired up to detonators. When the bomb was fired the detonators would set off the charges and these would press in on the heart of the device, forcing the two hemispheres of fissile material together to make a single critical mass. Also, to make doubly sure that there was no delay in the release of neutrons, an 'initiator' was built in between the two hemispheres. This consisted of polonium and beryllium, two rare elements which spontaneously produce neutrons when they are mixed. That mixture would take place as the implosion brought together the two fissile hemispheres; the nuclear reaction would be started; and within a fraction of a second the greatest man-made explosion the world had known would take place.

At least, that was the theory. It was the theory to which the Los Alamos workers put the final touches towards the end of 1944, and it was still only a theory when, during the first days of July 1945, there arrived in New Mexico sufficient plutonium for the theory to be put to the test. Oak Ridge was already producing Uranium 235, and it was expected that enough for a bomb would be ready for use in a cannon-type weapon by mid-July. But the success of that solitary weapon, and of a second plutonium bomb for which supplies of the fissile plutonium were already arriving at Los Alamos, depended on the answer to one question: Would a nuclear weapon work at all?

More than a year before the summer of 1945, General Groves had already taken the first steps to answer that question – by approving a test site on the Alamogordo bombing range, a desolate stretch of desert in the southern part of New Mexico. Some 200 miles from Los Alamos, 20 miles from the nearest small towns, the Alamogordo site was conveniently isolated, and by the autumn of 1944 plans were drawn up for 'Trinity', the code-name chosen by Oppenheimer for the test of the world's first atomic bomb.

By the beginning of July 1945, Trinity Camp had become the centre of a network of communications linking the observation points around 'ground zero', at which point a tall steel tower rose from the desert. At various distances around the tower there stood a variety of recording devices and instruments, each wired back to a central recording point. By the evening of Sunday, July 15, more than 250 scientists had gathered at the Trinity base.

As preparations were completed for testing the 'Fat Man', as the plutonium bomb was called owing to its shape, a closely guarded load was already being moved across the United States to the *Indianapolis* – most of the components of 'Little Boy', the uranium bomb that was already being shipped to the Pacific. For even on this crucial point, events forced the men behind the Manhattan Project to take risks that would never have been taken in any other enterprise. There was enough plutonium to test one weapon, and also enough for a second which was already being fabricated. But there was not enough separated Uranium 235 to make both a test and an operational uranium bomb. The uranium 'Little Boy' had to be shipped to the plane waiting on Tinian in the Pacific even before the success or failure of a nuclear weapon had been settled in the plutonium 'Fat Man'.

The plutonium hemispheres arrived at Trinity from Los Alamos. They were mounted in the bomb-casing and the assembly was then driven out across the desert to the test-tower where it was slowly, an inch at a time, raised to the top of the tower. Then, and only then, was the encircling sphere of explosive charges put in place. The electric firing leads were still attached only to a dummy mounted at the top of the tower.

At observation dugouts around the tower, the nearest of them more than 5 miles away, there gathered the cream of the world's nuclear physicists – Oppenheimer, Fermi, Chadwick, Frisch, Lawrence, and a score of others.

The night of Sunday the 15th was wet and windy. Groves and Oppenheimer were worried that rain might carry radioactive materials over inhabited areas. It seemed likely that the two observation planes would be grounded. But for a variety of reasons postponement was to be avoided at all costs.

Soon after 2 am the weather began to clear. High up, light winds began to disperse the clouds. Just before 5 am the weather experts reported that conditions would hold for two hours and Groves gave the final order for explosion – at 5.30 am.

On the tower, the final checks were made. The electric firing leads were connected. The floodlights illuminating the tower for the observation planes were switched on, and the members of the arming party drove from the tower in jeeps.

Soon after 5 am the countdown began, with the voice of the officer-in-charge relayed to the men in the observation dugouts and to the control room. Fermi had been taking bets on the possibility of the bomb setting light to the atmosphere and destroying the whole planet. Others had been betting that the bomb would fail.

Now, at five-minute, then one-minute intervals, the count went on. Then at one-second intervals.

The voice continued unemotionally, 'four, three, two, one – now'.

The first mushroom-cloud

Many of the men lying on the ground, eyes protected, shielding their faces, have described the world's first nuclear explosion. Few have given a more vivid description than Otto Frisch, who less than seven years previously had with his aunt Lise Meitner worked out how it would happen.

'Suddenly, and without any sound, the hills were bathed in brilliant light, as if somebody had turned the sun on with a switch', he has written. He waited for a few seconds and then turned towards Trinity. Although some 20 miles away, the explosion was too bright to keep his eyes on, although a small brilliant core could be discerned. 'After some seconds I could keep my eyes on the thing and it now looked like a pretty perfect red ball, about as big as the sun, and connected to the ground by a short grey stem', Frisch continued. 'The ball rose slowly, lengthening its stem and getting gradually darker and slightly larger. A structure of darker and lighter irregularities became visible, making the ball look somewhat like a raspberry. Then its motion slowed down and it flattened out, but still remained connected to the ground by its stem, looking more than ever like the trunk of an elephant. Then a hump grew out of its top surface and a second mushroom grew out of the top of the first one, slowly penetrating the highest cloud layers.'

After the glare there came the thunder, and the blast-wave. Fermi, dropping a handful of paper scraps as the air whipped round his party, calculated the force of the explosion.

Trinity had been a success. The weapon had produced the effects of an explosion of 20,000 tons of TNT. The $2,000,000,000 which had gone into the Manhattan Project had been scientifically justified and it was hoped they would now be militarily justified.

The news, subtly coded – 'Operated on this morning. Diagnosis not yet complete but results seem satisfactory and already exceed expectations' – was radioed to Potsdam where Truman and Churchill were in conference with Stalin.

And as the Japanese, whose codes had been broken years earlier by the United States, repeated in Moscow their efforts to negotiate a surrender, 'Little Boy', and a successor to the Trinity 'Fat Man', were moved towards Hiroshima and Nagasaki.

RONALD CLARK is an author who has written extensively on the application of science to war. His books include *The Birth of the Bomb,* the first account of the European work that led to development of nuclear weapons, and *The Rise of the Boffins,* which describes how Britain used her scientists during the Second World War. He is also the biographer of the late Sir Henry Tizard, scientific adviser to four successive Ministers of Aircraft Production. During the Second World War, Ronald Clark was attached as a war correspondent to British and Canadian forces, landed in Normandy on D-Day, and covered the campaign in North-West Europe. He remained in Germany after the war, covering many of the War Crimes trials, and has travelled extensively.

US Air Force

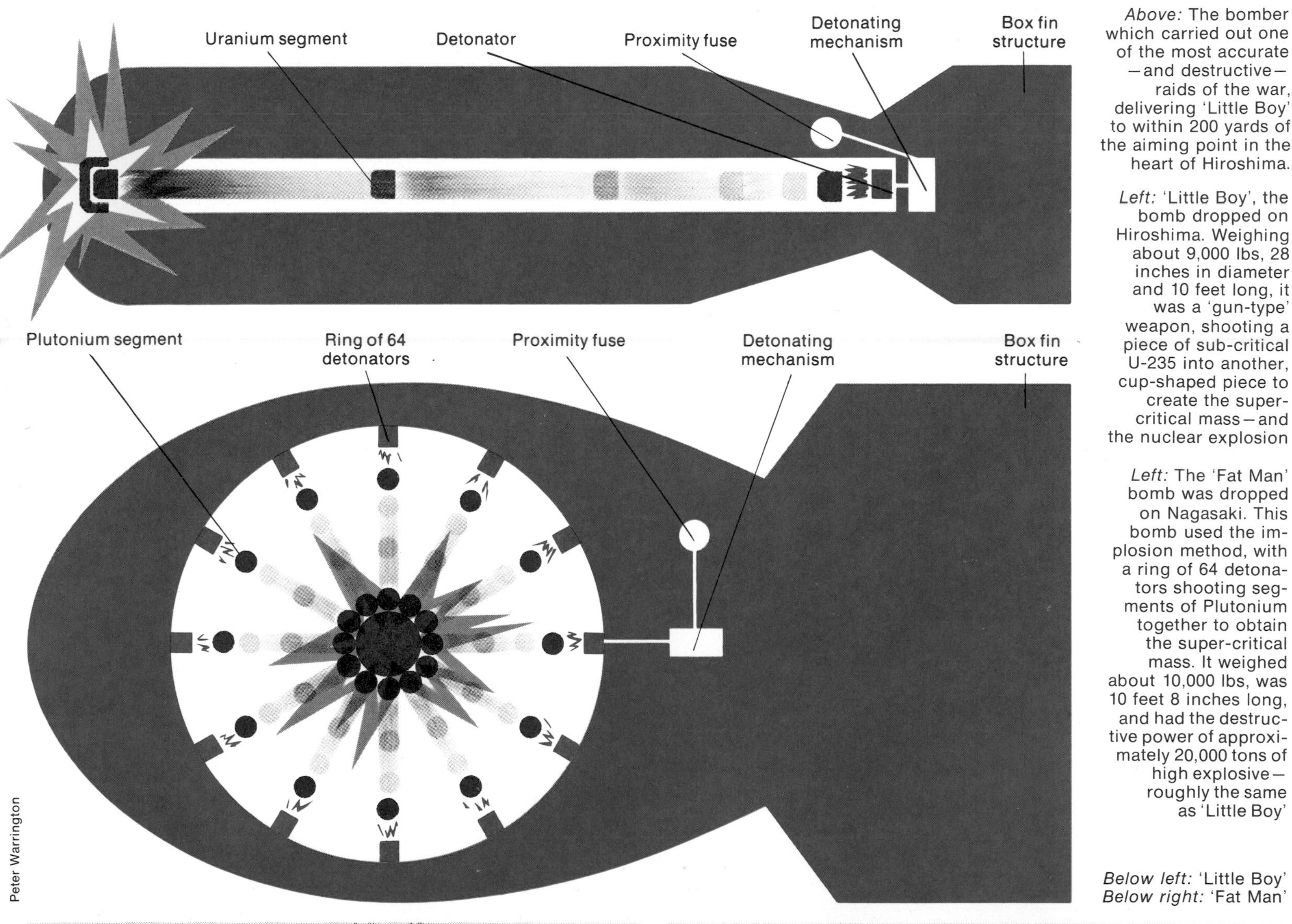

Peter Warrington

Above: The bomber which carried out one of the most accurate —and destructive— raids of the war, delivering 'Little Boy' to within 200 yards of the aiming point in the heart of Hiroshima.

Left: 'Little Boy', the bomb dropped on Hiroshima. Weighing about 9,000 lbs, 28 inches in diameter and 10 feet long, it was a 'gun-type' weapon, shooting a piece of sub-critical U-235 into another, cup-shaped piece to create the super-critical mass—and the nuclear explosion

Left: The 'Fat Man' bomb was dropped on Nagasaki. This bomb used the implosion method, with a ring of 64 detonators shooting segments of Plutonium together to obtain the super-critical mass. It weighed about 10,000 lbs, was 10 feet 8 inches long, and had the destructive power of approximately 20,000 tons of high explosive— roughly the same as 'Little Boy'

Below left: 'Little Boy'
Below right: 'Fat Man'

Fred Wolfe

US Air Force

PRINTED IN BELGIUM

proost Turnhout (Belgium)

Hiroshima: The Atomic Desert

There are deserts of sand, deserts of stone, deserts of ice. But since August 1945, Hiroshima—or more exactly the spot where Hiroshima once stood—has constituted a new, peculiar, and original sort of wilderness: an atomic desert, the handiwork of *homo sapiens,* and beneath its grey-black surface there still remain the traces of his activity and the pitiful remnants of his fellow-men . . .

Apart from the shadows of living creatures and of objects turned to charcoal by the heat of the atomic flash, one professor also collected hundreds of other specimens—materials which had not been destroyed, but only transmuted or changed in the huge blast furnace that had been the explosion. These included weirdly coloured earthenware tiles, bottles twisted into extraordinary shapes, singed fragments of cloth, and an ever-increasing quantity of stones. And what stones! Stones such as existed nowhere else on earth. In the uniquely high temperature produced by the atom bomb they had begun to 'weep' or to 'bleed'. This was clearly apparent when one of these stones was dissected. The deep black centre remained intact, but part of this core had forced its way through the light grey surface to emerge as boils or sores. It was as if the very stones had contracted mange or leprosy . . . [From *Children of the Ashes,* by Robert Jungk, published by Heinemann]

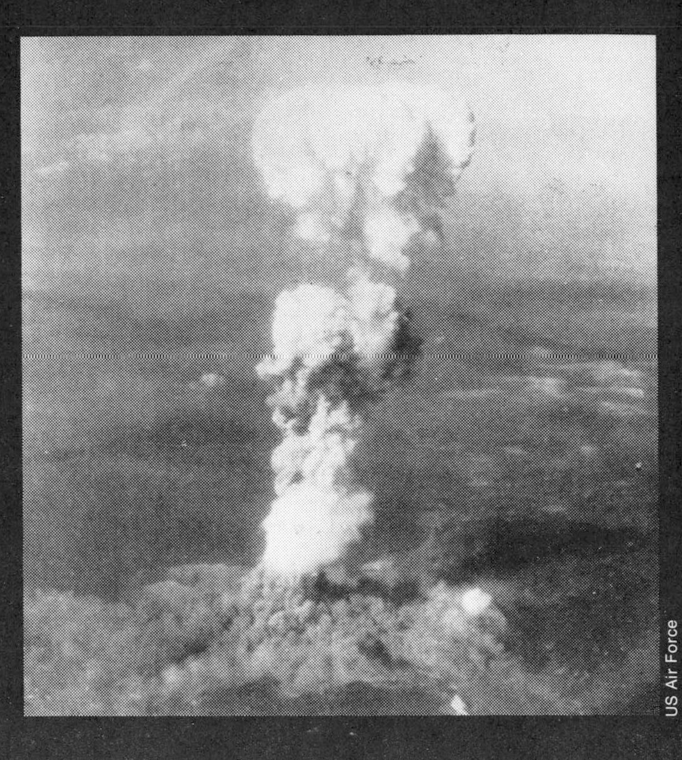

US Air Force

Orion Press-Opera Mundi